EL DORADO (MYTHS OF GOLD)

AMERICAS SOCIETY

Americas Society is pleased to present *El Dorado: Myths of Gold,* a two-part exhibition that will bring together artworks ranging from the pre-Hispanic period to the contemporary era. This groundbreaking exhibition explores the myth of El Dorado as a foundational narrative of the Americas. *El Dorado: Myths of Gold* presents artworks by more than forty different artists that challenge, reinforce, and question the continuity of the myth in the Americas into the present. Organized in collaboration with Fundación PROA in Buenos Aires, Argentina, and Museo Amparo in Puebla, Mexico, *El Dorado* offers new interpretations and interrogations on the myth from a hemispheric lens, engaging artists from across the continent and throughout its history.

I am grateful to Aimé Iglesias Lukin, Director and Chief Curator of Visual Arts, who brought this project to Americas Society and leads the gallery with exciting programming. Thank you also to the curatorial team, Edward J. Sullivan and Tie Jojima, who worked together with Iglesias Lukin on this presentation and to Karen Marta and Todd Bradway of KMEC Books for their editorial and production work on this and other Americas Society publications. Americas Society would also like to thank Esther Levy and Sarah Lopez for their research support for this exhibition and publication.

The presentation of *El Dorado* and related programming has been made possible by generous support from the National Endowment for the Arts and by public funds from the New York City Department of Cultural Affairs and New York State Council on the Arts with the support of the Office of the Governor and the New York State Legislature. Additional support was provided by Furthermore: a program of the J. M. Kaplan Fund.

Americas Society acknowledges the generous support from the Arts of the Americas Circle contributors: Amalia Amoedo, Almeida & Dale Galeria de Arte, Estrellita B. Brodsky, Virginia Cowles Schroth, Emily A. Engel, Diana Fane, Isabella Hutchinson, Carolina Jannicelli, Diana López and Herman Sifontes, Antonio Murzi, Gabriela Pérez Rocchietti, Vivian Pfeiffer, Phillips, Erica Roberts, Sharon Schultz, and Edward J. Sullivan.

SUSAN SEGAL
President and CEO, Americas Society/Council of the Americas

El Dorado: Myths of Gold is a tale of search and quest, of delirium and of violence. Since the arrival of the Spaniards in the Americas, rumors of a golden kingdom filled with gold quickly spread in Europe, driving conquistadores in their search to find it. Throughout the Caribbean and into the Amazon, the myth spread and evolved into many stories. Despite never being found, the mythical El Dorado has defined the continent as an empty land up for grabs. This exhibition is part of a much larger research project that brings together artworks and artists that engage with the myth to evaluate its continuity into the present, as well as how it defines who we are, offering a critical view and sometimes a path of resistance.

Since 2020, Americas Society in New York, Fundación PROA in Buenos Aires, and Museo Amparo in Puebla have joined efforts to conceptualize and bring to life the *Project El Dorado*. Dreaming of a collaborative exhibition project that discusses the myths and uses of gold and the legacy of extractivism and colonization over five centuries in the Americas, the curatorial teams of the three institutions started sharing their research and having regular meetings to discuss a show. The first step in the project was to organize a large convening of scholars, conceptualized and moderated by Professor Edward J. Sullivan—also a cocurator of this exhibition—which took place from Fall 2021 to Spring 2022. The convening brought together twenty-two scholars from all over the Americas, who presented papers on topics of interest to a selected audience, and it provided the groundwork for the development of the general concepts and themes for the project.

Two main conclusions were drawn from these scholarly discussions. First, that the contemporary artistic production around the subject was much bigger and richer than expected: this was not just a historical concern but a very current one. Second, that the scope of the project was too large to be encompassed by any specific exhibition, and that the histories and effects of the myth were very different for the audiences of each of these institutions. With this in mind we decided that each venue would organize its own exhibition, with a separate set of artworks, like chapters of a novel, in dialogue with the problematics of each audience and proposing new questions and theses on this rich topic.[1] This open-ended model of exhibition making allowed more curatorial freedom and at the same time allowed each institution to tell a different story and present a different angle on El Dorado. The collaboration between institutions is also demonstrated by shared public programs and exhibition catalogues: this current publication—the second in the series—invites a hemispheric discussion on the topic. Finally, the project will be accompanied by an illustrated reader, to be published in January 2024, which will include newly commissioned texts by scholars thinking through the myth of El Dorado beyond gold, as well as excerpts from historical texts addressing the myth from 1492 through the nineteenth century.

The project's being presented as an unfinished dialogue also allows something much more important: that the topic can keep growing with more research, exhibitions, and publications. Aiming to resituate the legend, the *Project El Dorado* presents these publications, public programs, and exhibitions to analyze and at the same time challenge the continuity of the myth in the Americas into the present.

AIMÉ IGLESIAS LUKIN
Director and Chief Curator of Art at Americas Society

1 The exhibition at Fundación PROA in Buenos Aires took place from April through August 2023; at Americas Society in New York, it is organized in two parts from September through December 2023 and January through May 2024; and at Museo Amparo in Puebla, it will run from August through December 2024.

V.

IMPERATOR

NOBILES SVOS OR-

ſi quando ad prandium vel

inuitare velit.

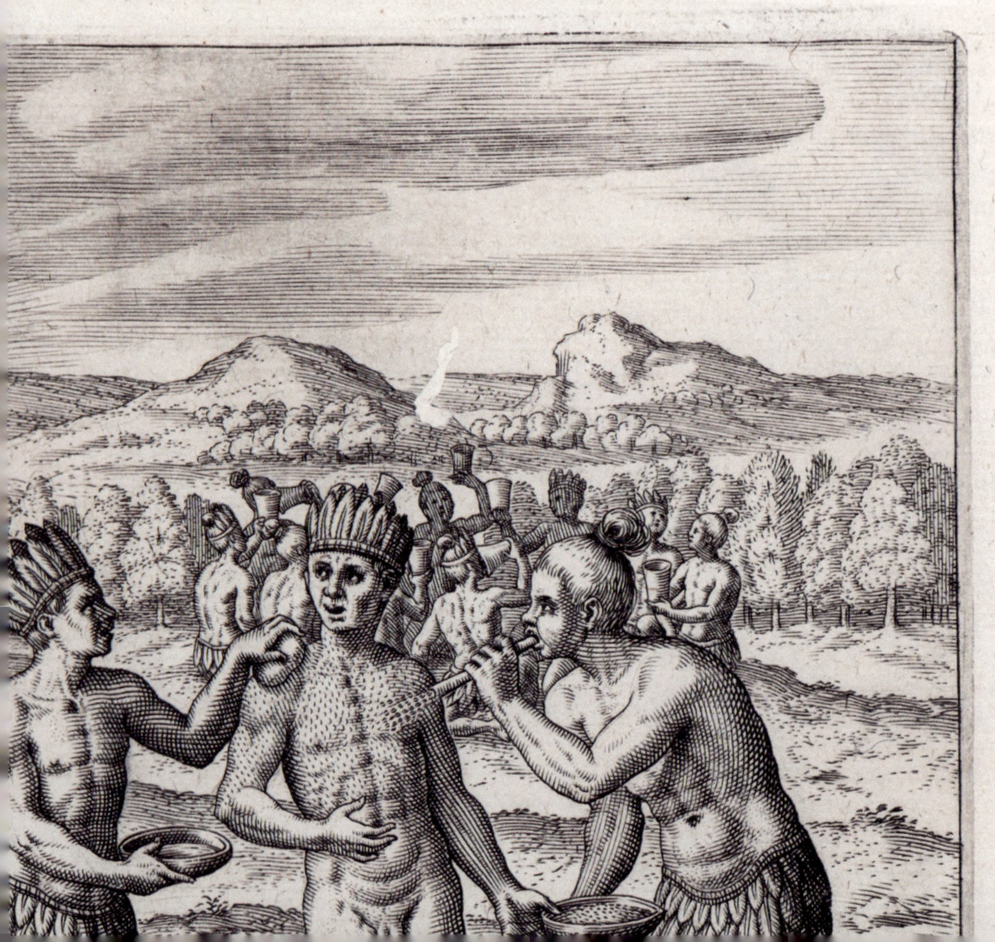

Theodor De Bry, *The Origin of the El Dorado Legend*, 1599

EL **DORADO**: MYTHS OF GOLD

AIMÉ IGLESIA LUKIN, TIE JOJIMA, and EDWARD J. SULLIVAN

Throughout time and within most societies, gold, in all its various manifestations and uses, functioned as a beacon of desire, a signifier of the sacred, and a descriptor of the marvelous. Myths of golden treasures galvanized European colonization and exploration of the Americas since 1492, serving as justification for the plunder of resources regardless of Indigenous lives, ancestral territories, and environmental concerns. The myth of El Dorado was one of those.[1] From the fifteenth through the eighteenth centuries, El Dorado was imagined as an Indigenous land rich in gold and precious stones. Though such a place was never found, the legend came to shape the colonization of the Americas as a foundational ethos for exploitation, which persists into the present. Not only does it explain the ambitions of the Europeans who colonized the Americas, but it also represents a powerful indication of how the Americas are still considered by locals and foreigners today as a territory for exploitation and individual enrichment. In the nineteenth century and beyond, the myth came to encapsulate the actual wealth of natural resources belonging to the emerging modern nations, including gold in Brazil and California, oil in Venezuela, silver in Bolivia, sugar in the Caribbean, and, more recently, lithium in Bolivia and Chile. Extracted from the land, these resources circulate globally, establishing national power within world geopolitics and bringing wealth to the political and economic elites while also driving the dislocation and migration of peoples across the continent.

As if by alchemy, the myth of El Dorado has further transformed from exchangeable products into more intangible, and equally powerful, personal and collective values, such as individualism, greed, and consumerism, that are central to contemporary societies. Like the dream of El Dorado, consumerism in contemporary culture is based on a promise of happiness achieved through the purchase of material goods and private property. The desire for wealth, status, and power is a major driving force, even if it is often impossible to attain. As we grapple with the enormous long-term sociopolitical and environmental effects of this operating dynamic, there is a pressing need to reevaluate its influence on our identification as human beings and members of a globalized society. Presenting artworks from the precolonial period to today, this exhibition complicates and reevaluates the idea of El Dorado, employing the myth as a framework for understanding the Americas both past and present. By placing historical and contemporary artworks together, the exhibition facilitates dialogues between past and present, in order to demonstrate how the myth has shaped the value of gold, as well as that of territories, bodies, religious beliefs, and nature.

TALES OF EL DORADO

For some pre-Hispanic civilizations in the Americas gold was not valued in the same way that it was elsewhere in the world. The material was used, like many other metals, as a symbol of status and for ritual purposes, but this was due more to its light-reflecting qualities than to any sense of rarity or trade value. Obsidian and other polished stones, such as jade, were often more highly regarded.[2] When the Spaniards arrived in the hemisphere, they noticed this disregard for gold in the accounts of their travels, using it as proof of the supposed naivete of the local population. The myth of El Dorado became a key element in this context, with the Spaniards believing they would find a treasure-filled land they could easily plunder without much local resistance. But as priest, historian, and social reformer Bartolomé de las Casas asserted in the early sixteenth century, El Dorado was also used as a diversion strategy by Indigenous populations, who often guided the conquistadores

1 For a brief history of the many myths of El Dorado see "The Myth of El Dorado," *History Workshop* 34 (1992): 1–15; Robert Silverberg, *The Golden Dream: Seekers of El Dorado* (Athens: Ohio University Press, 1996); Charlotte Rogers, *Mourning El Dorado: Literature and Extractivism in the Contemporary American Tropics* (Charlottesville: University of Virginia Press, 2019); Christian Kuchik, *La leyenda de El Dorado y otros mitos del descubrimiento de América* (Madrid: Ediciones Nowtilus, 2008); Massimo Livi Bacci, *El Dorado in the Marshes: Gold, Slaves and Souls between the Andes and the Amazon* (Cambridge: Polity, 2010).

2 Joanne Pillsbury, Timothy Potts, and Kim N. Richter, eds., *Golden Kingdoms: Luxury Arts in the Ancient Americas* (Los Angeles: J. Paul Getty Museum and Getty Research Institute, 2017).

to false locations in remote areas as a way of pushing them out of their territories.[3]

The most famous of the El Dorado legends, that of the Golden King, originated in what is now Colombia. It concerns a ceremony of power investiture among the Muisca people whereby a new leader was covered with gold dust and placed on a raft adorned with treasures that would then be submerged, along with many gold offerings, in Lake Guatavita, near contemporary Bogotá. This myth (described by Juan Rodríguez Freyle in his 1638 text *El carnero* and in other historical sources) was believed to have been confirmed by two discoveries in the nineteenth and twentieth centuries.[4] In 1856, a votive figure of a leader on a raft was found in Lake Siecha, about sixteen miles from Guatavita. The object had been sold to the ethnographic museum in Berlin but disappeared before leaving Colombia (fig. 1).[5] More than a century later, in 1969, a rural worker in the town of Pasca found a miniature golden raft in a local cave, topped with figures similar to the raft found in the Siecha lake. This piece, now one of the signature objects in the Museo del Oro of the Banco de la República in Bogotá, became a symbol of the authenticity of the legend (fig. 2).[6] The search for El Dorado is thus at the root of the formation of Colombia as a nation. The expeditions of Gonzalo Jiménez de Quesada in pursuit of this golden land were what led to the establishment of the Nuevo Reino de Granada in 1538, followed by another failed expedition in 1569 from which, after two years, only twenty-five of the original five hundred men returned.[7] But these were not the only imagined locations for the persistent myth of El Dorado.[8]

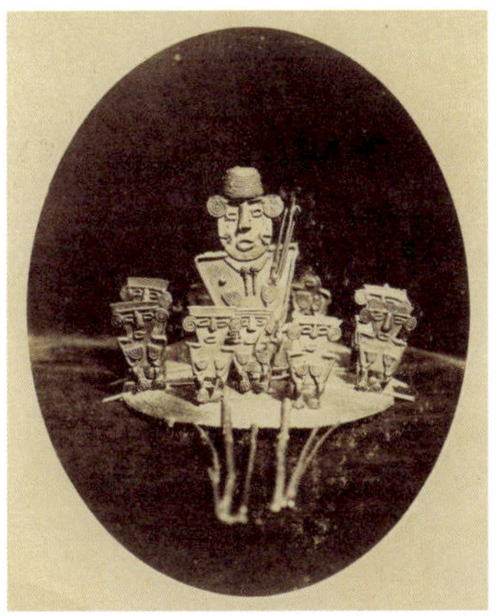

Fig 1. Nineteenth-century photograph of the Siecha raft. Albumen silver print, 7 3/4 x 5 1/2 in. (19.7 x 13.9 cm.) Museo Nacional de Colombia

3 "La gente toda, recién venida, no se descuidaba de preguntar dónde y cómo el oro con redes se pescaba, y, según yo creo, comenzó desde luego a desmayar como no vía las redes y aparejos con que se pescaba, ni hablar o tratar dello a cada paso; y así fue que, oídos los trabajos que los huéspedes les contaban haber pasado, y como el oro que tenían no era pescado, sino a los indios robado, y puesto que había muchas minas y muy ricas en la tierra, pero que se sacaba con inmenso trabajo, comenzaron luego a desengañarse y hallarse del todo burlados." Bartolomé de las Casas, *Historia de las Indias* (Caracas: Biblioteca Ayacucho, 1956), 222.

4 The myth appears in Rodríguez Freyle's 1636–8 book *El carnero – Conquista y descubrimiento del nuevo reino de Granada, de las Indias Occidentales del Mar Océano, y fundación de la ciudad de Santafé de Bogotá* (Caracas: Biblioteca Ayacucho, 1979). Rodríguez Freyle's father was a soldier in the Pedro de Ursúa expedition. Juan de Castellanos, who was part of that expedition, left a similar account. He was a priest in the campaign against the Muisca and wrote the poem "The Quest of El Dorado" in the mid-sixteenth century. See also Gonzalo Fernández de Oviedo y Valdés, *Historia general y natural de las Indias*, vol. I (Spain: Impr. de la Real academia de la Historia, 1851–2); Lopez Vaz, *The Expedition of Pedro de Ursua & Lope de Aguirre in Search of El Dorado and Omagua in 1560–1* (London: Hakluyt, 1570); and Gonzalo Fernández de Oviedo, *Historia general y natural de las Indias, islas y tierra-firme del mar océano* (Alicante: Biblioteca Virtual Miguel de Cervantes, 2007).

5 María Alicia Uribe Villegas and Héctor García Botero, "Una historia del coleccionismo y la investigación en el Museo del Oro (Banco de la República, Bogotá, D.C., Colombia)," *Boletín Museo Del Oro* 60 (2021): 5–117, https://publicaciones.banrepcultural.org/index.php/bmo/article/view/21803.

6 Liborio Zerda, "El Dorado," *Papel periódico ilustrado* (Boldan y Tamayo: 1882): 336–41.

7 Germán Arciniegas, *The Knight of El Dorado: The Tale of Don Gonzalo Jiménez de Quesada and His Conquest of New Granada, Now Called Colombia* (New York: The Viking Press, 1942).

8 Other myths that inspired expeditions include the legend of the Seven Cities of Gold" (Seven Cities of Cibola), which originated the 1548 New Mexico expedition by Francisco Vázquez de Coronado. The myth of the Seven Cities became intertwined with that of El Dorado. In 1603 the Portuguese Pêro Coelho de Sousa explored northward from Pernambuco, and the golden city of El Dorado was shown on maps of Brazil and the Guianas for years thereafter.

One of the first formal expeditions in search of El Dorado was launched from Cuzco, Peru, by Francisco Pizarro's brother Gonzalo in 1541. The expedition, which sought to discover the golden city across the Andes, in the Amazon, ended in failure and disaster—but also in discovery. In despair after not reaching his desired destination, Pizarro decided to divide his expedition into two parts, leaving the other half to his lieutenant, Francisco de Orellana. Pizarro returned to Cuzco, while Orellana continued to follow the river, eventually arriving at the Atlantic Ocean. He traveled up to the Caribbean and then to Spain, where he shared stories of his expedition. His claims of having been attacked by female warriors similar to the ones from Greek myth led to the naming of the rainforest region as "Amazonas."[9]

Another famous expedition in search of the mythical city of Manoa or El Dorado was Walter Raleigh's 1595 voyage along the Orinoco River (fig. 3).[10] Offering a key testimony of Anglo-Saxon involvement in the early history of what is now known as South America, Raleigh's expeditions demonstrate the tensions between the Spanish and English Empires—at war at the time—in their attempts to control wealth in the Americas. While Raleigh did not find El Dorado and was judged for his exaggerated account and failed promises to Queen Elizabeth I, the alliances that the English expedition established with local populations would determine the future of colonization in that area (as narrated in Nobel Prize–winning author V. S. Naipaul's 1969 novel *The Loss of El Dorado*).[11]

Werner Herzog's *Aguirre, the Wrath of God* (1972) (fig. 4) is an iconic cultural rendering of the loss of sanity one can suffer in an unrestrained quest for power.[12] The film is based on the true story of Lope de Aguirre, a violent Spanish colonizer who, in 1560, joined the expedition led by Pedro de Ursúa in Peru to find El Dorado, which was believed to be at the headwaters of the Amazon. Soon after the beginning of the expedition Aguirre led a rebellion that ended with the killing of Ursúa. He then assassinated Ursúa's successor, Fernando de Guzmán, and took over the expedition. As leader, Aguirre raided towns and spread terror, killing members of his own company—including his daughter—before arriving at what is now Venezuela, where he was captured and killed by the Spanish.[13] Herzog's film illustrates the futility of the search itself: even if such a land exists to be

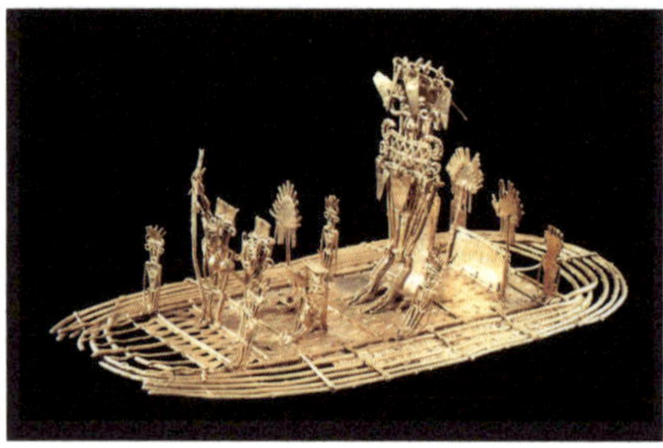

Fig 2. Unknown Muisca artist, *raft*, 600 – 1600 CE. Cast gold alloy. Museo del Oro, Banco Nacional de la República, Bogotá, Colombia

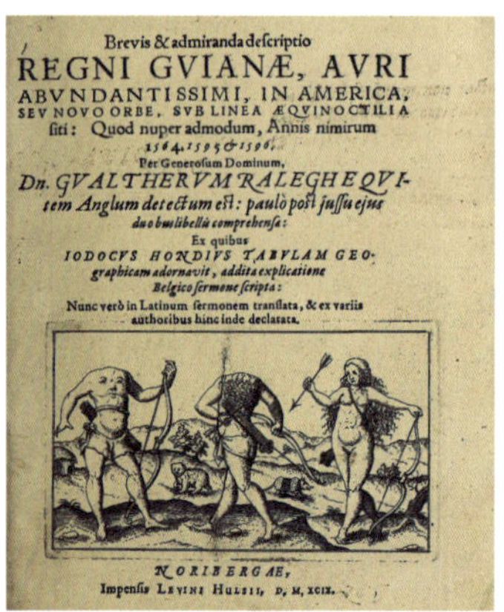

Brevis & admiranda descriptio
REGNI GVIANÆ, AVRI
ABVNDANTISSIMI, IN AMERICA,
SEV NOVO ORBE, SVB LINEA ÆQVINOCTILIA
siti: Quod nuper admodum, Annis nimirum
1564. 1595 & 1596.
Per Generosum Dominum,
Dn. GVALTHERVM RALEGHEQVItem Anglum detectum est: paulò post jussu ejus
duobus libellis comprehensa:
Ex quibus
IODOCVS HONDIVS TABVLAM GEOgraphicam adornavit, addita explicatione
Belgico sermone scripta:
Nunc verò in Latinum sermonem translata, & ex variis
authoribus hinc inde declarata.

NORIBERGAE,
Impensis LEVINI HULSII, D, M, XCIX.

Fig 3. Cover of *Walter Raleigh's Brevis & admiranda descriptio regni Guianae, avri abundantissimi, in America*, 1599

9 Kuchik, *La leyenda de El Dorado*, 40–59.

10 Walter Raleigh, *The Discouerie of the Large, Rich, and Bevvtiful Empyre of Guiana: With a Relation of the Great and Golden Citie of Manoa (which the Spanyards Call El Dorado) and the Prouinces of Emeria, Arromaia, Amapaia, and Other Countries, with Their Riuers, Adioyning: Performed in the Yeare 1595* (London: Robert Robinson, 1596).

11 V. S. Naipaul, *The Loss of El Dorado: A History* (London: Deutsch, 1969). In 2016 the Venezuelan government created the Orinoco Mining Arc (OMA), a large-scale mining project primarily focused on extracting valuable minerals. With an extension of 111,843.70 km², the OMA was created to create economic development and generate revenue for the country. However, the project has been subject to criticism and controversy due to its negative effects on the environment and Indigenous rights.

12 Werner Herzog (director), *Aguirre, the Wrath of God* [motion picture] (Germany: Werner Herzog Filmproduktion and Hessischer Rundfunk, 1972).

13 For more on Herzog's film, see Julia Bozer, "'An Unfinished Country': Werner Herzog's Amazonian Films," in "Traveler-Artists in the Old New World, 1968–1982" (PhD Diss., Institute of Fine Arts, New York University, 2021), 189–226.

found, the explorer always gets lost in their ambition. And history repeats itself, first as tragedy and then as farce. In Ana María Millán's video installation *Dinastía* (Dynasty, 2014) [PL. 94], the artist's friends and colleagues read dialogue taken from Herzog's film, accompanied by comical images of animals and strange objects that highlight the absurdity not only of the original story but also the Herzog film itself, which, by giving more voice to Aguirre than to the land's Indigenous inhabitants, perpetuated the narratives that guided conquest.

SHAPING TERRITORY

The El Dorado expeditions were fundamental for the European creation of maps of the Americas from the sixteenth to the eighteenth centuries. These maps served the purpose of organizing land into intelligible forms, marking the sites of rivers and mountains, and attributing names to them. Mapmaking facilitated different methods of domination and reflected the projections of Europeans onto a land they considered free for the taking. As they invaded the Americas, they produced knowledge, with the aid of native populations, that was then made visible, including scientific data on animal and plant species and information about natural resources, geological formations, and more. While conveying all this information in visual form, maps also established geopolitical divisions of the land and reflected the speculative location of various sites—including that of El Dorado.

Inspired by accounts of Raleigh's trips, Thomas Hariot's sixteenth-century map [PL. 66] and the seventeenth-century map *Guiana sive Amazonum Regio* [PL. 68] of the Guianas (present-day Venezuela) represent the apocryphal Lake Parime as an enormous rectangular site in the middle of the Amazon, with the town of "Manoa, or El Dorado" located in its northwest.[14] Although these earlier depictions reflected the belief in the existence of this mythical place, by the mid-eighteenth century, with the rise of scientific explorations in the Americas, the physical location of El Dorado began disappearing from maps. The myth had been debunked by Alexander von Humboldt and Aimé Bonpland after their 1799–1804 expedition (fig. 5). They concluded—repeating an argument made by Bartolomé de las Casas two centuries earlier—that the myth of El Dorado had been adapted and used by Indigenous peoples to disorient the Spaniards. The story, as malleable as gold itself, could serve many purposes and opposing goals, escaping the control of those who claimed to own it.[15]

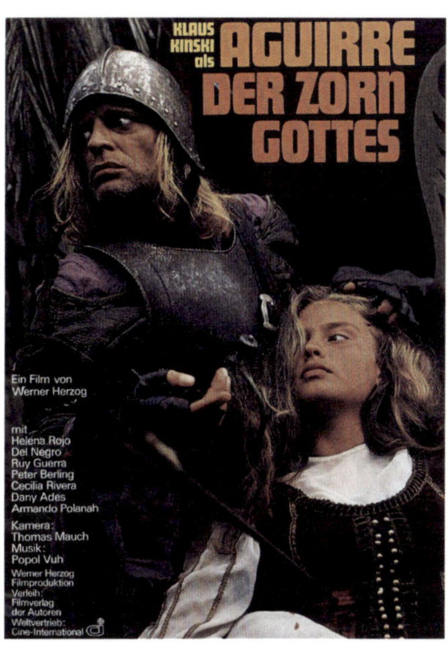

Fig 4. Poster of Aguirre: *The Wrath of God*, directed by Werner Herzog, 1972. Werner Herzog Filmproduktion. Photo: Alamy

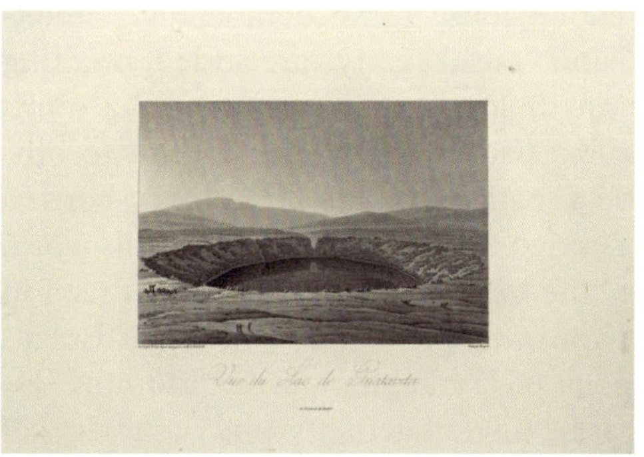

Fig 5. View of Lake Guatavita, engraving published in Alexander von Humboldt and Aimé Bonpland, *Vues des cordillères et monumens des peuples indigènes de l'Amérique*, 1810

14 The belief in the existence of this lake was perpetuated by accounts of explorers, especially Walter Raleigh's *The Discouerie of the Large, Rich, and Bevvtiful Empyre of Guiana*.

15 According to Joachim Eiback and Tobias Haller, Humboldt was skeptical of myths in general, but he paid attention to myths of Indigenous groups and speculated that they used the myth of El Dorado to disorient and divert the Spaniards. See Eiback and Haller, "Pioneering Political Ecology: Perceptions of Nature, Indigenous Practices and Power Relations during Alexander von Humboldt's Travels in Latin America," *Journal of Political Ecology* 28 (2001): 663–77.

However, the quest for El Dorado had already established an ethos of exploitation in the Americas, and, according to Charlotte Rogers, "rather than fading away, El Dorado became a concept signifying a variety of sources of wealth."[16]

Nineteenth-century landscape paintings and prints depicting different places in the Americas also offered visual representations of the colonizers' stereotypes of the land and its people. Charles Bentley's *Twelve Views in the Interior of the Guianas* was created from sketches drawn during the expedition of the Royal Geographic Society of London, led by Robert H. Schomburgk from 1835 through 1839 [PL. 87]. The expedition was organized just two years after the Guianas became part of the British Empire. The prints were published alongside textual information written by Schomburgk. While they were supposed to be truthful accounts of what the expedition encountered, they also reproduced the projections of the British over the territory, such as stereotypical views of Indigenous peoples and the land as an untouched site filled with riches and dangers.

In this exhibition, the juxtaposition of historical and contemporary maps and landscapes allows us to see the continuity of colonial violence from the past to the present. Contemporary artists engaging with maps speak to this long tradition of the visual representation of land, upending it to reveal different dynamics of power. One example is Jaime Lauriano's map *Novus orbis: democracia racial, melting pot e pureza de razas* (Novus orbis: racial democracy, melting pot, and race purity) [PL. 72], in which the artist appropriates Hans Holbein's 1532 map *Novus Orbis Regionum*, which depicts Indigenous peoples as cannibals devouring parts of human bodies.[17] In Lauriano's version, drawn in black *pemba*, a chalk used in Umbanda rituals, the expressions "racial democracy," "melting pot," and "racial purity" are added, pointing to other mythologies that constitute the modern Brazilian nation, and which extend to other American nations. At the upper right corner, the artist added the Yoruba word *axé*. This word, meaning "life force," is widely used in Brazil in different contexts, including in the Afro-Brazilian religions of Umbanda and Candomblé. By incorporating the materiality and language of Afro-Brazilian cultures into his map, Lauriano highlights the connection of Black populations with their ancestral roots, as well as their active resistance to colonialism up to the present.

GOLD AND ART: PAST AND PRESENT

Gold is a highly malleable material that never tarnishes and never disintegrates. It is a virtually everlasting substance that has spawned innumerable legends and myths in practically every culture, and it has been used since ancient times in Asia, Africa, and Europe for its material value, as currency for trade, and as a symbol of power.[18] In terms of art and visual culture in the Americas, the use of gold in ancient civilizations and across the development of European and American art is central to the imaginaries of many contemporary artists who seek to refashion the past in ways that connect to contemporary identities and complicate foundational historical narratives.

In early Christian Europe, gold was the denominator of the divine. Byzantine churches from Ravenna and Venice in the West to Constantinople in the East glowed with mosaics created with tin sulfide, which was applied to surfaces from metal to wood to produce an ethereal glow (fig. 6). The gold that was used in thirteenth- and fourteenth-century paintings came from Africa, in many cases arriving into the Italian peninsula with traders who covered vast territories, both extracting and selling the precious substance. In medieval Europe, gold was also extracted closer to home, through mining or panning in various parts of the continent, especially in the vicinity of the Rhine River. As time progressed, it continued to be essential as a symbol of sacredness. The backgrounds of the gold ground paintings and frescos of the Italian (especially the Florentine) Renaissance are created entirely with gold leaf. This signified that the religious dramas depicted therein were

16 Charlotte Rogers, *Mourning El Dorado: Literature and Extractivism in the Contemporary American Tropics* (Charlottesville: University of Virginia Press, 2019), 33.

17 Yobenj Aucardo Chicangana-Bayona, "Canibais do Brasil: os açougues de Fries, Holbein e Münster (século XVI)," *Tempo* 14, no. 28 (2010): 165–92.

18 For more on the history of gold and the arts, see H. G. Bachman, Steven Lindberg, and Jorg Vollnagel, *The Lure of Gold: An Artistic and Cultural History* (New York: Abbeville Press, 2006) and Shannon L. Kenny, *Gold: A Cultural Encyclopedia* (Santa Barbara: ABC-CLIO, 2011).

sanctified scenes, enactments of vignettes of the vast liturgical dramas of biblical and saintly derivation, from the Creation to the life of Christ and those of the saints (fig. 7).

Renaissance and Baroque portraits, as well as the thousands of religious images that adorned churches, chapels, and private homes, both imposing and modest, were also enhanced by gold leaf, which created an aura of grandeur and an atmosphere of sanctity when embellishing scenes of religious history. In these works, the garments of holy figures are flecked with gold, enlivening the painted surfaces and attesting to their sacredness. The powerful series of acrylic and pencil on paper drawings (*Serie A.M.O.*, 2020) by New York–based Venezuelan artist Esperanza Mayobre, in which bars of pure gold color alternate with basketlike, woven patterns, recall the gilded patterns on the clothing of innumerable Baroque saints and Virgins, while posing political critiques to wealth extraction [PL. 17]. Renaissance and Baroque artists and collectors who wished to further accentuate the dazzling qualities of the paintings surrounded them with—often spectacular—gold frames.

Many contemporary artists, like Mayobre, have continued to evoke and complicate gold's spiritual qualities in their work. One such artist, the German-born Mexican architect, sculptor, and painter Mathias Goeritz, created golden abstract works that evoked spirituality. Many of his works made after 1958—collectively entitled *Mensajes* (Messages)—are wood-based pieces that are covered with gold leaf. They are often punctured by nails, which leave networks of small holes on the surfaces [PL. 60]. Although these pieces contain no overt references to any specific spiritual phenomenon, they nonetheless recall, for some observers, Mexican Baroque evocations of the sorrows of Christ and the Virgin Mary. Thus the spiritual legacy of gold becomes, especially in works like *Cruz en la caja* (Cross in a box) [PL. 54], a cojoining of both exaltation and pain.

At the time of the "first contact" (a euphemism for the beginning of colonialism), the greed for gold on the part of the Europeans and the reverence for it as a substance of ritual and religious expression among Indigenous peoples clashed like two explosive meteors in the heavens. A late sixteenth-century print by Flemish artist and printer Theodore de Bry (fig. 8) purports to show the landing of Christopher Columbus on what was called Guanahani by the Lucayans, the original inhabitants of the island in the Bahamas archipelago and the first of many Indigenous groups in the Caribbean to be enslaved by the Spaniards. Columbus called the place San Salvador, the name it bears today. In the foreground of de Bry's print, which appeared in the book *America* (1594), the Indigenous inhabitants approach the foreigners with armloads of gifts, presumably of gold, while the Spaniards plant a cross in the background. The viewer intuits that the exchange is far from fair. Contemporary Barbadian artist Alberta Whittle engages with de Bry's prints in her series *Jamestown Mythology: Amonute* (2023) [PL. 75], reinterpreting and altering de Bry's engravings, including the gold embossing of a snail trail, to highlight the mythological distortion of these representations of Indigenous Americans and the violence they imply.

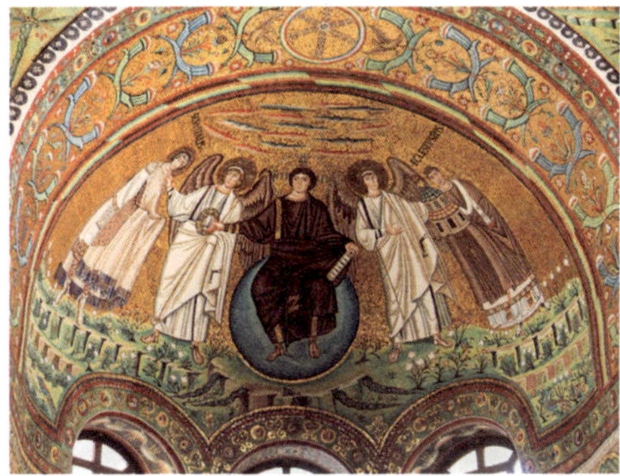

Fig 6. Mosaic of *Christ Astride the World* in the Basilica of San Vitale, Ravenna, Italy. Photo: Hal Bera

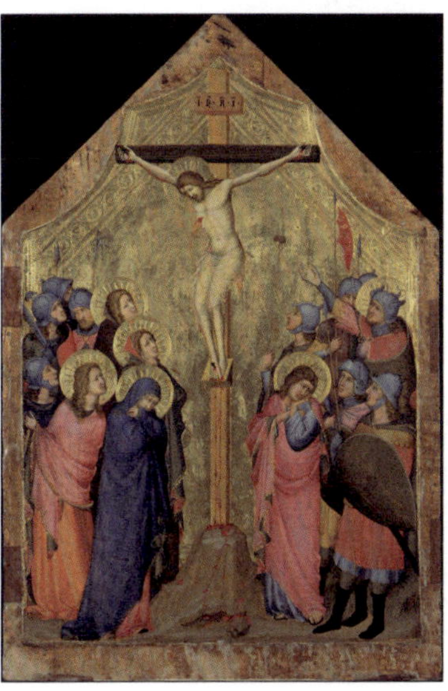

Fig 7. Master of the Codex of Saint George (Italian, active Florence, ca. 1315–35), *The Crucifixion*, ca. 1330–35. Tempera on wood, gold ground, 18 × 11 ¾ inches (45.7 × 29.8 cm). The Metropolitan Museum of Art

With the inclusion of the cross, de Bry alludes to the catechizing fervor of the first European friars in the early sixteenth-century Americas, which soon gave way to the highly organized bureaucracy of the Church.

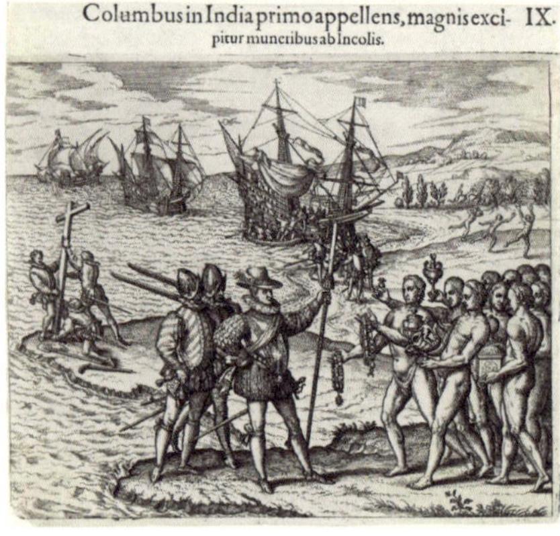

Fig 8. Theodor de Bry, *Christopher Columbus Arrives in America*, 1594, etching and text in letterpress, 78 1/4 × 7 3/4 in. (18.6 × 19.6 cm.) From *Collected Travels in the East Indies and West Indies* (Collectiones peregrinationum in Indiam occidentalem), vol. 4: Girolamo Benzoni, Americae pars quarta. Sive, Insignis & admiranda historia de primera occidentali India à Christophoro Columbo (Frankfurt am Main: T. de Bry, 1594) Rijksmuseum, Amsterdam

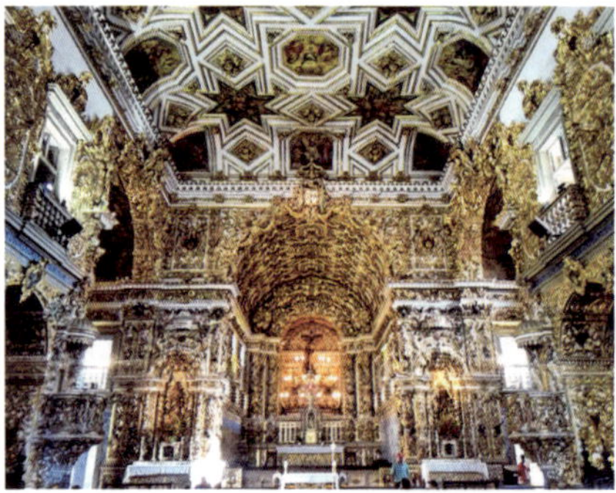

Fig 9. Interior of Igreja de São Francisco in Salvador, Brazil. Photo: Maiquel Jantsch

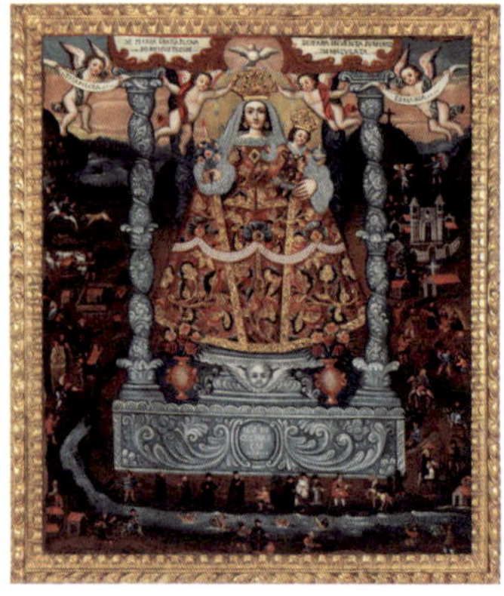

Fig 10. Unidentified Workshop, *Our Lady of Cocharcas*, 1751. Oil and gold on canvas, 50.4 × 41.5 inches (128 × 105.4 cm). Collection of Carl and Marilynn Thoma. Public domain, courtesy of the Carl & Marilynn Thoma Foundation. Photo: Jamie Stukenberg

The power of the Catholic religion from the start of the colonial era to the age of liberation and independence in the nineteenth century relied, to a great extent, upon the use of symbols, colors, grandiose structures, and rituals in an attempt to reconfigure the spiritual and everyday practices of Indigenous civilizations. From the first mission churches to the cathedrals in large and small urban centers and rural outposts, gold became a vehicle that served the purposes of conversion and the always-uncomfortable melding of two highly distinct cultures (fig. 9). In service to both the Church and secular authorities, artists produced tabernacles, altarpieces, priestly vestments, and vessels such as chalices and patens with the excess of gold in the colonies [PL. 46]. The precious metal also played an important role in the religious imagery of the vast numbers of sacred figures, including the Virgin Mary [PL. 44]. During the Spanish colonial period, the Virgin, distinguished by her gold leaf halo and glittering garments, was often depicted alongside Indigenous people in specifically American landscapes, all contained within sophisticated and complex golden frames (fig. 10). The historical association between power and religion, embodied by the image of the golden Virgin as paragon of admiration and worship, is complicated by contemporary artists such as Jamaican-born Ebony G. Patterson, who appropriates the genre to depict Black men and question issues of masculinity [PL. 50]. In similar fashion, Afro-Cuban American artist Harmonia Rosales uses this visual vocabulary to represent deities from African religions [PL. 41].

In the Spanish colonial era, foreign-imposed aesthetic and practical standards became the rule, but in some of the principal centers of artistic creativity, including Mexico, Peru, Nueva Granada, and Río de la Plata, criollo and Indigenous artists fashioned extraordinary images, both religious and secular, based upon a hybridity of pre-Hispanic and European forms of subjects, media, and themes. The Cuzco School of the late seventeenth and eighteenth centuries is one example of this dynamic fusion.[19] The work of Los Angeles–based Latino artist Eamon Ore-Giron, who is of Peruvian and Irish descent, aims for a similar kind of cross-cultural hybridity. One of his principal intentions is to overturn the hegemonic perception of spatial representation that comes from a European-based Cartesian system of so-called rational, geometric space. Often employing gold as a principal color in many of his abstract canvases, Ore-Giron draws inspiration from a variety of sources, including the patterns found on ancient Peruvian pottery and textiles, Amazonian fiber works, and pre-Hispanic objects [PL. 53]. The gold-infused tapestries and installations of Colombian artist Olga de Amaral offer another compelling take on this theme, her frequently monumental textile and fiber works serving as abstract points of visual and spiritual contact for their audiences [PL. 73].

More so than in perhaps any other region in the world, it is in the Americas where the legacy of the past is a near-constant presence within the creative processes of contemporary artists, where it continues to propel the formulation of cultural debates that move forward national and transnational conversations about ownership, indigeneity, heritage, and the rights of contemporary Indigenous populations. In 2023 Costa Rican artist Priscilla Monge created a series of Polaroid photographs covered with gold leaf [PL. 18]. Her own description of these works connects them directly with the ancient heritage of Central America: "In pre-Hispanic cultures in Costa Rica, the healers or shamans used ceramic or golden figures that represented a person and their sickness. If they wanted to heal a person with headaches, they would do something to the figure, like breaking it or smashing the head. So, these little Polaroids are something like those little golden figures the healer used."[20] By contemplating the cultural vestiges of the ancient past, as Monge does, and the clash of cultures beginning in the late fifteenth century, American artists can begin to assess the catastrophes of colonialism, as well as imagine possibilities for evolving new understandings.

BEYOND EL DORADO, BEYOND EXTRACTION

Contemporary artists' engagement with the legacy of El Dorado and the allure of gold not only poses critiques of the colonial violence perpetrated by extractivist capitalism. It also sheds light on alternative modes of existence within a state of coloniality, along with different ways of narrating colonial history. If the methods through which colonial powers structured and organized land, peoples, and nature are ingrained into how the Americas were conceived as modern nation-states, so are the counter-narratives and modes of resistance that operate within colonial and postcolonial societies. Scholars such as Macarena Gómez-Barris and Silvia Rivera Cusicanqui shed light on ideas of relationality, contradiction, and coexistence, all of which allow us to move away from a totalizing or dualistic view of colonization and to look at the flaws inherent within the colonial project.[21] Art is one way in which alternative modes of existence can symbolically disseminate these questions, and in which history can be retold and engaged with critically.

In the sixteenth century, the myth of El Dorado was fostered by the finding and plundering of Indigenous goldwork from Peru to Tenochtitlán. Oftentimes the gold was melted into bars to facilitate its transportation to Europe. By the nineteenth and twentieth centuries, these ancient relics, of which they had historically been robbed, became national symbols for the newly independent nations, ones that differentiated them from their European colonizers. Contemporary artists engaging with pre-Hispanic goldwork address the complex history of these objects, including how they were weaponized to further specific views of nationhood based on white supremacist values and narrow racial discourses. For his *Tesoros especulativos* (Speculative treasures, 2020–22) Colombian artist Juan Covelli created software that generates infinite numbers of images based on 3D scans of thousands of ancient gold objects from the collection of the Museo del Oro in Bogotá.

19 Gabriela Siracusano, *El poder de los colores: de lo material a lo simbólico en las prácticas culturales andinas: siglos xvi–xviii* (Buenos Aires: Fondo de Cultura Económica, 2005). See also Donna Pierce, Rogelio Ruiz Gomar, and Clara Bargellini, *Painting a New World: Mexican Art and Life, 1521–1821* (Denver, CO: Frederick and Jan Mayer Center for Pre-Columbian and Spanish Colonial Art, Denver Art Museum, 2004).

20 Priscilla Monge, email exchange with the authors, June 14, 2023.

21 See Macarena Gómez-Barris, *The Extractive Zone: Social Ecologies and Decolonial Perspectives* (Durham, NC: Duke University Press, 2017); Silvia Rivera Cusicanqui, "The Potosí Principle: Another View of Totality," Hemispheric Institute of Performance & Politics, New York University, https://hemisphericinstitute.org/en/emisferica-11-1-decolonial-gesture/11-1-essays/the-potosi-principle-another-view-of-totality.html.

In this work, the artist not only touches upon the violence of archaeological and museological work but also lends visibility to the imagined and artificial nature of national values [PL. 08 and 09]. In addition, Carlos Motta, another artist from Colombia, is interested in how these ancient goldworks speak to the imposition of Western sexual and gender systems onto subaltern populations, as well as how they can emphasize the voyeuristic and appropriative gaze toward these objects [PL. 35].

Extraction lies at the center of the appropriation of pre-Hispanic Indigenous icons, knowledges, and cultures, which feeds into the symbolic cultural values of modern nations; it is also at the center of the exploitative systems of labor, such as enslavement, imposed on subjects to remove material wealth from the land. Afro-Brazilian artist Tiago Sant'Ana references the history of mining in colonial Brazil in the video *Chão de estrelas* (Ground of stars, 2022) [PL. 82]. Filmed at Chapada Diamantina in the State of Bahia, a historical site of gold and precious metal extraction, the video depicts Black men panning for gold in a river. Yet instead of holding pans or sieves, they hold mirrors. Addressing how the history of enslavement constructed the subjectivity of Black people in Brazil, the video also tells of strategies of survival, suggesting other possible narrative paths. In a similar vein, Afro-Brazilian artist Bruno Baptistelli emphasizes the role of gold in ancestral Black civilizations with his golden sculptural works. In his *Manus* and *Pedites* (2023), in which sculptural body fragments are displayed as precious objects in delicate boxes, he also explores the importance of gold for the construction of subjectivity, such as in hip-hop culture, while also speaking to a longer history of exploitation in its extraction [PL. 28 and 29].

The extraction of gold in the Americas has taken different forms. The process often involves large-scale operations and a complex economic system behind them, from the individual working on site in open mining pits in the Amazon to the storefronts of luxury jewelry shops in global capitals. The effects of gold mining on the environment are enormous, causing negative ecological, social, and political impacts. Not only does it demand large amounts of water, causing long-term water contamination with heavy metals, but it also requires the clearing of forests, which leads to soil degradation and erosion. For some artists of Indigenous descent, these ecological catastrophes are the subject of urgent inquiry. In her work *Kuêra* (2021), Moara Tupinambá, from the Tupinambá people, juxtaposes deforested areas of the Amazon with historical and present-day representations of Indigenous people, pairing the exploitation of the natural environment with disease and the deaths of Indigenous populations [PL. 106].

The human costs of gold extraction are concentrated in Indigenous communities. Local populations—for example, the Yanomami in the Brazilian Amazon—who live in areas rich in gold are often targeted by miners, governments, and corporations who continue to see their land as an empty space up for grabs. The subsequent displacement, famine, and illness constitute a grave humanitarian crisis for these vulnerable populations. Facing the vast variety of extractive practices in the Americas, contemporary artists shed light on the nefarious continuity of the mythic allure of material wealth. In his video *Azougue 80* (2019), Denilson Baniwa, from the Baniwa people, performs the ingestion of contaminated water and fish over the sound of a speech given by the former president of Brazil, Jair Bolsonaro, in which he defends the benefits of gold mining for the country [PL. 92]. Works like these and many others that critique extraction as an ethos in the Americas create and reflect new cultural imaginaries that envision a sustainable relationship between humans and nature, one which grows in the cracks of the extractivist system. The Colombian artist duo Mazenett Quiroga, for instance, created precious boxes with gilded seeds of the Guayacan trees, which are considered sacred by Indigenous groups in their country [PL. 34], while Brazilian artist Laura Vinci created golden leaves and tree trunks [PL. 20]. By gilding these natural objects, she addresses their status in contemporary Western culture, which values gold much more than it values nature. Perhaps these artists are pointing toward environmental protection as a new El Dorado, a utopian view that is hardly attainable in a world driven by the greed of contemporary capitalism. On the other hand, and more positively, these artworks, along with the numerous voices of artists, activists, and scholars, point to a necessary shift in how we can conceive of the Americas moving forward, beyond the aid of myth.

The Americas embody not one but many ideas.[22] Encompassing a large range of cultures, languages, and histories across populations that, though they may share a colonial past and postcolonial present, have seen them manifested differently, "America" is a homogenizing term that can sometimes flatten the richness and diversity of the continent. It could even be considered too broad to be used in any productive sense. Something similar could be said today about El Dorado, and the shared intangible quality might also explain why the myth expanded so much and for so long throughout the continent. Still, both El Dorado and the Americas are as abstract as they are concrete and real, as evinced by the material, even corporeal, consequences of the violence that was accomplished and is still done in their names. Through their use of gold, both physical and metaphorical, the artists in this exhibition emphasize to us the ambivalent power of myth in conditioning who we are as a region, opening space for us to resist extractive systems and to reconsider what we are seeking.

22 In his seminal book *The Idea of Latin America* (Malden, MA: Blackwell, 2005), Walter Mignolo argues that the concept of Latin America was constructed by European colonizers to serve their own interests, perpetuating a Eurocentric narrative. He calls for a decolonial perspective that challenges this imposition and embraces diverse local histories and epistemologies.

GOLD, VALUE, AND THE BODY

Goldwork held a significant place in the history and culture of pre-Hispanic societies. Alongside other materials valued for their shiny properties, such as obsidian, shell, jade, and silver, gold was valued for its symbolic associations with the sun; for example, for the Mexica, gold was considered the sun's excreta. Gold was widely used in bodily ornaments, including earrings, nosepieces, masks, and pendants, each of which carried a different meaning according to specific iconographies. These included abstract forms and shapes of animals such as eagles, frogs, bats, and crocodiles. The pre-Hispanic goldworks in this section, originating from different cultures located in present-day Peru, Colombia, Costa Rica, and Panama, were mostly used as adornments for the body, or make direct reference to the human figure. Such emphasis on the body is a rich connector between these pre-Hispanic goldworks and contemporary artworks also emphasizing bodies, whether they be human, animal, or natural. The works here also point to the intrinsic relativity and abstract nature of value, from ancient to contemporary times.

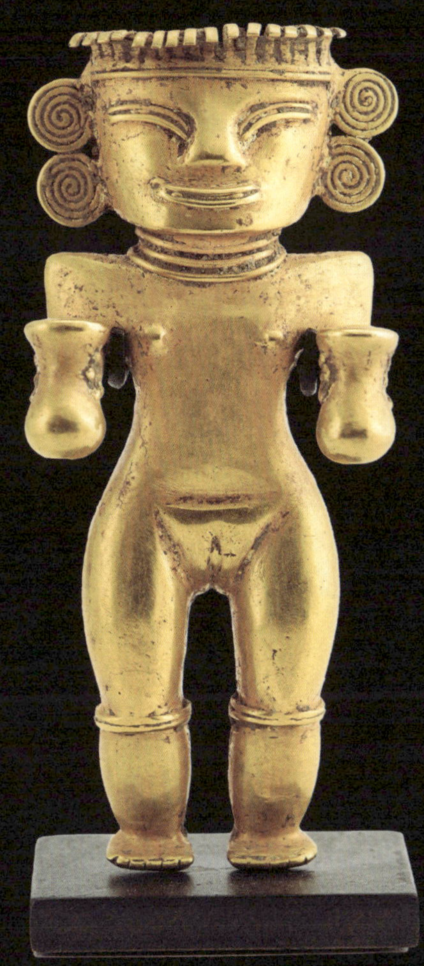

Unknown Quimbaya style artist, Colombia, *Female Figure Holding Poporos*, 600–1400 CE

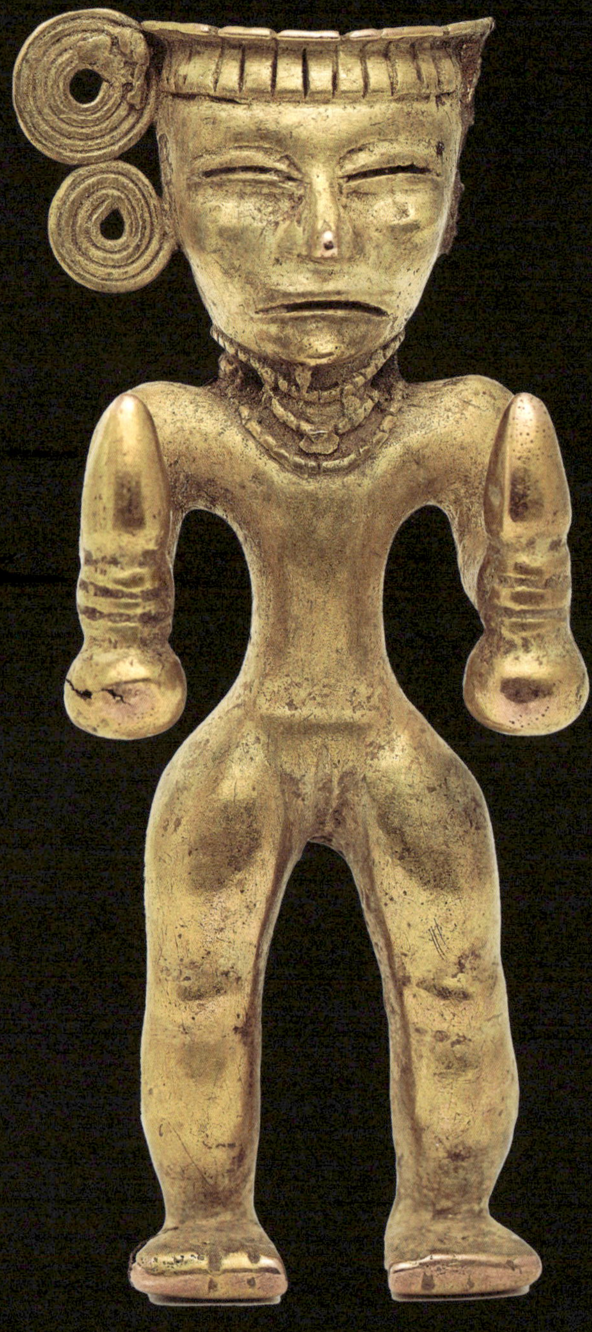

Unknown Quimbaya style artist, Colombia, *Female Figure Holding Poporos*, 600–1400 CE

Juan Brenner, *San Juan Comalapa, Chimaltenango, Guatemala*, from T*onatiuh Series*, 2017–19

↓ [PL. 03]

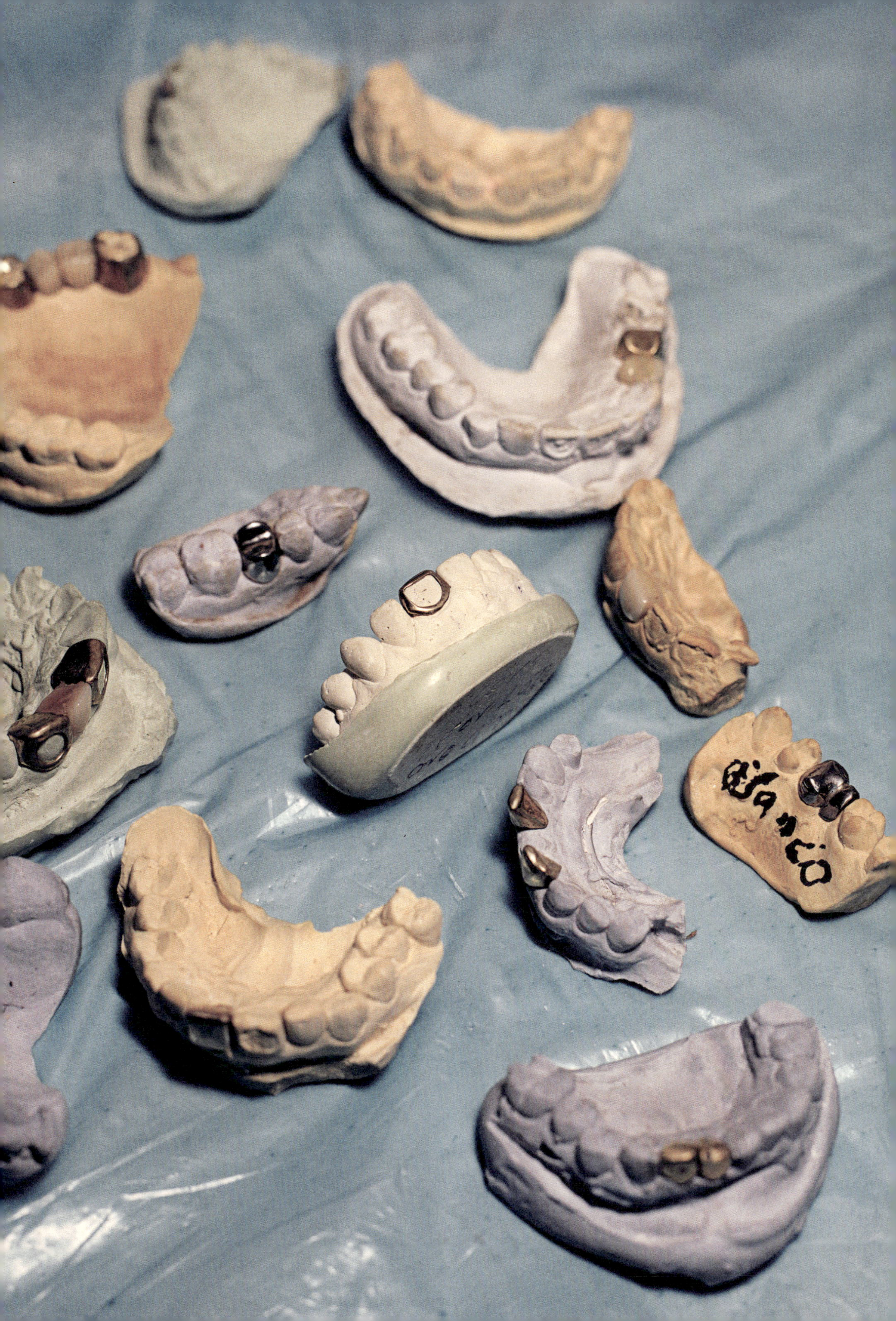
Bianco

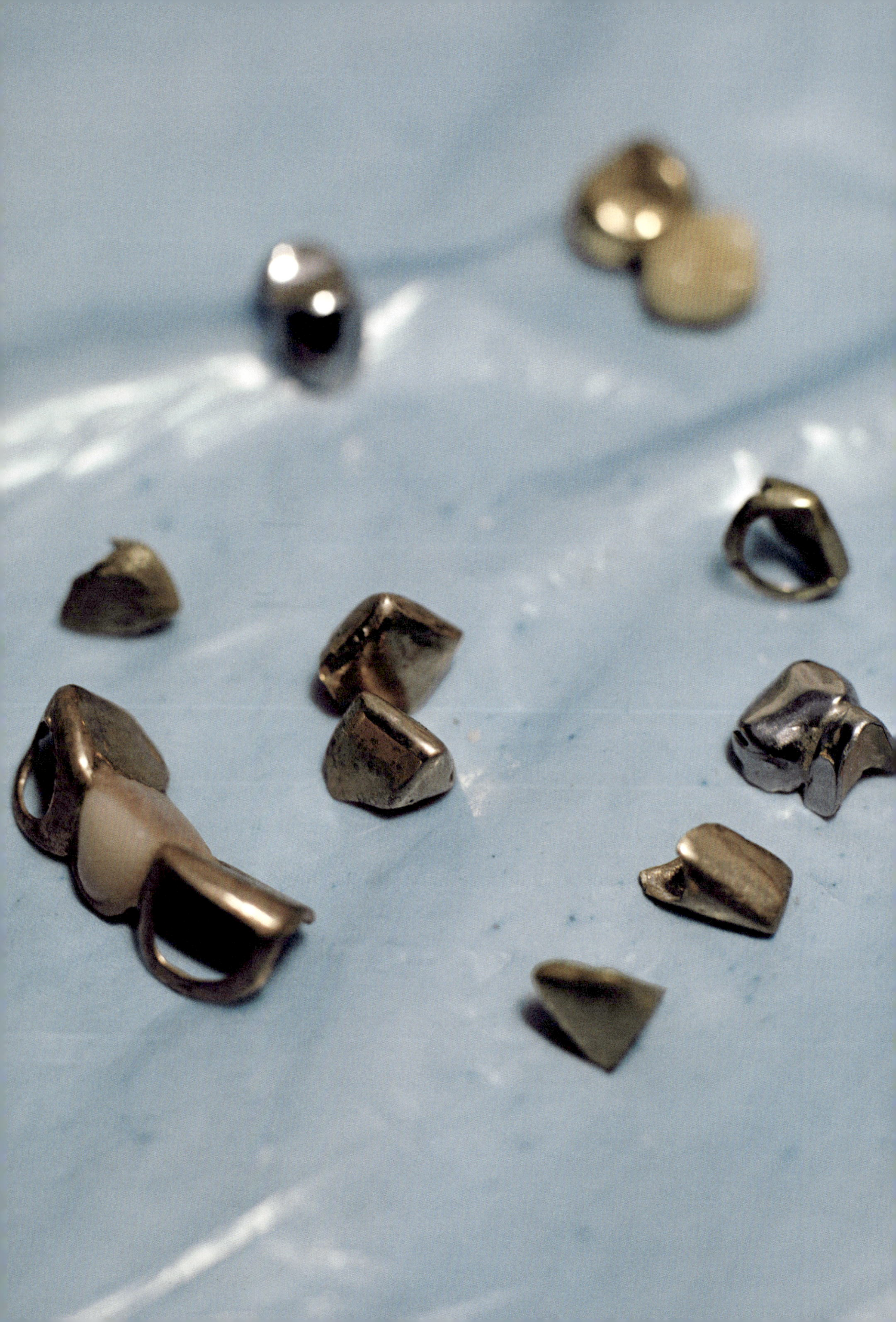

Juan Brenner, *San Juan Comalapa, Chimaltenango, Guatemala*, from *Tonatiuh Series*, 2017–19

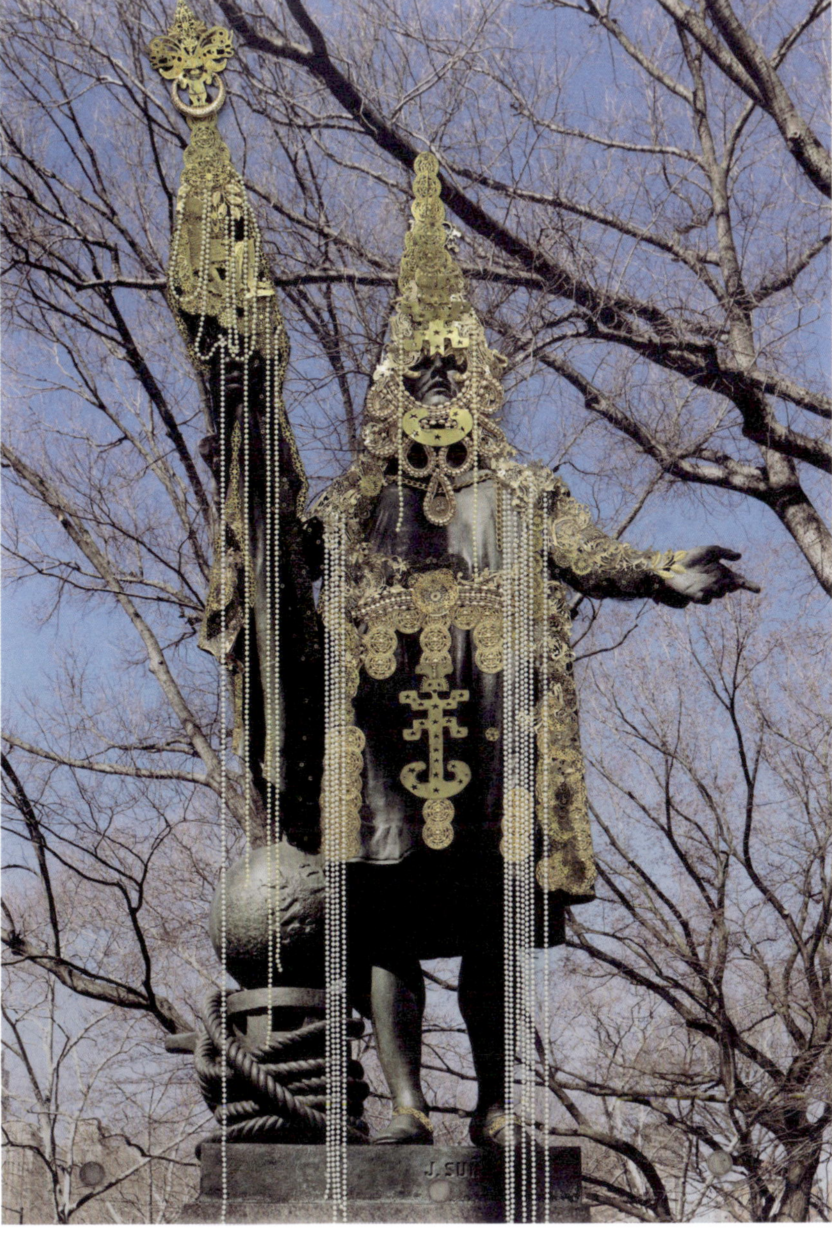

Hew Locke, *Columbus, Central Park*, 2018

↑ [PL. 04]

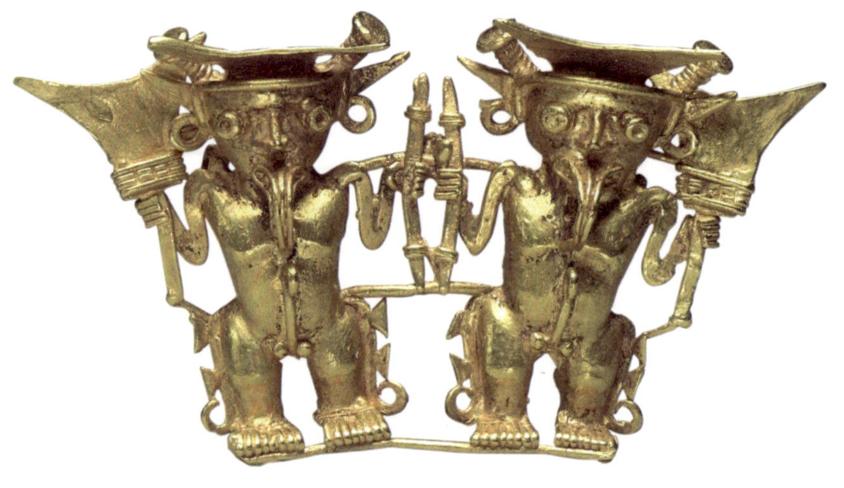

Unknown Coclé artist, Central Panama, *Double Warrior Pendant*, 1150–1400 CE

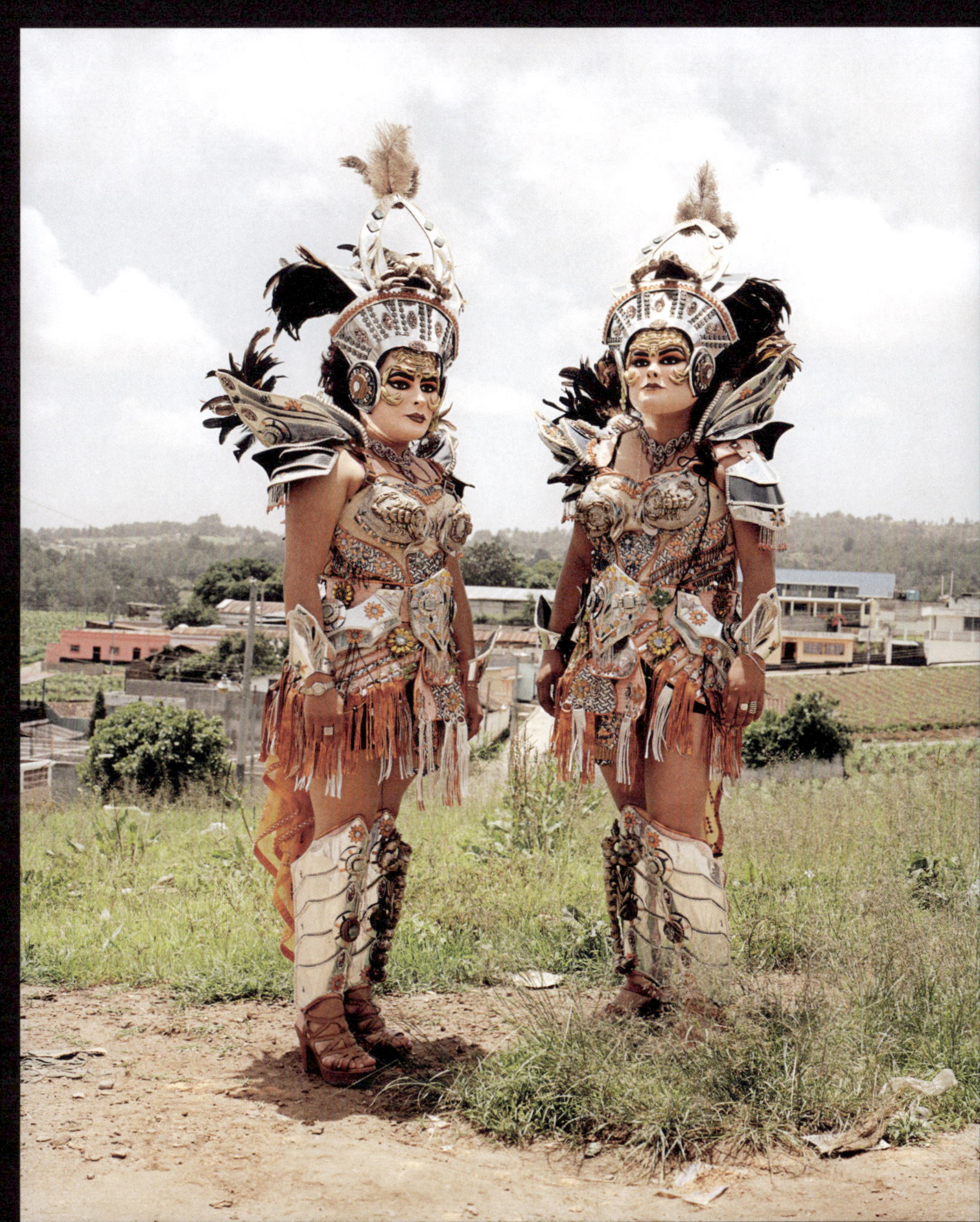

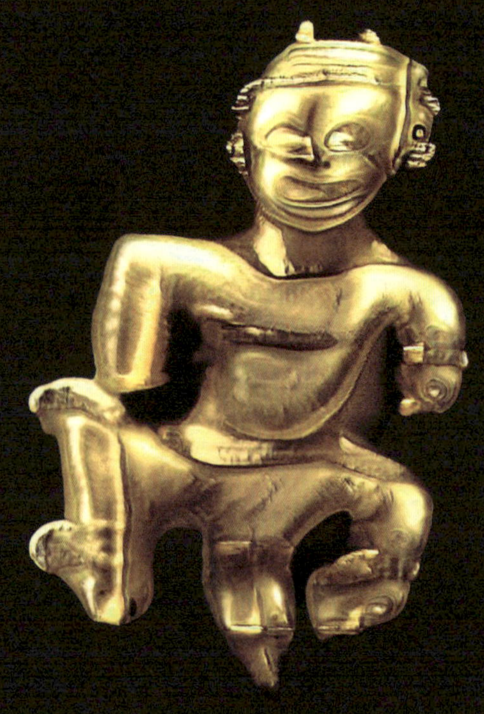

Juan Covelli, *Tesoros especulativos* (Speculative treasures), 2020–22

[PL. 09]

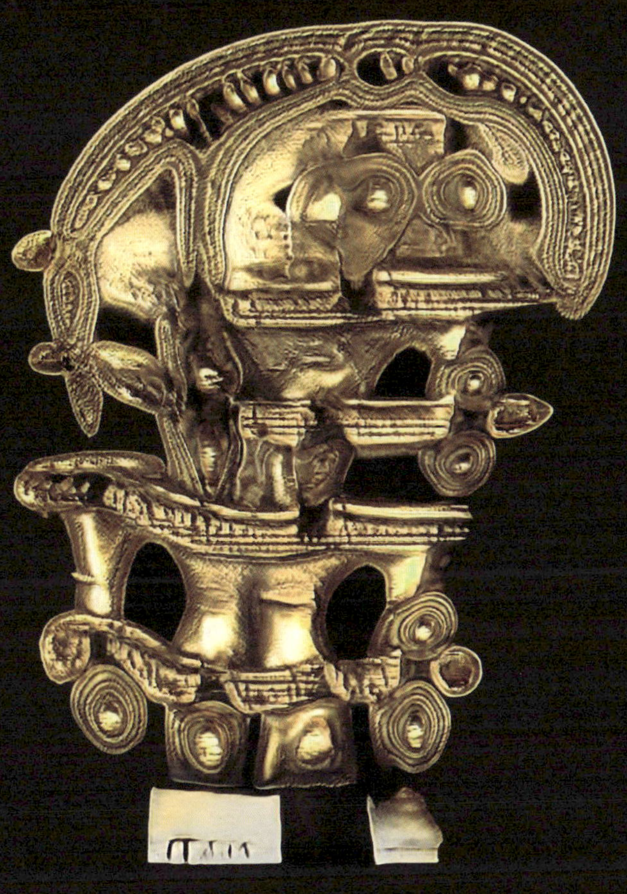

Juan Covelli, *Tesoros especulativos* (Speculative treasures), 2020–22

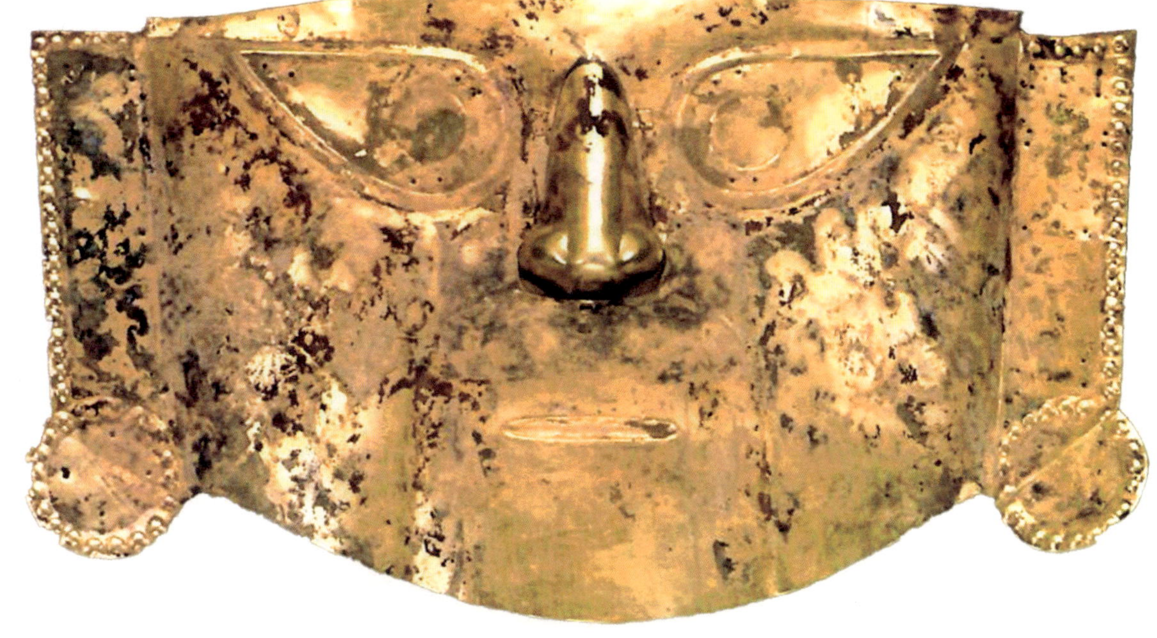

Unknown Lambayeque artist, north coast of Peru, *Gold Mask*, 900–1100 CE

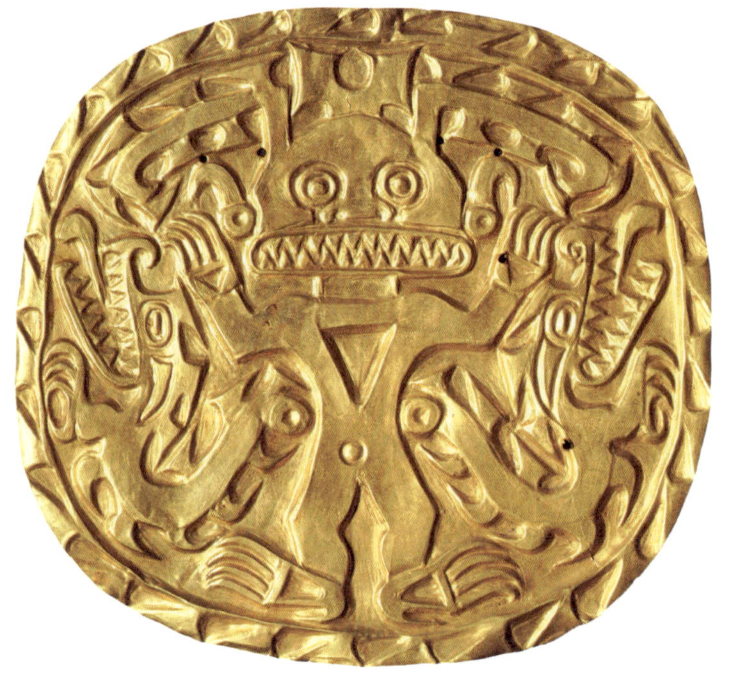

Unkown Coclé artist, *Plaque with Crocodile Deity*, ca. 700–900 CE

Carlos Rojas, *Yo, Midas*, 1989-1990

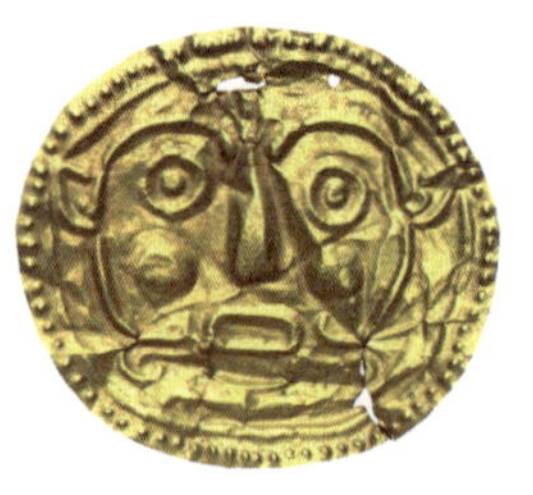

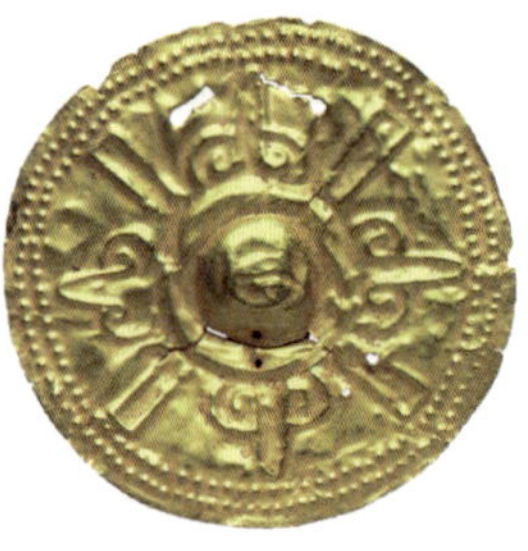

Unknown Greater Chiriquí artist, Costa Rica, *Gold Disk with Embossed Face*, 800–1522 CE
Unknown Greater Chiriquí artist, Panama. *Disk with Directional Symbol*, 700–1000 CE

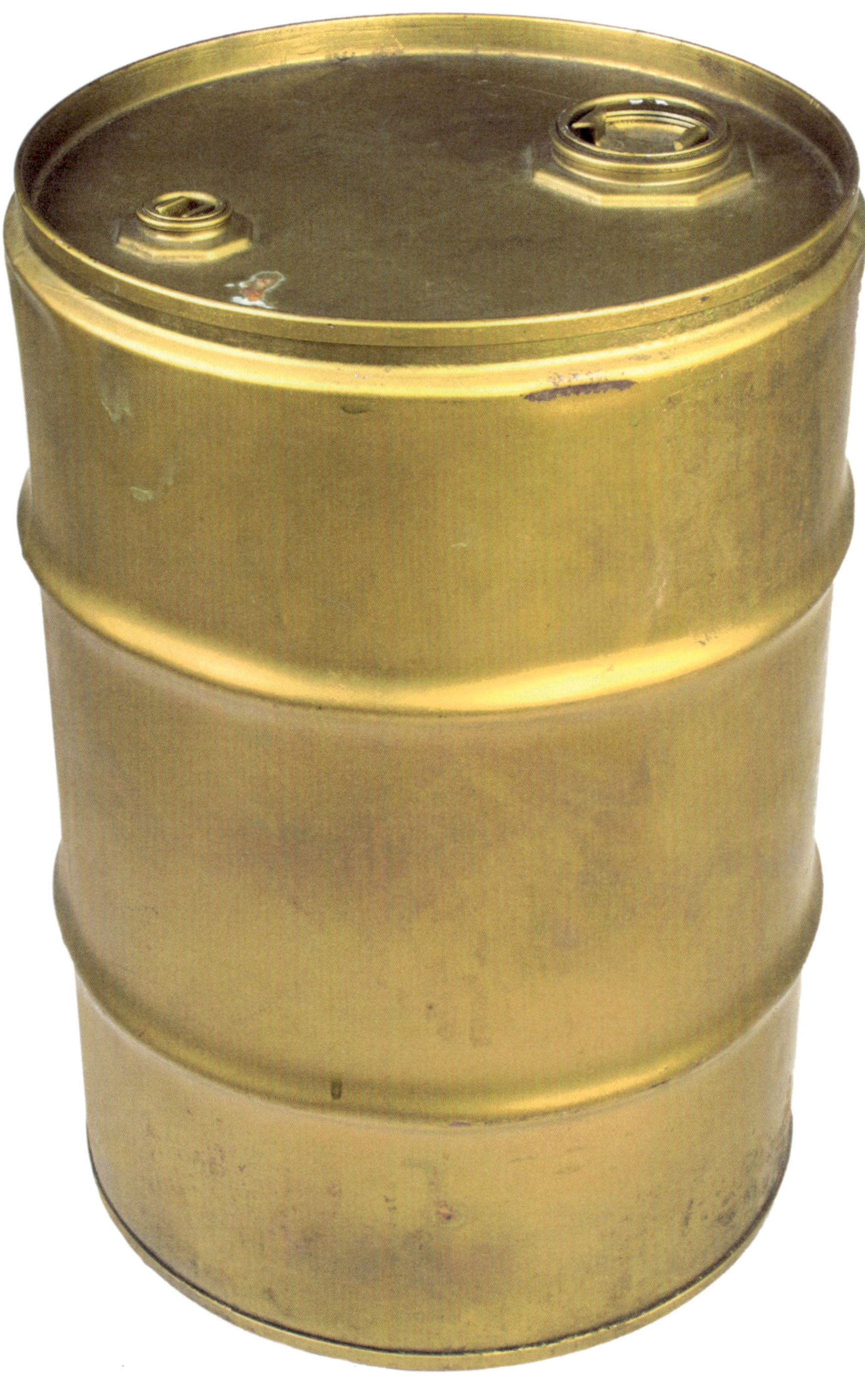

Rolando Peña, *El barril encontrado* (The found barrel), 1975

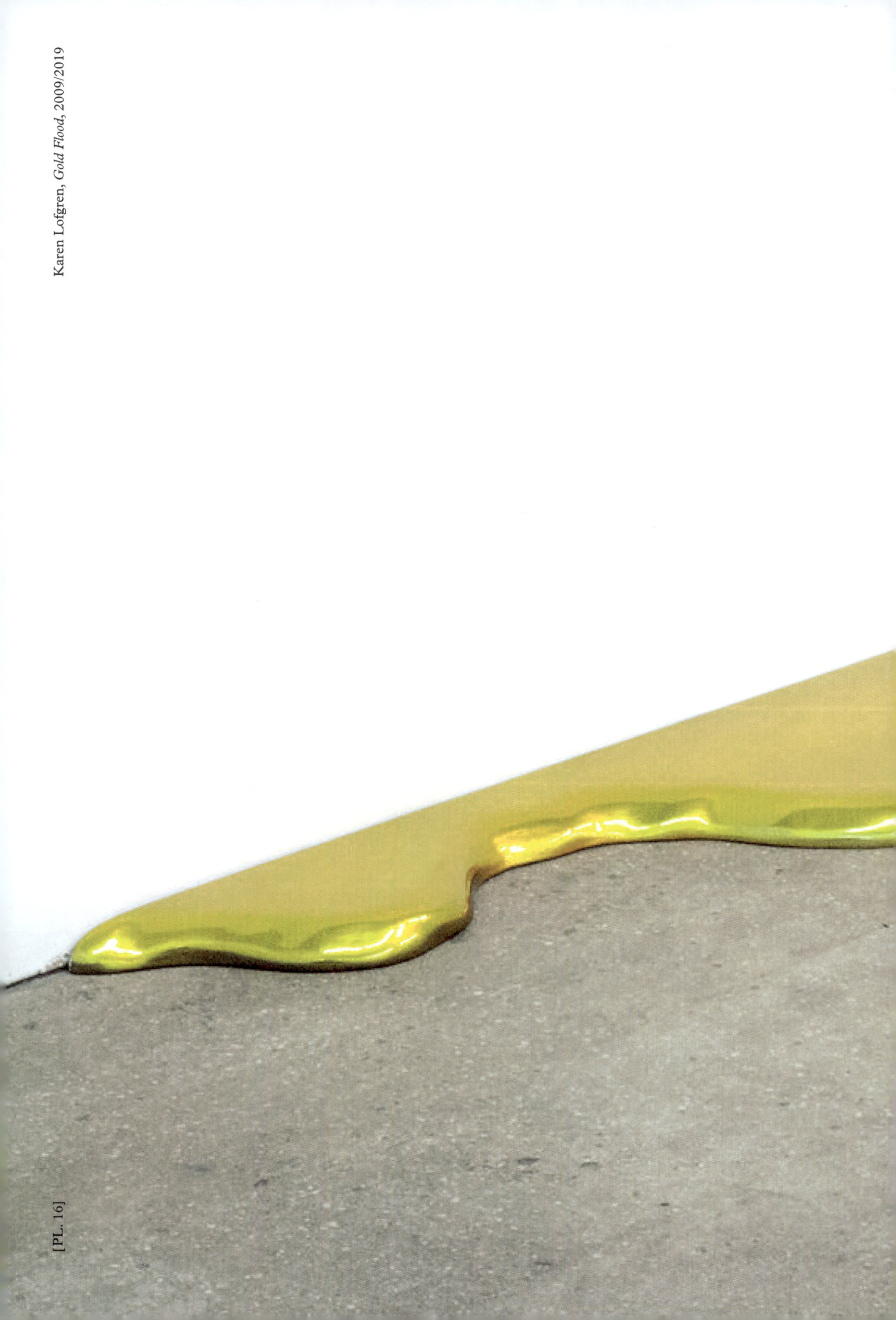

Karen Lofgren, *Gold Flood*, 2009/2019

[PL. 16]

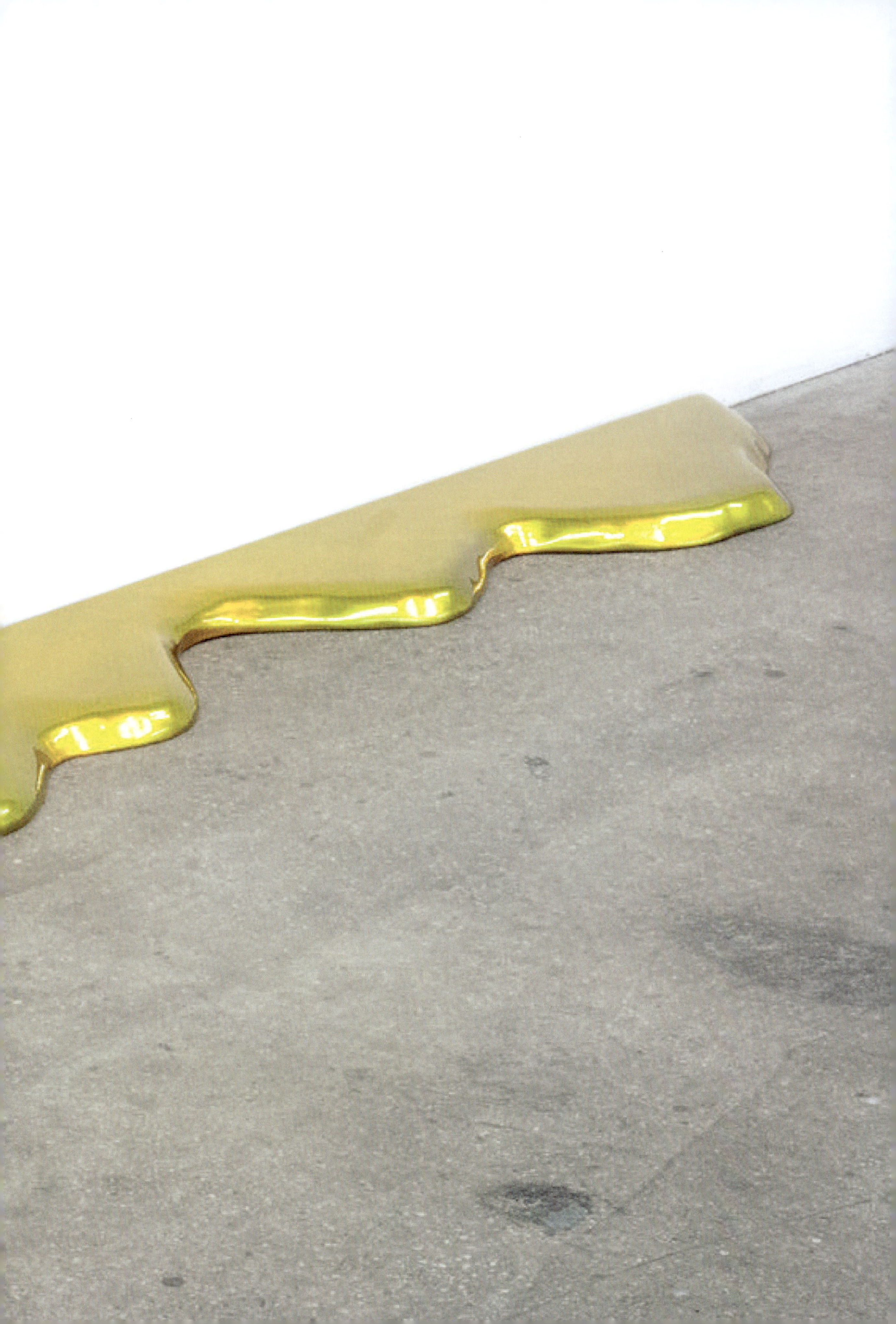

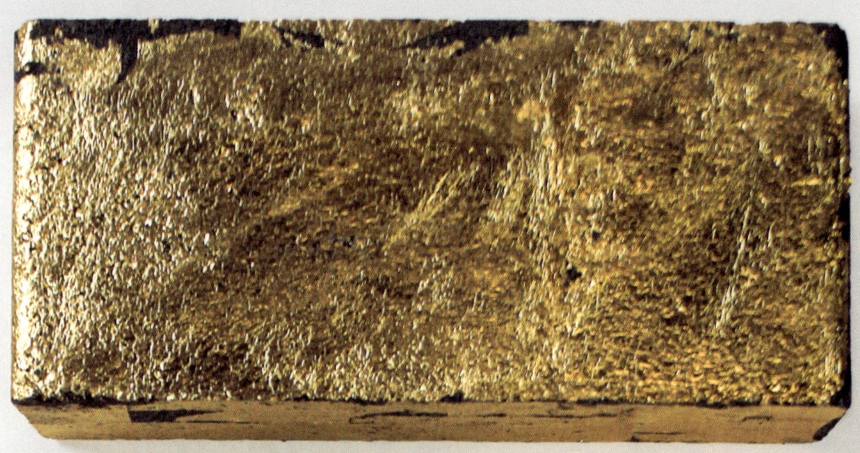

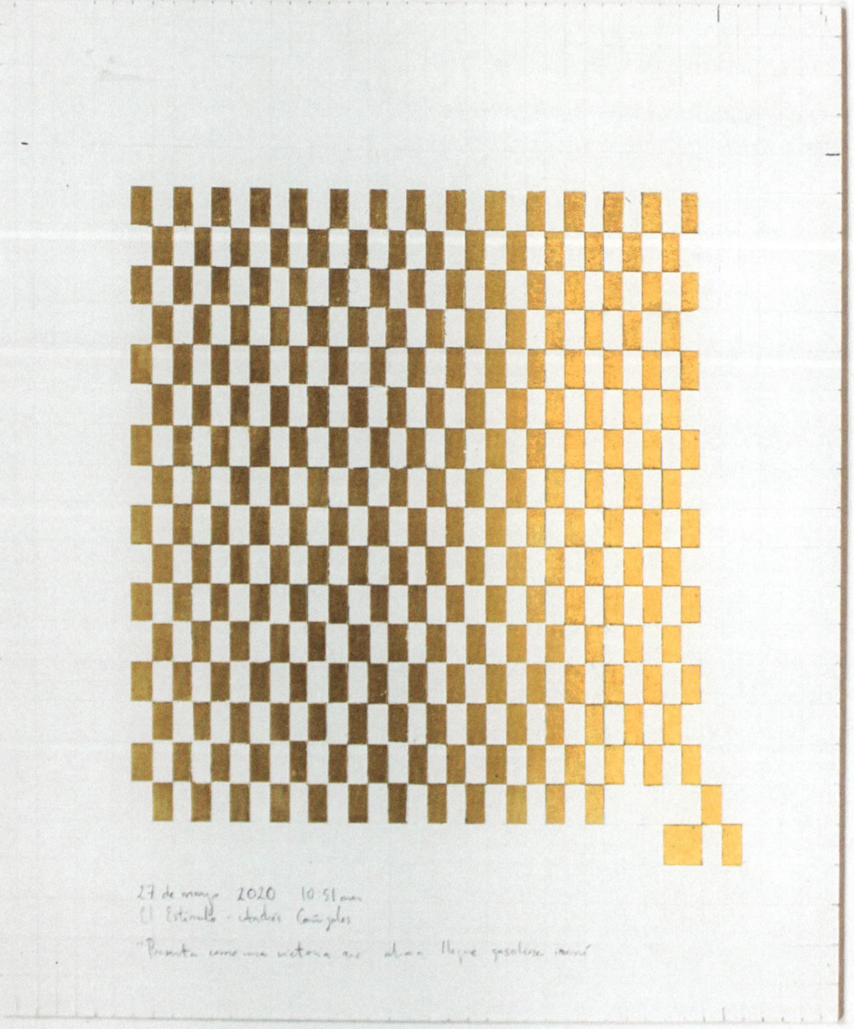
27 de mayo 2020 10:51 am

[PL. 18]

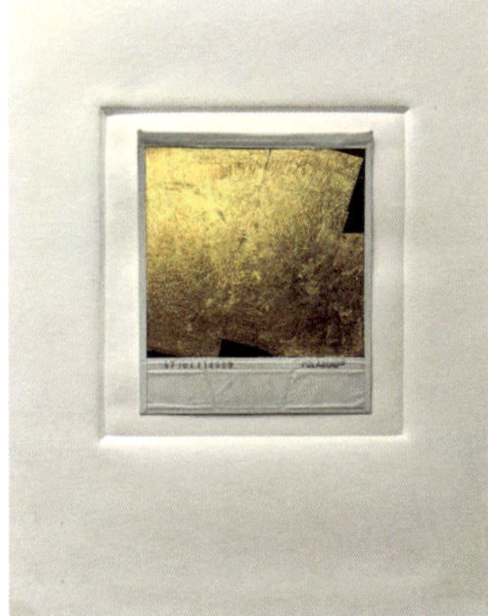

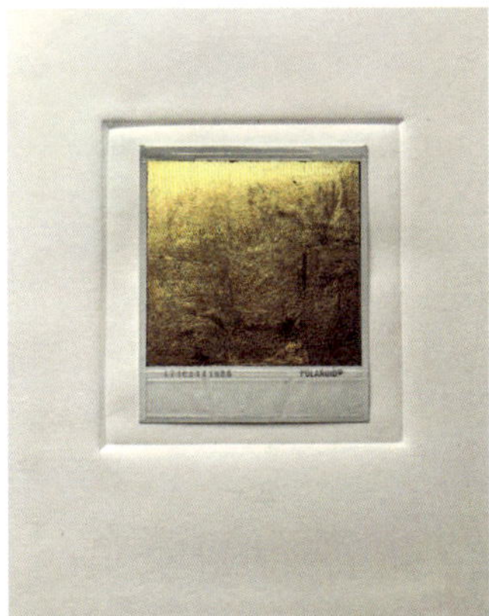

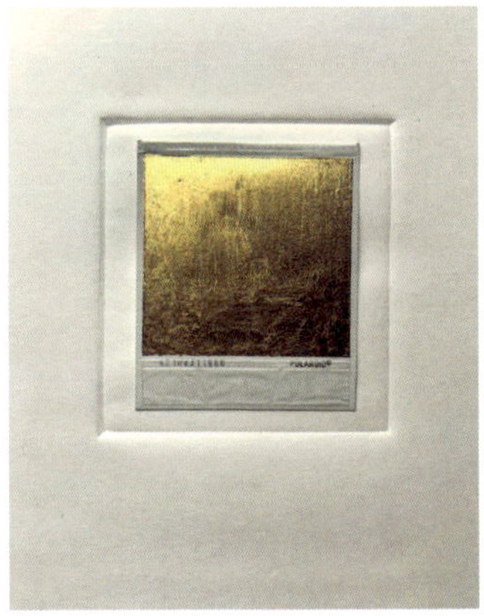

Priscilla Monge, *Healing Surfaces*, 2023

(Top) Esperanza Mayobre, *Serie A.M.O.* 2020

(Bottom) *Serie A.M.O. (They present as a victory that Iranian gasoline now arrives. March 27th, 2020. Caracas,Venezuela.)*, 2020

↑ [PL. 17]

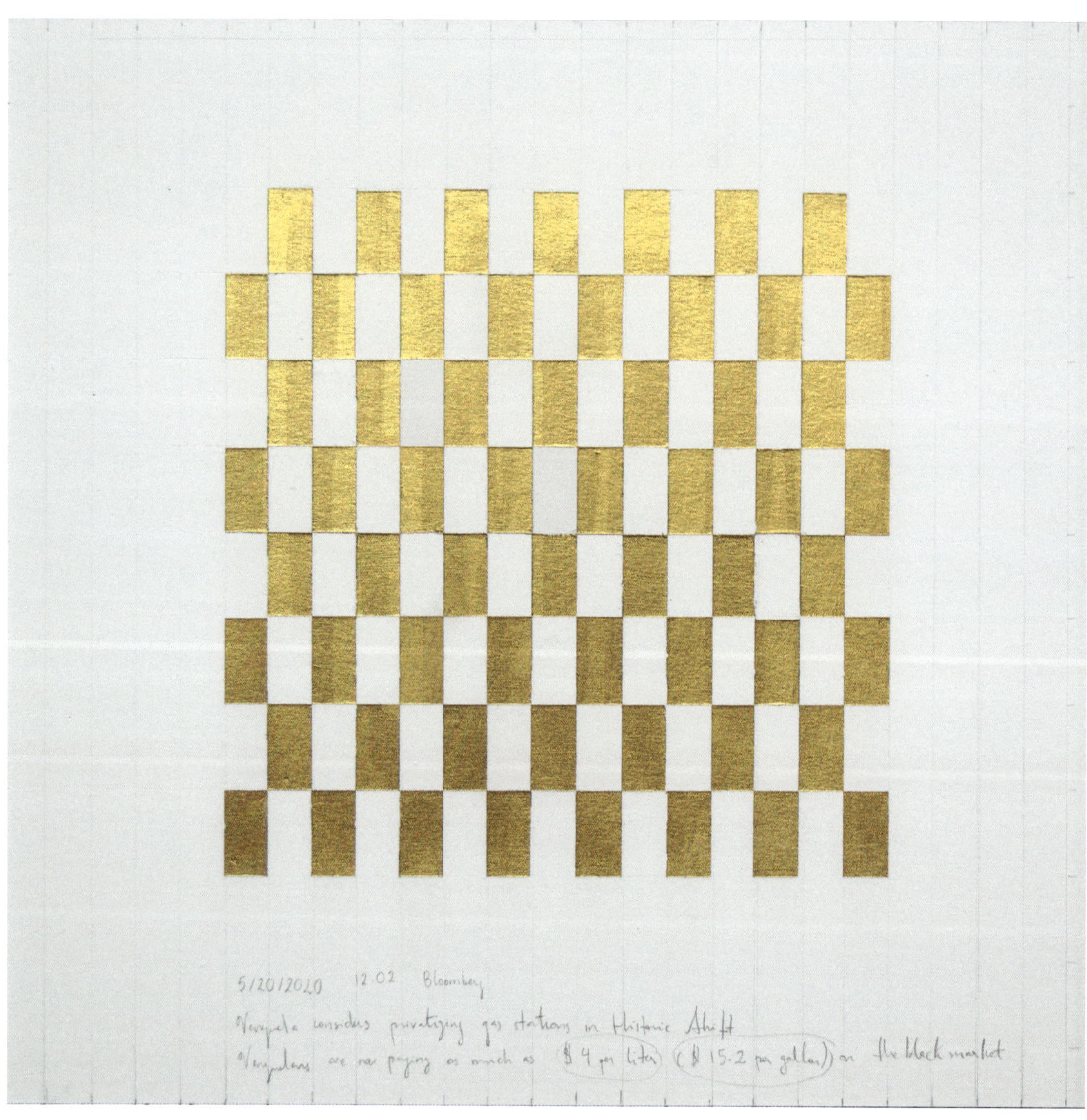

Esperanza Mayobre, *Serie A.M.O. ($15.20 por galón en el mercado negro)* ($15.2 per gallon in the black market), 2020

Laura Vinci, *Folhas avulsas # 1 e # 2* (Loose leaves #1 and #2), 2018

↓ [PL. 20]

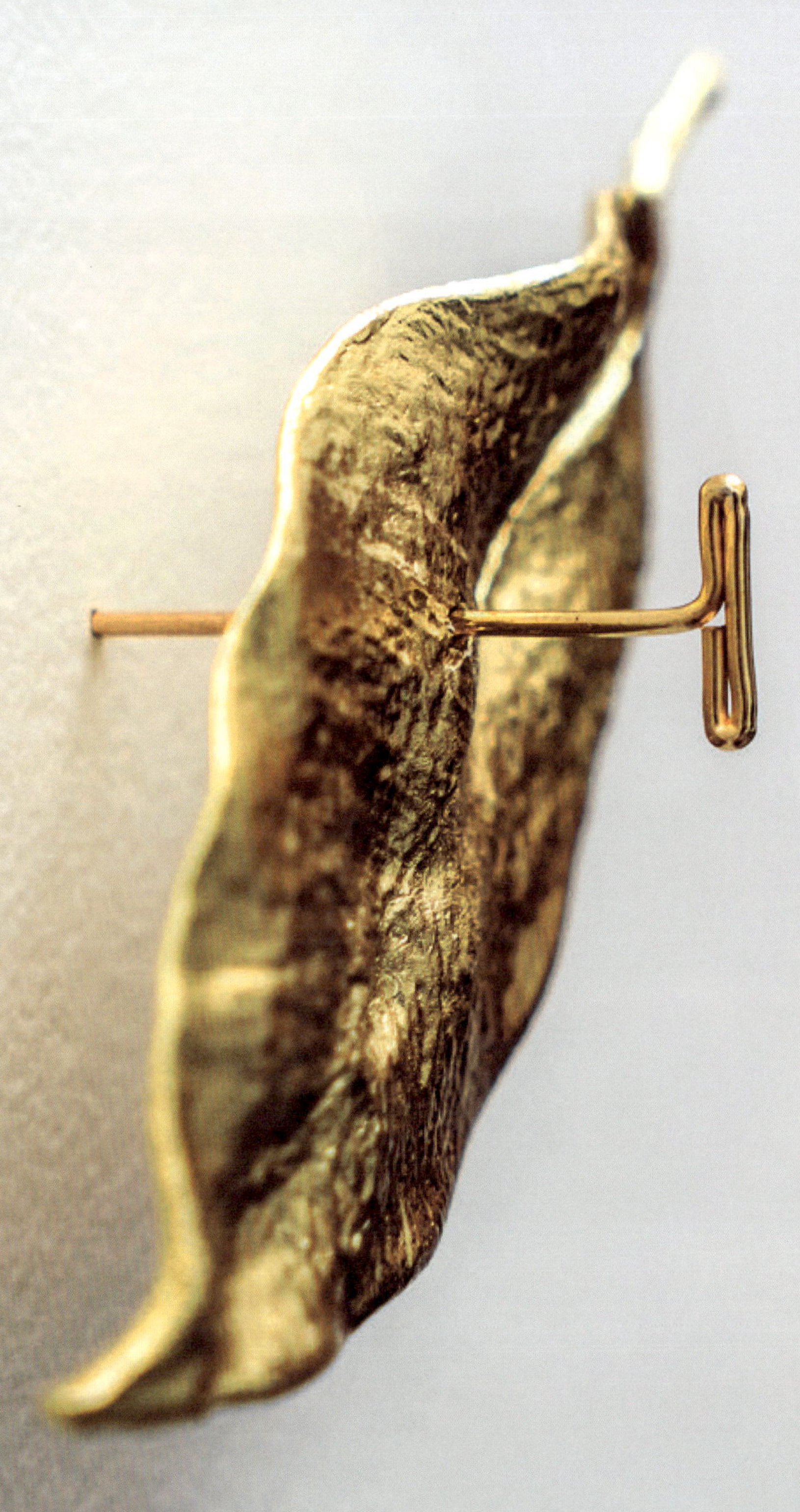

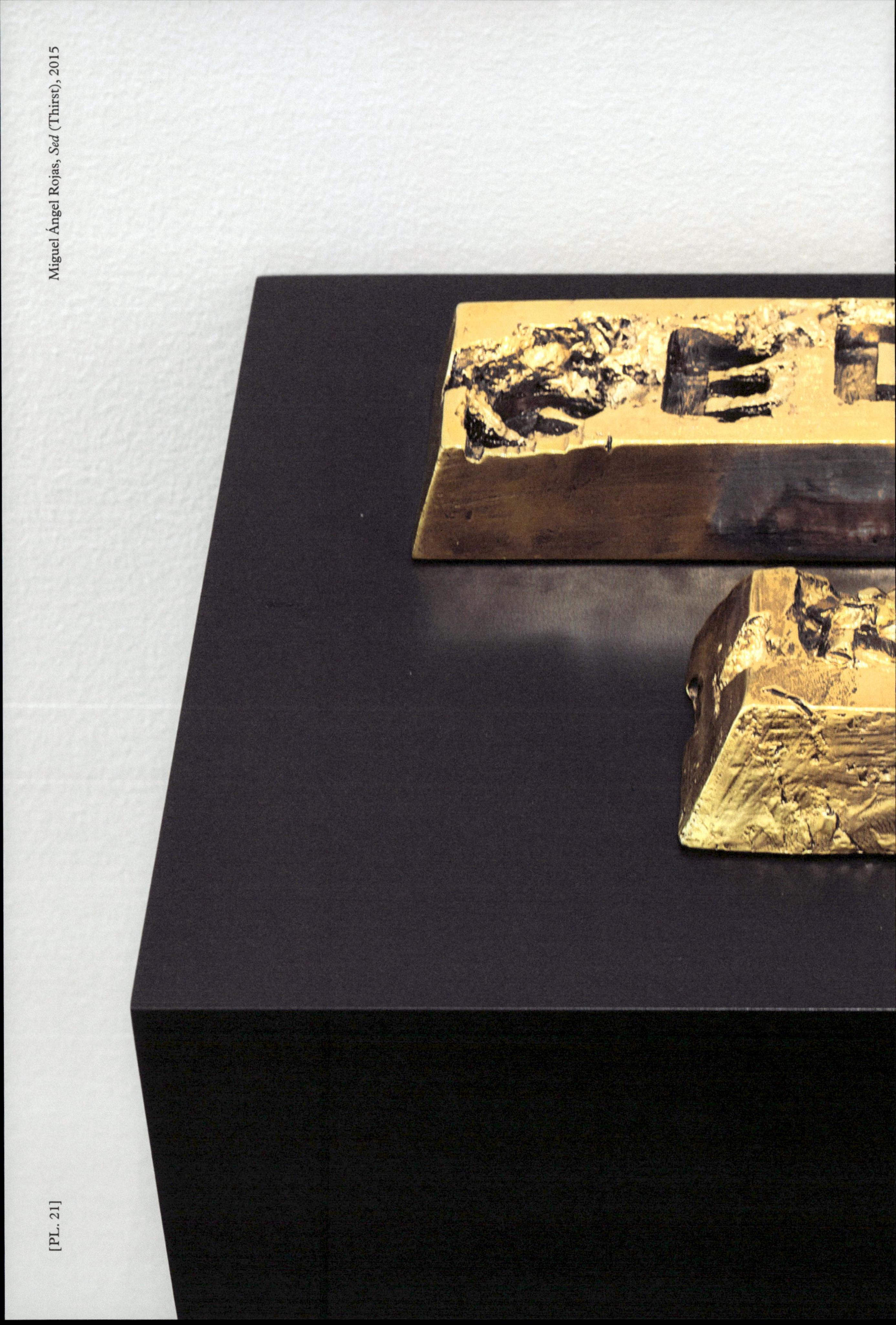

[PL. 21] Miguel Ángel Rojas, *Sed* (Thirst), 2015

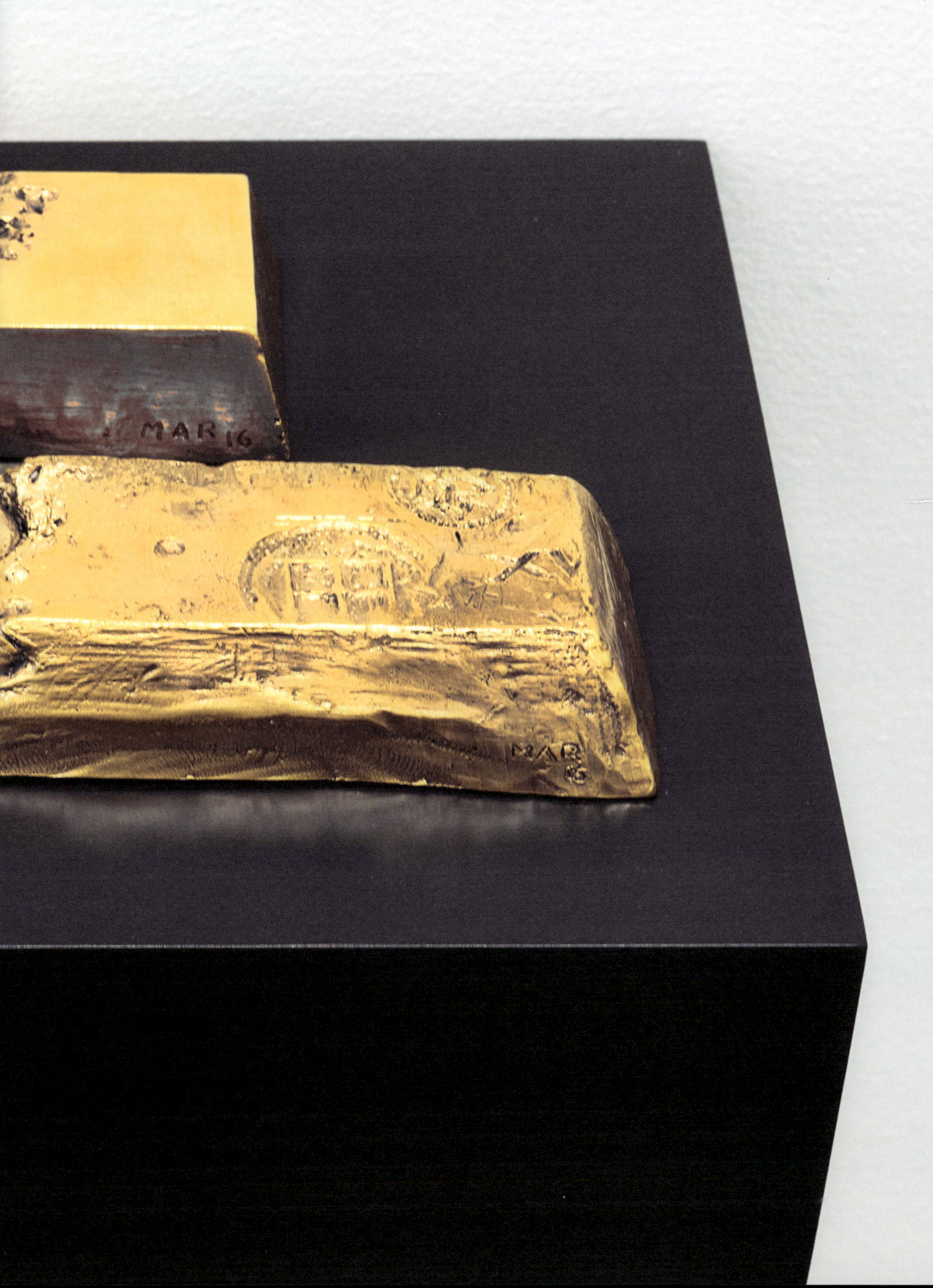
MAR16

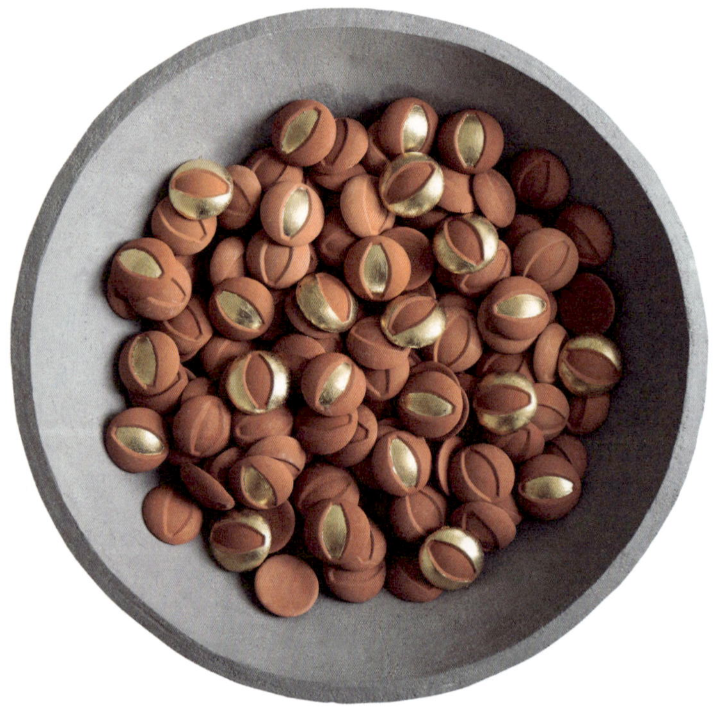

Sara Mejia Kriendler, *Inner Visions (Visiones) I*, 2021

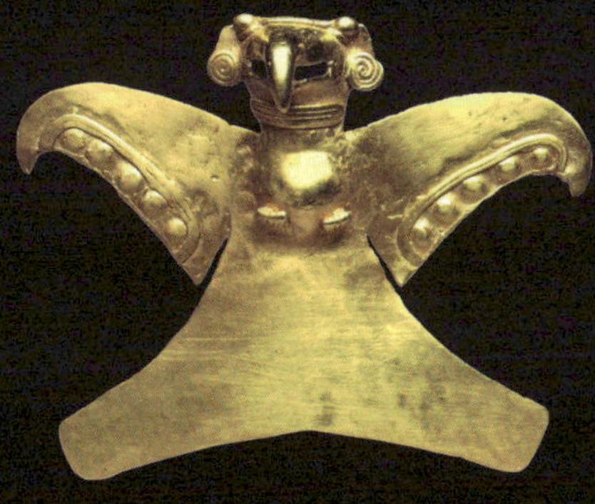

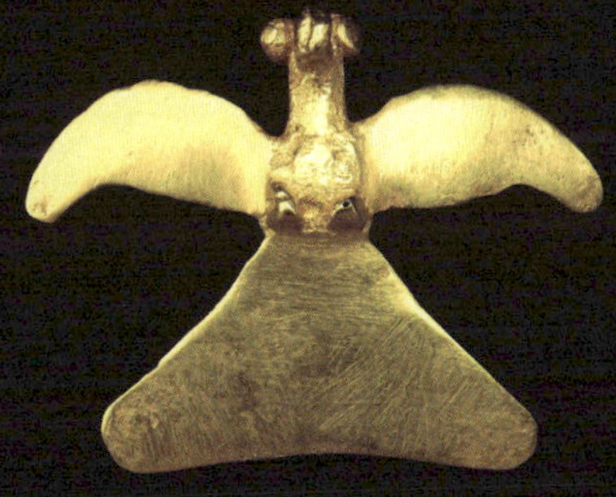

Unknown Greater Chiriqui artist, Costa Rica, *Eagle Pendant*, 800–1522 CE
Unknown Greater Chiriqui artist, Costa Rica, *Eagle Pendant*, 800–1522 CE

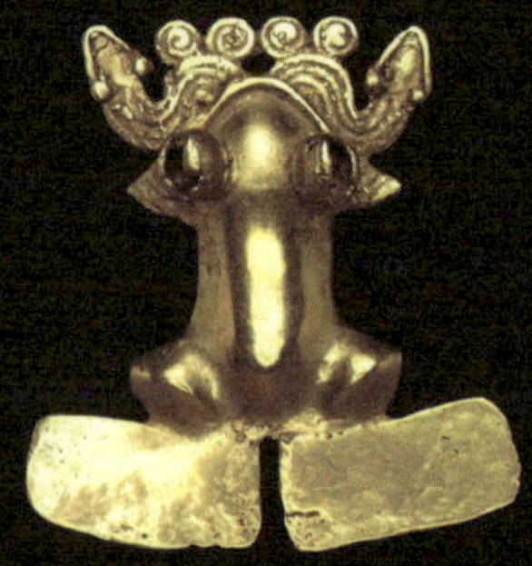

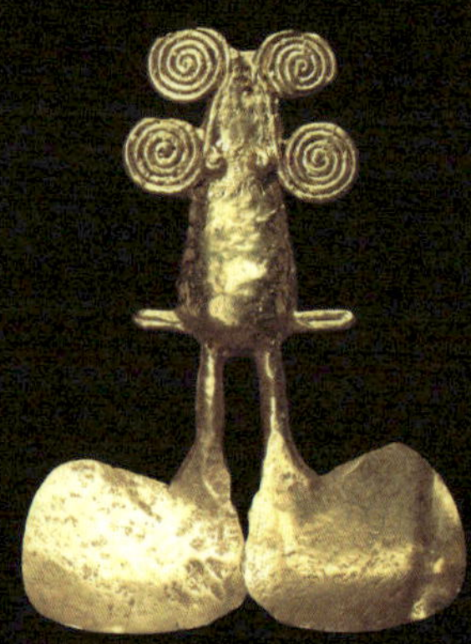

Unknown Greater Chiriquí artist, *Frog Pendant*, 800–1522 CE
Unknown Panamanian artist, Panama. *Pendant*, 500–1520 CE

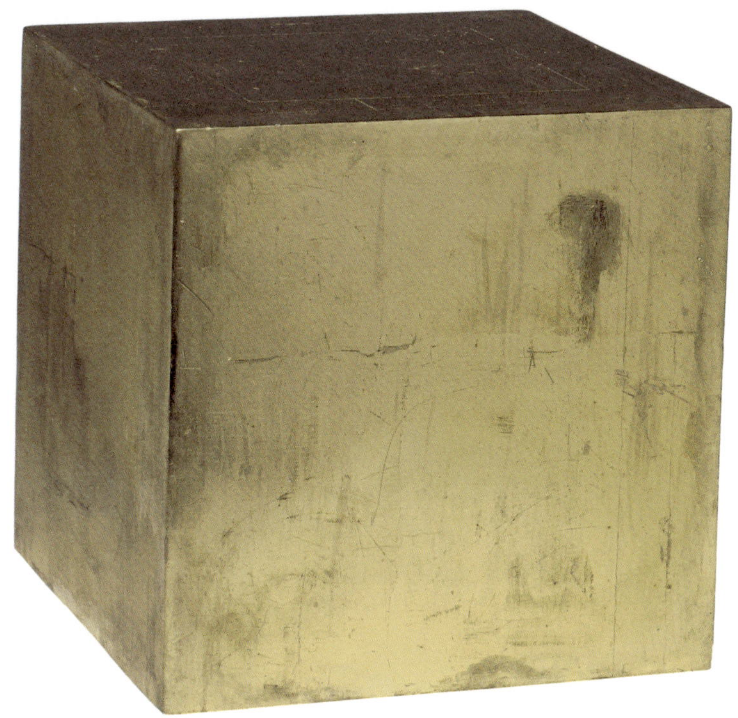

Mathias Goeritz, *Figura geométrica* (Geometric figure), 1961

Denilson Baniwa, *Série mimética e resistência 2. Mercúrio: dias de um futuro esquecido* (Series mimetics and resistance 2. Mercury: days of a forgotten future), 2022

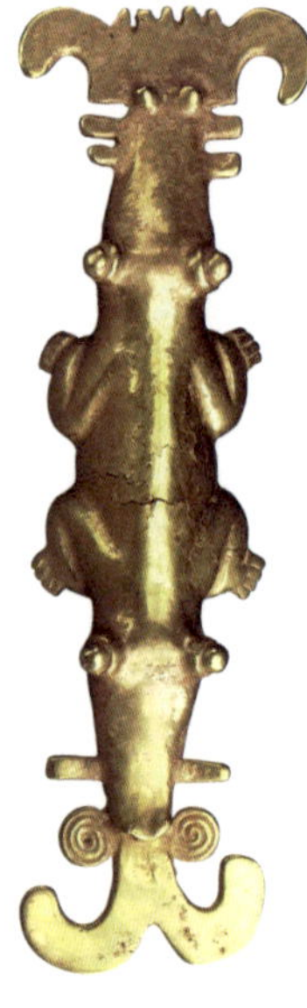

Unknown Coclé artist, Panama, *Double-Headed Crocodile*, 1150–1400 CE

↓ [PL. 27]

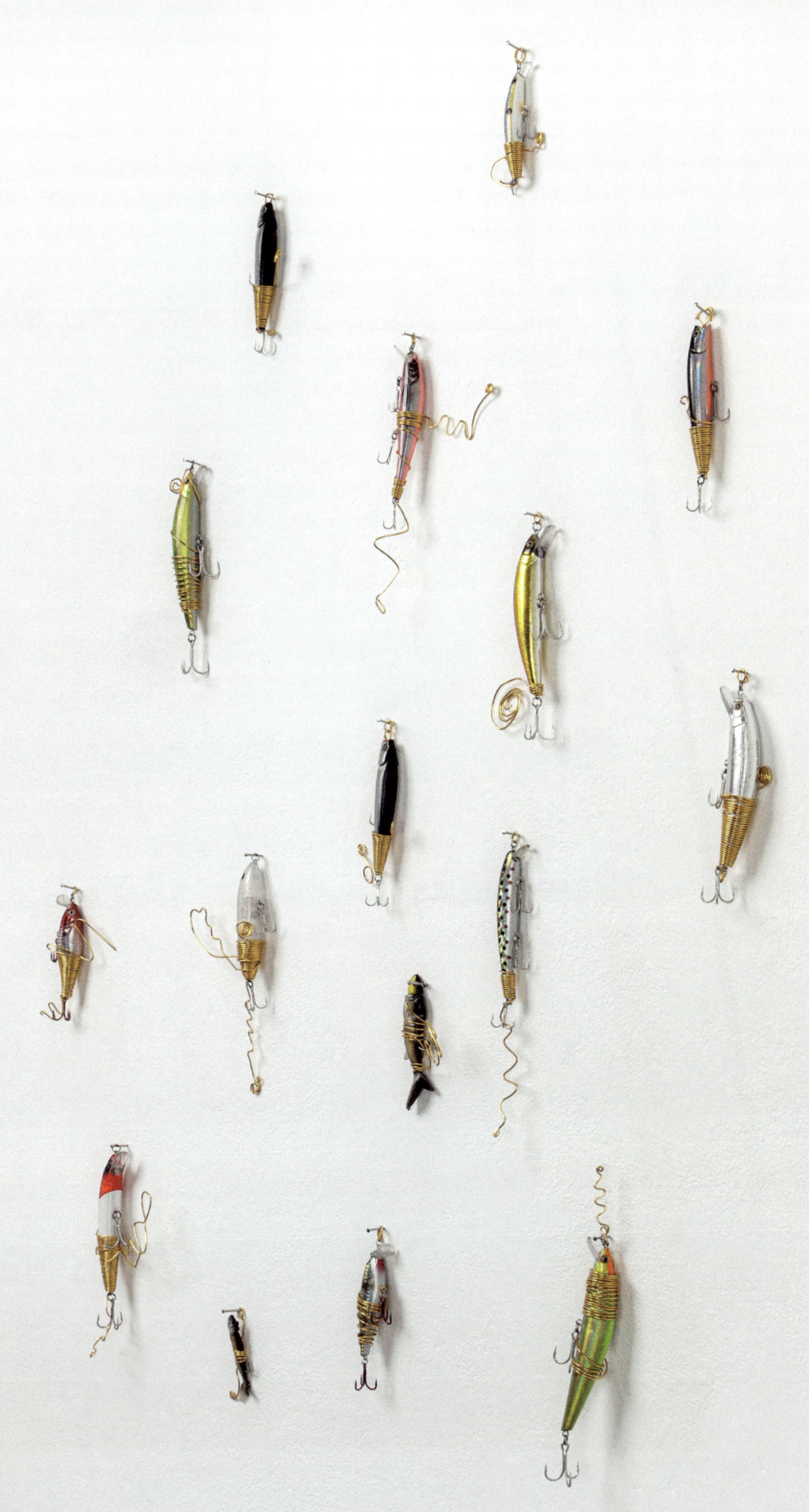

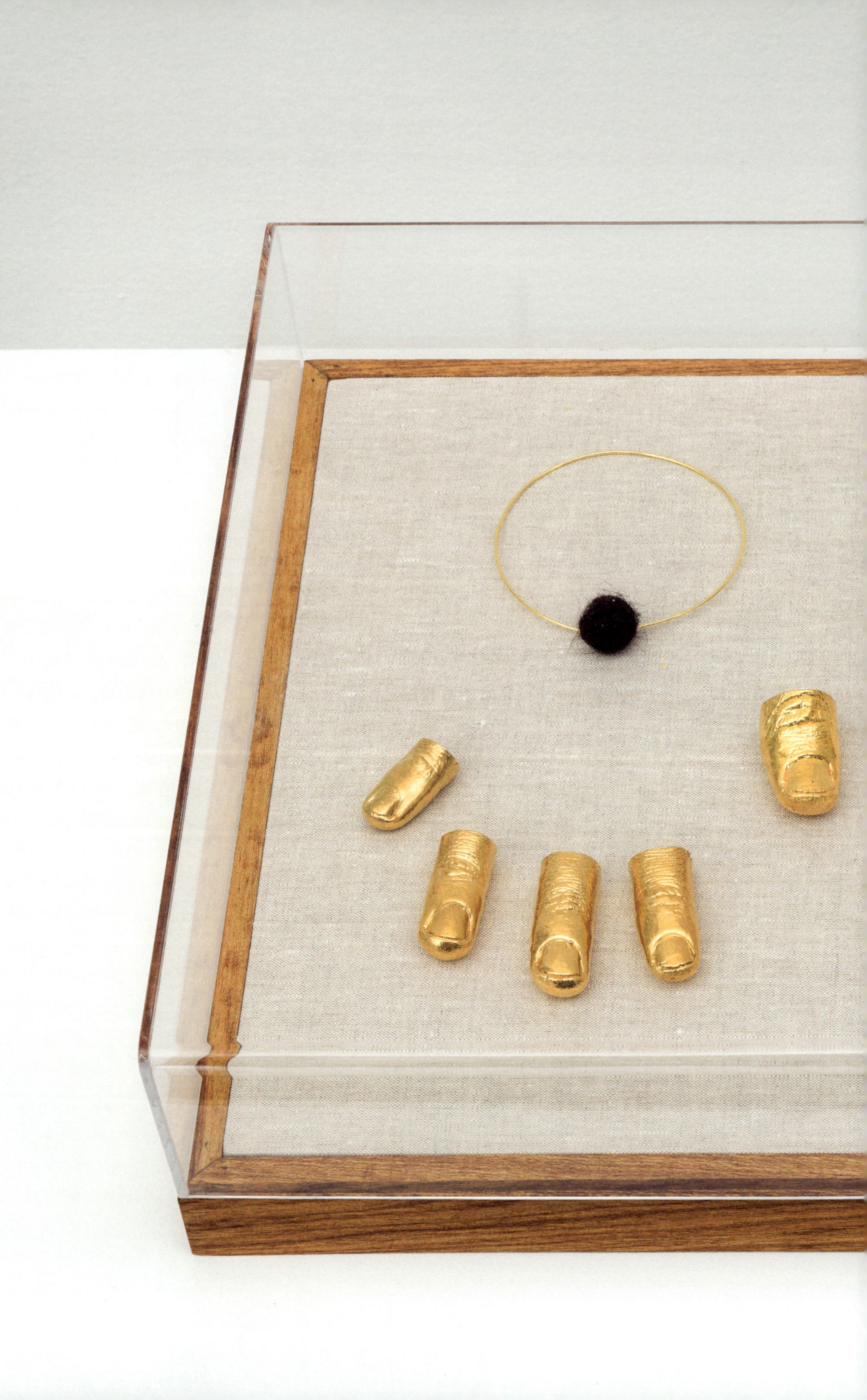

Bruno Baptistelli, *Untitled (Manus)*, 2023

[PL. 28]

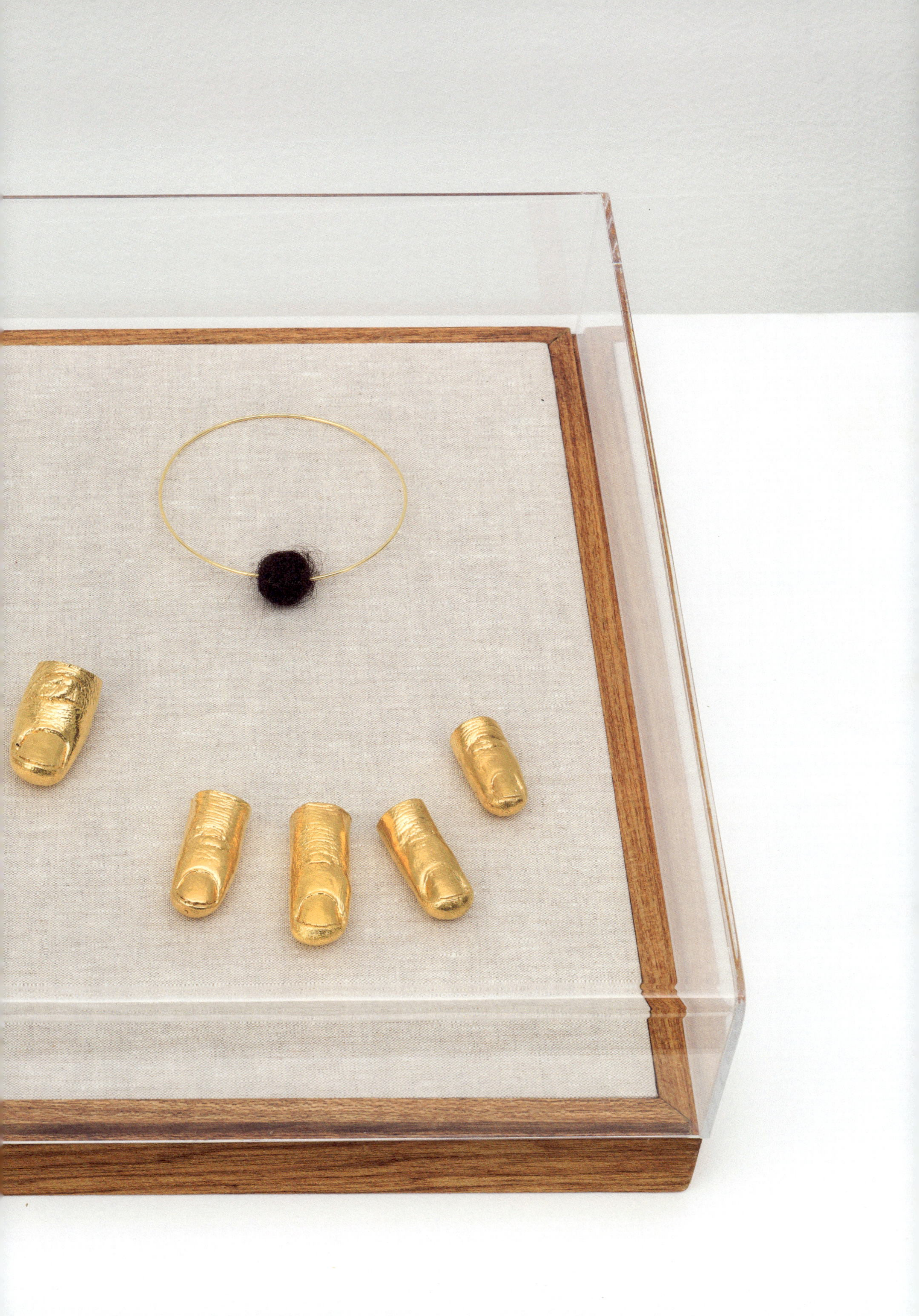

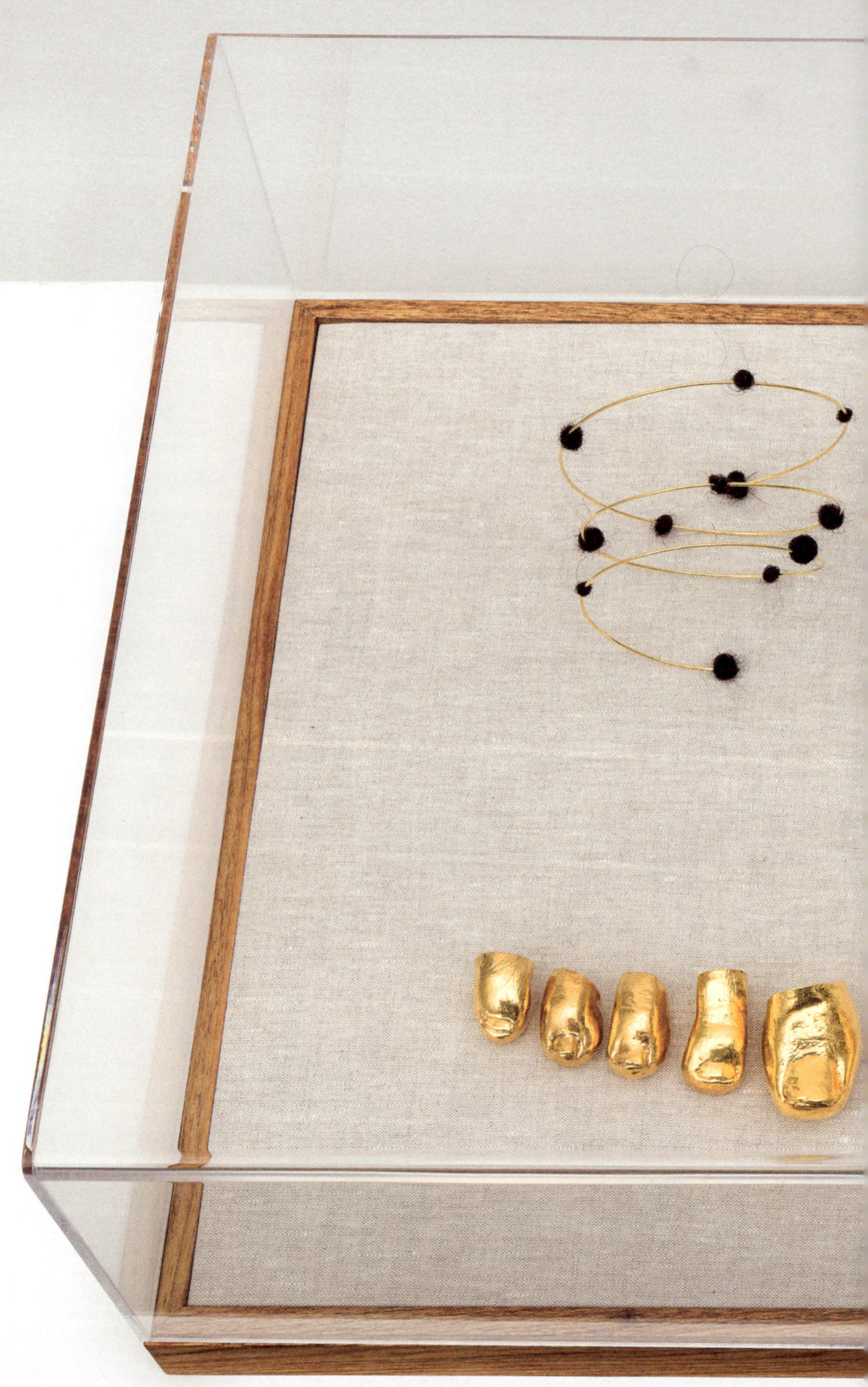

Bruno Baptistelli, *Untitled (Pedites)*, 2023

[PL. 29]

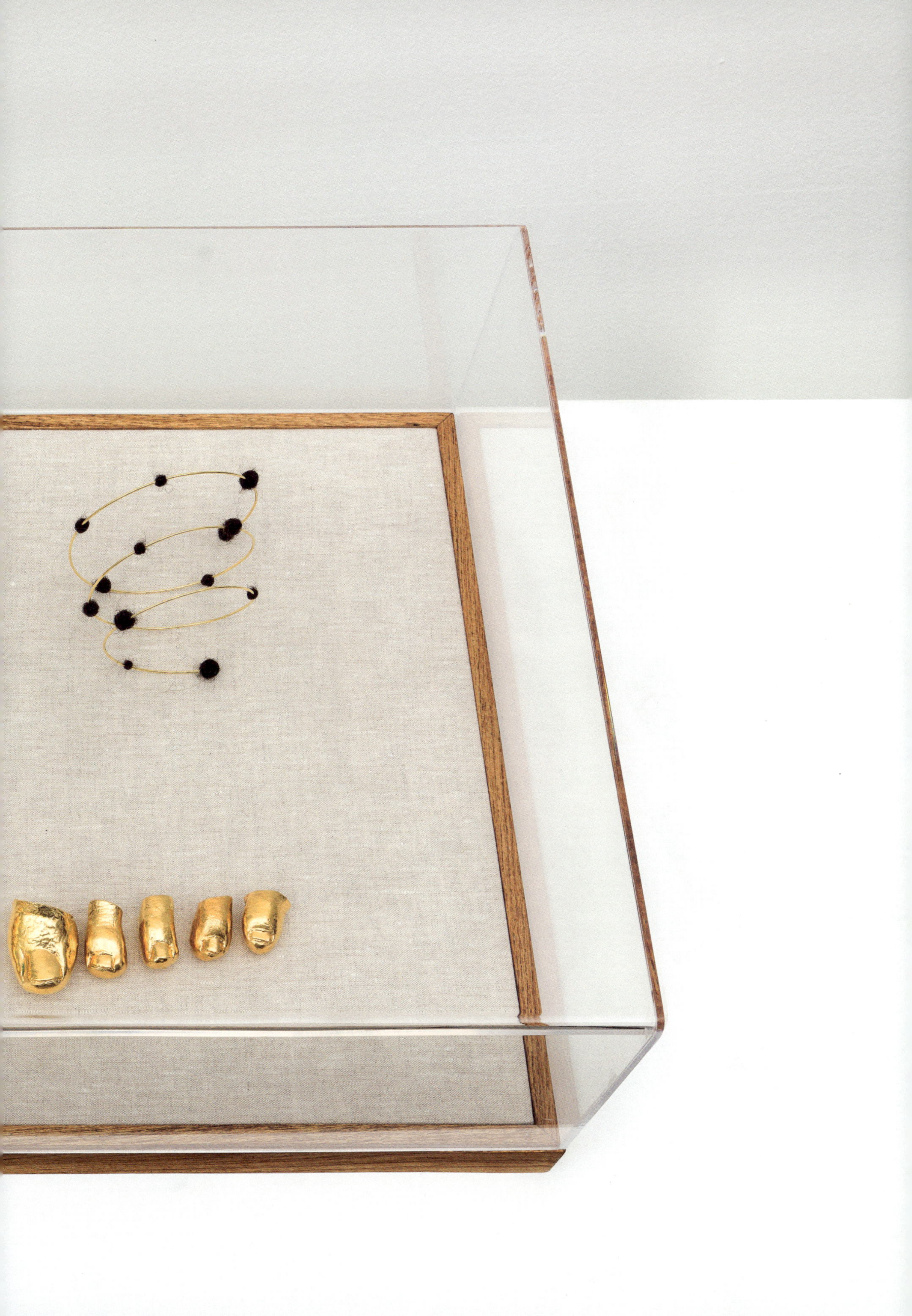

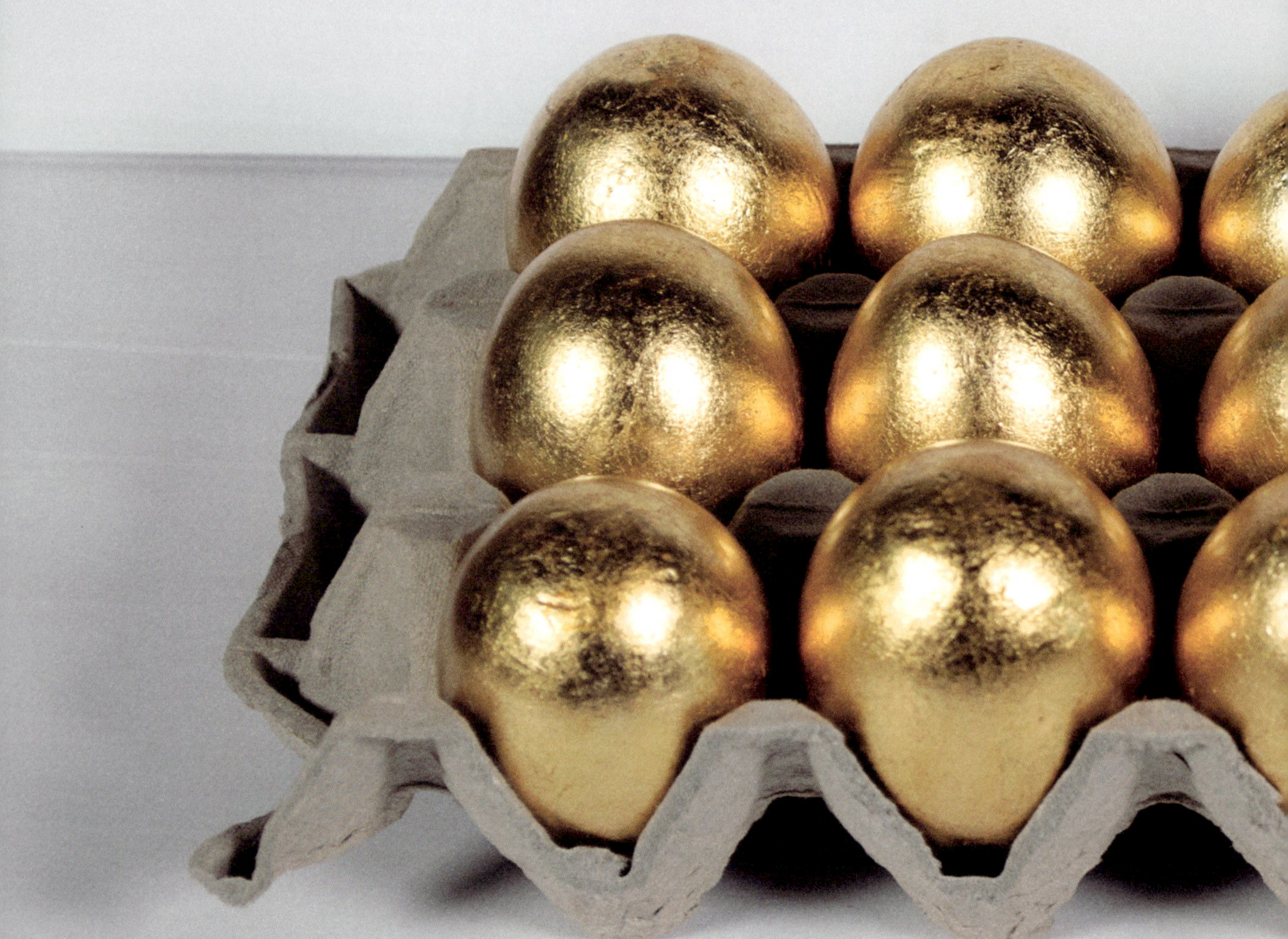

Priscilla Monge, *Huevos de oro* (Golden eggs), 1998

[PL. 30]

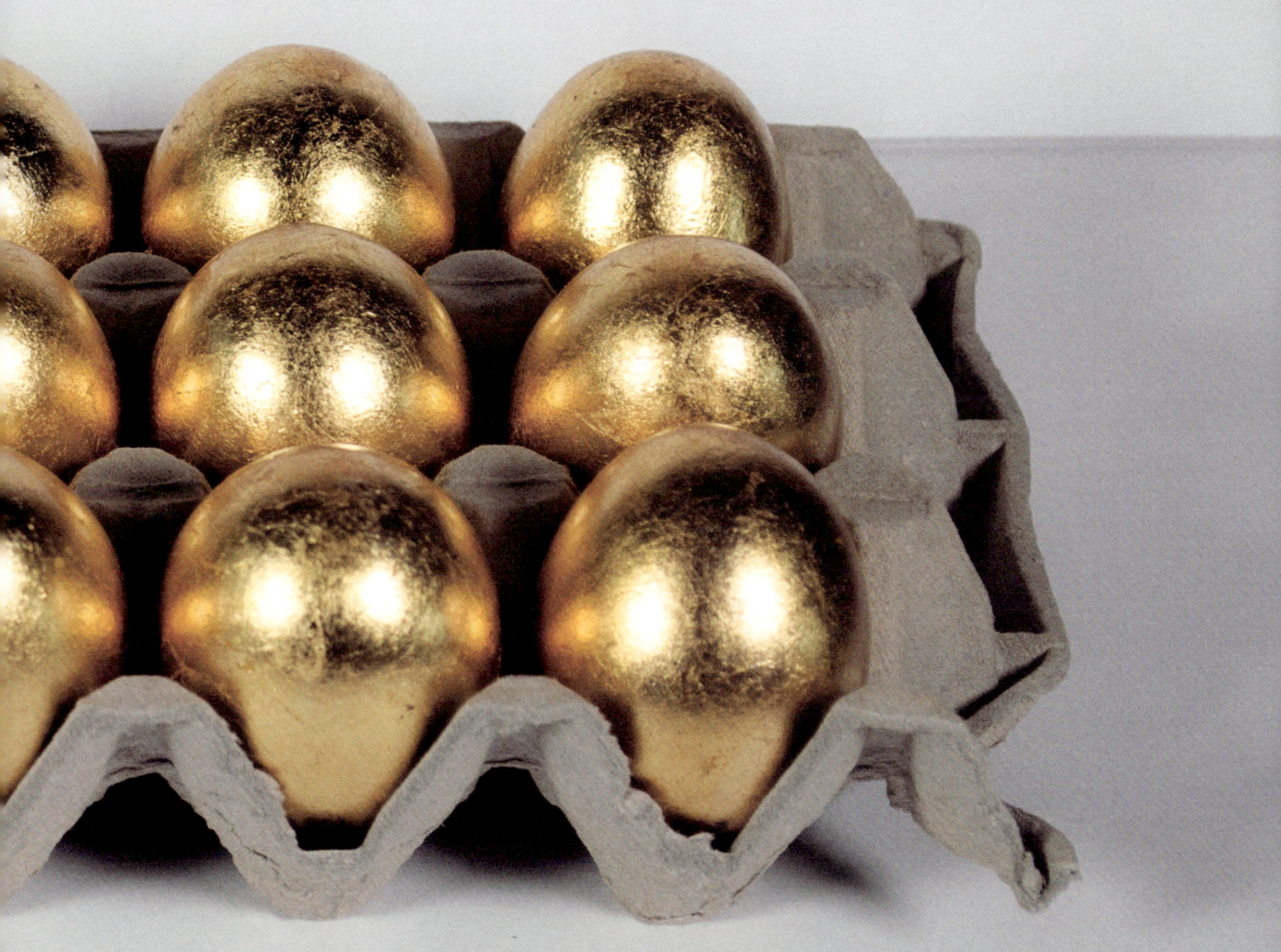

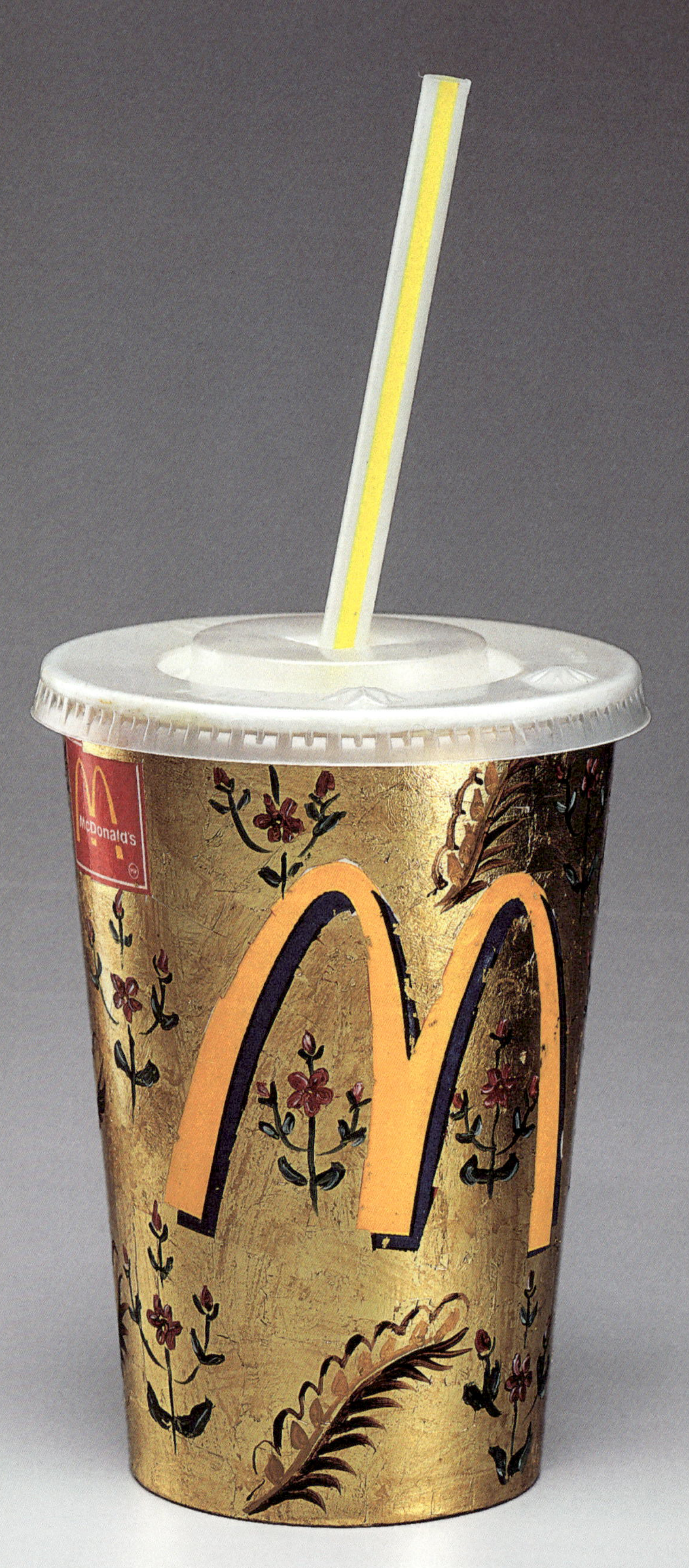
McDonald's

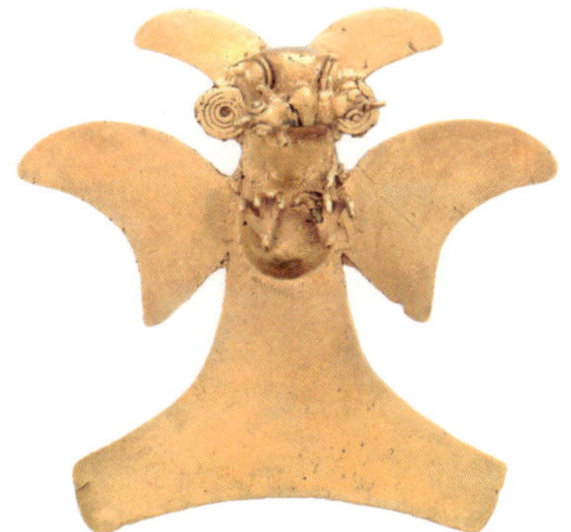

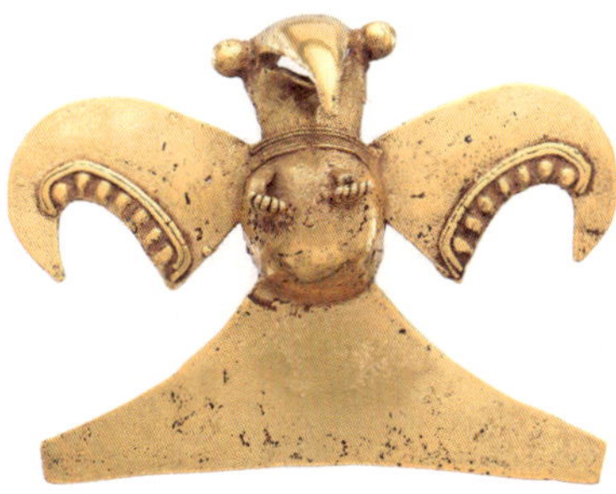

Unknown Chiriquí artist, Costa Rica, *Eagle Pendant*, 800–1519 CE
Unknown Veraguas artist, Colombia, *Eagle Pendant*, eleventh–sixteenth century

↑ [PL. 31]

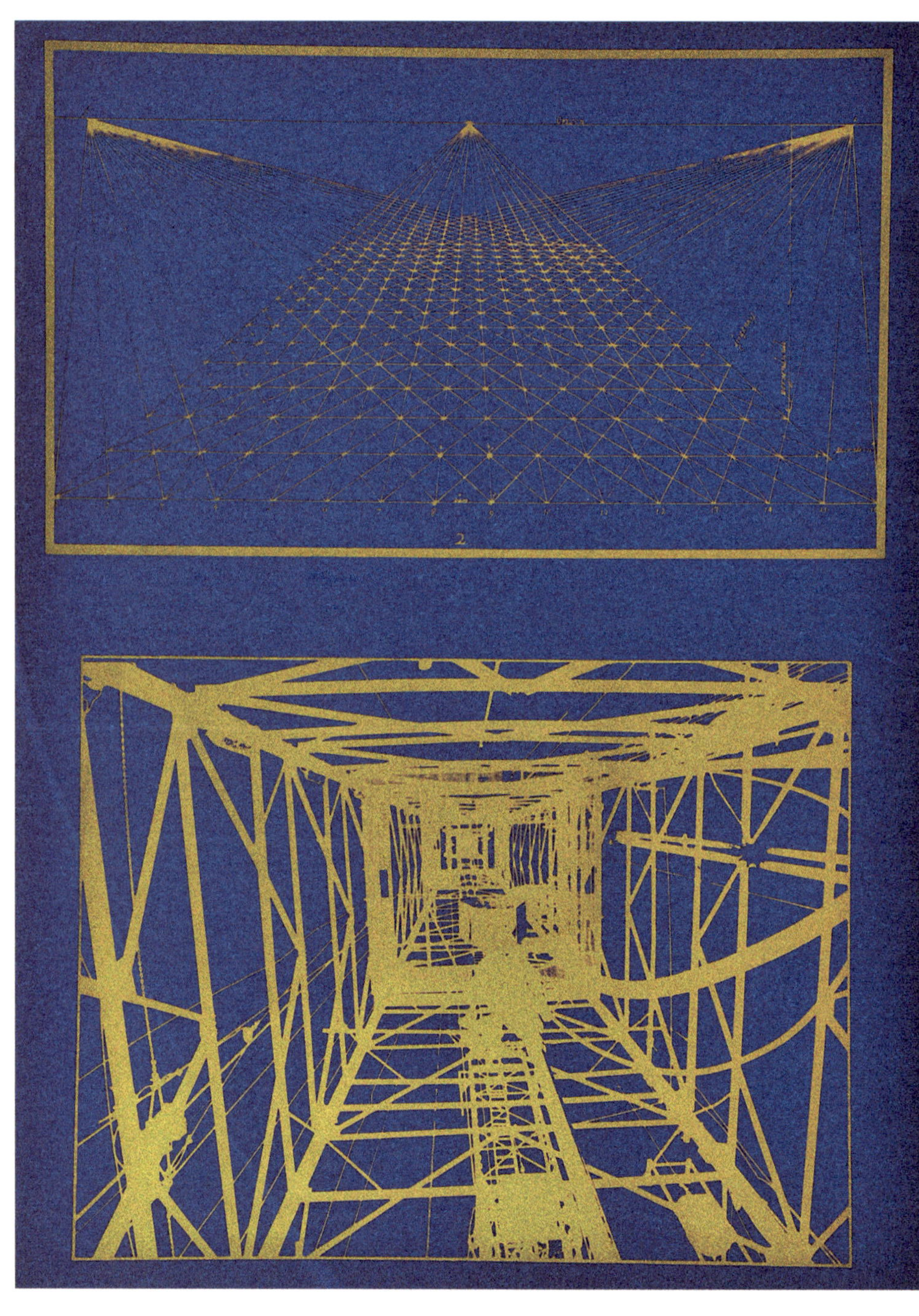

(Top) Mazenett Quiroga, *Semillas de estrellas (Nogal)* (Star seeds [Nogal]), 2015
(Bottom) *Semillas de estrellas (Yarumo)* (Star seeds [Yarumo]), 2015

↓ [PL. 34]

Rolando Peña, *Mene*, 1982

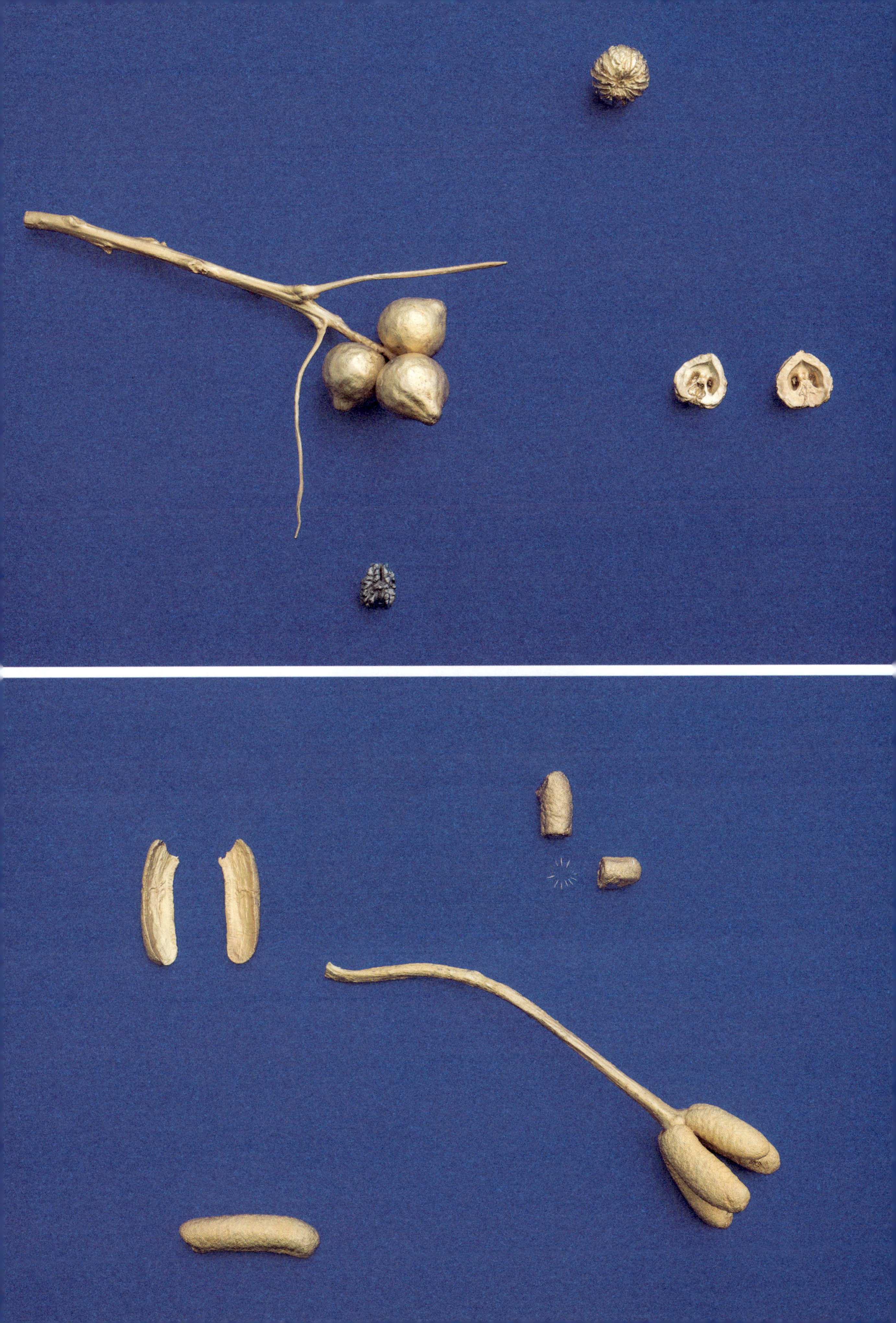

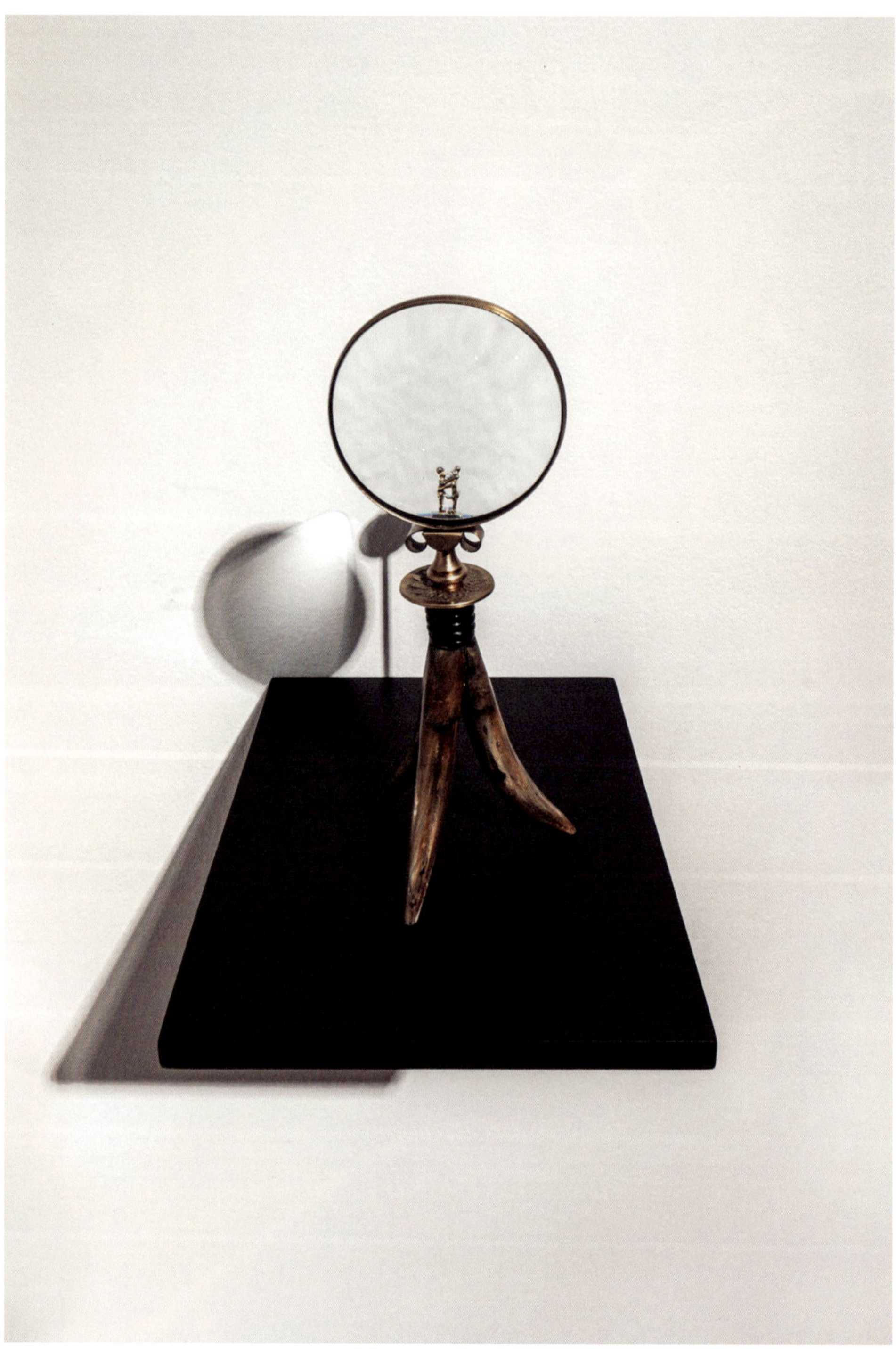

Carlos Motta, *Contra natura*, 2019

↓ [PL. 36]

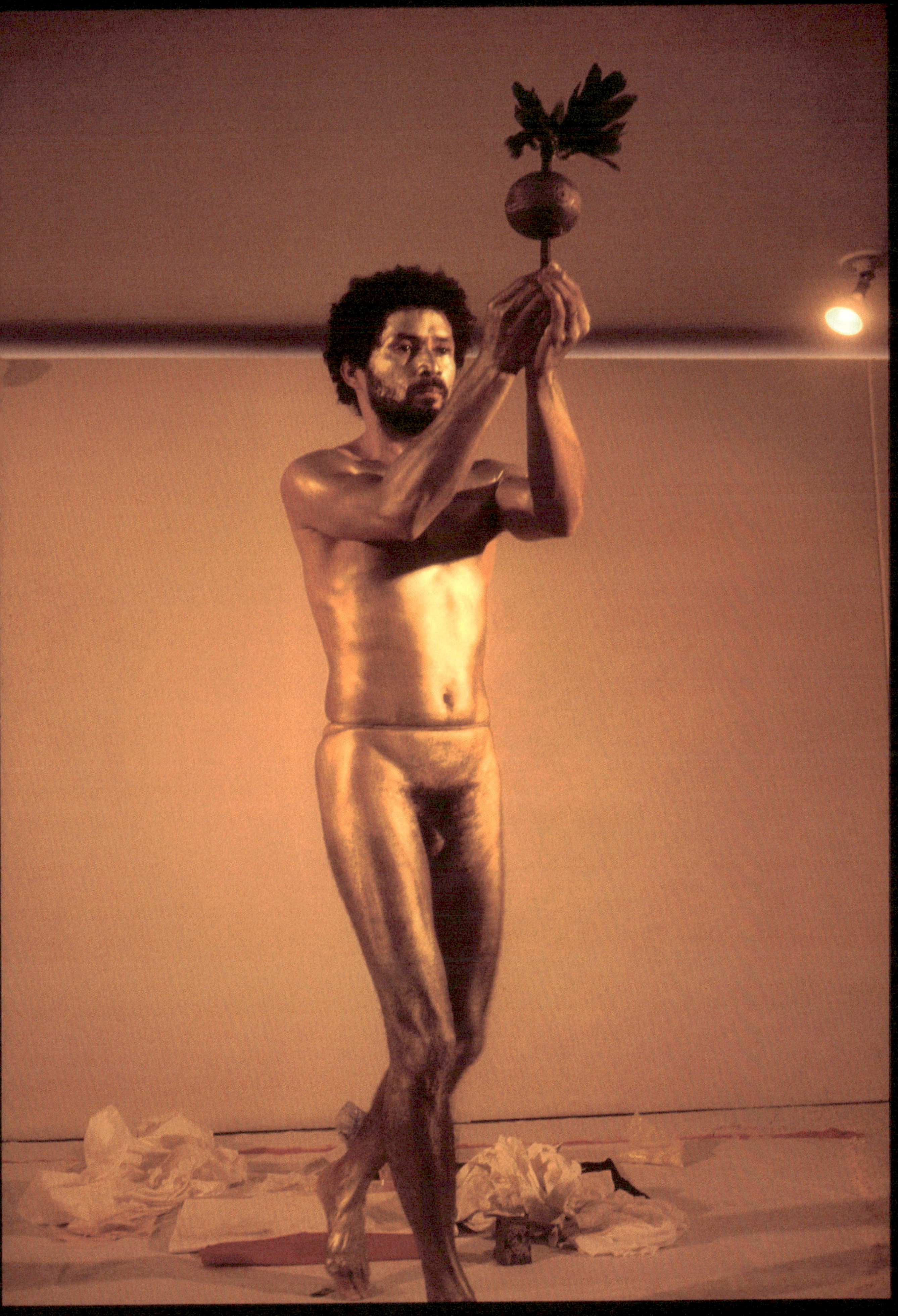

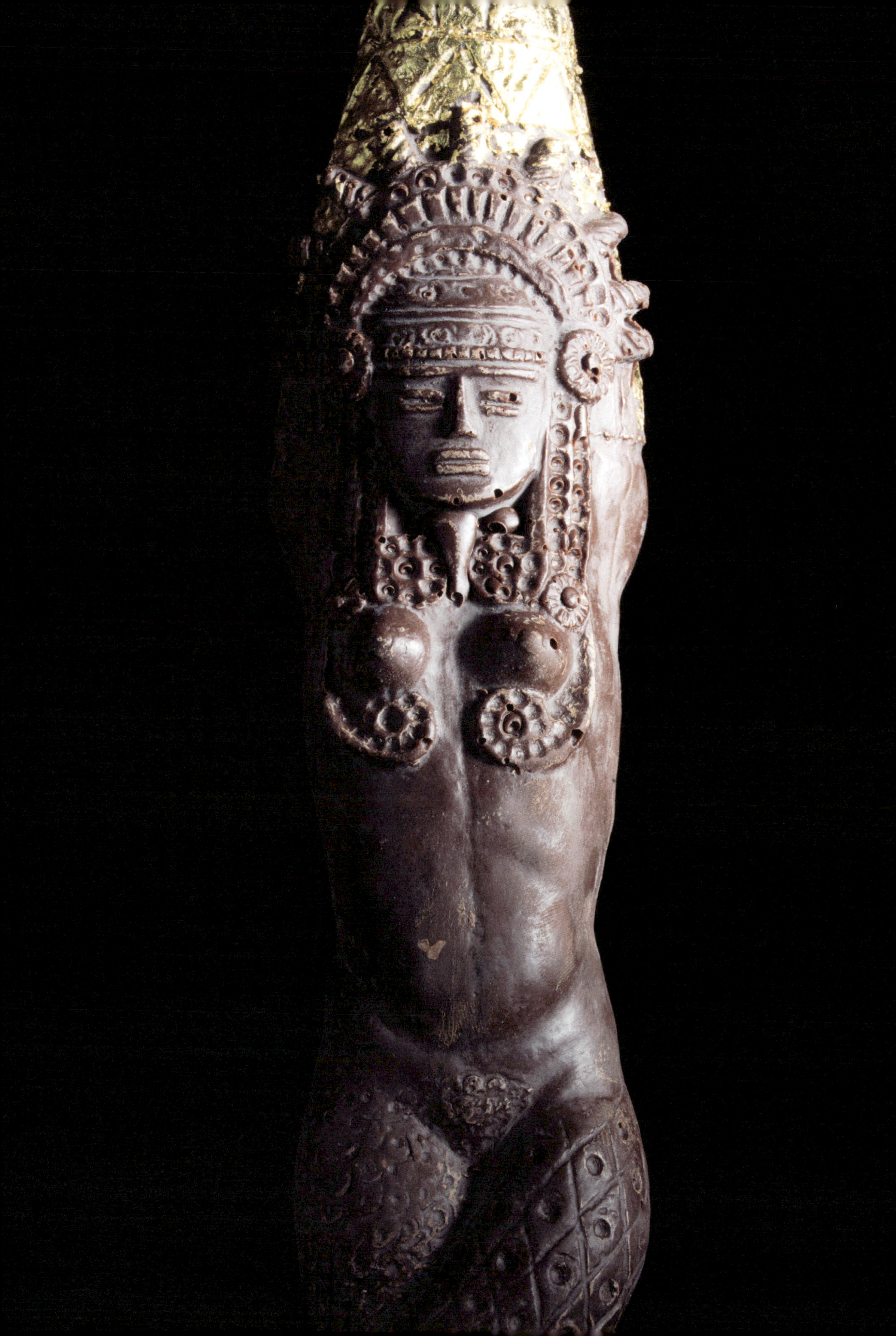

[PL. 38]

Santiago Montoya, *La Bachué en chocolate* (Chocolate Bachué), 2023

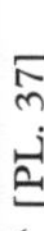
↑ [PL. 37]

Ana Mercedes Hoyos, *Laguna de Guatavita* (Guatavita lake), 1981

El Dorado: The Myth of Gold was organized in two parts. The first part was on view from September 6 to December 16, 2023 and the second part from January 24 to May 18, 2024. See indications in parentheses at the beginning of each caption.

PL. 01 P. 19
Unknown Quimbaya style artists, Colombia

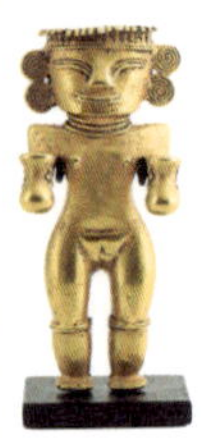

PL. 02 P. 20

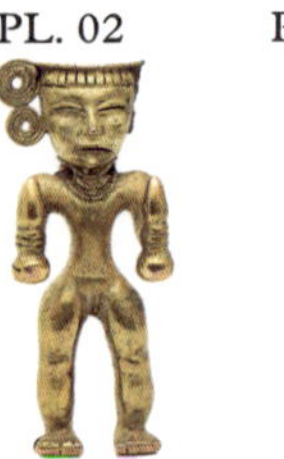

(I)
Female Figure Holding Poporos,
600–1400 CE.
Gold, 2 ¼ × 1 × ⅜ inches
(5.8 × 2.5 × 1 cm).
Colección Patricia Phelps
de Cisneros.
Photo: Arturo Sánchez

(I)
Female Figure Holding Poporos,
600–1400 CE.
Gold, 3 × 1 ⅜ × 1 inches
(7.5 × 3.5 × 2.5 cm).
Colección Patricia Phelps
de Cisneros.
Photo: Arturo Sánchez

← Indigenous metalworkers in what is now Colombia likely cast these gold objects—possibly pendants—using a metallurgical technique called the lost wax method, a process wherein a carefully modeled wax mold is first covered in clay, then filled with molten metal. The objects seen here depict standing female figures with eyes partially or completely closed. Both figures are thought to be holding, in each hand, a schematic representation of a *poporo*, a hollow vessel used throughout South America to carry powdered lime made from finely crushed limestone or seashell. Indigenous communities have consumed this powder alongside the leaves of the coca plant for thousands of years to soothe gastric maladies. Many pre-Hispanic cultures considered these materials to be sacred, their import rivaling that of precious metals like gold and silver. Powdered lime and coca leaves were so valuable to Indigenous communities that sixteenth-century Spanish authorities failed to suppress their usage, even after the Catholic Church denounced them as idolatrous paraphernalia. Metals, moreover, were seldom used as currency in the pre-Hispanic period and therefore carried little monetary value. Gold and silver were instead sought out for their shine and color, especially in South America, where such hues were closely associated with celestial entities like the sun and the moon. What is more, some pre-Hispanic cultures may have regarded alloys like *tumbaga*—a mixture of gold and copper—more highly than pure metals, due to the enhanced malleability and high tensile strength commonly seen in alloyed materials.

–Mary Seo

PL. 03 P. 21
Juan Brenner

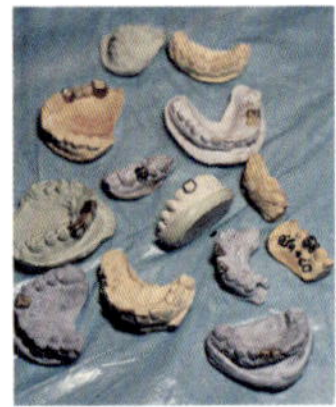

PL. 04 P. 22

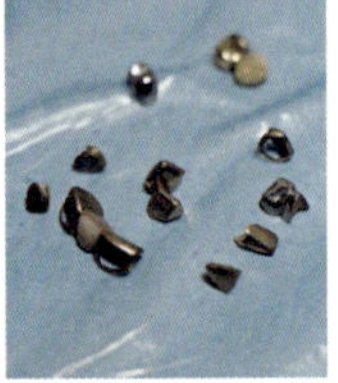

PL. 07 P. 25

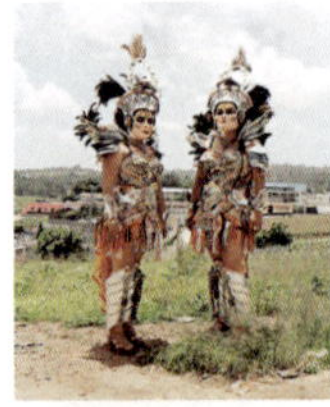

(I)
San Juan Comalapa, Chimaltenango, Guatemala,
from *Tonatiuh Series*, 2017–19.
Photographic print,
dimensions variable.
Courtesy of the artist

(I)
San Juan Comalapa, Chimaltenango, Guatemala,
from *Tonatiuh Series*, 2017–19.
Photographic print,
dimensions variable.
Courtesy of the artist

(I)
San Pedro Jocopilas, Quiché, Guatemala, from *Tonatiuh Series*, 2017–19.
Photographic print,
dimensions variable.
Courtesy of the artist

(I)
Olintepeque, Quetzaltenango, Guatemala, from *Tonatiuh Series*, 2017–19.
Photographic print,
dimensions variable.
Courtesy of the artist

← Juan Brenner (b. 1977, Guatemala City) is a Guatemalan artist working primarily with photography. In his work the artist explores themes such as identity, memory, and social issues within the context of Guatemala's complex colonial history and its effects in contemporary society. His photographic series *Tonatiuh* explores the history of the colonizer Pedro de Alvarado, who invaded Guatemala in 1524 and who was named "Tonatiuh" or "the Sun" by the Tlaxcalan people. In the mid-sixteenth century, priests created "The Dance of the Conquest," an allegorical dance that taught natives about religion, battles, and the importance of *Tonatiuh*, a dance still performed during special celebrations today. The series is focused on the depiction of contemporary Guatemalan society seen through the lens of the legacy of Tonatiuh.

–Tie Jojima

PL. 05 P. 23
Hew Locke

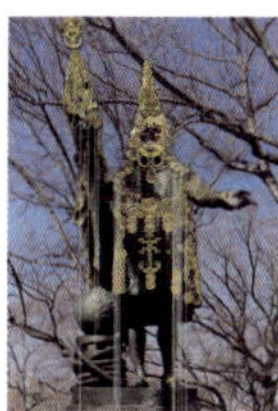

Hew Locke (b. 1959, Edinburgh) is a sculptor and multimedia artist, who grew up in Guyana, and whose works engage themes of history and colonialism. In the series *Patriots,* the artist lavishly decorates photos of public monuments of historical figures, creating images that allude to the individuals' fraught histories. While at first the figures may appear to be sumptuously decorated in precious metals and pearls, a closer look indicates a far more complex narrative. In *Columbus, Central Park,* Locke embellishes the figure of Christopher Columbus with strands of pearls and golden filigree, fashioned to form a priestly staff, crown, and robe. The skirt and crown feature golden figures that resemble Mesoamerican-style goldwork figures, evoking the imagery of those whose homeland he colonized. This idea is further compounded by the detail work present in the highly embellished gold staff, featuring another Mesoamerican stylized figure crowning a golden cage that holds a seated, golden skeleton. Gold and pearls—two precious commodities historically used as symbols of status and wealth in fifteenth- and sixteenth-century Europe—drip from Columbus's figure like blood. Locke melds both European and Mesoamerican goldsmithing styles, suggesting the historical theft of resources from Indigenous Americans by Europeans.

–Esther Levy

(II)
Columbus, Central Park, 2018.
C-type photograph with mixed media, 72 × 48 inches (182.9 × 121.9 cm).
Courtesy of the artist and P·P·O·W, New York.
Photo: Angus Mill

PL. 06 P. 24
Unknown Coclé artist, Central Panama

(II)
Double Warrior Pendant, 1150–1400 CE.
Gold alloy, 2 ⅜ × 4 ⅜ × ¾ inches (6 × 11.1 × 1.9 cm).
Denver Art Museum: Gift of Frederick and Jan Mayer, 1996.111. Photography © Denver Art Museum

PL. 08 P. 26
Juan Covelli

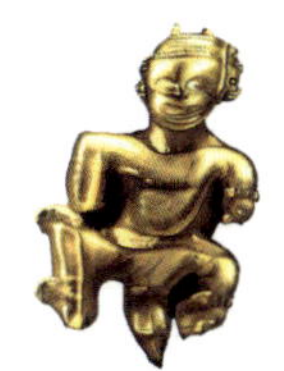

PL. 09 P. 27

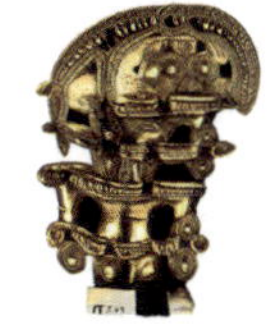

PL. 93 P. 145

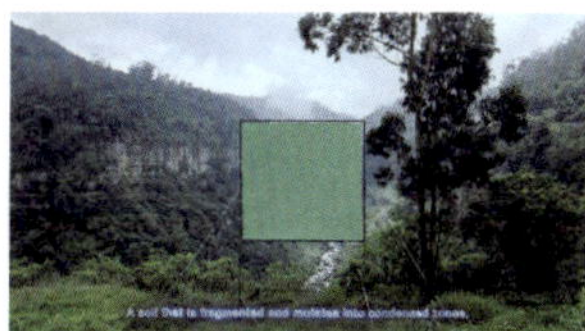

(II)
Tesoros especulativos (Speculative treasures), 2020–22.
Video, 5 minutes.
Courtesy of the artist

(I)
El salto (The jump), 2021.
Video, 12 minutes, 36 seconds.
Courtesy of the artist

← Juan Covelli (b. 1985, Bogotá,) creates artwork that engages with technology, archaeology, and colonialism. In *Tesoros especulativos,* the artist 3D scanned the collection of ancient goldwork held at the Museo del Oro in Bogotá and programmed an artificial intelligence algorithm that generates new images based on those scans. The works are shown in a perpetual state of transformation, constantly morphing into the next and perpetually building upon one another to produce imagined historical artifacts. Covelli touches on historical and contemporary taxonomical practices in museum institutions through his remodeling of the Museo del Oro's collection, while also referencing the "speculative treasures" held in the imagined city of El Dorado.

In another of Covelli's video works, titled *El salto,* the artist utilizes the landscapes of the Bogotá River to discuss the history of colonial resource extractivism in Colombia. The narrator explains that history in conjunction with that of the river, and the role of nineteenth-century German explorer and geographer Alexander von Humboldt in representing landscapes in the Americas. The artist juxtaposes technology, nature, historical imagery, and rich narration to delve into the region's complex history and its ties to contemporary resource extractivism in Colombia.

–Esther Levy

PL. 10 P. 28
Armando Queiroz

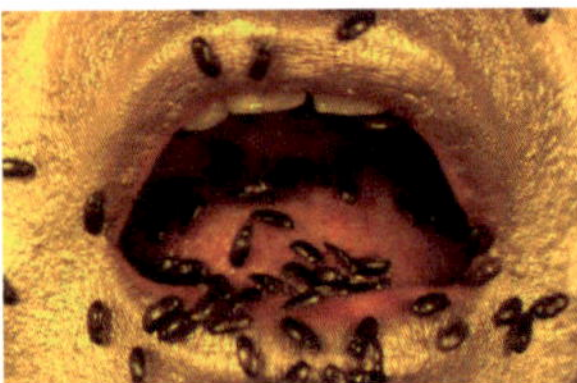

Armando Queiroz (b. 1968, Belém) is a Brazilian artist who lives in Serra Pelada in the state of Pará in the Amazon, where the largest gold mine in Brazil is located. The artist came of age during the Brazilian gold rush of the 1980s, when thousands of miners migrated to the region in search of gold. Having grown up listening to stories of people striking it rich and then losing everything, as well as television images reporting on the *fomigueiro humano* (human anthill), an image of thousands of men carrying bags of dirt out of the mine in inhuman conditions, the artist began exploring issues of mining in his practice. Interested in the human consequences of mining, he began interviewing those who stayed in the region after the "gold fever." Based on these stories, he created the series *Ouro de tolo* (Fool's gold) with works that reflect on those experiences. The video *Midas* partially depicts a golden face, focusing on the mouth and the act of eating. Referring to the Brazilian art historical narrative centered on *Antropofagia* (cultural cannibalism), the work resituates such a narrative by centering a mythical subject—Midas, who had the power to turn everything into gold—in the abject act of eating insects or being eaten by those creatures.

–Tie Jojima

(I)
Midas, 2009.
Video, 10 minutes.
Courtesy of the artist.
Video: Marcelo Rodrigues

PL. 11 P. 29
Unknown Lambayeque artist, north coast of Peru

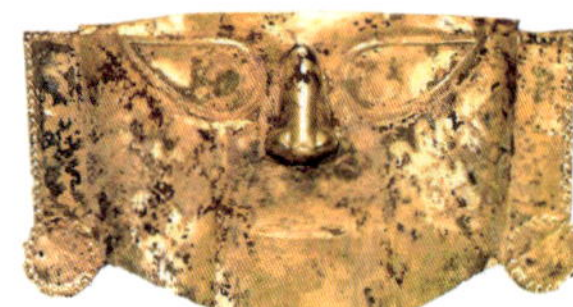

← This gold mask, made by the Lambayeque sometime between 900 and 1100 CE, still bears traces of the red pigment that once covered much of the hammered metal surface. The Lambayeque, also known as the Sicán, flourished on what is now the northern Pacific coast of Peru, a region rich in precious metals like gold and silver. Such a landscape has attracted *huaqueros,* or grave robbers, for hundreds of years, including sixteenth-century Spanish conquistadores driven by myths like El Dorado. Just as the lords of the Muisca (600–1600 CE, present-day Colombia) are said to have covered their bodies in gold dust, so too did the Lambayeque adorn themselves in precious metals, as evinced by extraordinary numbers of gold and silver body ornaments found in high-status tombs. One such object is the mask seen here, which features pointed ovoid eyes and a three-dimensionally modeled nose, the defining characteristics of the so-called Sicán Deity, who is thought to have conferred aspects of his power to those donning his image. Indeed, skewer-like projections once attached to the eyes of the mask likely represented piercing vision, while colorful feathers and mineral pigments painted onto the surface may have alluded to celestial flight and divine authority. Masks in many collections, however, now lack such embellishments, which were likely removed in modern times to expose and accentuate the gold underneath. This appetite for precious metals is further evidenced by the thousands of crude looters' pits still seen throughout the Lambayeque region today.

–Mary Seo

(I)
Gold Mask, 900–1100 CE.
Gold, 10 ¼ × 18 ¾ × 3 inches (26 × 47.6 × 7.6 cm).
Private Collection, in care of Americas Society.
Photo: Arturo Sánchez

PL. 12 P. 30
Unknown Coclé artist

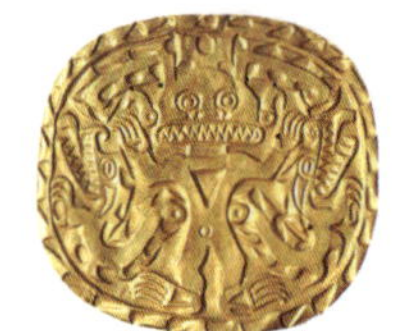

(II)
Plaque with Crocodile Deity, ca. 700–900 CE.
Gold, 8 ½ × 9 inches (21.6 × 22.9 cm).
Brooklyn Museum, Museum Expedition 1931, Museum Collection Fund, 33.448.12

← This hammered plaque was made by a once-known artist in Greater Coclé and represents a central anthropomorphic figure flanked on either side by saurian or reptilian creatures in profile. Six small holes are drilled into the plaque, indicating that at one point it would have been worn on the body or possibly attached to a textile as a dangling element. Due to this area's high humidity, textiles and other organic materials like feathers have not survived in great quantities compared to their more durable metal and ceramic counterparts. The central figure stands on two legs but is highly stylized, possibly suggesting a hybridization of both human and animal attributes. Its hands and feet are rendered with enormous claws, its fanged jaw is opened wide, and it looks straight out to the viewer with focused eyes. The artistic design of mirroring two reptilian creatures in profile links this plaque to the rest of the Isthmo-Colombian (or Intermediate) Area, as artists in this region rendered their metalwork with symmetry and iconographic balance in mind. These creatures may represent "animal metaphors," emanations of the central deity's predatory power and fearsome aggressiveness. When the plaque was worn by an elite ruler in life, that individual would symbolically embody these divine qualities, visually manifesting their prowess and right to rule to others in the community. This fearsome animal iconography became standardized in ancient Panamanian art around 500 CE and can be seen throughout many works in ceramic, metal, shell, and stone. Some research suggests that designs like these may also have been tattooed onto the body for individual recognition or group affiliation.

This plaque was discovered in 1931 in the region known as Greater Coclé, near Parita Bay in what is today eastern Panama. Sponsored by Harvard University, archaeologist Samuel K. Lothrop uncovered a plethora of ancient Coclé artworks there, in situ and in various tombs. Lothrop's findings have greatly contributed to the modern understanding of ancient Panamanian art broadly construed and are invaluable for modern art historical analysis of these extraordinary works.

–Eric Mazariegos

PL. 13 P. 31

Carlos Rojas

Carlos Rojas (1933 - 1997, Facatativá) was a Colombian geometric and abstract painter and sculptor. Rojas' work aims to articulate the geometric basis of the world and is characterized by a vibrant use of color and a strong awareness of architectural space. For Rojas, geometric abstraction was both a historical and contemporary visual language that was closely connected to pre-Columbian forms and the current artistic production of local craftsmen. In the 1990s, Rojas began creating a series of work called El Dorado, in which the surface of each canvas was filled with golden textures representing symbols of the sun, cosmic dust, and faith. The title of the work *Yo, Midas* (I, Midas), refers to the mythical King Midas and his ability to turn all that he touched into gold. The gold surface appears textured and tarnished, giving a sense that the canvas was imperfectly covered with liquid gold.

–Sarah Lopez

(II)
Yo, Midas, 1989-1990. Mixed media on canvas, 31 ½ × 31 ½ × 2 inches (80 × 80 × 5 cm). Private collection. Courtesy of Casas Riegner. Photo: Manuel A. Hernández

PL. 14 P. 32

Unknown Greater Chiriquí artists

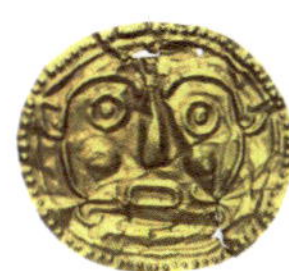

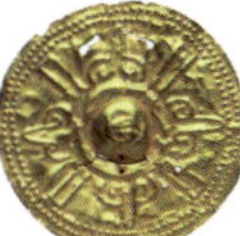

(II)
Unknown Greater Chiriquí artist, *Disk with Embossed Face*, 800–1522 CE.
Gold, 2 ⅝ × 2 ⅞ inches (6.6 x 7.3 cm). Denver Art Museum: Gift of Frederick and Jan Mayer, 1995.637. Photography © Denver Art Museum

(II)
Unknown Greater Chiriquí artist, Panama, *Disk with Directional Symbol*, 700–1000 CE.
Gold alloy, ⅛ × 2 ¾ inches (0.3 × 6.9 cm).
Denver Art Museum: Gift of Frederick and Jan Mayer, 1995.650.
Photography © Denver Art Museum

←The metal disks and plaques in this exhibition were manufactured throughout the region of Greater Chiriquí, geographically spanning what today is Costa Rica. Though they follow a basic schematic form, these disks are distinguishable from each other by differences in visual iconography, material composition, or technique of manufacture. Most were made of gold, using a variety of techniques like hammering (repoussé), continuously adding and removing heat to increase the metal's plastic workability (annealing), and cold-working. By processing small grains of gold in this way, they could be stretched to incredibly large surface areas. The disks depict a wide array of iconographic variability, including alert faces and simple geometric motifs. *Gold Disk with Embossed Face* [PL. 14, top] is notable for the substance that seems to fill the central figure's cheeks. In the ancient Americas, and especially throughout the geographic areas spanning the central Andes from Peru to Costa Rica, a common custom practiced by many individuals was to chew the leaves of the coca plant, a species native to western South America. After masticating these leaves, they would be bunched up into the cheeks of one's mouth and kept there for continuous release of their analgesic, stimulating properties. The wide-open eyes and mouth may signal that this individual was in a state of trance-like excitement caused by this organic substance. The crumbled appearance on some disks may also suggest their ritual context, indicating that they may have been ceremonially "destroyed" and subsequently buried, perhaps alongside their wearers in life. In the Maya area of Mesoamerica, metal objects from as far away as Colombia have been found interred in sacred *cenotes* (wells), indicative of long-distance trade and communication by these ancient artisans.

–Eric Mazariegos

PL. 15 P. 33

Rolando Peña

PL. 33 P. 56

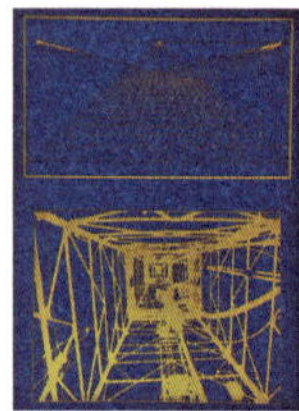

Rolando Peña (b. 1942, Caracas) is a pioneer of the Latin American underground scene of the 1960s and 1970s in New York and has remained a key figure in Venezuelan contemporary art throughout his career. Peña takes up social and political subjects across various media, including drawing, prints, sculpture, video, and performance. Peña's artistic practice stems from how he addresses social, political, and economic concerns, namely the theme of crude oil. For nearly forty years, Peña has made crude oil a focal point of his work. *El barril encontrado* (1975) presents a gold-painted oil barrel placed upon a pedestal. Peña has created the oil barrel to function as the divine power that oil holds over us. *Mene* (1982) is a silkscreen depicting an oil drill rig in orange against a blue background. *Mene* is the word used for oil by the Indigenous population of Venezuela.

–Sarah Lopez

(II)
El barril encontrado (The found barrel), 1975.
Barrel of petroleum and acrylic paint, 15 ¾ × 11 ¾ × 11 ¾ inches (40 × 30 × 30 cm).
Courtesy of Henrique Faria, New York.
Photo: Nelson Garrido

(II)
Mene, 1982.
Silkscreen, 36 × 24 inches (91.4 × 60.9 cm).
Courtesy of the artist

PL. 34 P. 57

Mazenett Quiroga

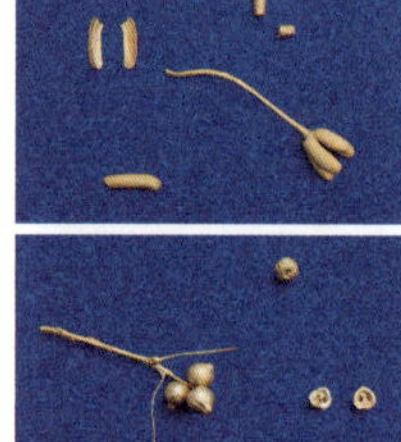

PL. 64 P. 108

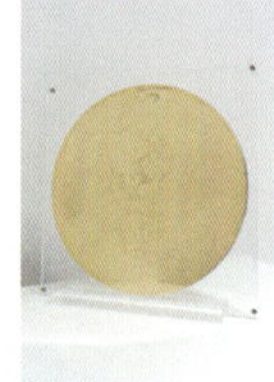

PL. 74 P. 125

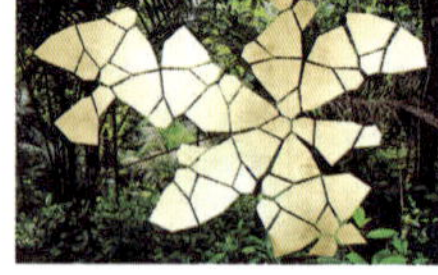

(I)
Semillas de estrellas (Yarumo) (Star seeds [Yarumo]), 2015.
Bronze foundries with 24-karat gold bath of guayacan seed (Indigenous sacred tree in Colombia), 23 ⅝ × 19 ⅛ × 4 inches (60 × 48.5 × 10 cm).
Courtesy of the artists and Instituto de Visión

(I)
Semillas de estrellas (Nogal) (Star seeds [Nogal]), 2015.
Bronze foundries with 24-karat gold bath of guayacan seed, (Indigenous sacred tree in Colombia), 23 ⅝ × 19 ⅛ × 4 inches (60 × 48.5 × 10 cm).
Courtesy of the artists and Instituto de Visión

(II)
Sun Disc, 2019.
Engraved and gold-plated bronze disk, diameter 16 ⅞ inches (43 cm).
Courtesy of the artists and Instituto de Visión

(II)
Selva intervenida (Pacífico colombiano) (Intervened jungle [Colombian Pacific]), 2018.
Digital printing and gold leaf, 49 ¼ × 33 ⅞ inches (125 × 86 cm).
Courtesy of the artists and Instituto de Visión

← The artistic duo known as Mazenett Quiroga consists of Colombian artists Lina Mazenett (b. 1989, Bogotá) and David Quiroga (b. 1985, Bogotá), who have been working collaboratively since 2014. The two embrace natural elements and their representations to interrogate the colonial basis of the Western production of knowledge. In *Sun Disc* (2019) the artists created a dual-sided spherical map, perforated at the coordinates of points throughout the world where gold is extracted. On one side, a map is visible to indicate the sites of gold mining, while the other side, devoid of geographic locations, instead resembles a star chart and uses these same perforations to create an imagined constellation of these points. In doing so, the artists represent dual viewpoints on the same data: while one side marks distinguishable geographic coordinates, the other forms a celestial alignment, connecting the earthly sites of gold with the universe beyond. Mazenett Quiroga's other works, such as *Semillas de estrellas*, further probe questions of colonization and taxonomy by depicting the sacred trees of different Colombian Indigenous groups, such as the *nogal* tree that is sacred to the Muisca people. The duo further draws a connection between the plant life and Indigenous peoples of Colombia by casting the work in 24-karat gold, utilizing the pre-Hispanic Indigenous practice of lost wax casting. The use of gold as a medium in which to depict the delicate beauty of botanical forms imbues the plants with the durability and value of gold, further underscoring the denotation of value of natural resources to Indigenous peoples, in contrast to those who colonized their ancestral territories.

–Esther Levy

PL. 16 PP. 34–35

Karen Lofgren

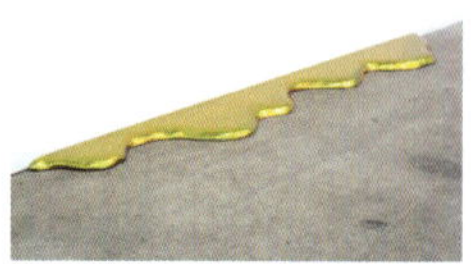

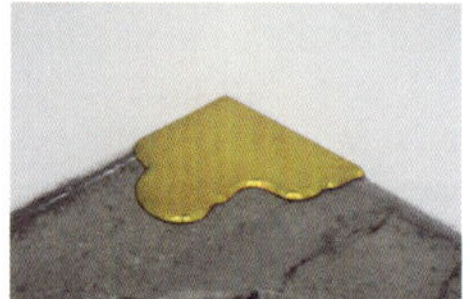

Karen Lofgren (b. 1976, Toronto) utilizes sculpture and installation to explore a wide range of contemporary issues, including environmental degradation, humans' relationship to nature, traditional medicine, and ecology, from an ecofeminist and decolonial perspective. Lofgren's *Gold Flood* (2009/2019) is a series of site-specific sculptures made from plywood and automotive paint that carefully create the effect of liquid gold puddles or spills. The power of *Gold Flood* comes from its ability to raise questions about the power and value that we give the substance and the volatility of that value.

–Sarah Lopez

(II)
Gold Flood, 2009/2019.
Plywood, automotive paint, ¾ × 46 ½ × 6 ¼ inches (1.9 × 118.1 × 15.9 cm).
Courtesy of the artist and Royale Projects

(I)
Gold Flood, 2009/2019.
Plywood, automotive paint, ¾ × 16 × 17 inches (1.9 × 40.6 × 43.2 cm).
Courtesy of the artist and Royale Projects

PL. 17 P. 36
Esperanza Mayobre

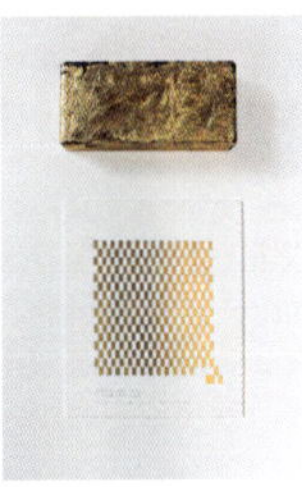

PL. 19 P. 38

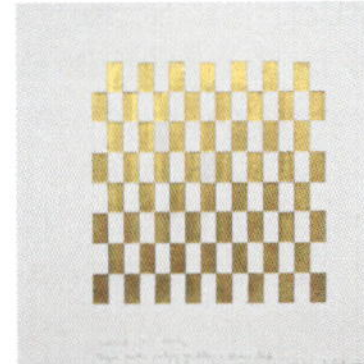

← Esperanza Mayobre (b. 1974, Caracas) is a Brooklyn-based artist whose work often conceptualizes the political and economic events that have led her home country of Venezuela into economic and moral ruin. Mayobre's *Serie A.M.O.* are commentaries on the ongoing financial crisis in Venezuela as the government continues to deforest the Amazon and cause lasting ecological and financial harm to the local population. *A.M.O.* refers to the Arco Minero del Orinoco (Orinoco mining arc), a resource-rich area in Venezuela known for being a hub of illegal mining. The gold-painted grids represent statistics related to the gold extractive practices in the Orinoco. Some of the names given to each work in the series are seemingly drawn from newspaper headlines: *They present as a victory that Iranian gasoline now arrives. March 27th, 2020. Caracas, Venezuela.* These works were based on Indigenous weaving practices and childhood memories of watching weavers from the Orinoco River.

–Sarah Lopez

PL. 20 P. 39
Laura Vinci

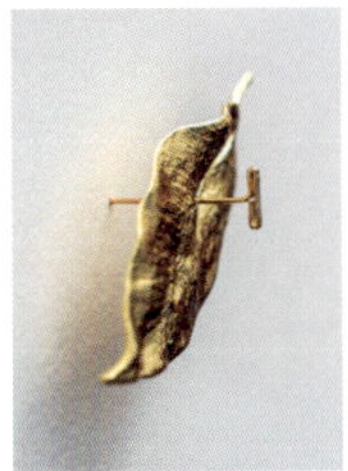

PL. 69 P. 115

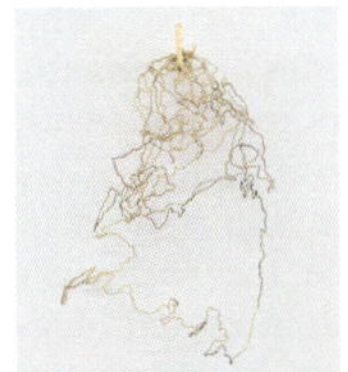

← Laura Vinci (b. 1962, São Paulo) is best known for her interventions, sculptures, and site-specific installations that explore the relationship between the body, ephemerality, and space. Also working as a theater and artistic director, Vinci observes space as a complex entity that mediates the body and is subject to the continual passage of time. Her projects typically investigate the processes of change or movement and invite the audience to reconsider the environment that surrounds them. *Folhas avulsas # 1 e # 2* (2018) is composed of numerous golden sculptures in the shape of leaves. Vinci's leaves are attached to the wall with thin pins and replicate the movement of a light breeze. *Morro mundo pin* (2018) is a miniature gold-plated outline of the world that is visibly contorted and pinned to a wall. The word *morro* in the title means "hill" in Portuguese but is also a verb in the present tense, meaning "to die." The small sculptural work seems to suggest that the world is in an increasingly fragile state.

–Sarah Lopez

(II)
Serie A.M.O. 2020.
Brick covered in gold leaf,
2 ¼ × 7 ⅝ × 3 ⅝ inches
(5.6 × 19.3 × 9 cm).
Courtesy of the artist

(II)
Serie A.M.O. (They present as a victory that Iranian gasoline now arrives. March 27th, 2020. Caracas, Venezuela.), 2020.
Drawing on paper, 10 × 8 ¼ inches (25.4 × 20.9 cm).
Courtesy of the artist

(II)
Serie A.M.O. ($15.20 por galón en el mercado negro) ($15.2 per gallon in the black market), 2020. Drawing on paper,
10 × 8 inches (25.5 × 20 cm).
Courtesy of the artist

(I)
Folhas avulsas # 1 e # 2 (Loose leaves #1 and #2), 2018.
Gold-plated brass,
5 ⅛ × 4 ¾ × 2 inches each
(13 × 12 × 5 cm).
Courtesy of the artist and Nara Roesler Gallery

(I)
Morro mundo pin (Pin world hill), 2018.
Brass plated in gold,
4 ⅜ × 7 ½ × 2 ⅛ inches
(11 × 19 × 5.5 cm).
Courtesy of the artist and Nara Roesler Gallery

PL. 21 PP. 40–41
Miguel Ángel Rojas

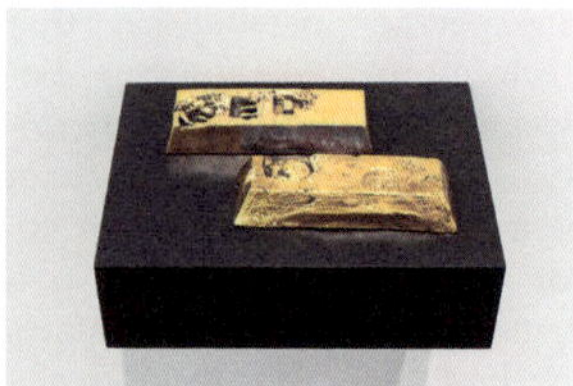

Miguel Ángel Rojas (b. 1946, Bogotá) is a multimedia artist whose work includes drawing, painting, photography, installations, and video and addresses themes of subjective experience, identity, sexuality, and politics. Ángel Rojas considers it a responsibility of artists to confront world issues through their work and has used his practice to condemn international drug trafficking and violence, as well as focus on experiences of marginality. *Sed* (2015) is a gold-plated bronze sculpture that takes the form of two gold bars that have been altered and damaged. The title *Sed*, or "thirst," is a criticism of the insatiable thirst for gold that has been the motivation and cause for many cultural ills, including the looting of Indigenous graves, melting down of pre-Hispanic artwork by the Spanish, gold mining, and continuous environmental destruction.

–Sarah Lopez

(I)
Sed (Thirst), 2015.
Bronze casted, gold and mercury-plated, 1 ⅛ × 7 ½ × 3 inches (3 × 19 × 7.5 cm).
Courtesy of Sicardi | Ayers | Bacino, Houston, TX.
Photo: Paul Hester

PL. 22 P. 42
Sarah Mejia Kriendler

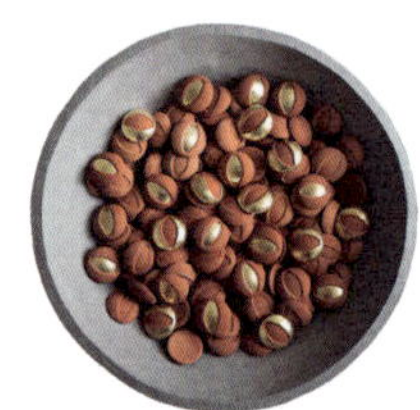

Sarah Mejia Kriendler (b. 1983, New York) is a Colombian American artist who primarily creates multimedia sculptural work that deals with themes of history, nature, and humanity. Her works in gold often reference the material's history in Colombia, employing gold's spiritual properties while also paying homage to Indigenous artmaking such as goldsmithing and pottery. In *Inner Visions* Kriendler filled a stoneware bowl with small terracotta sculptures resembling eyes leafed with gold. The stoneware vessel, in the shape of an offering bowl, forges the work's engagement with spiritual practices and their connection to the body and earth. The repetitious, circular design of the eyes and bowl suggest a paten of communion wafers, representing the body of Christ, ready to be blessed and consumed. Kriendler's work engages multiple dialogues that come together in viewership of this work by engaging the past, present, and future of artmaking practices in the Americas.

–Esther Levy

(I)
Inner Visions (Visiones) I, 2021.
Stoneware, terracotta, gold leaf, 14 × 14 × 4 inches (35.5 × 35.5 × 35.5 cm).
Courtesy of PROXYCO and the artist

PL. 23 PP. 43
Unknown Greater Chiriquí artists

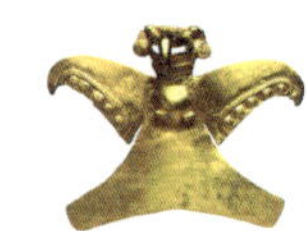

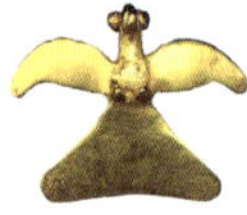

PL. 32 PP. 55

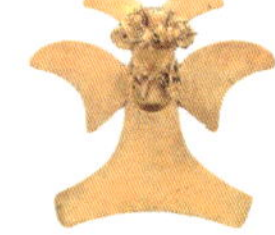

Unknown Veraguas artist, Colombia

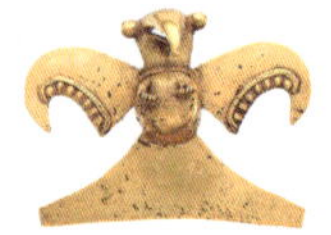

(II)
Unknown Greater Chiriquí artist, Costa Rica, *Eagle Pendant*, 800–1522 CE.
Gold, 3 × 3 ⅝ × ¾ inches (7.6 × 9.2 × 1.9 cm).
Denver Art Museum: Gift of Frederick and Jan Mayer, 1995.659. Photography © Denver Art Museum

(II)
Unknown Greater Chiriquí artist, Costa Rica, *Eagle Pendant*, 800–1522 CE.
Gold, 1 × 1 ¼ × ⅜ inches (2.5 × 3.1 × 0.9 cm).
Denver Art Museum: Gift of Frederick and Jan Mayer, 1995.890. Photography © Denver Art Museum

(II)
Unknown Chiriquí artist, Costa Rica, *Eagle Pendant*, 800–1519 CE.
Gold, 5 ⅝ × 5 ¾ × 2 ⅛ inches (14.3 × 14.6 × 5.4 cm).
The Metropolitan Museum of Art

(II)
Unknown Veraguas artist, Colombia, *Eagle Pendant*, eleventh–sixteenth century.
Gold, 2 ¾ × 4 × 1 ⅜ inches (7 × 10.2 × 3.5 cm).
The Metropolitan Museum of Art

← Portable and wearable pendants depicting birds in flight were common objects made by artists throughout the ancient Isthmo-Colombian (or Intermediate) Area (encompassing modern Costa Rica, Panama, and Colombia). Some researchers have suggested that these bird pendants would have been worn by high-ranking individuals, metaphorically granting a wearer shamanic powers of flight and preternatural communication. Some of the examples in this exhibition may be taxonomically identified as representing the harpy eagle, a species endemic to Central and South America. Both naturalistic and stylized, these pendants depict the flamboyant crest of feathers characteristic of this predatory bird, as well as the change in color on the bird's neck denoted by decorative, geometric bands. These pendants also showcase high degrees of artistic creativity and dynamic expression. For example, in the *Eagle Pendant* [PL. 23, top] the artist depicted swirling motifs at either side of the eagle's head to denote the harpy's crest of feathers. Hybrid, transformational, and stylized imagery such as this was favored throughout the Isthmo-Colombian region; similar spiraling forms representing serpents are also seen in Colombian *cacique* pendants made by Tairona artists.

These pendants were all made using the lost wax, or cire perdue, casting technique, a process practiced in many parts of the ancient Americas but perfected in Isthmo-Colombia. By mixing unique combinations of metal (known as alloys), varying tonalities between bright pink, deep red, saturated yellow, and dark gold could be achieved. A particular mixture preferred in this region was *tumbaga* (or *guanín* in the ancient Antilles), an alloy of copper and gold. *Tumbaga*'s melting point is lower than either copper or gold alone, and it is usually lighter weight than higher-karat gold objects, which can be heavy and dense. In some of these metalworks, reddish hues of copper are more prominent, highlighting these artworks' dynamic and shifting chromatic qualities.

–Eric Mazariegos

PL. 24 P. 44
Unknown Greater Chiriquí artist

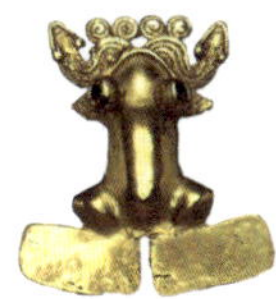

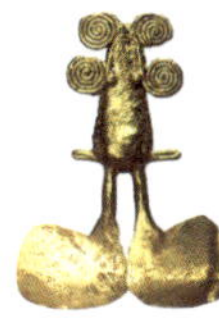

← Perhaps even more ubiquitous than their avian counterparts, small pendants in the shape of frogs abound in the ancient Americas, particularly in the Isthmo-Colombian (or Intermediate) Area. From a plethora of materials—such as metal, shell, and stone—artists and artisans cast, carved, and worked pendants in this basic form to great degrees of experimental stylization. The pendants in this exhibition are simultaneously naturalistic and abstract; their rotund bodies give the impression of fleshy weight, while their completely flattened legs are completely abstracted and geometric. Spiraling decorations emerge from the heads of these frogs, such as in the *Frog Pendant* [PL. 24, bottom], where coiling bands of metal terminate in triangular shapes that resemble serpentlike heads. These spiral elements artistically locate the pendants in Isthmo-Colombia and the broader ancient Greater Caribbean, where artists commonly rendered curvilinear, sinuous, and flowing forms in a wide array of media.

The highly abstracted and stylized imagery on these frogs may allude to a change in one's vision under the influence of psychotropic substances. In the ancient Americas, representations of frogs and toads may have held hallucinogenic connotations; the species known as *Bufo marinus* is endemic to the area and is known for the thick, saplike excretions produced on the surface of its skin. When ingested, this exudate causes a mild hallucinatory effect and may have been utilized at one point by high-ranking individuals in rituals or ceremonies to grant a kind of sacred, shamanic vision. The emanations that arise from the heads of these metallic frog pendants may be physical visualizations of hallucinatory manifestations and experiences.

–Eric Mazariegos

(II)
Unknown Greater Chiriquí artist, Costa Rica, *Frog Pendant*, 800–1522 CE.
Gold, 2 ⅜ × 2 ⅛ × ¾ inches (6 × 5.39 × 0.95 cm).
Denver Art Museum: Gift of Frederick and Jan Mayer, 1995.614.
Photography © Denver Art Museum

(II)
Unknown Panamanian artist, Panama. *Pendant*, 500–1520 CE. Gold, 2 ⅜ × 1 ¾ × ⅜ inches (6 × 3.17 × 0.95 cm).
Denver Art Museum: Gift of Frederick and Jan Mayer, 1995.667. Photography © Denver Art Museum

PL. 25 P. 45
Mathias Goeritz

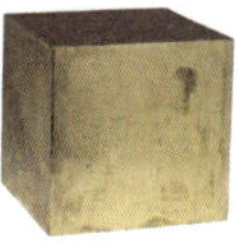

PL. 57 P. 96

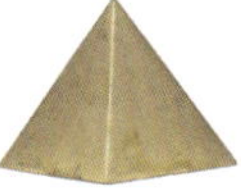

PL. 39 P. 75

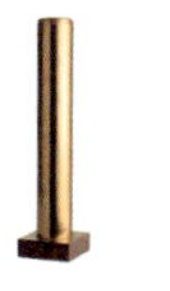

PL. 60 P. 99

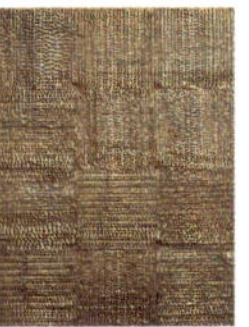

PL. 54 PP. 90–91

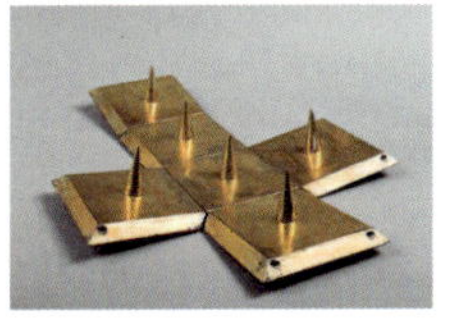

← Mathias Goeritz (1915–1990, b. Gdańsk) was a German emigree living in Mexico who became an important figure in the Mexican modern art and architecture milieu. Inspired by the European tradition of gold ground panel painting and its symbolic associations with transcendence and the divine, the artist incorporated gold in monochromatic works, sometimes adding nails to the canvas surface to create textural effects. In his series *Mensajes* (Messages) the artist explores the quality of gold as a substance that evokes a sense of awe and creates an emotional impact on the viewer.

–Tie Jojima

(I)
Figura geométrica (Geometric figure), 1961.
Wood on gold leaf, 10 × 9 ⅞ × 9 ⅞ inches (25.4 × 25.1 × 25.1 cm).
Private Collection, Courtesy of Henrique Faria, New York

(I)
Figura geométrica (Geometric figure), 1961.
Wood on gold leaf, 10 × 9 ⅞ × 9 ⅞ inches (25.4 × 25.1 × 25.1 cm).
Private Collection, Courtesy of Henrique Faria, New York

(I)
Untitled, 1969.
Wood on gold leaf, 23 ⅝ × 5 ⅞ × 5 ⅞ inches (60 × 15 × 15 cm).
Private Collection, Courtesy of Henrique Faria, New York

(I)
Untitled, ca. 1958–9.
Mixed media: perforated brass mounted on wood, 32 ⅛ × 23 ⅞ inches (81.5 × 60.5 cm).
Estrellita B. Brodsky Collection.
Photo: Arturo Sánchez

(II)
Cruz en la caja (Cross in a box), 1960–61.
Wood, gesso, gold leaf, paint, brass, steel, and magnets, 28 ¼ × 22 × 3 ⅛ inches (71.8 × 55.9 × 8 cm).
Tate Americas Foundation, courtesy of the Latin American Acquisitions Committee 2015

PL. 26 P. 46

Unknown Coclé artist, Panama

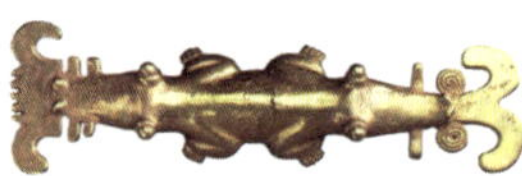

(II)
Double-Headed Crocodile, 1150–1400 CE. Gold alloy, 4 ⅛ × 1 ¼ × ¾ inches (10.4 × 3.1 × 1.9 cm). Denver Art Museum: Gift of Frederick and Jan Mayer, 1996.117. Photography © Denver Art Museum

← This pendant was made by an artist in the Greater Coclé region of ancient Panama, using the lost wax, or cire perdue, casting process with a combination of hammering and false filigree techniques. It represents two bilaterally positioned saurian or reptilian creatures symmetrically mirroring each other and conjoined at their abdomens. These creatures may be stylized representations of crocodiles, animals which held great symbolic and spiritual significance in the ancient Panamanian worldview. Beginning at around 500 CE, the iconography of the so-called Crocodile God became standardized and was frequently represented in ceramic vessels and hammered metal disks throughout the region of Greater Coclé. Archaeological and art historical analyses of these artworks have shown a common reverence for other marine creatures as well, such as sharks, catfish, crabs, and even seahorses.

This piece showcases bilateral and symmetrical form, a common artistic attribute in artworks from the ancient Isthmo-Colombian (or Intermediate) Area. However, intricate details emerging from the mouths of these crocodiles break this balance, pointing to the artist's individual agency and proclivity toward experimentation. These curving extensions are seen elsewhere in the corpus of ancient Coclé art, such as when artists represented the sinuous whiskers of the Panamanian catfish. These decorative elements placed onto the crocodile's snout may hint at stylistic animal hybridity and transformation, where the metalsmith wanted to showcase attributes of more than one animal form simultaneously in a single piece.

–Eric Mazariegos

PL. 27 P. 47

Denilson Baniwa

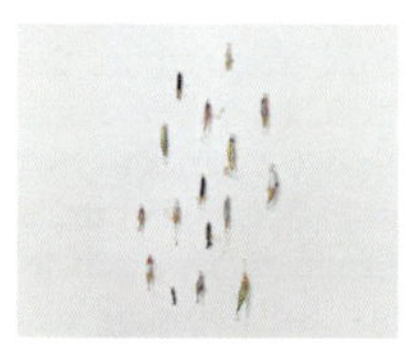

PL. 92 P. 144

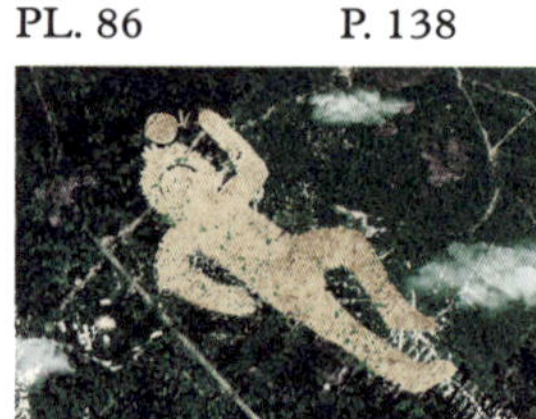

PL. 86 P. 138

(II)
Série mimética e resistência 2. Mercúrio: dias de um futuro esquecido (Series mimetics and resistance 2. Mercury: days of a forgotten future), 2022. Hooks, plastic, and golden wire, dimensions variable. Courtesy of the artist and A Gentil Carioca Gallery

(II)
Azougue 80, 2019. Video, 4 minutes 29 seconds. Courtesy of the artist and A Gentil Carioca Gallery

(I)
Natureza morta 1 (Still life 1), 2016. Digital photography, dimensions variable. Courtesy of the artist and A Gentil Carioca Gallery

← Denilson Baniwa (b. 1984, Amazonia) is an Indigenous artist from the Baniwa people in Brazil, whose multimedia artistic practice is rooted in his heritage and cultural identity. In his works Baniwa explores themes of Indigenous knowledge, cosmology, culture, and representation, as well as ecology and environmental justice. In his video *Azougue 80* the artist performs the ingestion of contaminated water and fish to reference the negative, life-threatening impact of gold mining on Indigenous communities, while listening to a speech by former Brazilian president Jair Bolsonaro defending the benefits of gold mining for the country. The artist counters and rejects the politician's discourse with his performative eating and spitting out of contaminated objects. In the work *Natureza morta 1* (2016)—which can be translated as "still life" or "dead nature"—the artist depicts a deforested area of the Amazon in the shape of a silhouetted body like those made by the police to mark a murder scene. In the work he juxtaposes the exploitation of the natural environment with the death of Indigenous populations.

–Tie Jojima

PL. 28 PP. 48–49
Bruno Baptistelli

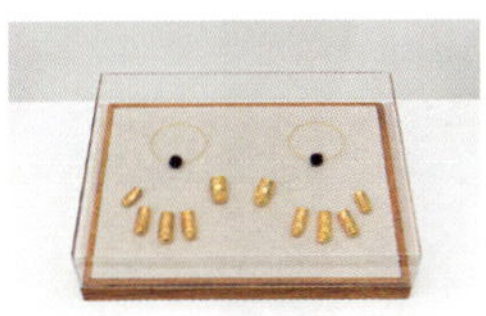

PL. 29 PP. 50–51

In his golden sculptural works, Afro-Brazilian artist Bruno Baptistelli (b. 1985, São Paulo) recovers the importance of gold for ancestral Black civilizations such as the Egyptians. In his *Manus* and *Pedites* works, comprised of fragments of the body, the artist taps into the history of archaeology as well as the role of museums (or perhaps galleries) in reproducing power dynamics based on colonial relations. These precious objects in delicate boxes allude to the importance of gold in one's construction of subjectivity—for instance, in hip-hop culture. The focus on fragmented hands and feet, however, also speaks to the bodies of those affected by the exploitation of gold.

–Tie Jojima

(II)
Untitled (Manus), 2023.
Resin, copper, and nickel, plated in 18-karat gold, 13 ¾ × 17 ¾ × 1 ⅝ inches (35 × 45 × 4 cm).
Courtesy of Galeria Luisa Strina and the artist.
Photo: Ana Pigosso

(II)
Untitled (Pedites), 2023.
Resin, copper, and nickel, plated in 18-karat gold, Foot: 2 × 4 inches (5 × 10 cm), anklet: 2 × 4 inches (5 × 10 cm). Courtesy of Galeria Luisa Strina and the artist.
Photo: Ana Pigosso

PL. 18 P. 37
Priscilla Monge

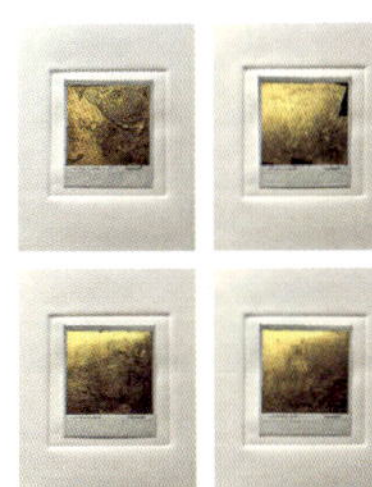

PL. 30 P. 52–53

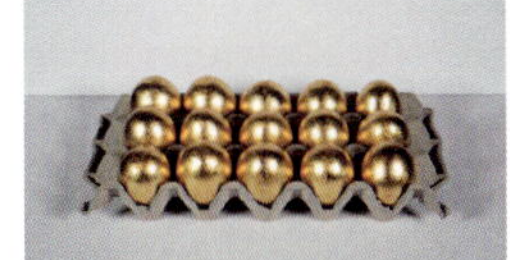

(I)
Healing Surfaces, 2023.
Polaroid with applied 23-karat gold leaf, 4 ⅜ × 3 ½ inches each (11 × 9 cm each).
Courtesy of Hutchinson Modern & Contemporary

(II)
Huevos de oro (Golden eggs), 1998. Gold leaf on chicken egg, 5 ⅞ × 5 ⅞ inches (15 × 15 cm).
Courtesy of Hutchinson Modern & Contemporary

← Priscilla Monge (b. 1968, San José) works with a range of materials to rethink the representation of everyday objects and their relationships to dominant power structures. In works such as *Huevos de oro* (1998) Monge laminates chicken eggs with gold leaf, displaying them in their familiar paper carton. Monge engages with the multivalent symbolism of the egg as both a commonly used item in the domestic kitchen and a symbol of fertility and creation, while also signifying the Spanish euphemism *huevos* and its connection to masculine virility.

Monge's *Healing Surfaces* (2023) presents four Polaroids, leafed in 23-karat gold to create a luminous, textured field of brilliant metallic color. Like the alchemist's quest to transform lead into gold, Monge utilizes the transformative process of Polaroid film and suggests the miraculous transmutation of the image into gold. Monge further engages with gold's magical properties by referencing Indigenous healing practices in Costa Rica, where a shaman would use golden or ceramic figures as representatives of the individual and what ailed them.

–Esther Levy

PL. 31 P. 54
Dario Escobar

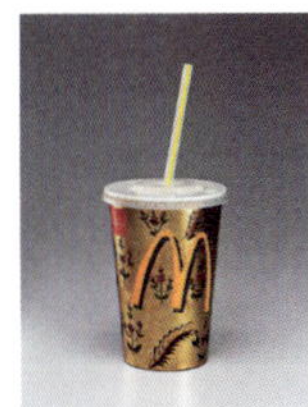

Dario Escobar (b. 1971, Guatemala City) creates work characterized by the formal and conceptual examination of objects and their function in the visual arts. He is best known for combining mass-produced items with traditional Guatemalan artisanal techniques and mythological references, uniting the artistic history of Guatemala with contemporary visual culture. Through his practice, Escobar focuses on themes including the complicated relationships between globalization, aesthetics, colonialism, Modernism, and consumerism. *Untitled* (1998) is a sculpture that Escobar crafted to resemble a McDonald's cup. This popular object is juxtaposed with a floral motif and gold pigment, which further emphasize the iconic golden arches of the logo and transform the object into a modern-day chalice.

–Sarah Lopez

(II)
Untitled (from *Gold Bling* series), 1998.
Cardboard, plastic, gold, and pigments, 7 ⅞ × 3 ½ inches (20 × 8.8 cm).
Courtesy of Almine Rech Gallery NY.
Photo: Daniel Hernández-Salazar

PL. 35 P. 58
Carlos Motta

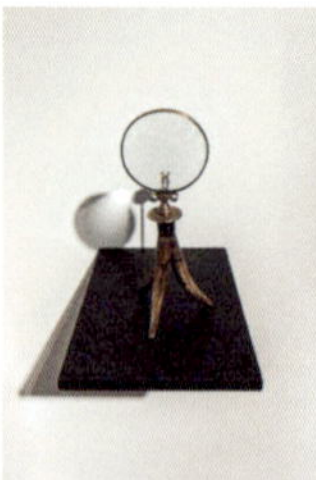

PL. 98 P. 152

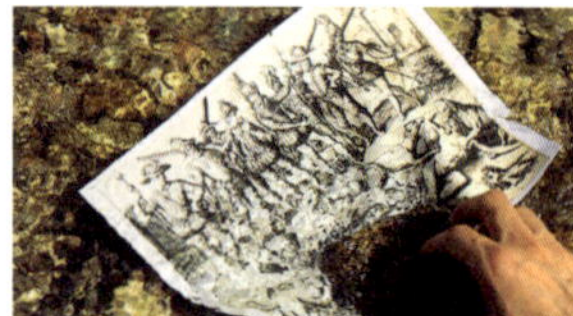

← Carlos Motta (b. 1978, Bogotá) is a multidisciplinary artist whose practice delves into themes such as gender and sexuality, colonialism, power, representation, historical discourse, and political activism. In his *Nefandus* series, he investigates the epistemic violence imposed on Indigenous cultures and individuals throughout the process of European colonization, particularly concerning the imposition of Western sexual and gender systems onto the subaltern populations in the colony. Such imposition involved the weaponization of sexuality as a normativizing tool to subjugate individuals. The work *Contra natura* (2019) consists of a minuscule golden sculpture of two individuals practicing anal sex and a magnifying lens that allows viewers to see the object in detail. While revealing a practice that has been demonized as a sin in the colonial period, the work also reveals our own gaze as a technique for study and control. The video *Nefandus Trilogy* presents two individuals on a boat (one is off camera, presumably the artist), floating along a crystalline river, and two monologues, one in Spanish and the other in Kogi, an Indigenous language, reflecting upon different forms of oppression of Indigenous peoples as a result of colonization, including sexual repression and epistemic erasures.

–Tie Jojima

(II)
Contra natura, 2019.
Gold and copper figure and magnifying glass on wooden shelf, 0.78 × 0.39 inches (2 × 1 cm).
Courtesy of the artist and mor charpentier

(II)
Nefandus Trilogy, Nefandus, 2013.
Video, color, sound, 13 minutes, 4 seconds.
Courtesy of the artist and Galeria Filomena Soares, Lisbon; Galerie mor charpentier, Paris; and P·P·O·W Gallery, New York and Galeria Vermelho, São Paulo

PL. 36 P. 59
Pedro Terán

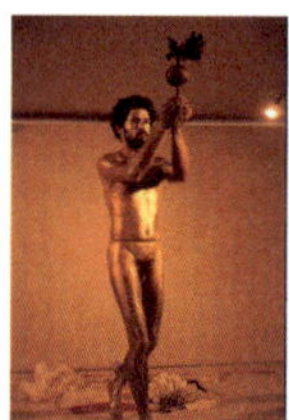

Pedro Terán (b. 1943, Barcelona) is a key figure in the Venezuelan Conceptual Art movement of the 1960s, known for using diverse visual language, including photography, performance, installations, and interventions in urban and rural public spaces. In his performances Terán aims to create an intimate connection between the viewer, the body, and subjectivity through ritual—often with the use of his body and strong gestures of masculinity. *Nubes para Colombia* was performed as a shamanistic ritual in which Terán, dressed in white, maneuvered canvases with red, yellow, and blue pigments (the colors of the Colombian and Venezuelan flags) and corresponding Polaroids. The artist then tore off his clothes, tied his genitals, and covered his body with gold dust, turning himself into a living sculptural depiction of the myth of El Dorado.

–Sarah Lopez

(I)
Nubes para Colombia (Clouds for Colombia), 1981.
Performance documentation.
Courtesy of the artist and Henrique Faria, New York

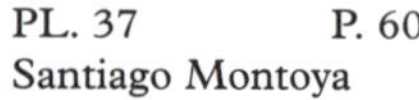

PL. 37 P. 60
Santiago Montoya

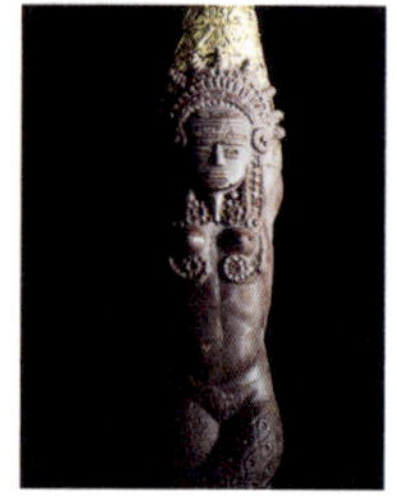

PL. 49 P. 85

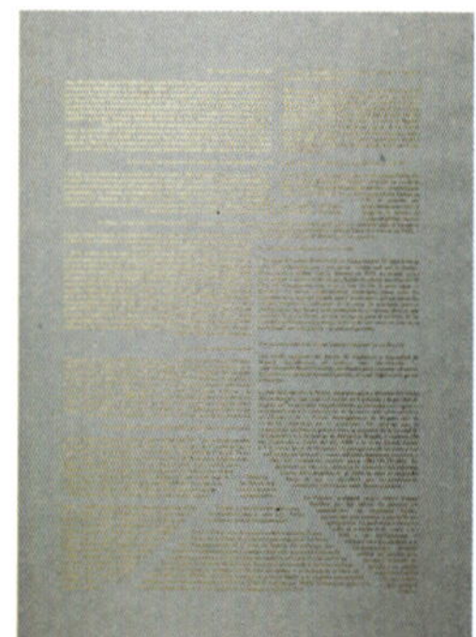

(I)
La Bachué en chocolate (Chocolate Bachué), 2023.
Chocolate, 24-karat gold leaf, batea, 16 × 16 × 17 inches (40.6 × 40.6 × 43.1 cm).
Courtesy of the artist.
Photo: Juan Manuel Garcia

(II)
Missteps and Other Paths, 2017.
Money paper, 24-karat gold leaf, 18 ½ × 12 inches (46.9 × 30.4 cm).
Courtesy of the artist.
Photo: Juan Manuel Garcia

← The work of Santiago Montoya (b. 1974, Bogotá) often utilizes a sardonic sense of humor to engage with themes of consumerism, colonialism, and notions of value. Montoya has created works made from a variety of materials, including paper money, neon signs, and chocolate. *La Bachué en chocolate* is an example of his sculptural works made with chocolate that address the history of art, resource extractivism, and national identity in Colombia. In this work, Montoya depicts the goddess Bachué, known as the mother of humanity to the Muisca people. Montoya references the iconic 1925 sculpture of Bachué by Colombian Modernist Rómulo Rozo, setting his own artwork in dialogue with earlier Colombian artists. Other works, such as *Missteps and Other Paths*, also engage with Colombian history and notions of national identity. Montoya creates four books that come together to form a map of the *Paso del Quindío*, a difficult and dangerous historical trek that has been used as a metaphor for the country's struggles to become a modem nation. This mountainous region of Colombia is home to many Indigenous groups and archaeological parks, along with remnants of European colonies that aimed to control the Indigenous communities that lived there.

–Esther Levy

PL. 38 P. 61
Ana Mercedes Hoyos

Ana Mercedes Hoyos (1942–2014, Bogotá) was a key figure in Colombian painting, with canvases that combine influences of the pop movement in themes that explore the national imaginary. From the late 1960s she produced abstract landscapes in oil where the use of subtle color variations connected the composition to specific places. *Laguna de Guatavita* depicts the famous lake near Bogotá where it was believed that the mythical Golden King from the Muisca culture performed the ritual in which he covered himself in gold and threw gold offerings into the lake. Instead of emphasizing the gold hue associated with the myth, Hoyos highlights the brown, thick mud of the lake soil. In doing this she reminds us of the real materiality of the lake that is so associated with Colombian identity.

–Aimé Iglesias Lukin

(I)
Laguna de Guatavita
(Guatavita lake), 1981.
Oil on linen, diameter 35 ⅜ inches (90 cm).
Courtesy of the Estate of the artist and Henrique Faria, New York

RELIGION AND TRANSCEN-DENCE

Abundant in religious artworks and artifacts, gold is a material that has been widely adopted in artworks from the colonial period for its association with the spiritual wealth of the Catholic Church, transcendence, and to reinforce the divine nature of saintly figures. For example, the use of golden halos or crowns indicates the aura of holiness surrounding a figure, and the golden frames often embellishing the artworks further emphasize their divinity. Gold has also symbolized the power and domination of the Catholic Church over subaltern peoples in the Americas. The figure of the Virgin and those of other local saints were sometimes represented alongside Indigenous people and a landscape that was typically American, indicating conquest through religious conversion. In this section, focused mostly on ideas of spirituality and transcendence, representations of the Virgin and of other Catholic saints are juxtaposed with contemporary works that elevate contemporary subjects and deities from Afrodiasporic religions as protagonists in this traditional iconography.

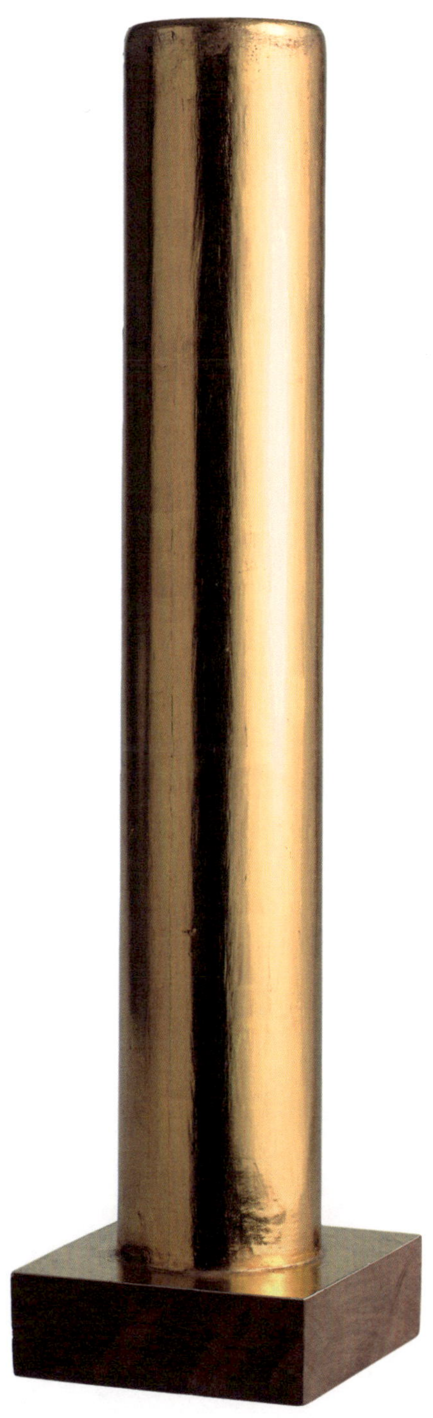

Mathias Goeritz, *Untitled*, 1969

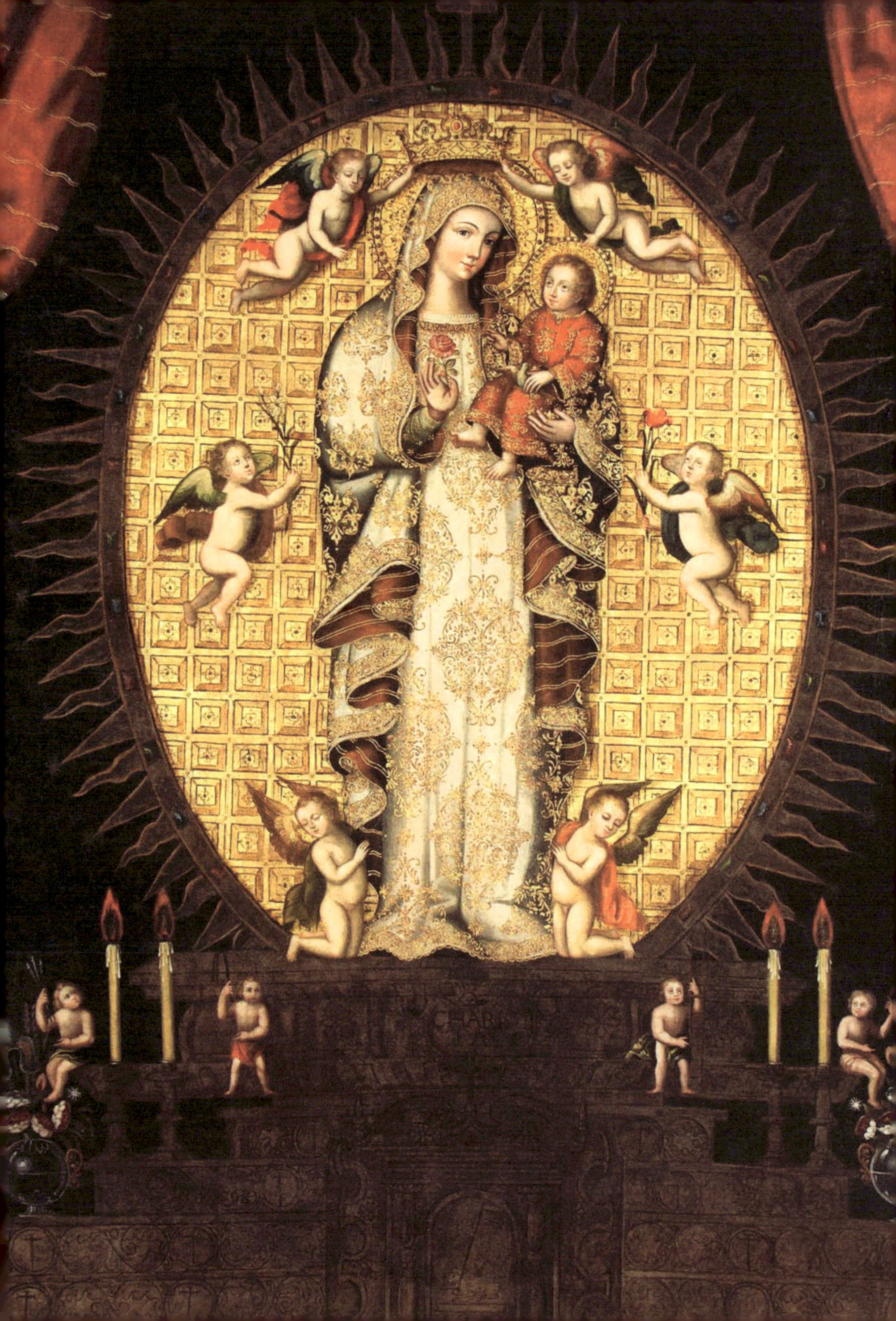

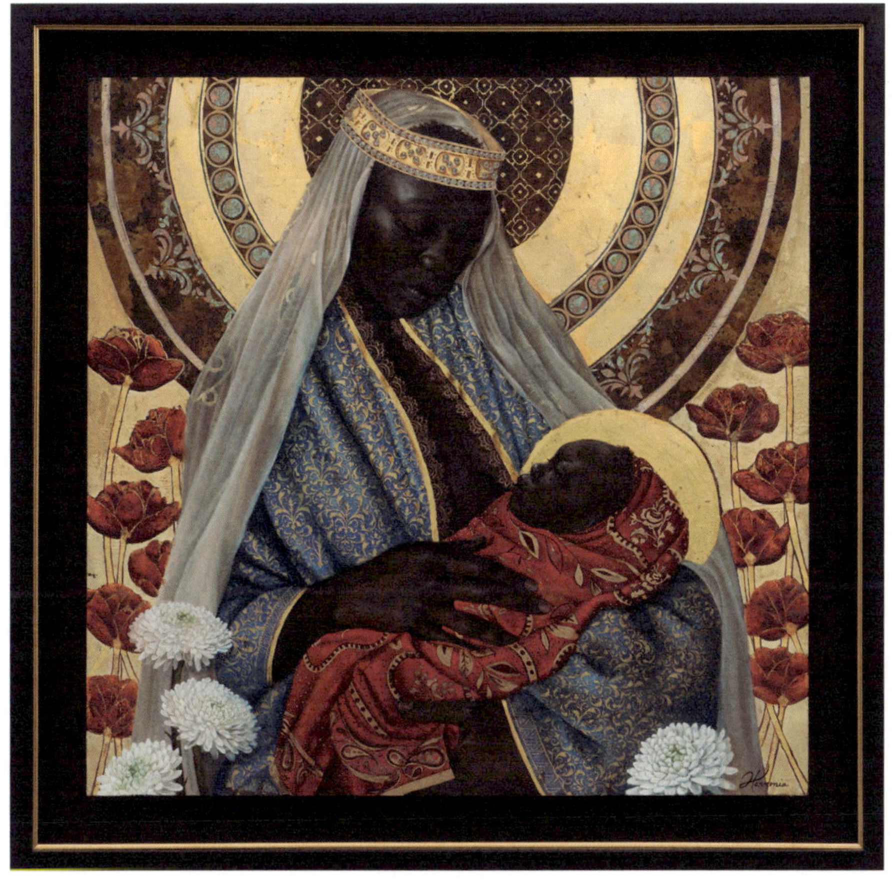

Harmonia Rosales, *Our Lady of Regla*, 2019

Unknown artist, Cuzco, Peru, *Our Lady of La Antigua*, eighteenth century

↑ [PL. 40]

Unknown artist, Mexico, *Virgin of Ocotlán (Tlaxcala)*, 1789

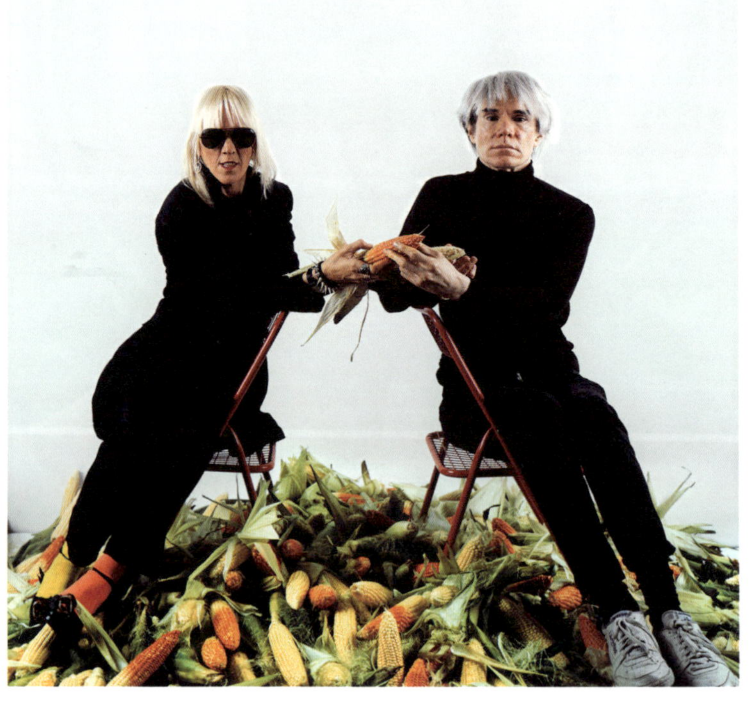

Marta Minujín, *Payment of the Argentine Foreign Debt to Andy Warhol with Corn, The Latin American Gold*, 1985

↓ [PL. 43]

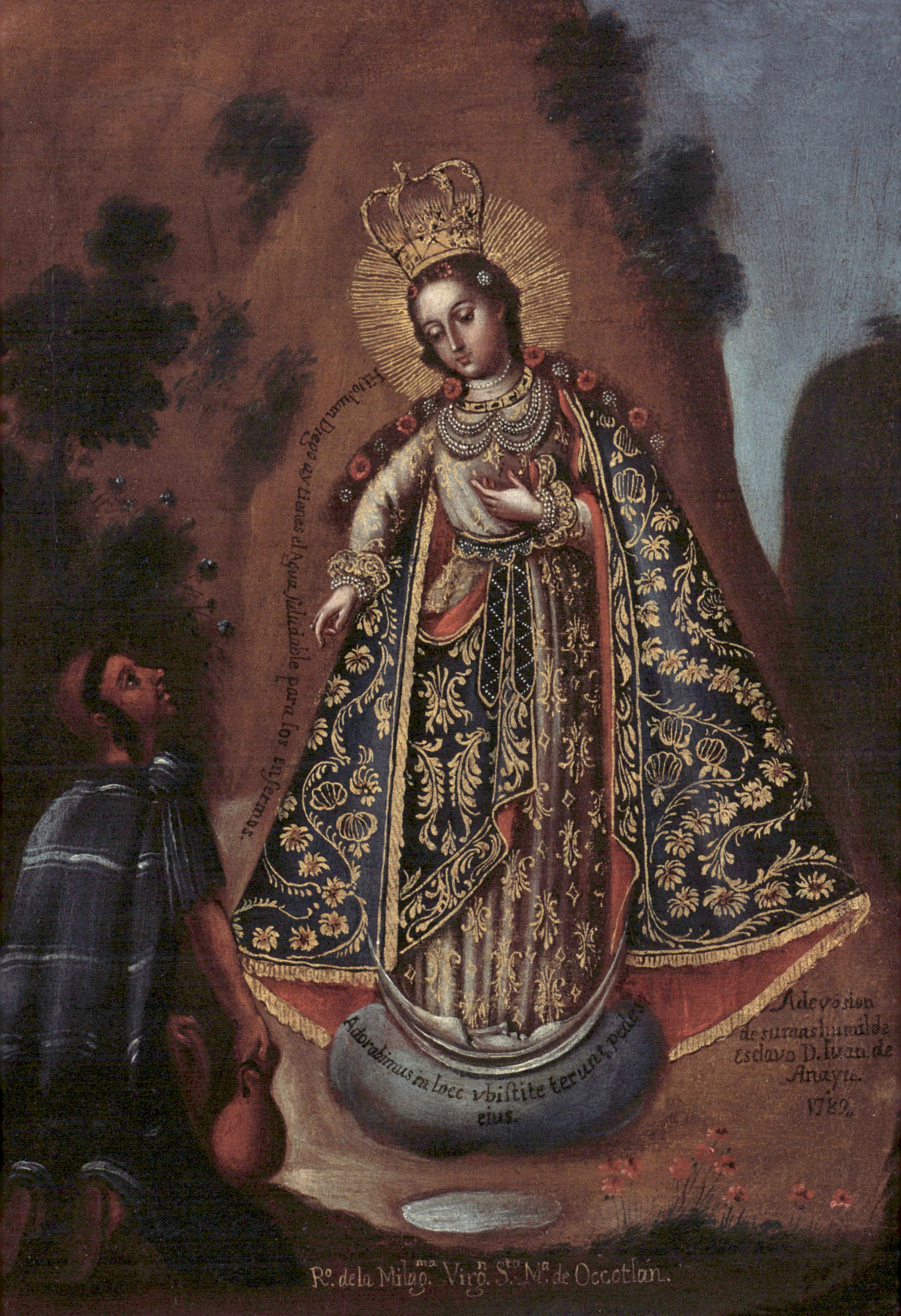
Hijo Juan Diego ay tienes el Agua saludable para los enfermos.
Adorabimus in loec vbistite terunt pedes eius.
A devosion de su mas humilde esclavo D. Juan de Anaya. 1789.
Rº. de la Milagª. Virg. Stª. Mª. de Occotlan.

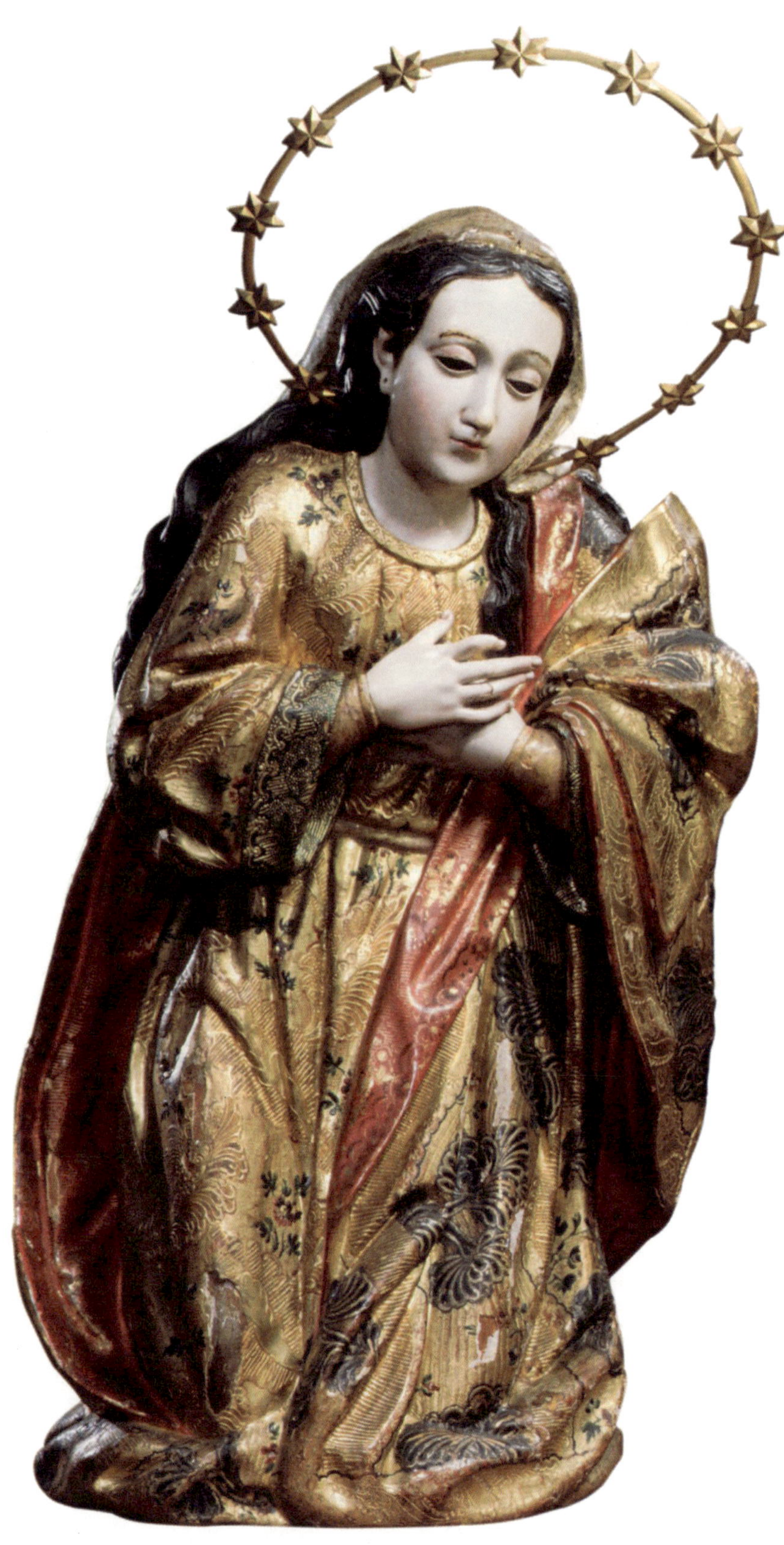

Unknown artist, Guatemala, *Mary (from Nativity)*, eighteenth century

[PL. 45]

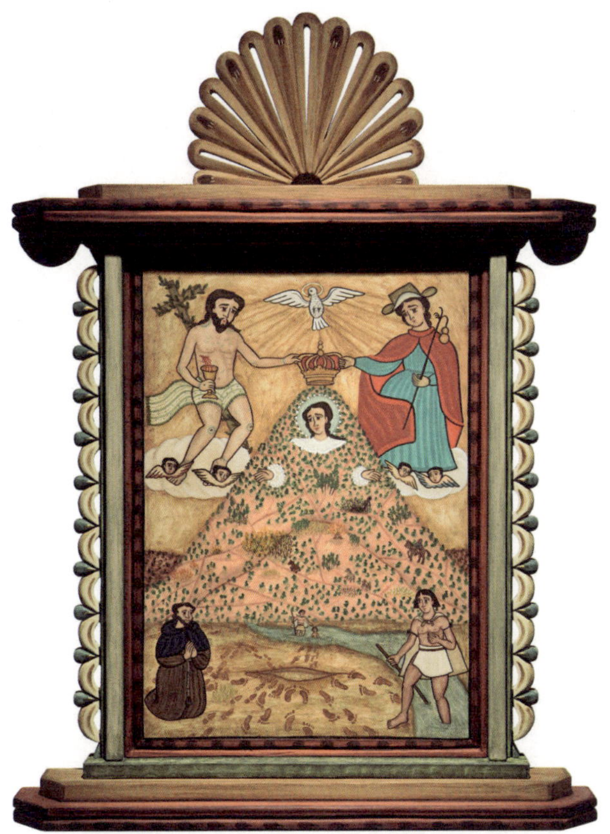

Vicente Telles, *Virgen del Cerro T'samajo / Chimayo*, 2023

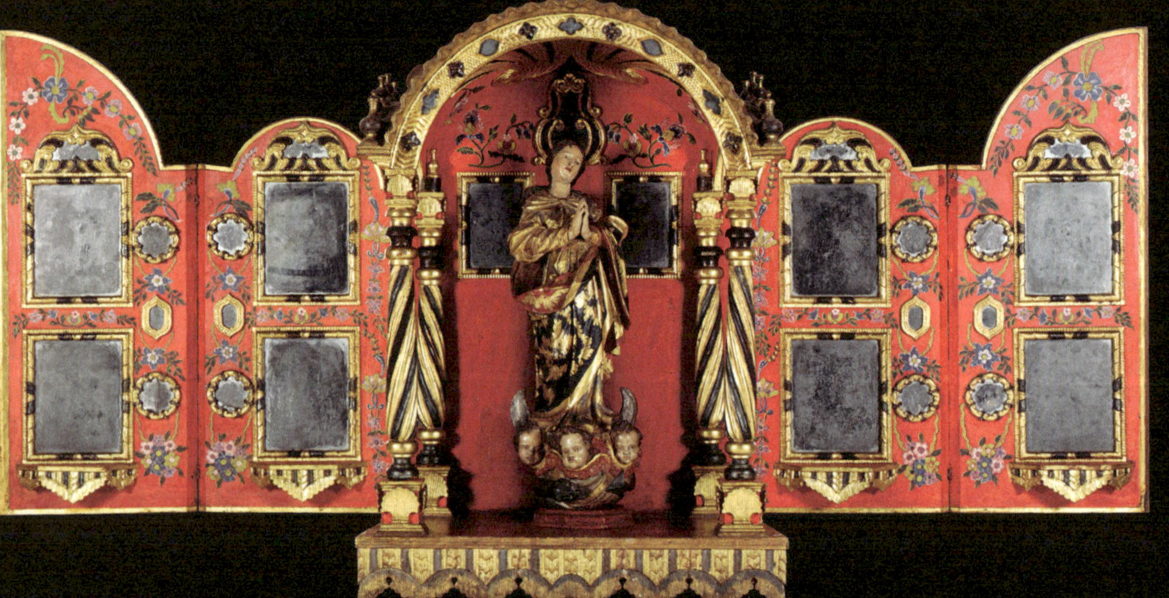

Unknown artist, Mexico, *Tabernáculo*, eighteenth century

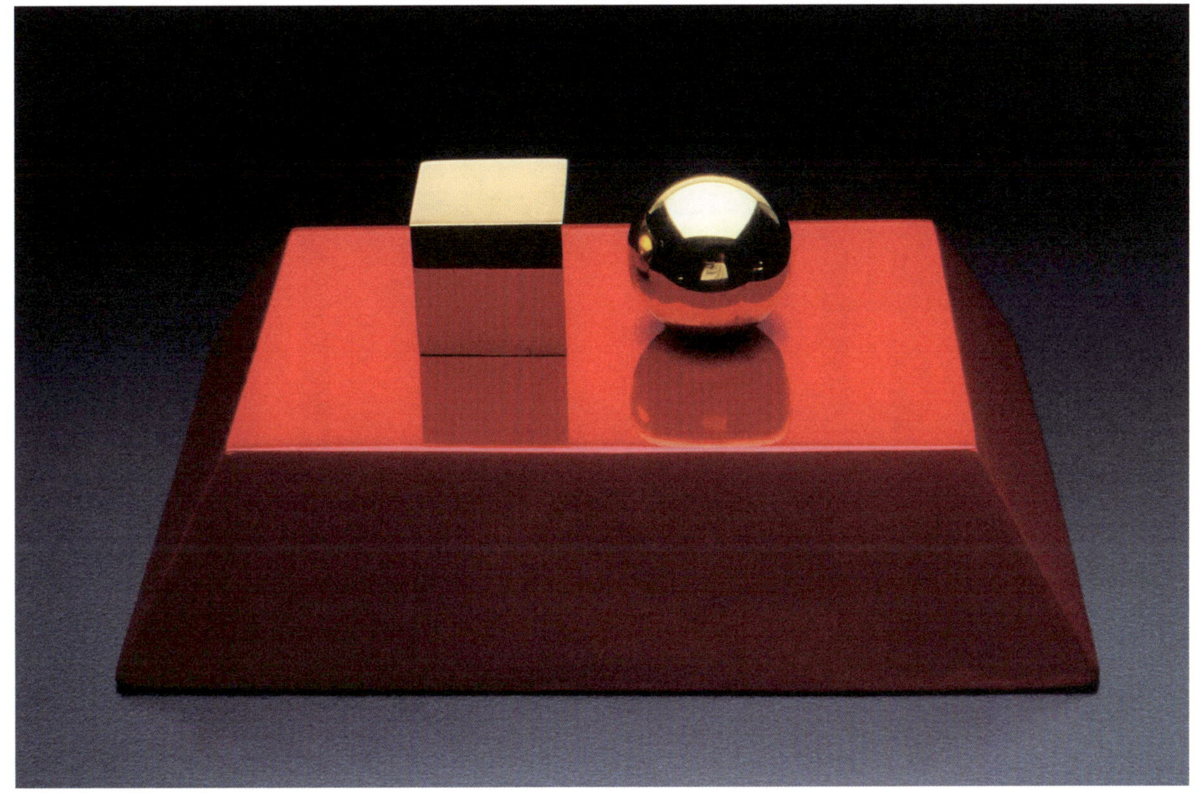

Liliana Maresca, *Objeto* / *Object*, from the series El Dorado - Ecuación, 1991

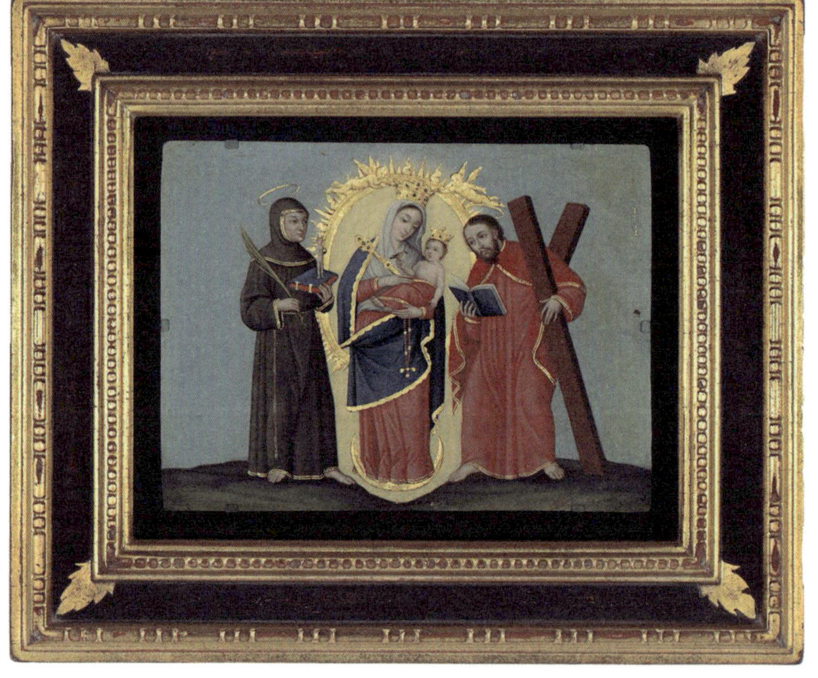

Joaquín Gutiérrez, *Our Lady of the Rosary of Chiquinquirá*, Bogotá, Colombia, before 1767

↓ [PL. 49]

40 años en espera del Metro

Hace 40 años el Ingeniero Virgilio Barco, como Alcalde de Bogotá, propuso reutilizar varias líneas ferroviarias abandonadas y que antes habían servido para salir de la ciudad. Su idea era aprovecharlas para iniciar un sistema rápido de transporte colectivo a superficie, con trenes a lo que llegó a llamar "Ferrocarril Central del Chicó". En esos 40 años Bogotá ha estado lejos el complejo de unirse a otras ciudades que tienen Metro, como Caracas o Medellín y cada bogotano mayor de edad, alcalde o no, ha creído ser dueño de la verdad en cuanto a transporte masivo. Otro ingeniero y alcalde, Enrique Peñalosa, adelantó lo más concreto y avanzado: [illegible] Transmilenio, pero lo dejó inconcluso porque es [illegible]. Ahora la ciudad está en un caos como nunca en su [illegible] urbano y [illegible] rieles que la nación comenzó a abandonar hace medio siglo. Frente a las voces que siguen pidiendo el Metro, se ha ofrecido ceder las rutas ferroviarias al Distrito [illegible] trenes de cercanías". La condición es una "espera prudencial" [illegible].

Luego de diez años, por fin abrirán el deprimido de la 94

Uno de los símbolos de la corrupción en la ciudad. Este [illegible], el alcalde Enrique Peñalosa tiene previsto entregar la obra que le costó a la ciudad [illegible] millones, cuatro veces su costo inicial. El mandatario ofrecerá excusas a la ciudadanía. [illegible] trabajadores, las decenas de maquinarias [illegible] directora del Instituto de Desarrollo Urbano (IDU), [illegible] tradiciones, enterró [illegible] de la calle 94 con Av. NQS, uno de los monumentos de [illegible] de la contratación en la ciudad.

El túnel de La Línea no estaría listo [illegible]

Cámara Colombiana de la Infraestructura dice que [illegible] 1,2 billones. [illegible]

[illegible]

El [illegible]

[illegible]

En [illegible] de Transmilenio [illegible]

[illegible]

78 años de estudios: [illegible] en TransMilenio

Más viejo que el metro de México y no existe. Por más de 78 años, han estado listos los estudios para hacer el metro de Bogotá, pero como bien sabemos, en la realidad ha sido puro "niño, tilín y nada de paletas". Hicieron primero el de Ciudad de México, en 1969. Pero durante todos estos años, las noticias de "ahora sí", o en tantos años estará "el metro de Bogotá" han sido recurrentes en las primeras páginas de los diarios. Los anuncios han venido de alcaldes y presidentes, porque como bien nos señaló Hidalgo, el "metro es un proyecto nacional hecho en Bogotá", se necesita de ambas administraciones para lograrlo algún día.

La 'venta' de la primera [illegible] de La República en 1954

En los años 50, el entonces presidente Gustavo Rojas Pinilla, dijo que tenía contratado el metro mediante concesión con una firma japonesa, pero por aquello del golpe de estado se canceló el tema. Luego, con el alcalde de turno, Hernando Durán Dussán en 1981, se presentó una propuesta de tener una red integrada de sistema de transporte público masivo, el [illegible] SITP, que incluiría el metro y troncales para el transporte [illegible]. El plan era entregar la primera línea del metro en 1986, y costaría 737 millones de dólares en ese entonces.

El aeropuerto, el gran elefante blanco

El aeropuerto Gustavo Rojas Pinilla de Tunja cumplió 57 años desde su primera inauguración, pero sigue siendo incierto cuál será su destino. Desde la construcción, que se terminó en 1955, ha tenido varias intervenciones en la pista de aterrizaje, dejó de funcionar por al menos 40 años, fue reinaugurado tres veces y hoy en día la pista sigue en abandono. La actual administración municipal, como todas las anteriores, tiene su propuesta para que el aeródromo vuelva a operar. La Alcaldía proyecta la utilización de la zona de aterrizaje para el entrenamiento de pilotos y mantenimiento de aeronaves, pero en este momento, la única certeza es que no opera para el servicio de las aeronaves y el espacio que ocupa la pista de aterrizaje es una zona verde donde crece la maleza y se pasea el ganado.

Fiscalía imputará cargos por 'elefante blanco' de la Policía

Fue citado exgerente del Fondo de Vigilancia y Seguridad de Bogotá. Actualmente, el edificio está abandonado. La Administración Distrital realizó un estudio para constatar el estado del mismo y su posible reestructuración, lo cual implica más gastos al Distrito.

La Fiscalía General de la Nación imputará cargos a Mauricio Fernando Solano Sánchez, exgerente del Fondo de Vigilancia y Seguridad de Bogotá, por las presuntas irregularidades presentadas en el contrato correspondiente a la construcción de la nueva sede administrativa del Comando de la Policía Metropolitana de Bogotá, que se encuentra suspendida en la actualidad. De acuerdo con la investigación adelantada por una fiscalía seccional de la Unidad de Delitos contra la Administración Pública de Bogotá, el contrato 739 fue adjudicado a finales del año 2010, a la firma Castell Camel S.A.S., con un plazo de 15 meses y un presupuesto de cuarenta y tres mil setecientos noventa y cuatro millones doscientos cincuenta y siete mil trescientos sesenta pesos ($43.794.257.360). En diciembre de ese año, comenzó la ejecución del contrato. Cuatro años después, en el 2014, la obra se suspendió luego de que se descubrió que la construcción presentaba deficiencias como fisuras y grietas.

La Fiscalía imputará cargos contra Solano Sánchez por los delitos de contrato sin cumplimiento de requisitos legales, prevaricato por omisión y peculado por apropiación. La audiencia se llevará a cabo el próximo 9 de mayo, a las 9:00 a. m. Actualmente, el edificio está abandonado y la Administración Distrital realizó un estudio para constatar el estado del mismo y su posible reestructuración, lo cual traerá más gastos al Distrito.

Terminal del Norte, más de una década en construcción

Vecinos y comerciantes advierten incumplimiento y caos vial. Cerca funciona un paradero improvisado.

Hace casi doce años, la ciudad recibió el anuncio de que tendría una terminal de transporte para organizar los buses intermunicipales en el norte de Bogotá. Sin embargo, han pasado tres administraciones de cuatro años cada una y está a punto de comenzar una cuarta, y la obra sigue sin terminar así como el caos vial se ha incrementado en el norte de la ciudad. Aunque la promesa de la terminal se hizo en el 2004, cuando se propuso instalar una provisional y se incluyó en el Plan de Desarrollo en el 2008, en el cual se descartó esa primera opción y se propuso una terminal definitiva, sólo hasta noviembre del 2012 se firmó el contrato por 10.020 millones de pesos con [illegible] S.A. y se anunció la entrega para julio del 2013.

[illegible]

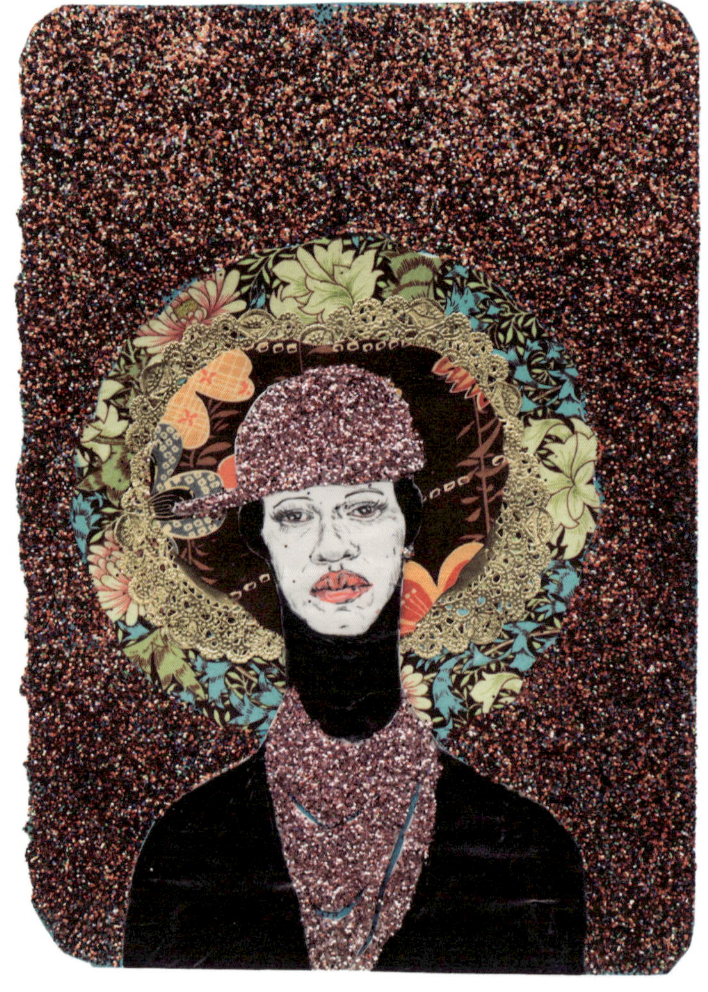

Ebony G. Patterson, *Untitled (Study of Khani)* from the *Disciplez series*, 2008

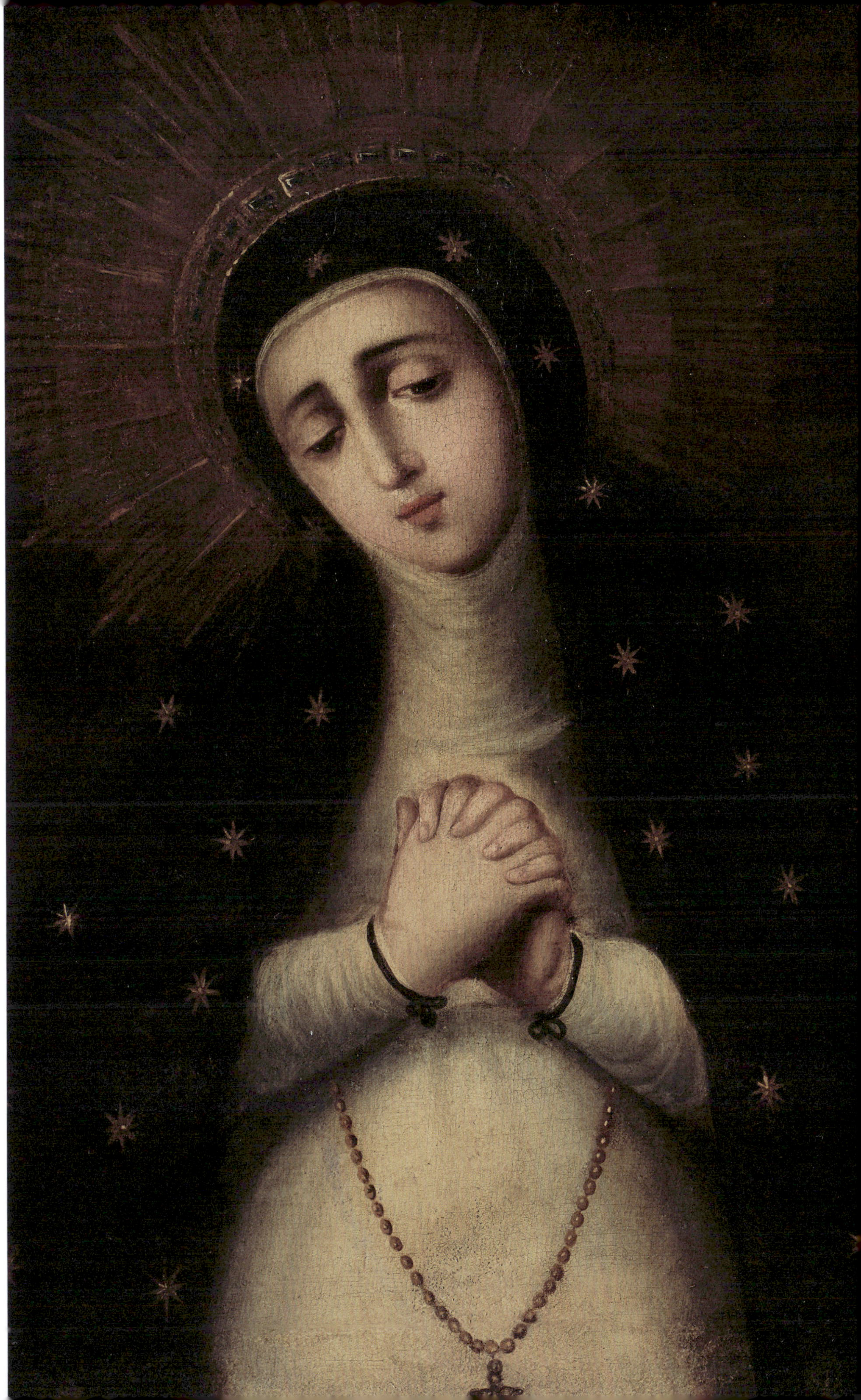

Juan Pedro López, *Nuestra Señora de la Soledad* (Our Lady of Solitude), eighteenth century

[PL. 51]

[PL. 52]

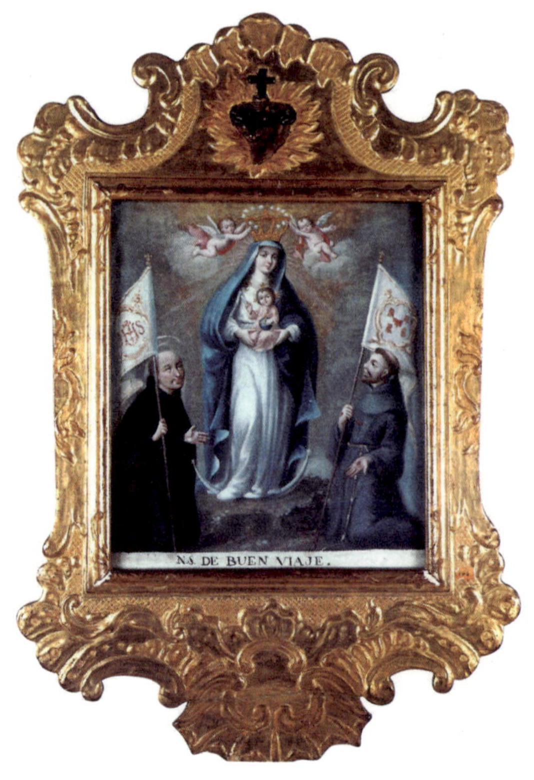

José Antonio Peñaloza, *Nuestra Señora del Buen Viaje* (Our Lady of Good Voyage), eighteenth century

[PL. 53]

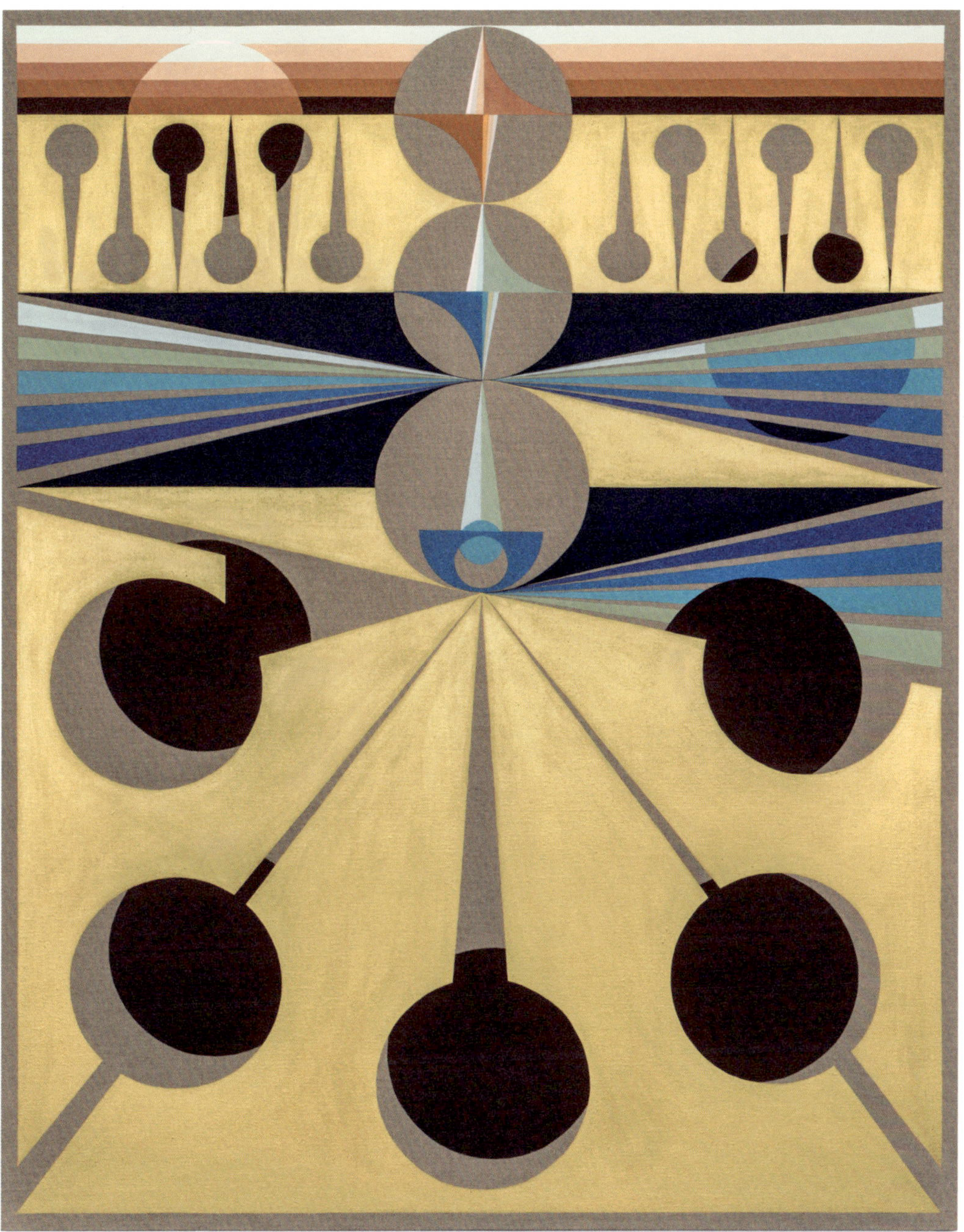

Eamon Ore-Giron, *Infinite Regress CC*, 2023

Mathias Goeritz, *Cruz en la caja* (Cross in a box), 1960–61

[PL. 54]

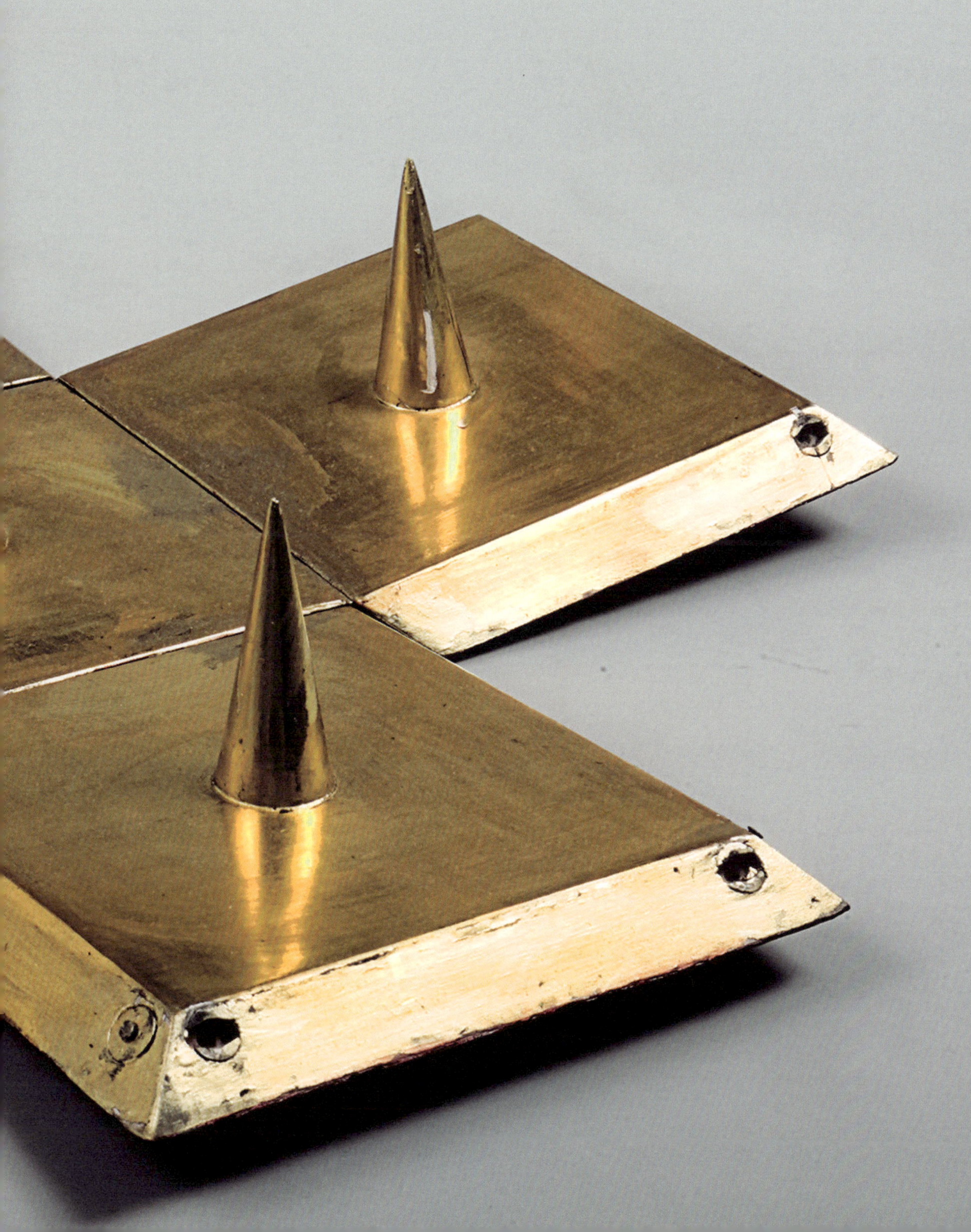

[PL. 55]

Freddy Rodríguez, *Casula*, 1993

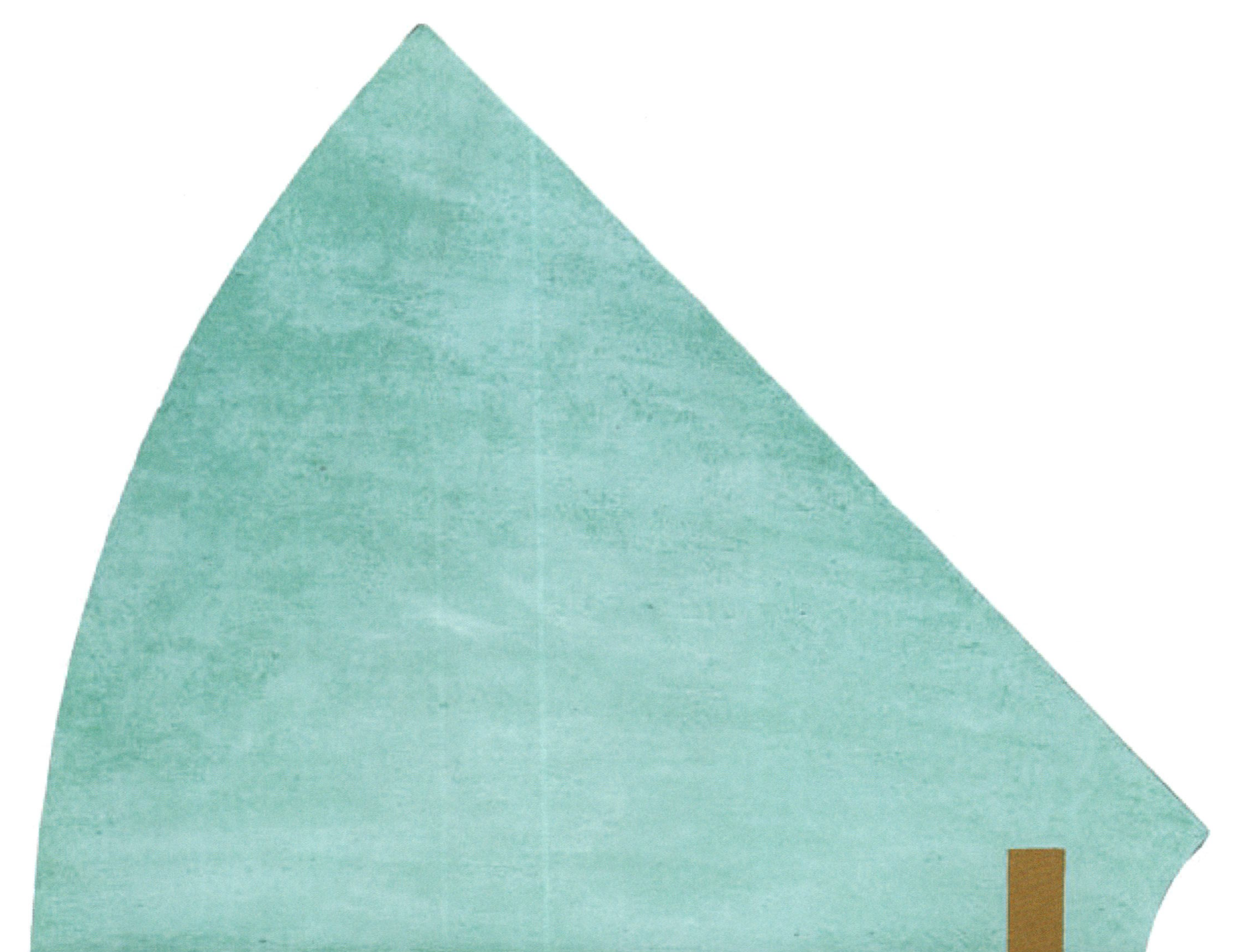

[PL. 56]

Freddy Rodríguez, *Gold or Investing in Art II*, 2015

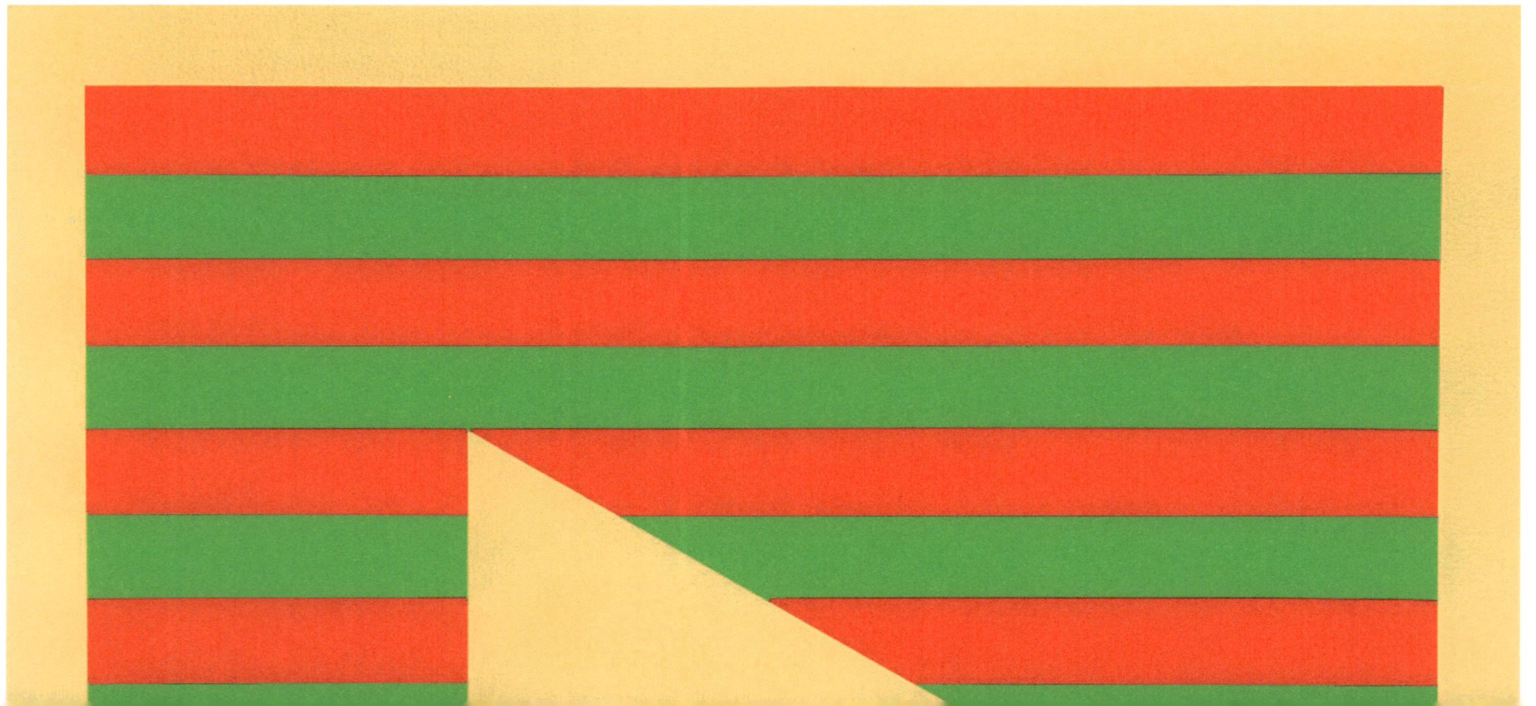

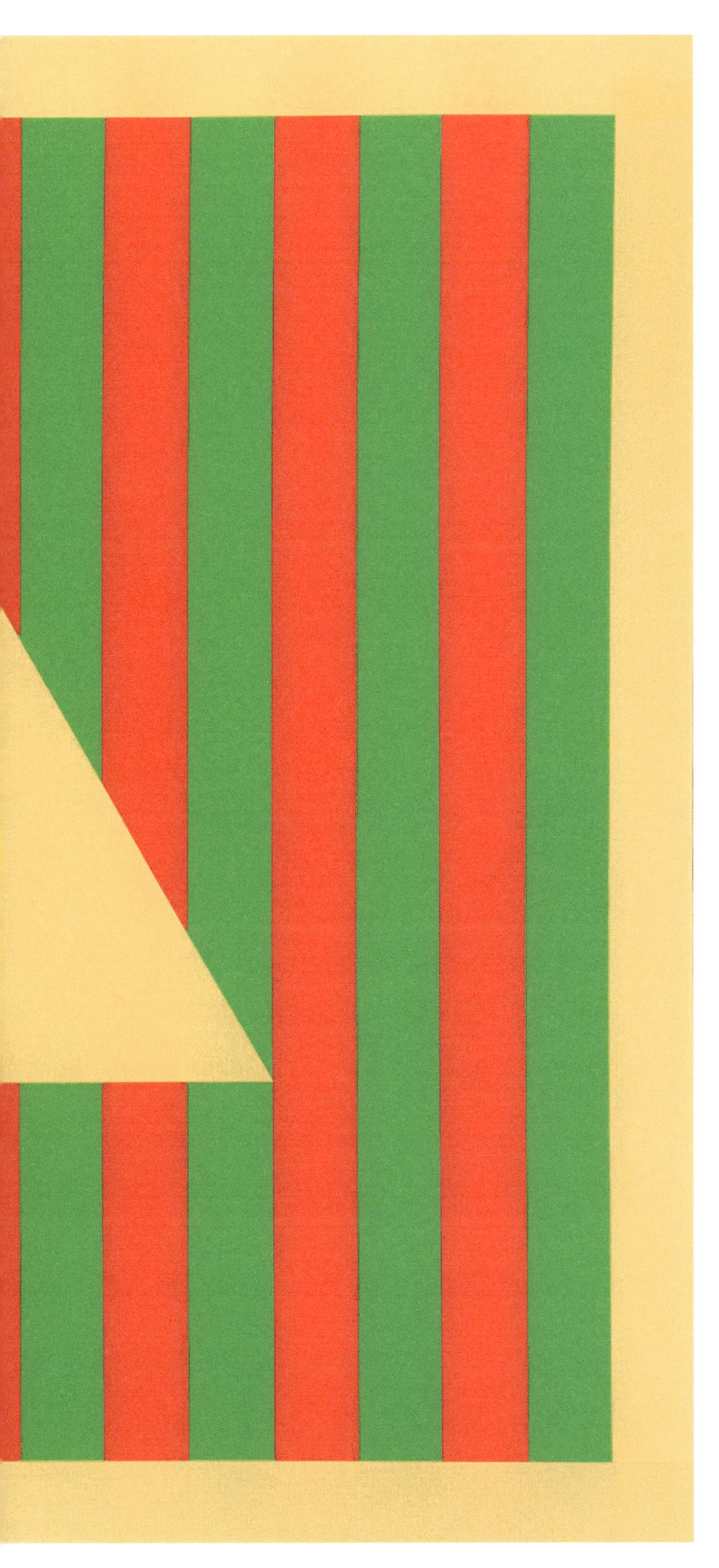

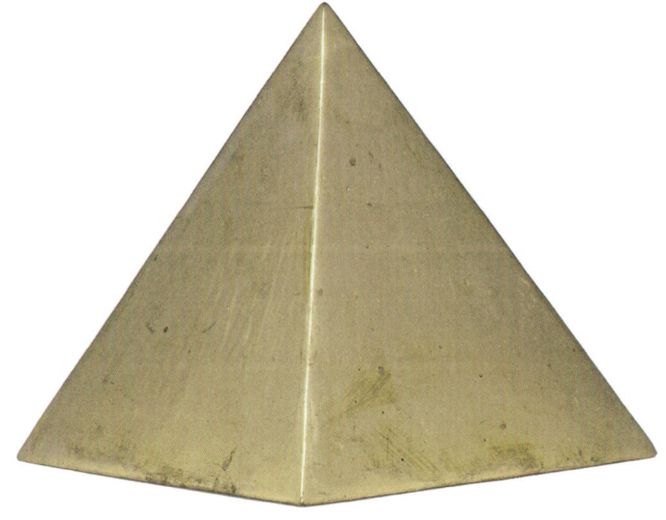

Mathias Goeritz, *Figura geométrica* (Geometric figure), 1961

[PL. 58]

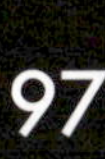

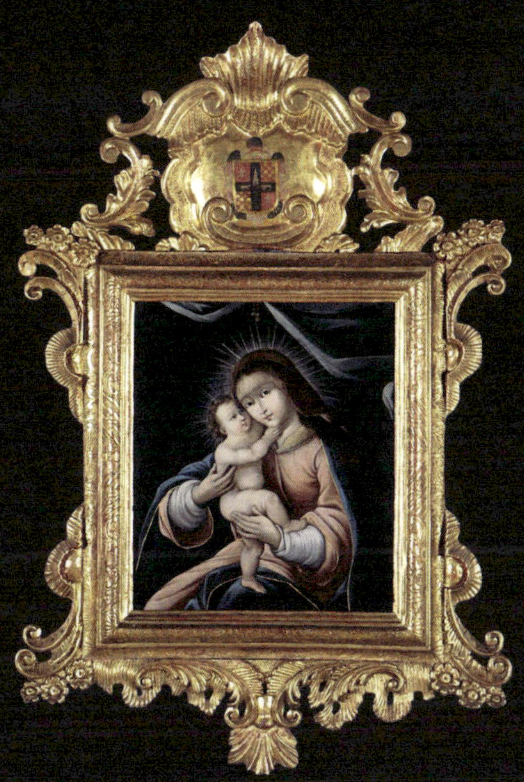

Unknown, Ecuador, *Nuestra Señora de Passau* (Our Lady of Passau), eighteenth century

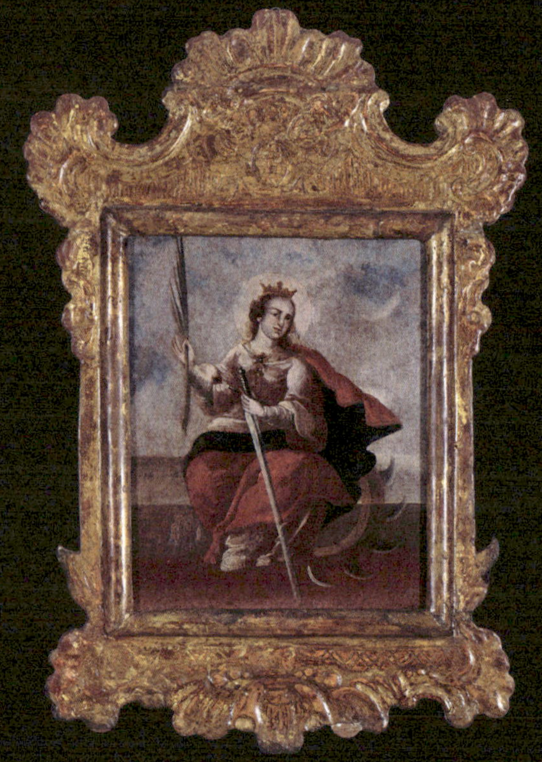

Unknown artist, Ecuador, *Santa Catalina de Siena*, eighteenth century

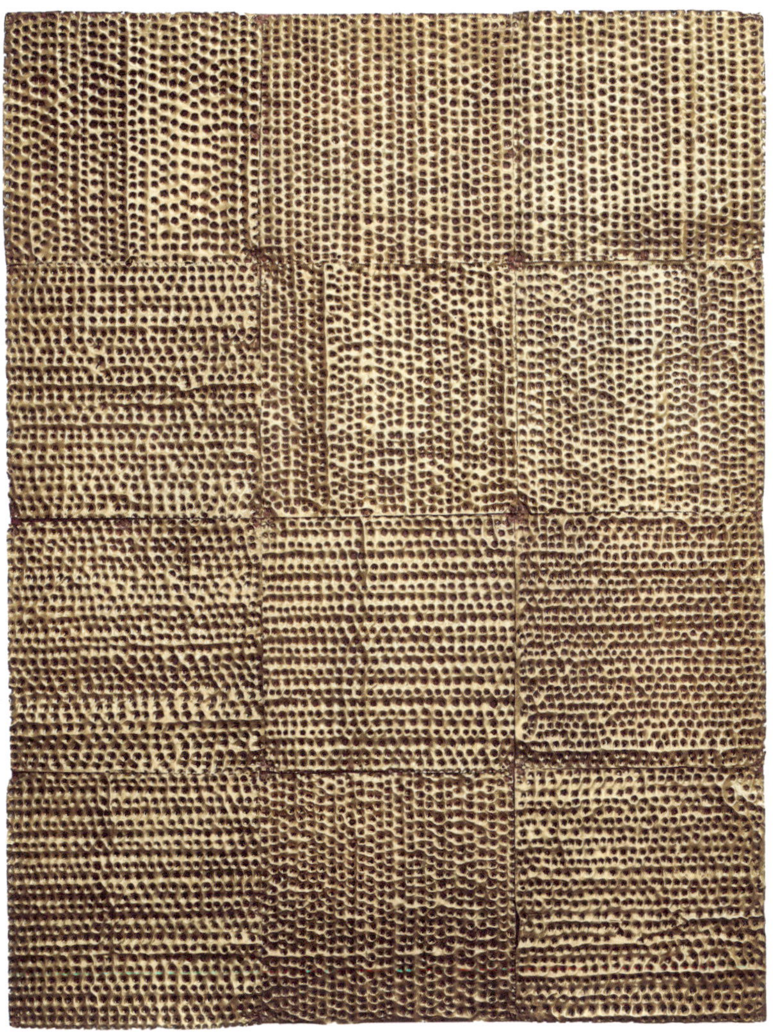

Mathias Goeritz, *Untitled*, ca. 1958–9

El Dorado: The Myth of Gold was organized in two parts. The first part was on view from September 6 to December 16, 2023 and the second part from January 24 to May 18, 2024. See indications in parentheses at the beginning of each caption.

PL. 40 P. 76

Unknown artist, Cuzco, Peru

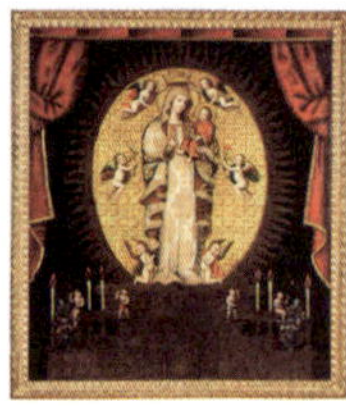

An object of devotion since the eleventh century, Our Lady of La Antigua was closely associated with Spanish victory over infidels. During the siege of Seville in 1248, King Ferdinand of Castile prayed to the Virgin, who promised him protection and victory over the Moors. An angel guided him through the city to an old painting of the Virgin Mary that was hidden from view, obstructed by the walls of the existing mosque. As he stood there, the image was revealed to him, and Ferdinand went on to take back the city.

In the New World, the veneration of this Virgin was appropriated to face new opponents. During his quest to find the City of Gold, Martín Fernández de Encisa and his troops found themselves outnumbered while fighting the natives in Panama. They swore an oath of fidelity and prayed to Our Lady of La Antigua for protection. If victorious, they promised to build a shrine in her honor—Santa María la Antigua del Darién—and send a large gift of the gold they were sure to find to La Antigua of Seville. In the middle of the sixteenth century, Don Juan Federegui, the Archdeacon of Seville Cathedral, had a copy of the painting made and sent it to the Cabildo of Lima. The new version, of similar dimension to the original, was framed in silver and installed in a an elaborately carved and gilded altarpiece in the Cathedral, where it is possible the maker of this image saw her likeness.

–Louisa Raitt

(II)
Our Lady of La Antigua,
eighteenth century.
Oil and gold on canvas,
63 ¾ × 54 3⁄16 inches
(161.92 × 137.63 cm).
Courtesy of Carl & Marilynn Thoma Foundation

PL. 41 P. 77

Harmonia Rosales

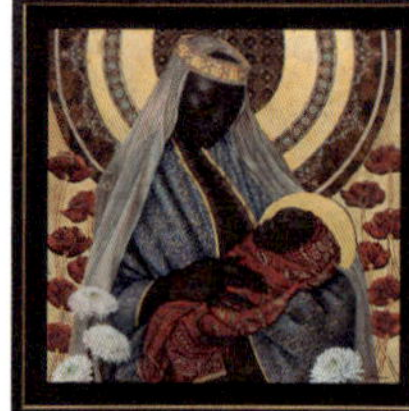

Harmonia Rosales (b. 1984, Chicago) creates sumptuous paintings that focus on Black female empowerment. Her work often references the works of Renaissance masters such as Michelangelo and Botticelli and recenters Black women as their subjects. She also often utilizes Afro-Cuban deities as replacements for Catholic religious figures in her reimagining of art history. Rosales's Renaissance stylization of Afro-Cuban religious figures reconfigures Catholic religious imagery to focus on bodies that have historically been exploited by the Church and colonization. A unique depiction of African diaspora is represented through Rosales's use of the techniques of the old masters to represent the rich history of Afro-Cuban religion, largely resulting from the slave trade. In *Our Lady of Regla*, Rosales depicts the Yoruba goddess Yemaya, crowned and veiled like the Virgin Mary. She is swathed in a richly embroidered blue robe, holding the infant Eve. Yemaya's scarred face suggests the physical and cultural effects of those impacted by the transatlantic slave trade. Yemaya looks down at the infant Eve, whose golden halo indicates the divinity and preciousness of her lineage.

–Esther Levy

(II)
Our Lady of Regla, 2019.
Oil, iron oxide, and 24k gold on wood panel 40 × 40 inches
(101.6 × 101.6 cm).
Private Collection

PL. 42 P. 78

Marta Minujín

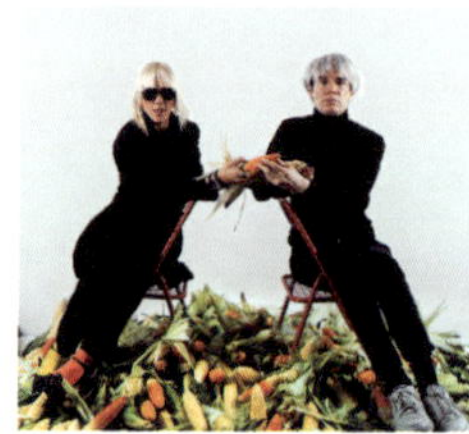

Marta Minujín (b. 1943, Buenos Aires) worked in New York in the late 1960s and early 1970s, where she pioneered in the neo avant-garde movements creating happenings, performance, and conceptual art. Many of her works explore the political implications of public participation in artworks, creating pieces such as interactive monuments that question authority by allowing the audiences to touch, enter, or even eat them. In this series of works, created on a visit by the artist to New York in 1985, she invited her friend Andy Warhol to participate in a photo-performance in which she paid the pop icon, a symbol of American culture, with the Argentine foreign debt represented in gold-sprayed corn, claiming that the region had already covered its debt to the first world with the "invention" of corn, a staple that today feeds millions worldwide. The witty but nonetheless quite serious proposal directly addresses the commercial colonialism that the Global South is subjected to by world powers such as the United States. By pairing herself on an equal footing with Warhol, the most famous artist at the time, Minujín also commented on the unequal trade of cultural capital in the art world. "Corn, the Latin American Gold" should balance these inequalities and put the world's regions on the same level, she claims.

–Aimé Iglesias Lukin

(I)
Payment of the Argentine Foreign Debt to Andy Warhol with Corn, The Latin American Gold,
1985. Photographic print,
36 ⅜ × 39 ¼ inches
(92.4 × 99.7 cm).
Private Collection, Courtesy of Henrique Faria, New York

PL. 43 P. 79

Unknown artist, Mexico

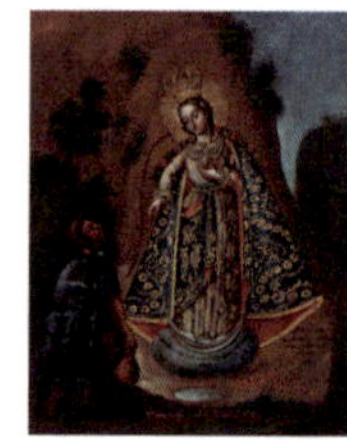

In 1541 a terrible epidemic struck the community of Ocotlán, a village near the city of Tlaxcala, east of Mexico City. According to legend, an Indigenous Tlaxcalan named Juan Diego, who served as a *topil* (altar server) at a nearby Franciscan monastery, was on his way to retrieve water from a nearby river that was believed to have healing properties when the Virgin Mary appeared to him. She instructed him to follow her down the mountain to a pine grove, where a spring of water would extinguish the calamity for all who drank from it. She then told him to return to the pine grove, where he would find a sculpted image of her, her true portrait, which should be placed in the church of St. Lawrence.

This painting shows Juan Diego kneeling before the miraculous apparition, affirming his Indigenous and Catholic identities simultaneously. While his gaze is cast in adoration of the Queen of Heaven, his head is shaved according to Tlaxcalan custom, and he wears a traditional *tilma* cloak. He carries an earthenware jug in his right hand to collect water from the curative pool, which glistens beneath the hovering Virgin. The Virgin herself is clothed in resplendent garments of gold brocade, embodying the text from Revelation which describes the Woman of the Apocalypse as "clothed with the sun, with the moon under her feet." This image reminds viewers not only of the material but also the spiritual riches to be extracted from the land in Spanish America.

–Louisa Raitt

(II)
Virgin of Ocotlán (Tlaxcala),
1789.
Oil on canvas, 13 x 9 ¾ inches
(33 x 24.7 cm).
Denver Art Museum:
Gift of Frederick and Jan Mayer, 2013.402.
Photography courtesy of Denver *Art Museum*

PL. 44 P. 80
Unknown artist, Guatemala

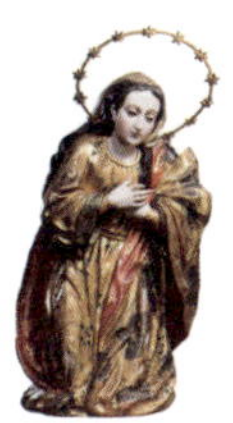

PL. 51 P. 87
Juan Pedro López

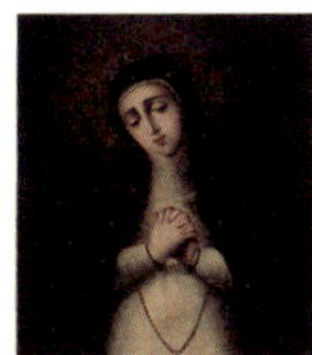

(II)
Unknown artist, Guatemala, *Mary (from Nativity)*, eighteenth century. Polychrome wood, gilt silver, and glass, 20 inches (height) (50.8 cm). The Metropolitan Museum of Art

(II)
Juan Pedro López, *Nuestra Señora de la Soledad* (Our Lady of Solitude), eighteenth century.
Oil on canvas, 20 × 16 ½ inches (50.8 × 41.9 cm).
Colección Patricia Phelps de Cisneros.
Photo: Arturo Sánchez

PL. 59 P. 98
Unknown artist, Ecuador

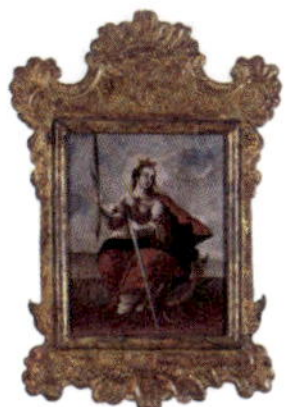

PL. 48 P. 84
Joaquín Gutiérrez

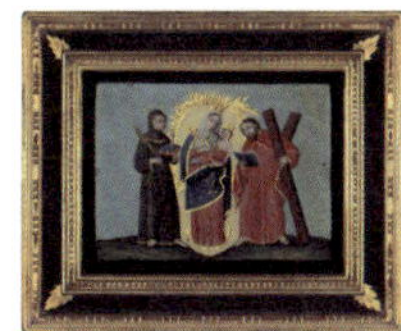

PL. 58 P. 97
Unknown artist, Ecuador

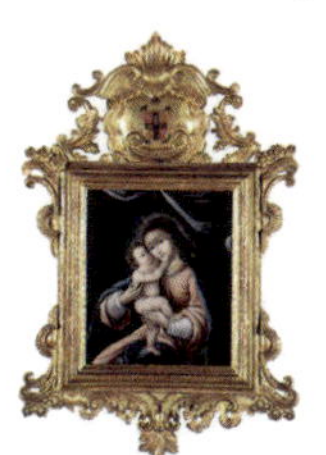

(II)
Santa Catalina de Siena, eighteenth century.
Oil on wood, 10 ¼ × 7 ⅞ inches (26 × 20 cm).
Colección Patricia Phelps de Cisneros

(II)
Our Lady of the Rosary of Chiquinquirá, Bogotá, Colombia, before 1767.
Oil and gold on copper, 8 × 10 ½ inches (20.5 × 26.8 cm). Collection of Carl & Marilynn Thoma.
Courtesy of Carl & Marilynn Thoma Foundation.
Photo: Jamie Stukenberg

(II)
Nuestra Señora de Passau (Our Lady of Passau), eighteenth century.
Oil on canvas, 21 × 18 inches (53.2 × 45.8 cm).
Colección Patricia Phelps de Cisneros

PL. 45 P. 81
Vicente Telles

Vicente Telles (b. 1983, Albuquerque) is a contemporary *santero*, or painter of saints, who aims to honor and reinterpret the traditional art of New Mexico. In *Virgen del Cerro T'samajo / Chimayo* the artist references the Andean mountains in Bolivia, which were considered sacred. The juxtaposition of the image of the saint with the shape of a mountain indicates the interrelation among a sacred space, femininity, and land as the provider of both resources and spiritual healing.

–Esther Levy

(II)
Virgen del Cerro T'samajo / Chimayo, 2023. Foraged mineral pigments, watercolor, gold leaf, and traditional gesso over carved basswood, 24 × 20 inches (60.9 × 50.8 cm).
Courtesy of the artist

PL. 46 P. 82
Unknown artist, Mexico

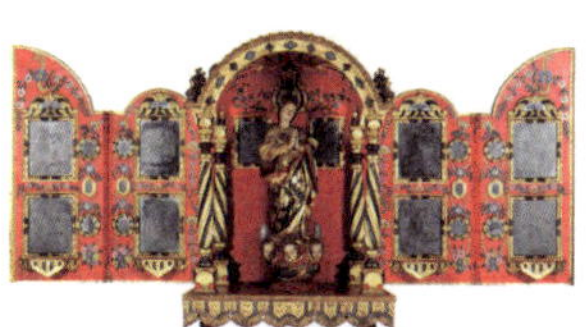

Made with a clientele of peninsular Spanish and Creole elites in mind, private religious objects, such as this luxurious tabernacle from New Spain, were displayed as an expression both of the owner's individual piety and of their personal wealth. Here, a delicately polychromed wooden statue of the Virgin of the Immaculate Conception stands encased within an elaborately painted and gilded shrine, the arms of which fold in to form a fully enclosed and transportable unit. The exterior of the enclosure is painted to resemble marble, while the interior, a red ground covered in vines of flowers, closely resembles the imported Asian textiles and Japanese lacquerware furnishings that flooded the market in eighteenth-century Mexico. Small shelves may have held flickering candles, the light from which would reflect off the mirrors behind causing the golden accents to shimmer, providing a dazzling vision of heaven on earth.

–Louisa Raitt

(II)
Tabernáculo, eighteenth century.
Polychrome wood, gold, and mirrors, 51 ⅛ × 36 × 19 ¾ inches (129.8 × 91.5 × 50.1 cm).
Colección Patricia Phelps de Cisneros.
Photo: Rodrigo Benavides

PL. 50 P. 86

Ebony G. Patterson

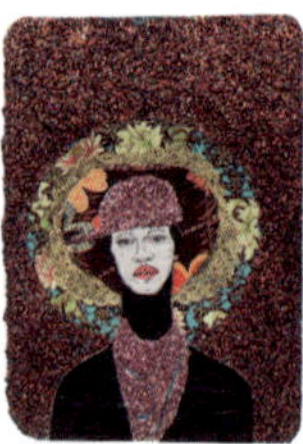

Ebony G. Patterson (b. 1981, Kingston) uses different media such as sculpture, painting, installation, and performance to address political and social injustices. The artist creates works that are both visually and symbolically multilayered, drawing the eye to a variety of details that form a complex web of meaning. In this work from the "Disciplez" Series, the artist renders a Black man depicted with a white face, wearing accessories, and pink lip-stick. The work toys with the construction of gender through the use of typically feminine crafting materials such as glitter, rhinestones, and doilies to grapple with the construction of Black masculinity in Jamaican dancehall and inner-city culture. The use of skin-bleaching creams and excessive bling have been associated with the beauty standards of Jamaican "gangsta" culture: at once posed as masculine while participating in stereotypically feminine forms of beautification. Patterson further emphasizes an element of femininity by creating a natural halo of flowers made vibrant by the contrast between the yellow greens and brown tones of the background. In doing so, the artist utilizes the visual tropes of religious iconography to connect this portrait to a lineage of religious painting while challenging ideas of masculinity.

–Esther Levy

(II)
Untitled (Study of Khani) from the *Disciplez series*, 2008.
Mixed media on paper, 20 × 15 ½ inches (50.8 × 39.4 cm).
Collection of Barbara Karp Shuster. Courtesy of the artist and Monique Meloche Gallery

PL. 47 P. 83

Liliana Maresca

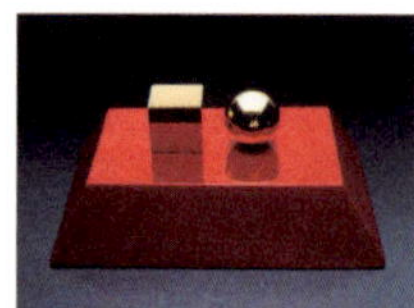

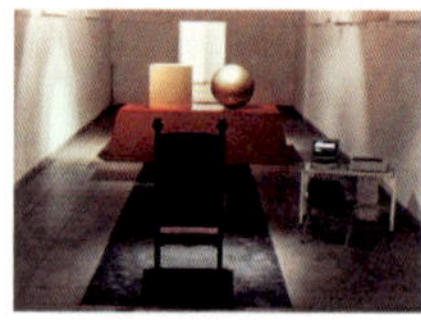

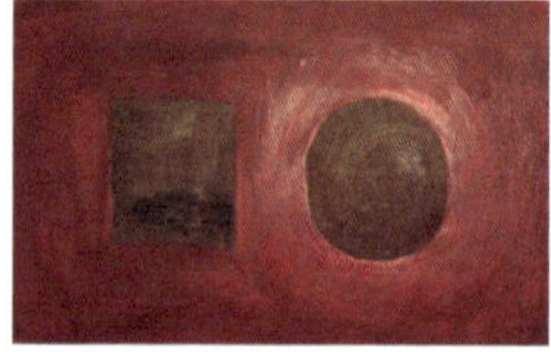

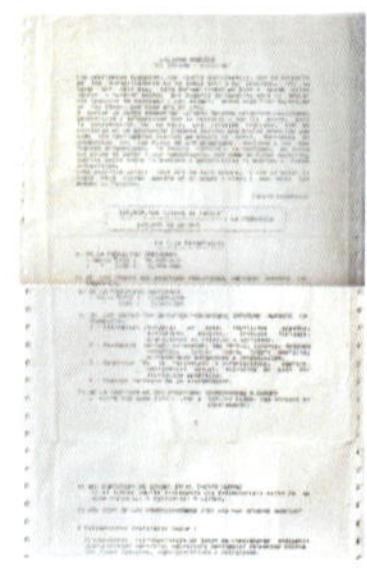

(II)
Objeto / Object, from the series *El Dorado – Ecuación*, 1991.
Lead and bronze plated wood, 7 ⅞ × 11 ¾ × 5 ⅞ inches (20 × 30 × 15 cm).
Private Collection, New York, courtesy of Sokoloff and Associates Art Advisors

(II)
El Dorado – Ecuación (Equation), 1991.
Inkjet print on RC paper, 11 ¾ × 7 ⅞ inches (30 × 20 cm) and video documentation.
Courtesy of Liliana Maresca Estate & Rolf Art Gallery

(II)
Dibujo from El Dorado – Ecuación (Drawing from El Dorado – Equation), 1991.
Mixed media on paper, 11 ¾ × 7 ⅞ inches (30 × 20 cm).
Courtesy of Liliana Maresca Estate & Rolf Art Gallery

(II)
Original printed document from the computer of El Dorado – Ecuación (Equation), 1991–2.
Archival document.
Courtesy of Liliana Maresca Estate & Rolf Art Gallery

← Liliana Maresca (1951–1994, Buenos Aires) worked with sculpture, installation, performance, and conceptual strategies to make works that questioned systems of power and gender inequalities in post-dictatorship Argentina. Around 1992, as part of a series of exhibitions that reevaluated the legacy of the Spanish invasion of the Americas during the five hundredth anniversary of the arrival of Christopher Columbus, Maresca created works that directly questioned the role of searching for gold during the conquest. Her installation *El Dorado – Ecuación*, presented in the late 1991 exhibition *La Conquista* at Centro Cultural Recoleta in Buenos Aires, presented a giant trapezoid structure in shiny red melanin wood, reminiscent of the base of a pyramid, supporting a golden cube and sphere, shapes alluding to alchemy. Presented as a royal banquet, the structure was connected by a rug with a thronelike chair, inviting the viewer to sit and "eat" the geometric gold. An office desk to the side included a computer, which regularly printed the results of an equation calculating the relation between the kilos of gold sent to Spain and the liters of Indigenous blood spilled during colonization. In this way, the work questioned the value of this mineral extraction by showcasing the losses it involved.

–Aimé Iglesias Lukin

PL. 52 P. 88

José Antonio Peñaloza

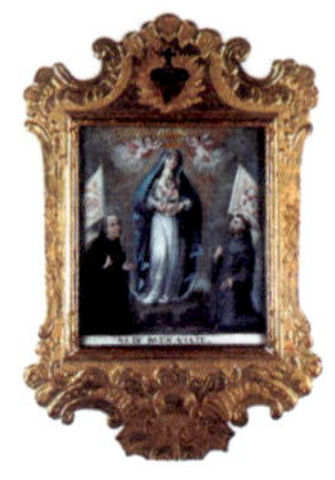

(I)
Nuestra Señora del Buen Viaje (Our Lady of Good Voyage), eighteenth century.
Oil on canvas, 13 ⅜ × 11 ⅜ inches (34 × 29 cm).
Colección Patricia Phelps de Cisneros

← Colonial expansion in the Americas would not have been possible without the successful proselytization of the Amerindian peoples. This composition features at its center Nuestra Señora del Buen Viaje, a title for the Virgin Mother that originated in seafaring communities in Spain and Portugal before spreading across the globe with expeditions of conquest. Two small cherubs are shown placing a gleaming crown atop her head while the Christ child she holds offers a gesture of blessing to viewers. Although Christ is depicted only as an infant, the blazing sacred heart adorning the top of the frame alludes to Christ's love for humanity made manifest through his sacrifice on the cross.

On the right side of the canvas, a reverent St. Francis of Assisi presents the stigmata on his left hand to the viewer and wields the flag of his order in the other. Saint Ignatius of Loyola kneels at left, brandishing a flag with the IHS symbol, a Greek monogram for the name of Jesus Christ that he adopted as the emblem for the Jesuit order. Although the Jesuits were expelled from the Spanish Empire in 1767, the inclusion of the leaders of the two most prolific monastic orders responsible for evangelizing Spanish America underscores the painting's devotional pedagogy.

This small-scale Venezuelan painting hangs in its original golden frame. Given that its maker worked in Caracas as both a painter and gilder, it is possible that he was also responsible for its ornate decoration.

–Louisa Raitt

PL. 53 P. 89
Eamon Ore-Giron

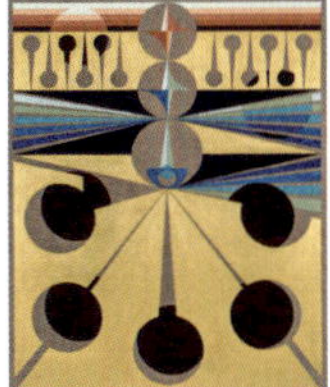

Eamon Ore-Giron (b. 1973, Tucson) creates brightly colored geometric and abstract paintings that gather a wide range of visual styles. Some of his influences include Native American medicine wheels, Amazonian tapestries, twentieth-century avant-gardes, Russian Suprematism, and Latin American Concrete Art, which he uses to create works that resonate across historical and cultural contexts. *Infinite Regress CC* (2023) is part of a series of works that Ore-Giron began out of interest in the formal qualities of the color gold. While producing the works, he became increasingly interested in the impact and history of gold, the value assigned to the material, and the ways in which the desire for gold has shaped our world.

–Sarah Lopez

(I)
Infinite Regress CC, 2023.
Mineral paint and flashe on linen, 69 × 54 inches (175.3 × 137.2 cm).
Courtesy of the artist and James Cohan, New York. Photo: Charles White / JWPictures.com

PL. 55 PP. 92–93
Freddy Rodríguez

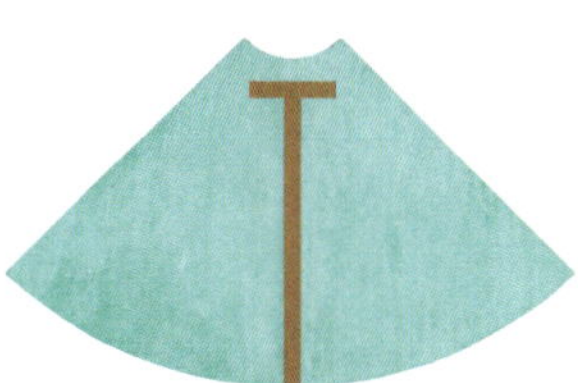

PL. 56 P. 94–95

(II)
Casula, 1993.
Acrylic and sawdust on canvas, 24 × 34 inches (61 × 86.4 cm).
Courtesy of Hutchinson Modern & Contemporary

(I)
Gold or Investing in Art II, 2015.
Acrylic on canvas, 36 × 36 inches (91.4 × 91.4 cm).
Courtesy of Hutchinson Modern & Contemporary

← Freddy Rodríguez (1945–2022, Santiago de los Caballeros) was a New York–based painter who drew inspiration from the prominent styles of the 1960s, including Abstract Expressionism, Minimalism, and Pop Art. In works such as *Gold or Investing in Art II*, the artist utilizes red and green to form crisp, vertical stripes. Atop these stripes, the artist has painted a gold frame and, in the center, a gold triangle. As the title suggests, the artwork engages with the historical and contemporary ideas of investment through the lens of artwork and gold. In *Casula,* the artist creates an abstraction of the liturgical vestment of the same name. In this work, Rodríguez utilizes sawdust to create the textured blue surface of the robes. Atop this textured blue tone, a golden T shape is formed. Compared to the highly ornate, silken casulas worn by priests, Rodríguez's rendition is simple: the golden T not quite forming a cross, while the textured blue surface suggests a coarse consistency. In both *Casula* and *Gold or Investing in Art II,* the artist utilizes abstraction as a means by which to raise questions and probe the cultural signifiers of wealth and power.

–Esther Levy

MAPS AND TERRITORY

The search for El Dorado played a crucial role in European mapmaking from the sixteenth to eighteenth centuries, shaping their understanding of the Americas. Maps served as tools of domination, organizing the land into intelligible forms and reflecting Europeans' projections and desires. Early maps even speculated about the site of El Dorado, locating it in the northwestern area of the apocryphal Lake Parime, an enormous rectangular lake imagined to exist in the middle of the Amazon. However, in the eighteenth century, scientific explorations began to discredit the myth. As El Dorado started to disappear from maps, the myth had already established the Americas as a land filled with wealth up for grabs. The juxtaposition of historical and contemporary works in this section addresses how maps and geography are political concepts deeply affecting our relationship with space, and how artists are challenging and questioning the established notions of borders, nation, territories, and power created by these objects.

105

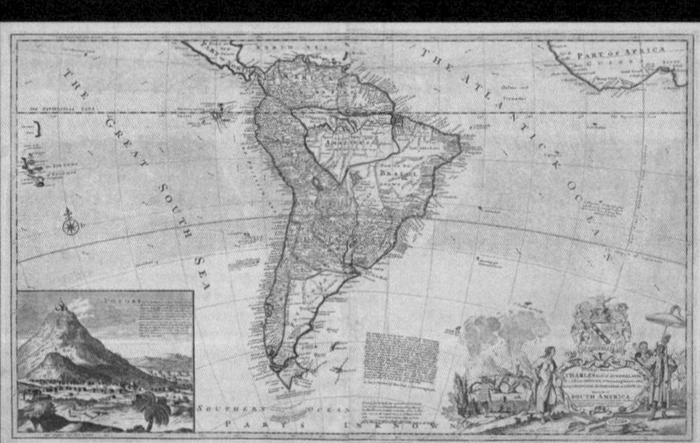

THE GREAT SOUTH SEA
THE ATLANTICK OCEAN
PART OF AFRICA
POTOSI
SOUTHERN OCEAN
PARTS UNKNOWN
SOUTH AMERICA

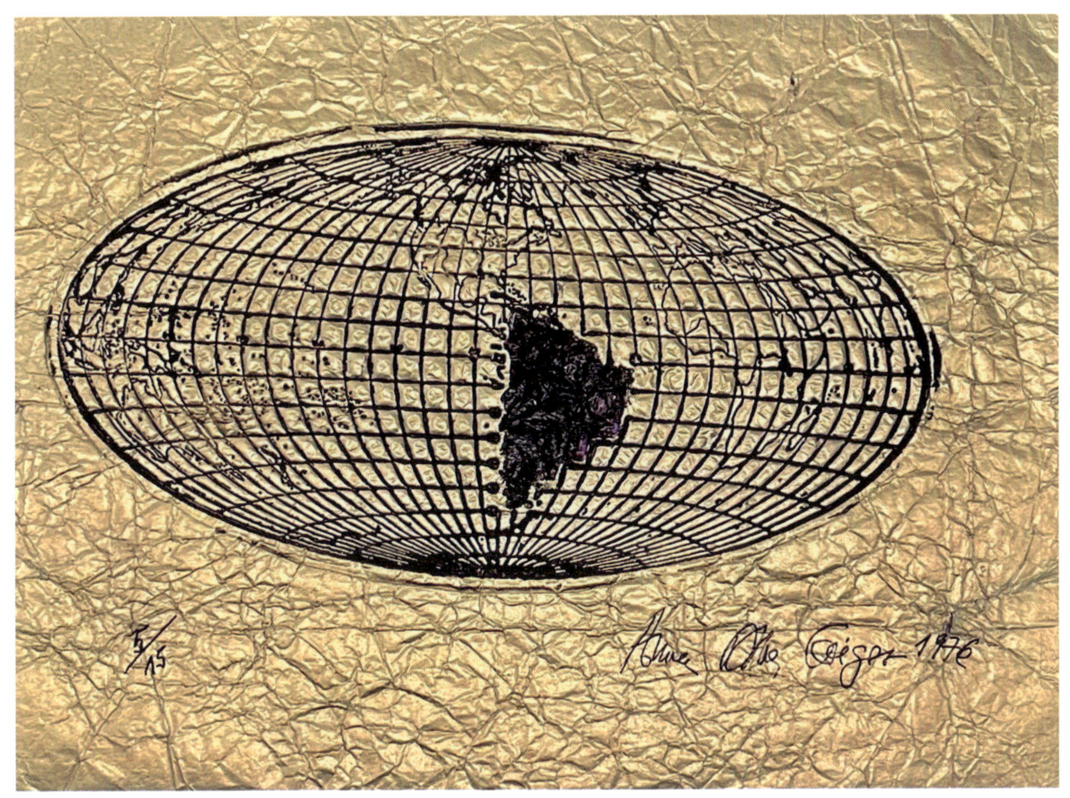

Anna Bella Geiger, *Local da ação n° 01* (Place of action n° 01), 1980

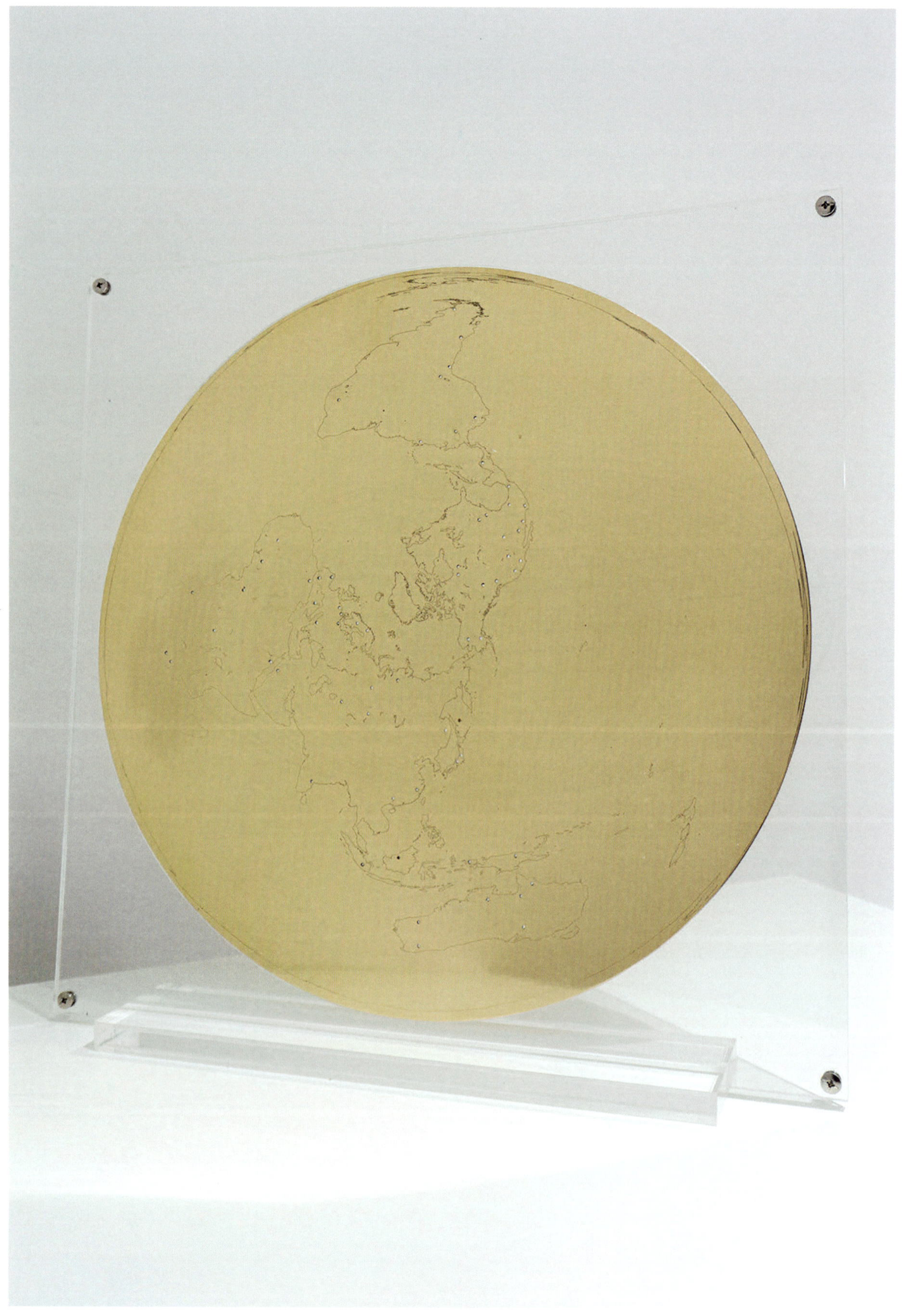

Mazenett Quiroga, *Sun Disc*, 2019

Covens & Mortier, Netherlands, *Archipelague du Mexique, ou sont les isles de Cuba, Espagnola, Lamaique, Etc.*, ca. 1700

↓ [PL. 65]

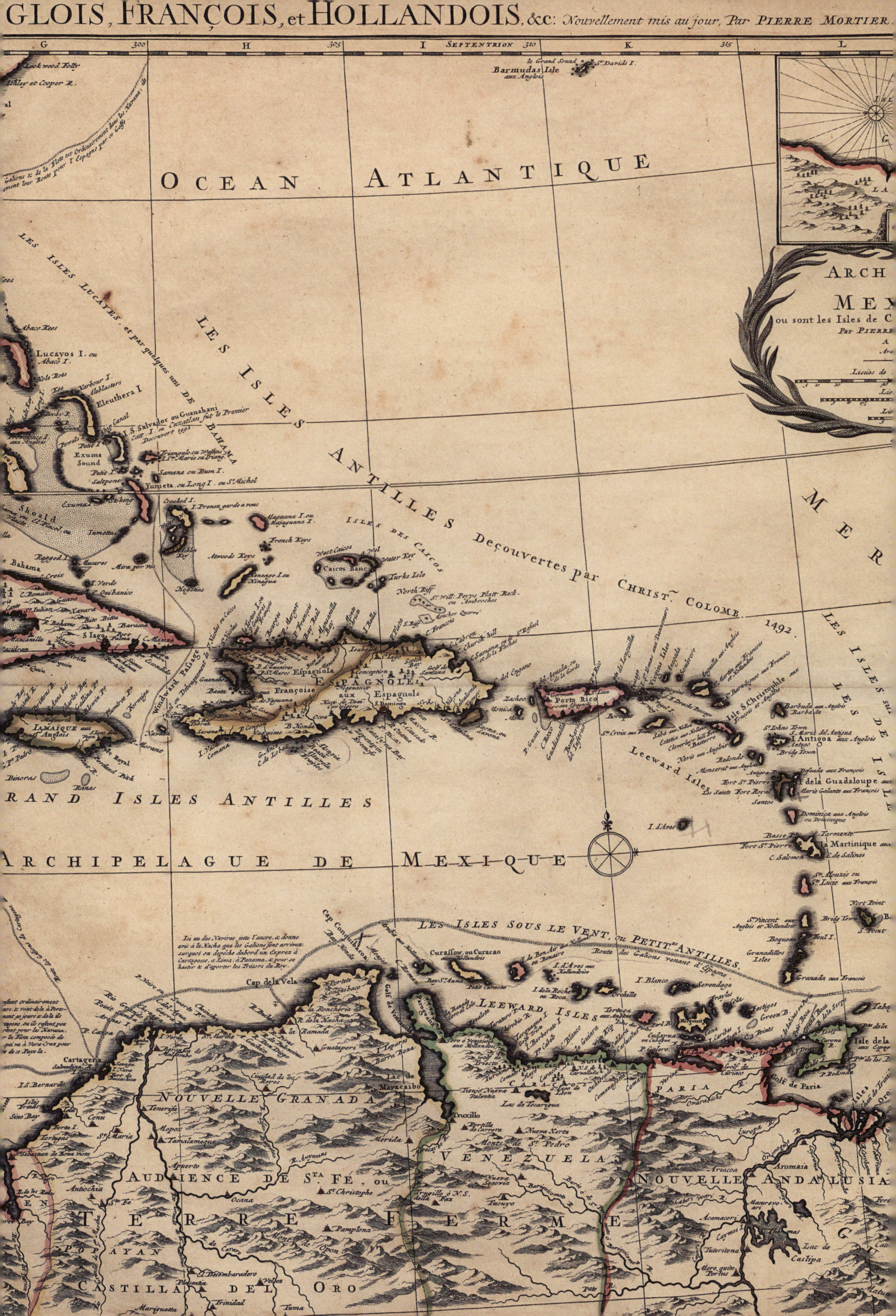

GLOIS, FRANÇOIS, et HOLLANDOIS, &c: Nouvellement mis au jour, Par PIERRE MORTIER.
SEPTENTRION
Barmudas Isle aux Anglois
OCEAN ATLANTIQUE
ARCH
MEX
ou sont les Isles de C
Par PIERRE
LES ISLES LUCAYES, et par quelques uns DE BAHAMA
LES ISLES ANTILLES Découvertes par CHRIST. COLOMB 1492.
ISLES DES CAICOS
Caicos Banc
Turks Isle
MER
Lucayos I. ou Abaco I.
Eleuthera I.
Exuma Sound
I. S. Salvador ou Guanahani
Samana ou Rum I.
Yumeta ou Long I. ou S.t Michel
Magnana I. ou Mayaguana I.
French Keys
Inagua
North Riff
Isabella
Espagnola
ESPAGNOLE
François
Espagnols
S. Domingo
Windward Passage
Porto Rico
Leeward Isles
Isle S. Christophle
Antigoa aux Anglois
Barbude aux Anglois
Guadaloupe
Dominica aux Anglois ou Dominique
Martinique
S.te Lucie aux François
S.t Vincent
Granada aux François
JAMAIQUE aux Anglois
GRAND ISLES ANTILLES
ARCHIPELAGUE DE MEXIQUE
LES ISLES SOUS LE VENT, ou PETIT.es ANTILLES
Curassow ou Curacao aux Hollandois
Route des Galions venant d'Espagne
LEEWARD ISLES
Cap de la Vela
Cartagena
NOUVELLE GRANADA
AUDIENCE DE S.TA FÉ, ou
TERRE FERME
VENEZUELA
NOUVELLE ANDALUSIA
PARIA
Golf de Paria
Isle de la Trinidad
Lac de Maracaibo
Truxillo
Merida
POPAYAN
CASTILLA DEL ORO

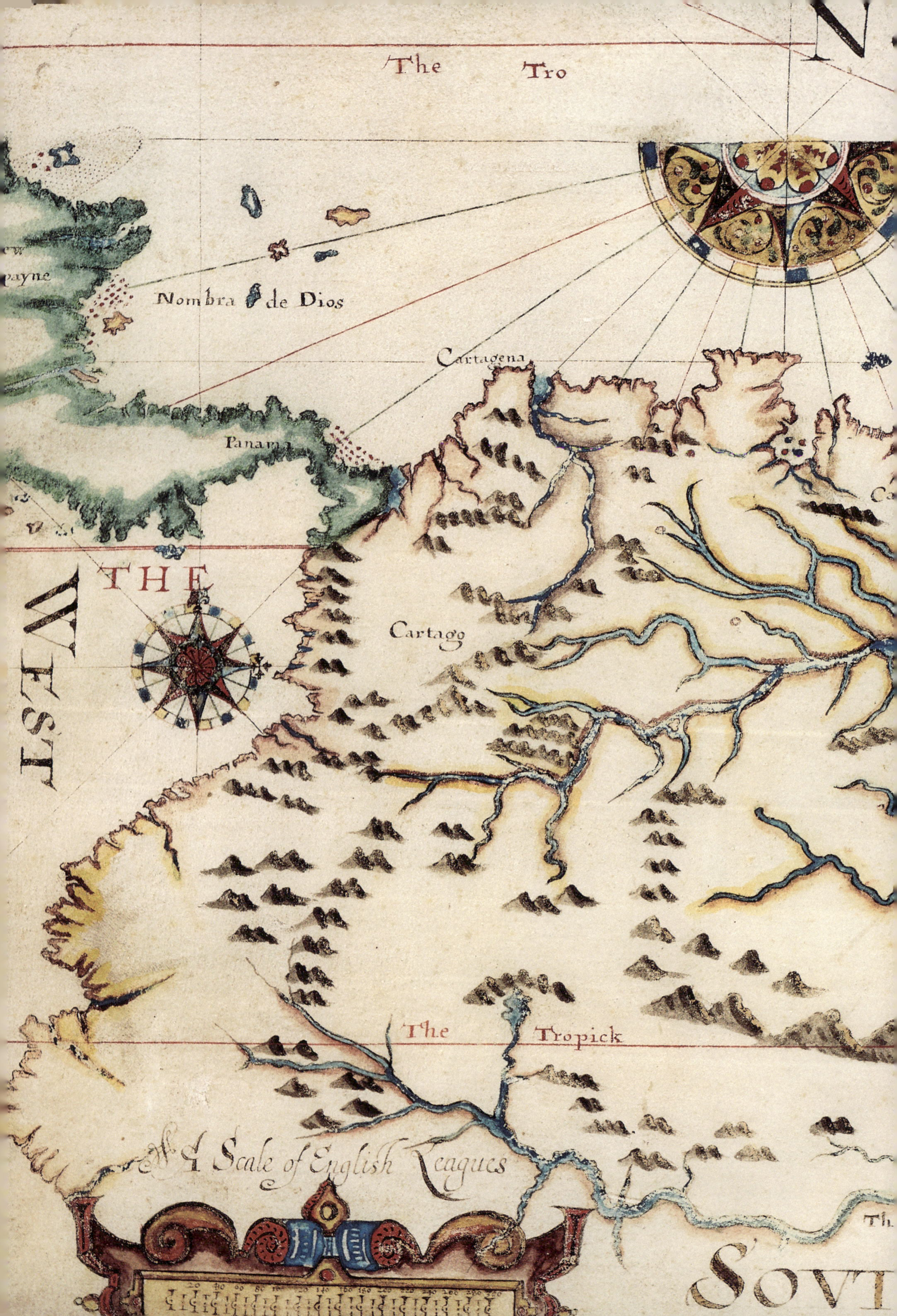

The Tro
Nombra de Dios
Cartagena
Panama
THE
WEST
Cartago
The Tropick
A Scale of English Leagues
SOVT

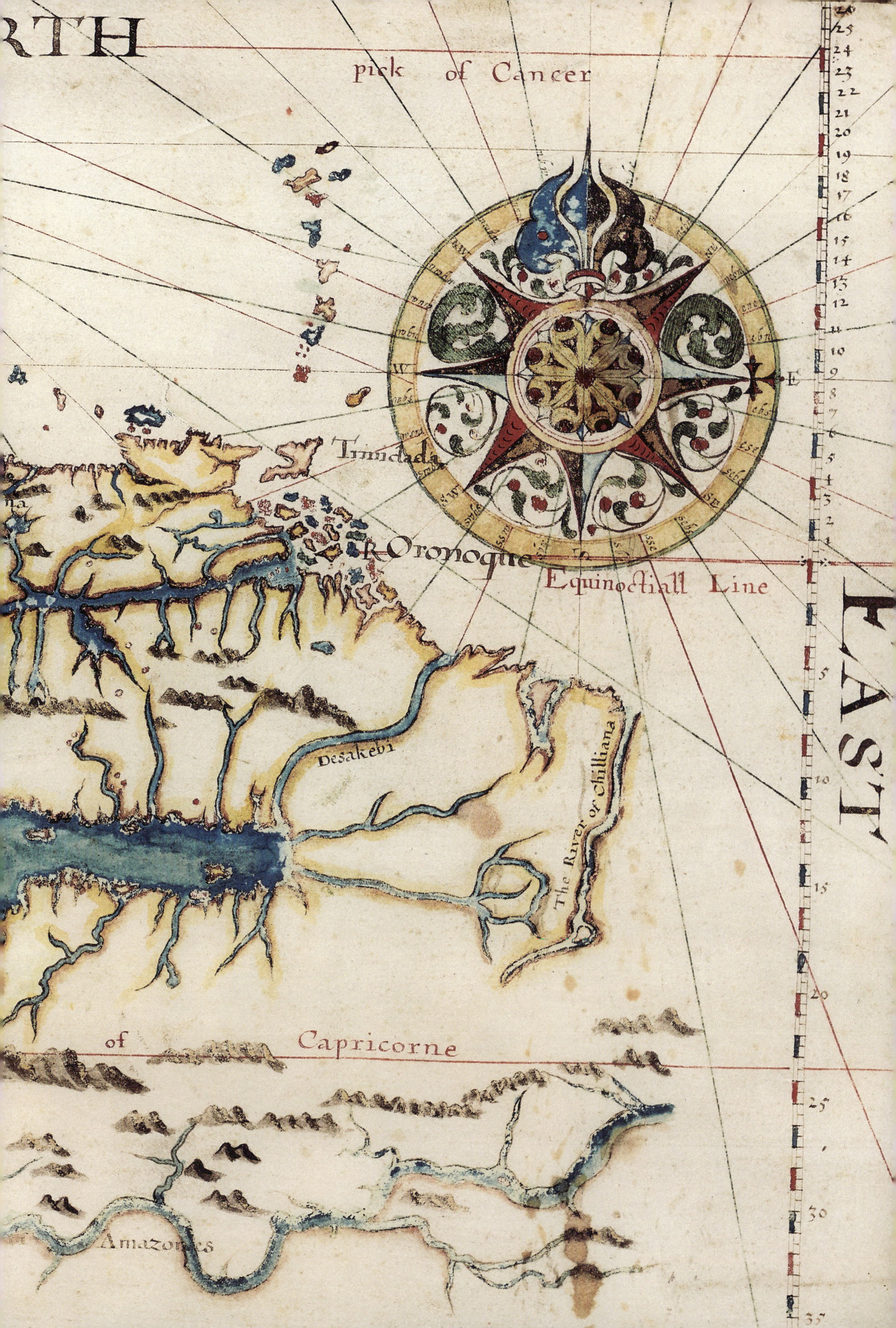

RTH
pick of Cancer
W
E
Trinidada
R. Oronoque
Equinoctiall Line
EAST
Desakebi
The River of Chilliana
of Capricorne
Amazones

↑ [PL. 66]
[PL. 67]

Thomas Hariot, *Magnificent Untitled Manuscript Map of the Guianas Region*, 1595–7
Leda Catunda, *Eldorado*, 2018

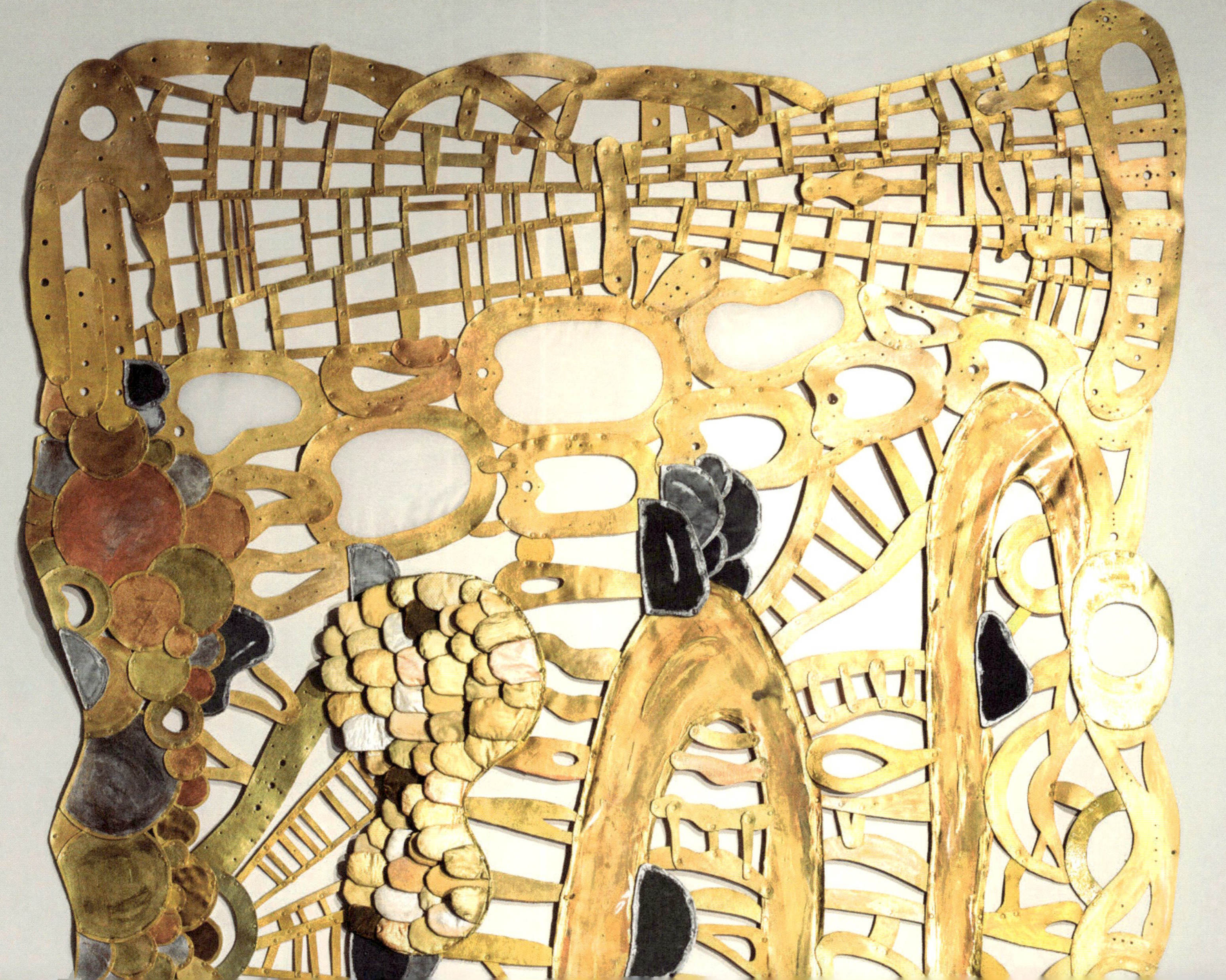

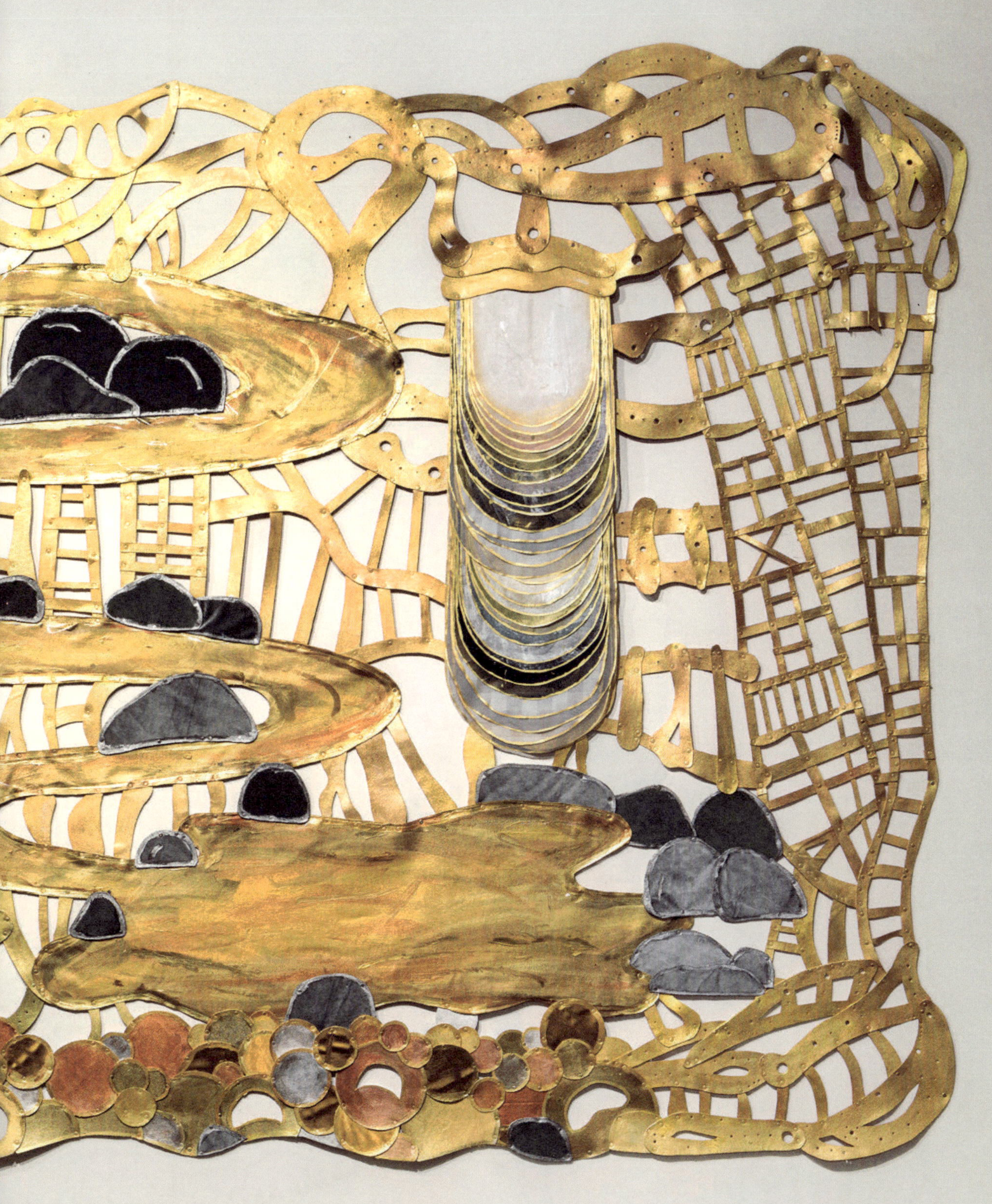

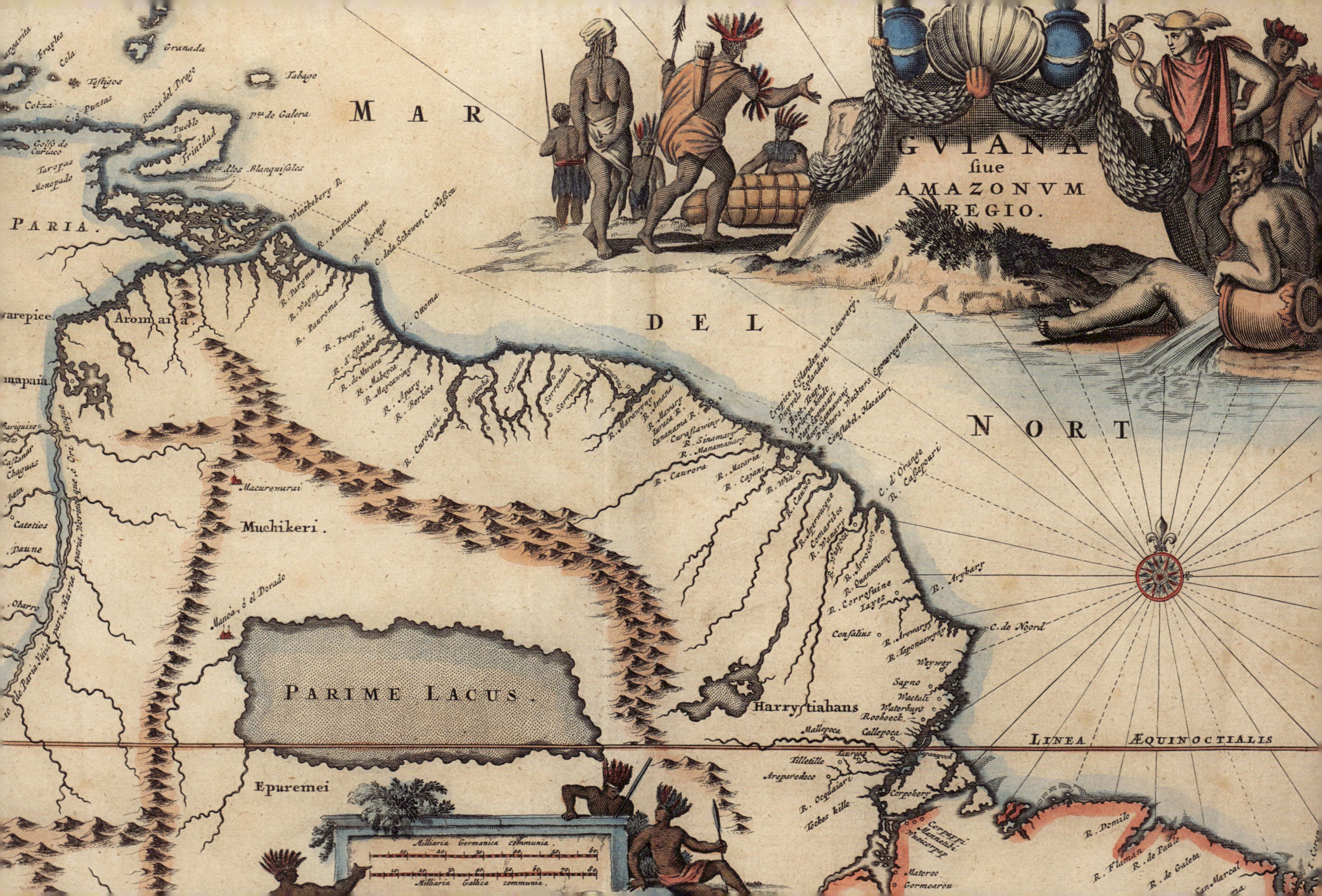
GUIANA
siue
AMAZONUM
REGIO.
MAR DEL NORT
PARIA.
Trinidad
Tabago
Granada
Aromaia.
Muchikeri.
Macuremurai
Manoa, ô el Dorado
PARIME LACUS.
Epuremei
Harrystiabans
C. de Noord
LINEA ÆQUINOCTIALIS
Milliaria Germanica communia
Milliaria Gallica communia

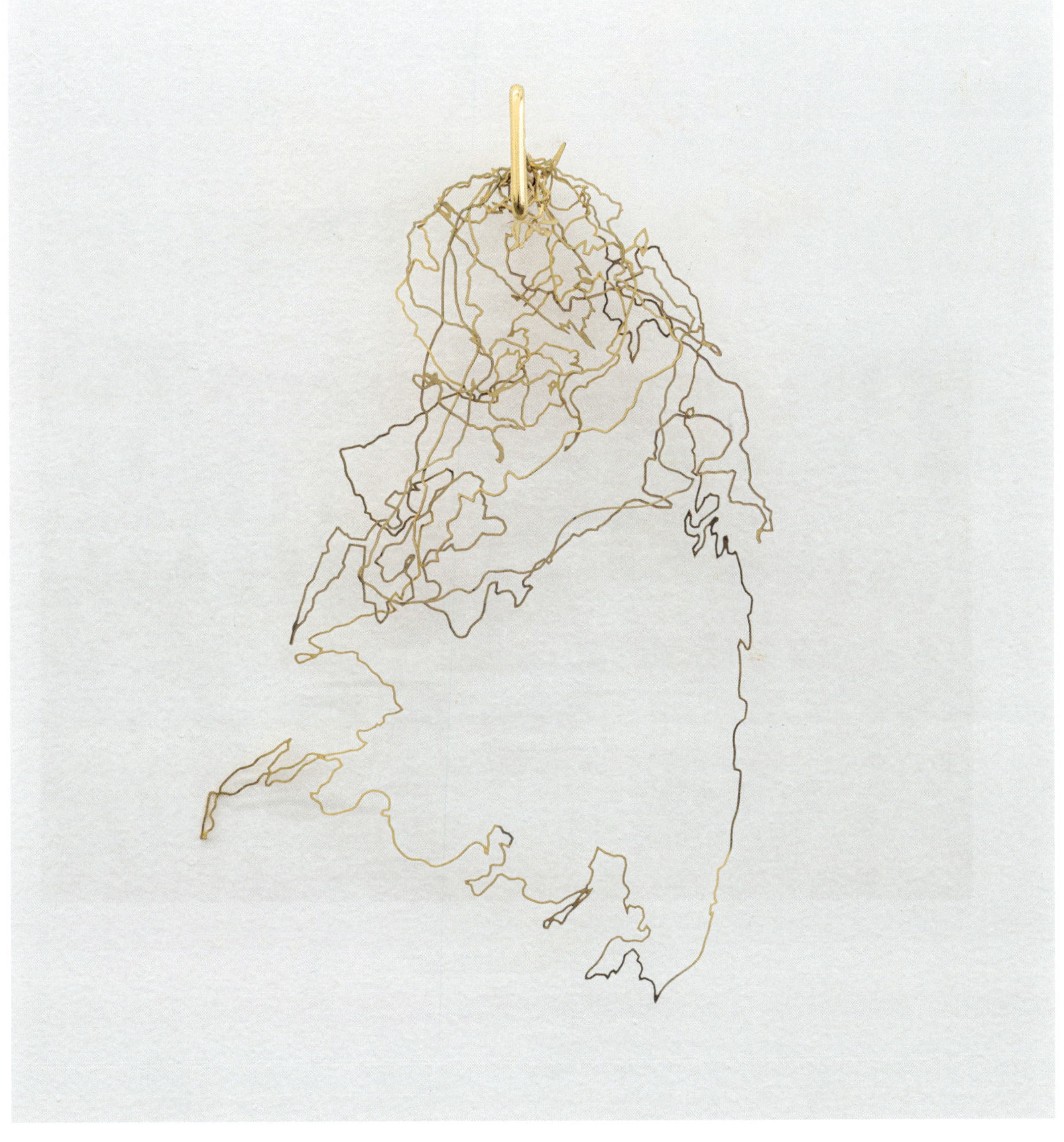

Laura Vinci, *Morro mundo pin* (Pin world hill), 2018

↑ [PL. 68]

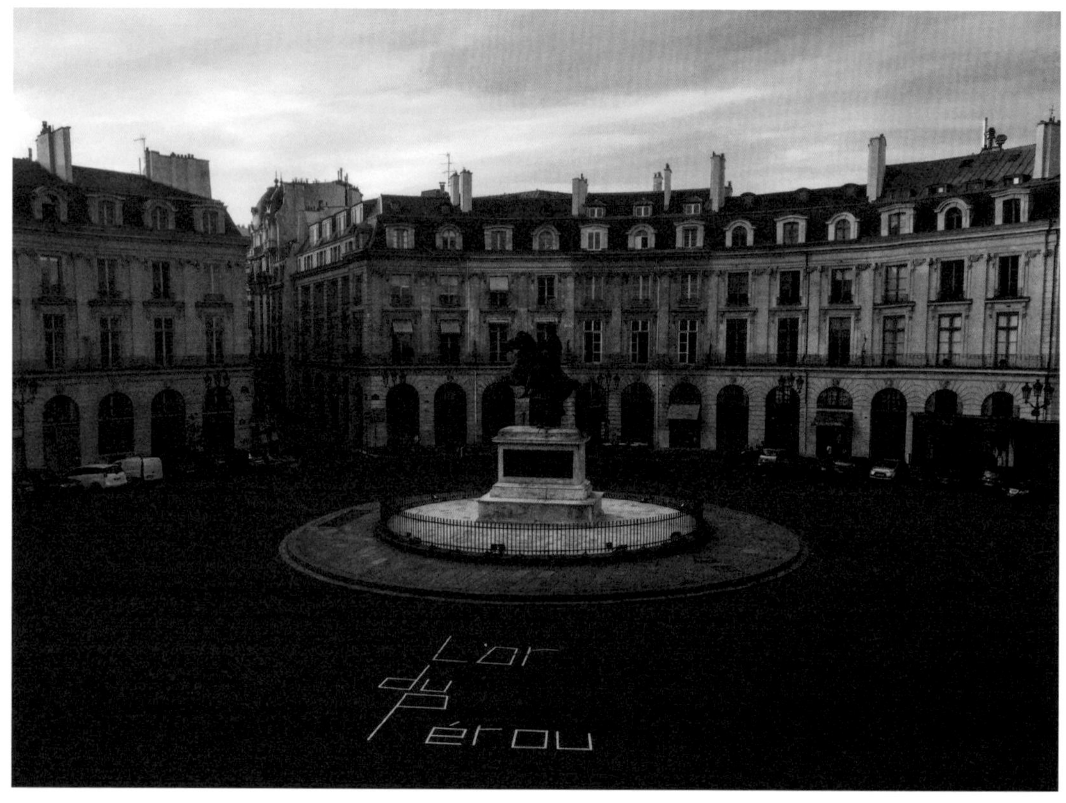

Mariano Leon, *L'Or du Pérou*, 2018

John Harris, *Plan of Lima*, 1746

A PLAN OF LIMA

Vol. 1. pa. 243.

1 The Royal Square.
2 The Vice Roy's Palace.
3 The Royal Court.
4 The Archbishop's Palace.
5 The Stone Bridge.
6 The Square of ye Inquisition.
7 The Inquisition.
8 The University & its Chappel.
9 The Mint.
10 The Flesh Market.
11 The Market for small Wares.
12 The Royal Gate of Callao.
13 The Gate of John Simon.
14 Matamendinga Gate.
15 S^t. Katharine's Gate.
16 Pisco Gate.
17 Gate of the Cercado or the Inclosure.
18 S^t. Clare's Gate.
19 Wickets or Sally gates.
20 A Powder and Corn Mill.
21 A Water Mill to beat Copper.
22 The Cathedral.
23 The Hospital for Sailors.
24 The Hospital for Blacks.
25 The Noviciate of the Jesuites.
26 The Meadow or Walking Place.
27 The Bethlehemites.
28 The Capucines.
29 The Trinitarian Nuns.
30 The Barefoot Friars.

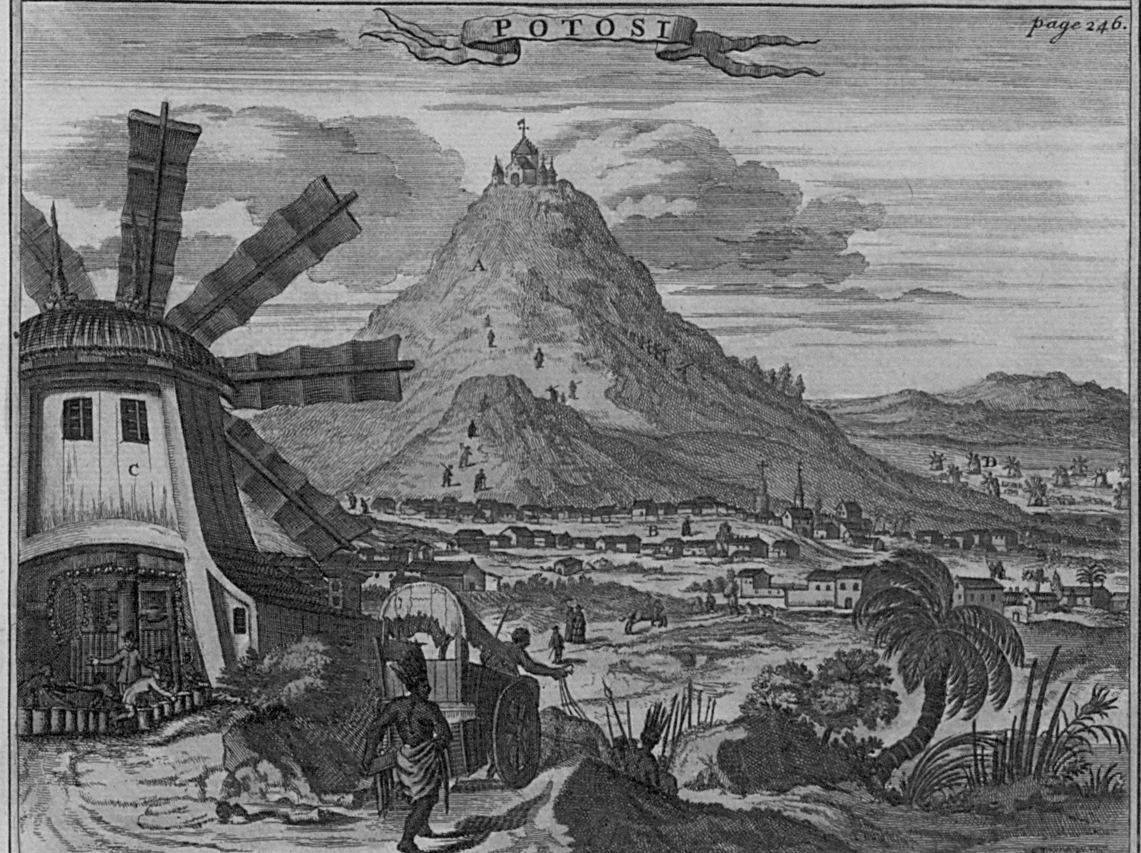

A. The mountain B The Town of Potosi. C. The Royal mill for grinding the Ore. D. Water mills for cleaning the Ore.

[PL. 71]

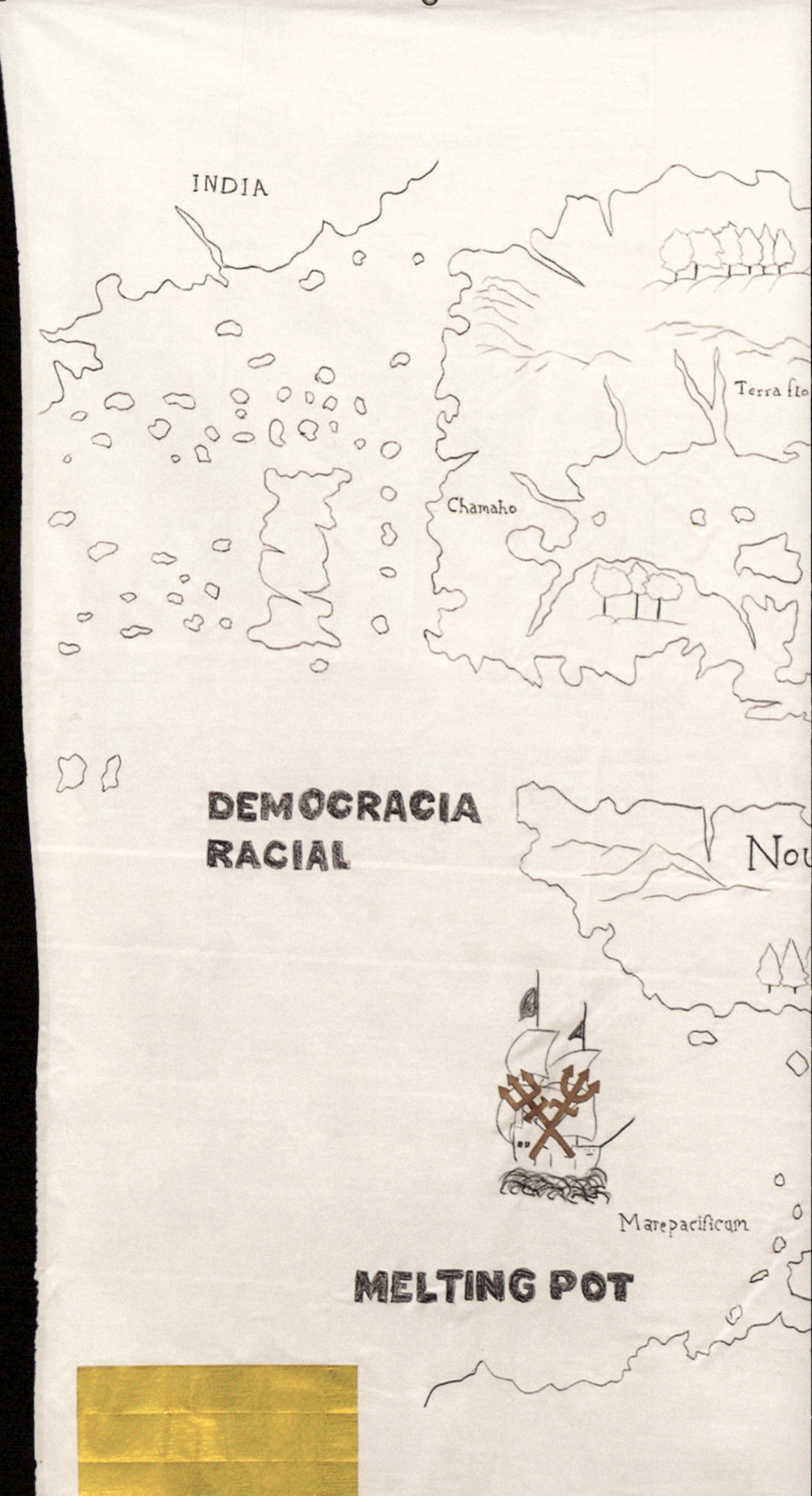

INDIA
Terra flo
Chamaho
DEMOCRACIA
RACIAL
Nou
Marepacificum
MELTING POT

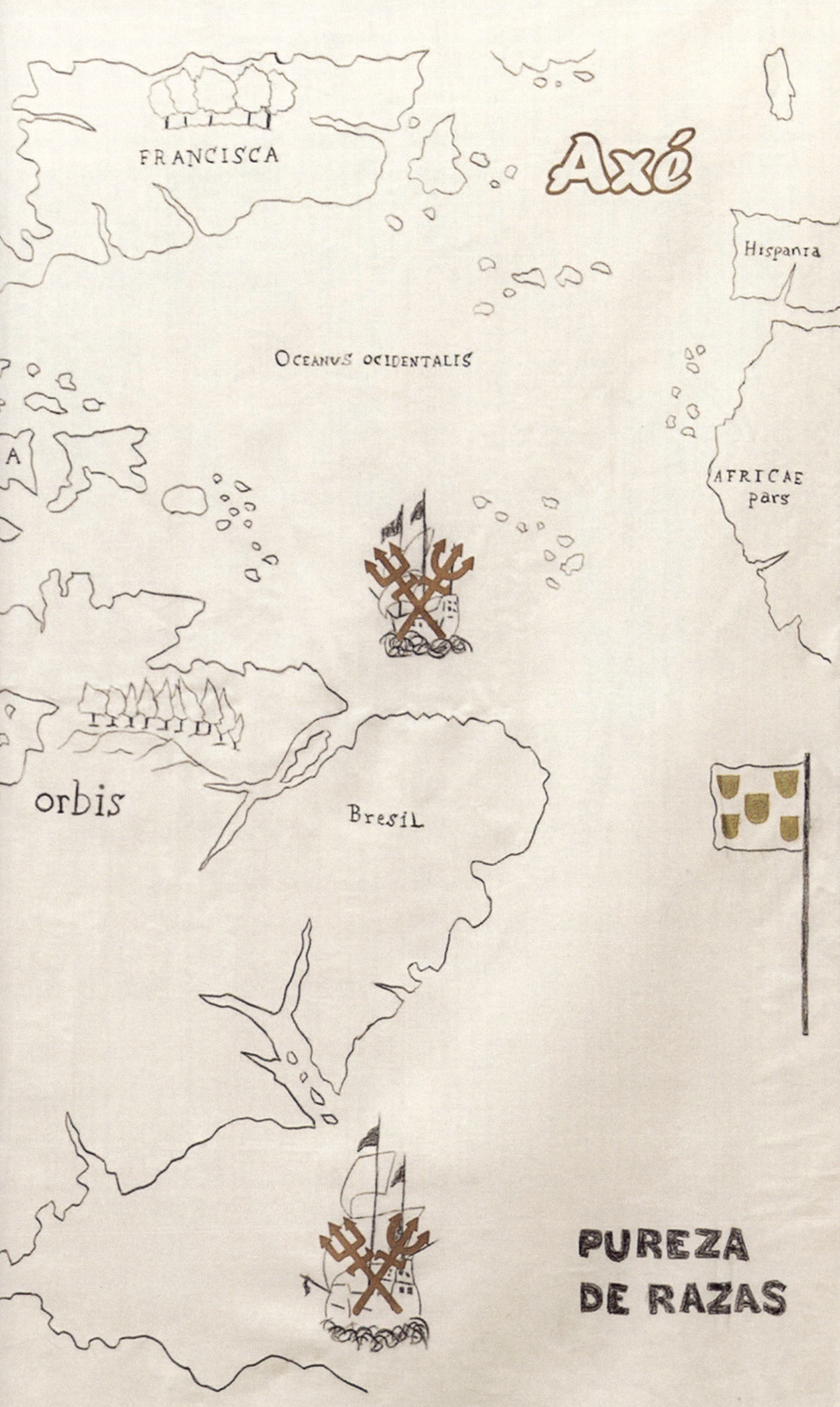
FRANCISCA
Axé
Hispania
OCEANUS OCIDENTALIS
AFRICAE
pars
orbis
Bresil
PUREZA
DE RAZAS

[PL. 73]

Olga de Amaral, *Núcleo 2* (Nucleus 2), 2015

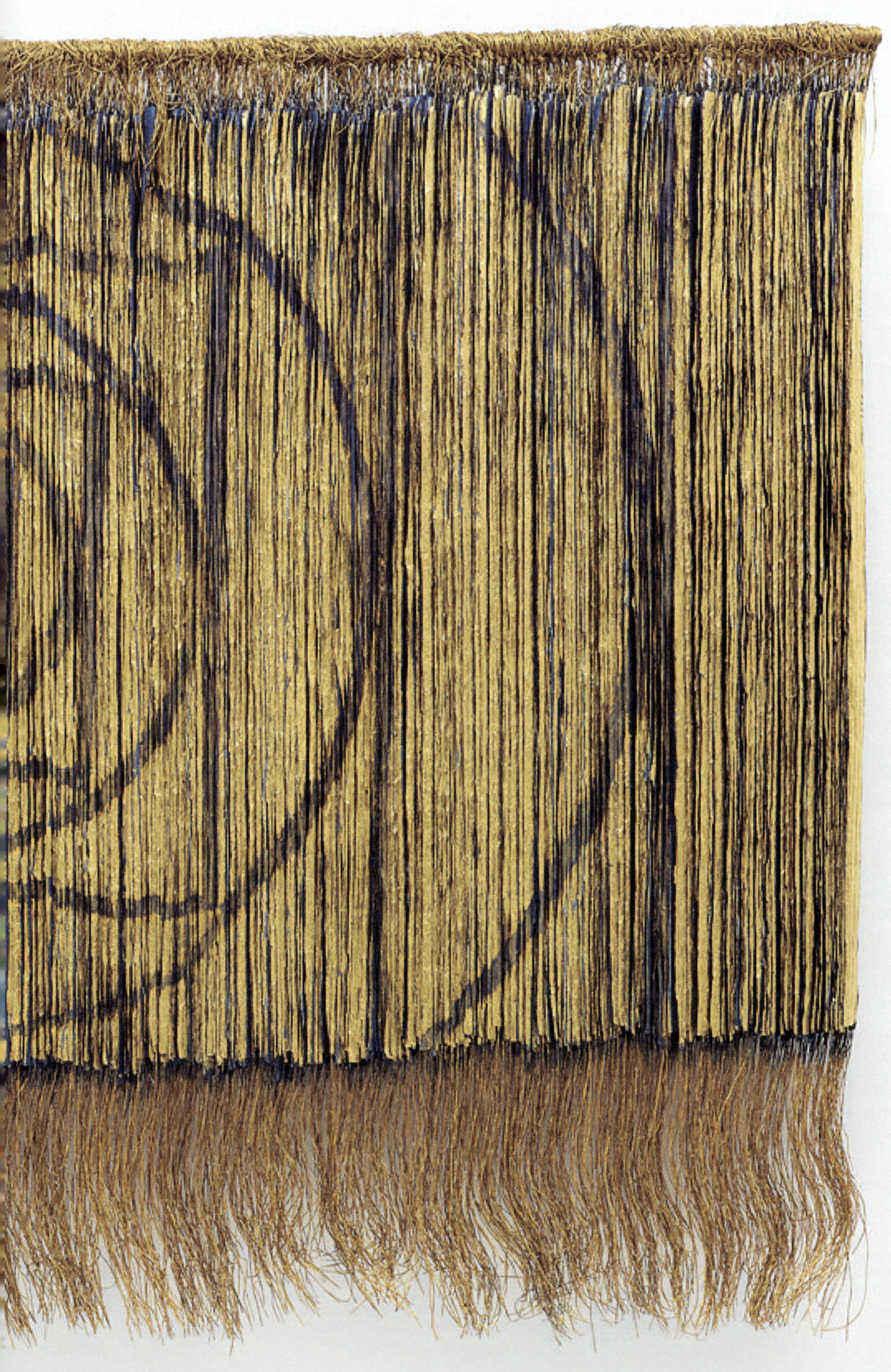

El Dorado: The Myth of Gold was organized in two parts. The first part was on view from September 6 to December 16, 2023 and the second part from January 24 to May 18, 2024. See indications in parentheses at the beginning of each caption.

PL. 61 P. 105
Rubén Ortiz-Torres

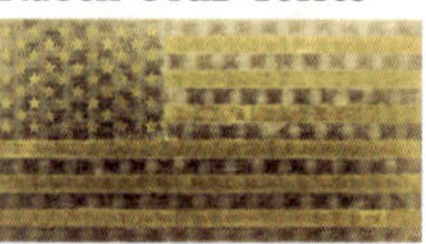

PL. 107 PP. 162–163

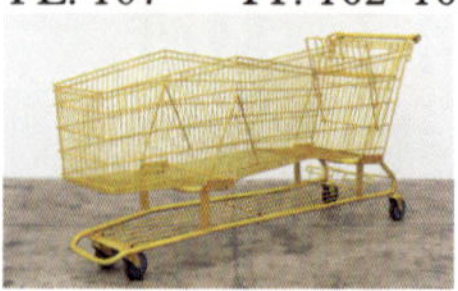

In *Long Shopper (Limo)* (2015), Rubén Ortiz-Torres (b. 1964, Mexico City) explicitly links car culture and consumerism by connecting shopping carts to create a "limo" cart finished with shimmering gold chromatic paint. In this work the artist connects gold and consumer culture connecting how the desire for gold is really the desire for the consumption of gold. In a later work, *La jaula de oro remastered* (2019), he creates the United States flag with golden car paint. In addition to suggesting consumerism as a foundation of US culture, the golden flag may also signal how the United States functions as a new El Dorado for immigrants from other parts of the world seeking real and perceived wealth in the US. The title of the painting also references a song by the Mexican band Los Tigres del Norte called "Jaula de oro" (1984), which tells the story of an undocumented immigrant. The narrator of the song laments, "Aunque la jaula sea de oro / No deja de ser prisión" (Even if the cage is made of gold / It is still a prison).

–Rachel Remick

(I)
La jaula de oro remastered (Golden cage remastered), 2019.
Gold, fake gold, urethane on wood, 37 ⅞ × 72 × 2 inches (96.2 × 182.9 × 5.1 cm).
Courtesy of the artist and Royale Projects

(II)
Long Shopper (Limo), 2015.
Chromatic paint on shopping cart, 42 × 81 × 23 inches (106.7 × 205.7 × 58.4 cm)
Courtesy of the artist and Royale Projects

PL. 62 P. 106
Herman Moll

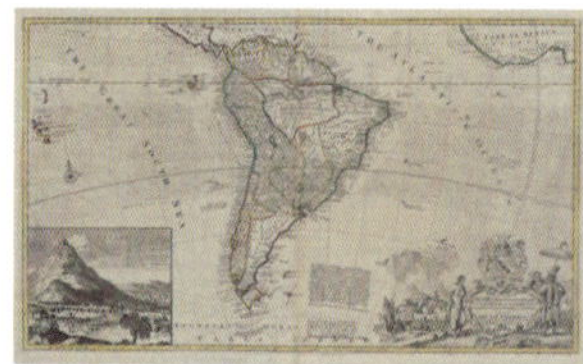

PL. 65 P. 109
Covens & Mortier, Netherlands

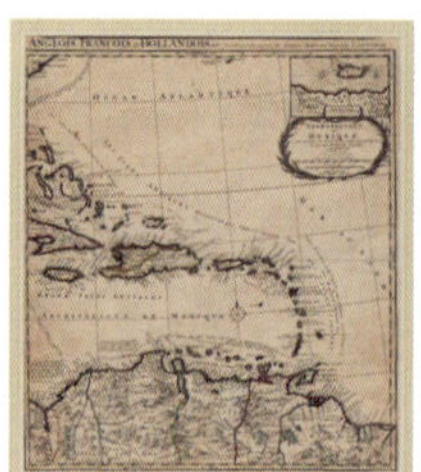

(I)
Herman Moll, *Map of South America*, c. 1725.
Copper engraving, 22 ⅞ × 37 ¾ (58 × 96 cm).
Proyeto Bachué Collection, Bogotá

(I)
Covens & Mortier, Netherlands, *Archipelague du Mexique, ou sont les isles de Cuba, Espagnola, Lamaique, Etc.*, ca. 1700.
Engraving, illuminated on edges, 23 ½ × 20 ¼ inches (59.69 × 51.44 cm).
Gustavo Cisneros map collection in the Colección Patricia Phelps de Cisneros.
Photo: Arturo Sánchez

PL. 66 PP. 110–111
Thomas Hariot

PL. 68 P. 114
Unknown artist

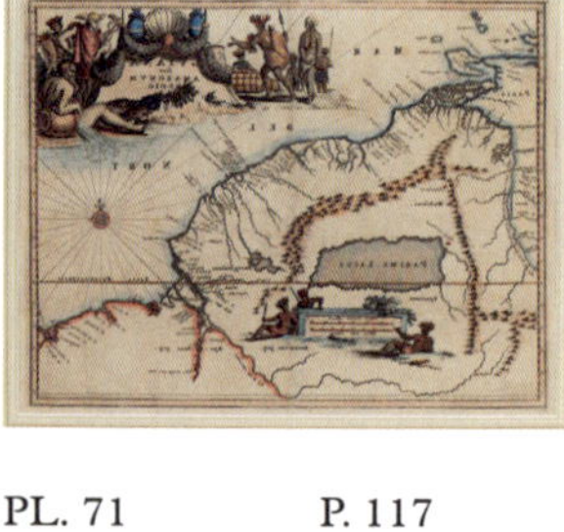

PL. 71 P. 117
John Harris

(I)
Thomas Hariot, *Magnificent Untitled Manuscript Map of the Guianas Region*, 1595–7.
Illuminated lithograph on parchment, 13 × 18 ½ inches (33 × 47 cm).
Gustavo Cisneros map collection in the Colección Patricia Phelps de Cisneros.
Photo: Arturo Sánchez

(I)
Unknown artist, *Guiana sive Amazonum Regio*, n.d.
Print and watercolor on paper, 12 × 14 inches (30.48 × 36.83 cm).
Gustavo Cisneros map collection in the Colección Patricia Phelps de Cisneros.
Photo: Arturo Sánchez

(I)
John Harris, *Plan of Lima*, 1746.
Intaglio print, 17 ⅞ × 9 ⅞ (45.5 × 25 cm).
Proyecto Bachué Collection, Bogotá

PL. 63 P. 107
Anna Bella Geiger

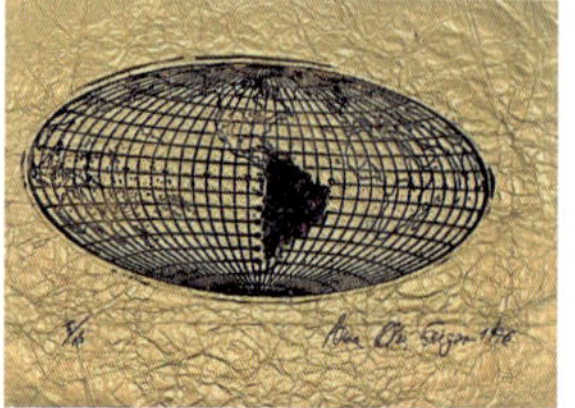

Brazilian artist Anna Bella Geiger (b. 1933, Rio de Janeiro) has widely engaged with mapmaking to explore how geographical representation can shape our understanding of the world and our emotional relationship to space, while revealing maps as social and political constructions. The artist often reinterprets maps, challenging given notions of borders and territories and questioning the assumption of objectivity of these objects.

In *Local da ação nº 01*, the artist reproduces the globe on a gold leaf. By removing the portion of South America, she represents it as an absence and as a space for wealth extraction, a commentary on the plunders of colonialism.

–Tie Jojima

(I)
Local da ação nº 01 (Place of action nº 01), 1980.
Engraving on gold leaf, 9 ¾ × 13 ¾ inches (24.9 × 34.9 cm). Courtesy of the artist and Henrique Faria, New York

PL. 67 PP. 112–113
Leda Catunda

PL. 105 P. 160

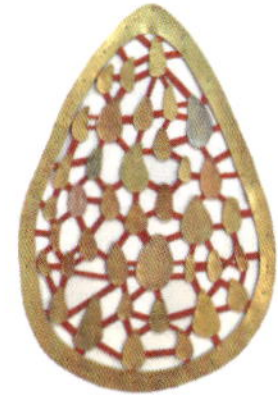

Leda Catunda (b. 1961, São Paulo) works with paintings and fabrics to create visually and tactilely appealing works that evoke fantasies of desire and consumption. Her series *Eldorado* directly addresses the idyllic space, sought by many and found by nobody, presenting a landscape with a wandering path finishing in a small lake, perhaps referring to Guatavita lake in Bogotá. The golden canvas is opened with sophisticated fretwork and accumulated layers and textures typical of the artist's work, which in this case also remind us of the jewelry and treasures that we wish to find in the search for gold. *Ovo Rei* uses the same techniques to present a golden egg, symbol of fertility, reproduction, abundance, and wealth, presenting it as the equivalent of a religious ritual object to be worshipped.

–Aimé Iglesias Lukin

(I)
Eldorado, 2018.
Acrylic on canvas, plastic voile, 113 × 185 ⅞ inches (287 × 472 cm).
Coleção Andréa e José Olympio Pereira, São Paulo.
Photo: Eduardo Ortega

(II)
Ovo Rei (King egg), 2018.
Acrylic on canvas, tissue, and plastic, 51 ⅛ × 35 inches (130 × 89 cm).
Courtesy of the artist

PL. 70 P. 116
Mariano León

Mariano Leon (b. 1976, Lima) is a multimedia artist interested in pre-colonial and contemporary systems of knowledge, as well as the colonial legacies of Peru. In *L'Or du Pérou,* the artist is interested in exploring the parallels between the Inka empire and the French Monarchy in the seventeenth century, particularly regarding the differences on how these two cultures valued gold. During an arts residency in France, León created a street intervention at the Place de Victoires in Paris, in which he wrote on the pavement "L'Or du Pérou" (The gold of Peru) to show the ultimate destination of gold extraction in Peru. The work also functions as a critique to the plunder of wealth by the Europeans as result of the process of colonization.

–Tie Jojima

(II)
L'Or du Pérou, 2018.
Inkjet print, dimensions variable.
Courtesy of Henrique Faria, New York

PL. 72 PP. 118–119
Jaime Lauriano

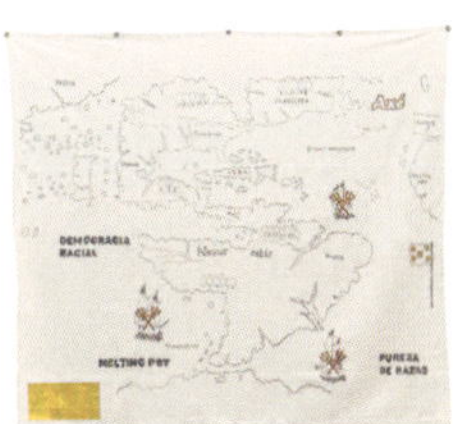

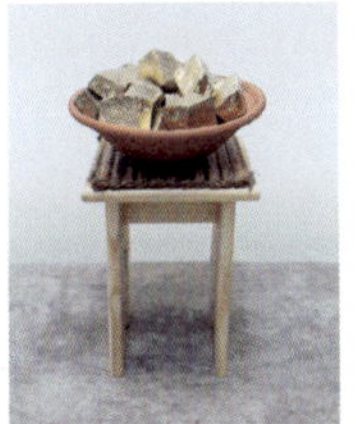

In his practice, Jaime Lauriano (b. 1985, São Paulo) critically engages with historical narratives, as well as social and political issues particularly related to the experiences of Afro-Brazilians. In *Novus orbis: democracia racial, melting pot e pureza de razas* (2023) the artist modifies Hans Holbein's 1532 map "Novus Orbis Regionum" to challenge the prevailing racial mythologies shaping the modern Brazilian nation. In the sculpture *Colonização #2* (2022) he appropriates elements of Candomblé and Umbanda, as well as those symbolic of colonization, such as the gilded Portuguese stones, to point to Afro-Brazilian forms of resistance throughout colonial history into the present.

–Tie Jojima

(I)
Novus Orbis: democracia racial, melting pot e pureza de razas (Novus orbis: racial democracy, melting pot, and race purity), 2023.
Drawing made with black pemba (chalk used in Umbanda rituals) and dermatographic pencil on white cotton, 63 ⅜ × 69 ⅞ inches (161 × 177.5 cm). Courtesy of the artist and Nara Roesler Gallery

(II)
Colonização #2 (Colonization #2), 2022.
Apoti (bench used in Candomblé terreiros), cattail straw mat, bowl, and twenty-eight Portuguese stones cast in brass, 20 ⅞ × 13 ⅜ × 13 ⅜ inches (53 × 34 × 34 cm). Courtesy of the artist and Nara Roesler Gallery

PL. 73 PP. 120–121
Olga de Amaral

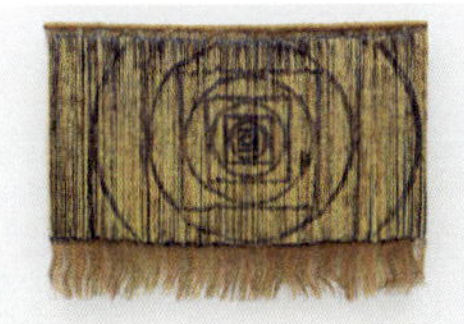

PL. 102 PP. 156–157

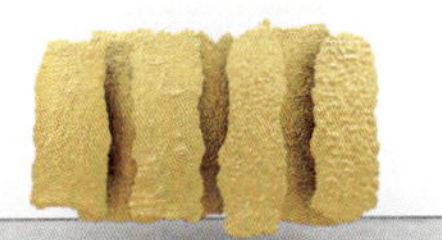

Olga de Amaral (b. 1932, Bogotá) is known for her site-specific installations woven from materials such as traditional fibers, fiber glass, paint, and gold leaf. Amaral's work is driven by her exploration of her own identity and the socio-cultural dichotomies of Colombia. Her interest in gold as a material comes from the interlaced histories of pre-Hispanic and colonial art, namely the material's religious and ceremonial uses in pre-Columbian society, and its subsequent plunder by the Spanish and appearance in colonial art. *Núcleo 2* (2015) is a tapestry crafted from linen, Japanese paper, plaster, acrylic, and gold leaf. The geometric design made of gold leaf on the face of the tapestry is made up of a series of concentric circles and squares. *Estelas* (1996–2018) is a series of structures typically presented in groups, which the artist crafted by experimenting with traditional weaving techniques. Each structure's face is covered with gold leaf and is made from numerous individual woven squares that have been hardened with gesso. The *Estelas* were inspired by the upright stones of the same name, often made in commemoration.

–Sarah Lopez

(I)
Núcleo 2 (Nucleus 2), 2015.
Linen, gesso, acrylic, Japanese paper, and gold leaf, 51 ⅛ × 70 ⅞ inches (130 × 180 cm).
© Olga de Amaral; Courtesy of Lisson Gallery / Numena

(II)
Estelas (Stelae), 1996–2018.
Linen, gesso, acrylic, and gold leaf, roughly 70 ⅞ × 31 ½ inches each (180 × 80 cm).
© Olga de Amaral; Courtesy of Lisson Gallery

EXTRACTION AND WEALTH

Driven by their thirst for gold and wealth, the conquistadores believed they would find El Dorado, a land filled with gold and other riches to be extracted, regardless of Indigenous lives, ancestral territories, and environmental concerns. El Dorado was never found, but the myth persisted in the Americas, taking different forms that continue to have negative social, political, and environmental consequences. Contemporary artists engaging with the myth, and by result, with gold as a material, often embrace it because of its polysemic quality. At the same time that gold is desired and can have positive meanings—for example, when it symbolizes affective bonds such as marriage—it also has negative connotations, such as excess, greed, and even death. Artworks in this section investigate the interconnectedness among gold, extraction, consumerism, and their nefarious consequences in people's lives, land, and the environment.

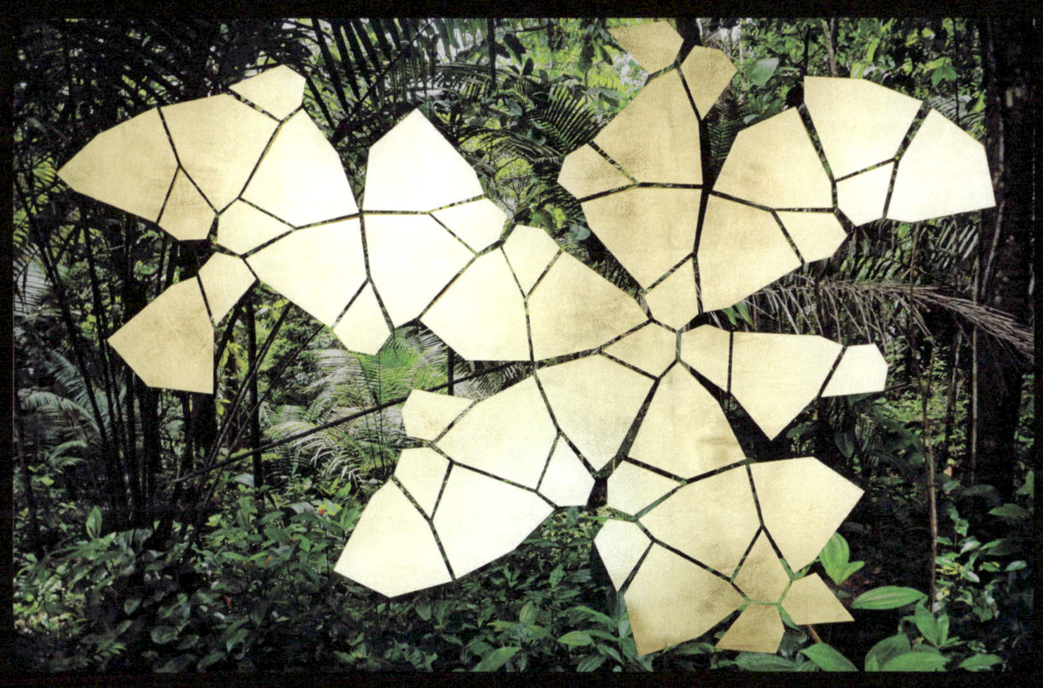

Mazenett Quiroga, *Selva intervenida (Pacifico colombiano)* (Intervened jungle [Colombian Pacific]), 2018

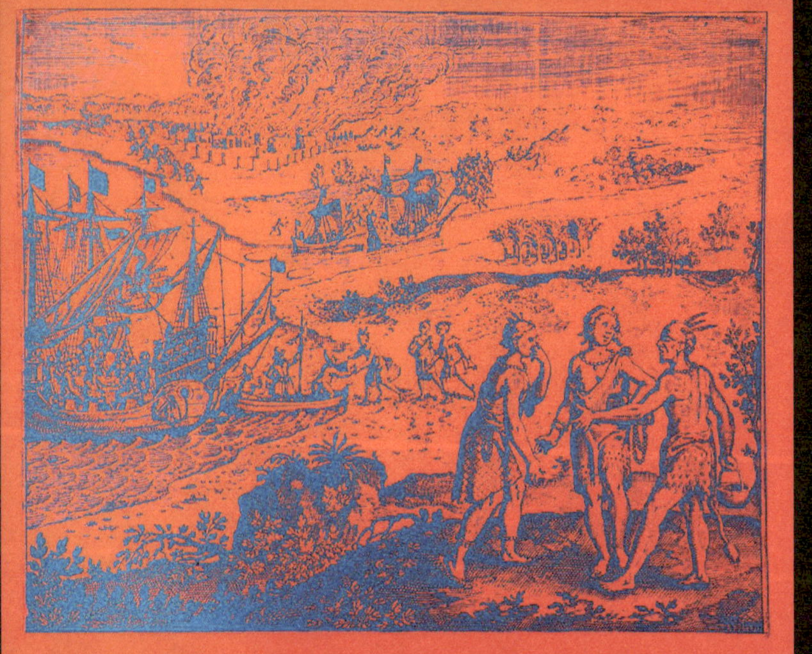

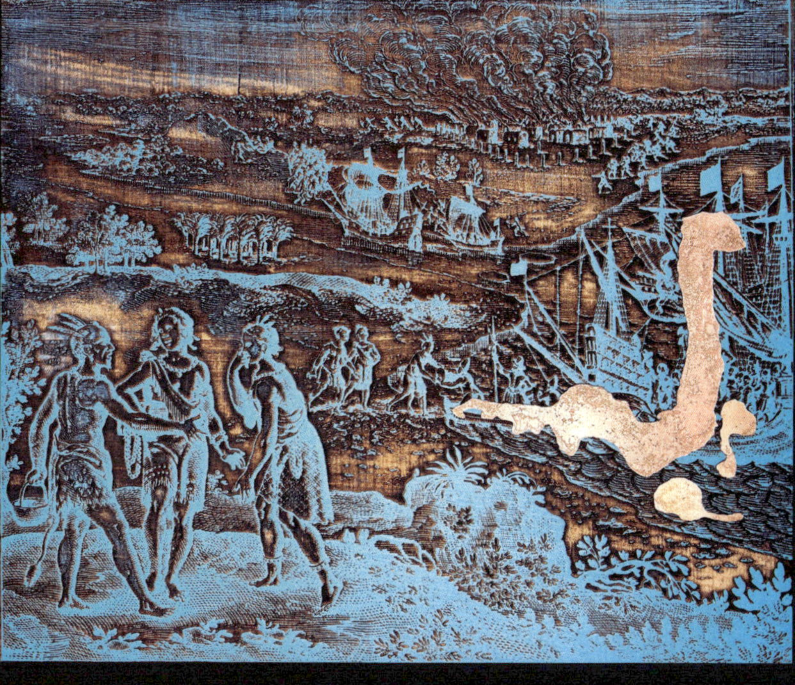

XV.

QVOMODO IMPERATOR REGNI GVIANÆ, NOBILES SVOS ORnare & præparare soleat, si quando ad prandium vel cœnam eos inuitare velit.

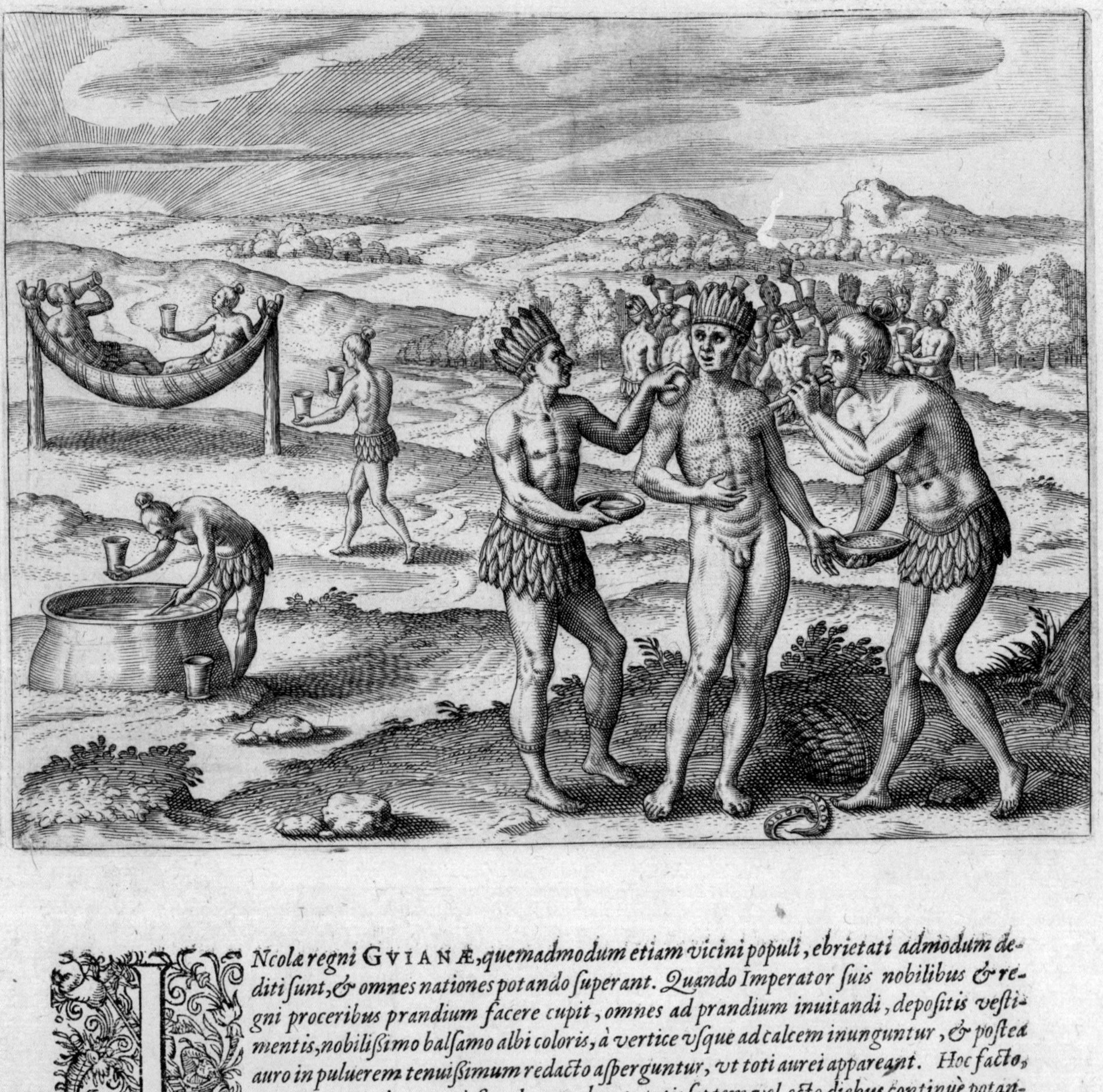

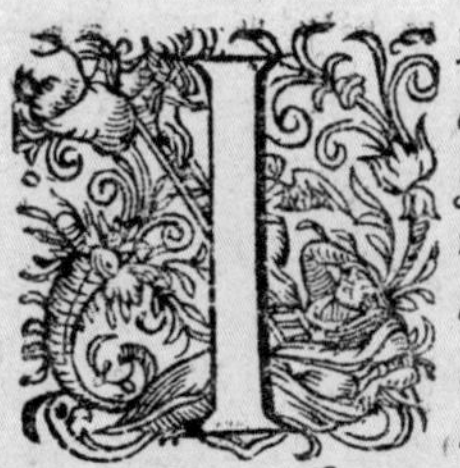

Ncolæ regni GVIANÆ, *quemadmodum etiam vicini populi, ebrietati admodum dediti sunt, & omnes nationes potando superant. Quando Imperator suis nobilibus & regni proceribus prandium facere cupit, omnes ad prandium inuitandi, depositis vestimentis, nobilissimo balsamo albi coloris, à vertice vsque ad calcem inunguntur, & postea auro in puluerem tenuissimum redacto asperguntur, vt toti aurei appareant. Hoc facto, quinquageni & centeni simul accumbunt, totis septem vel octo diebus continuè potantes, donec amplius non possint. Cum Angli aliquando ad* CASSIQVE TOPARIMACA *venissent, qui aliū quendam* CASSIQVE *inuitauerat, inuenerunt eos in* BRESILIENSI HAMACA *siue lecto simul sedentes, & strenuè potantes, ita vt quilibet vna vice tria pocula euacuaret, quæ à duabus mulieribus mensæ ministrantibus infundebantur. Potus ipsorum ex herbis quibusdam & varijs aromatibus conficitur, asseruaturq́ in vasis fictilibus, quorum amplitudo est 10 vel 12 vlnarum.*

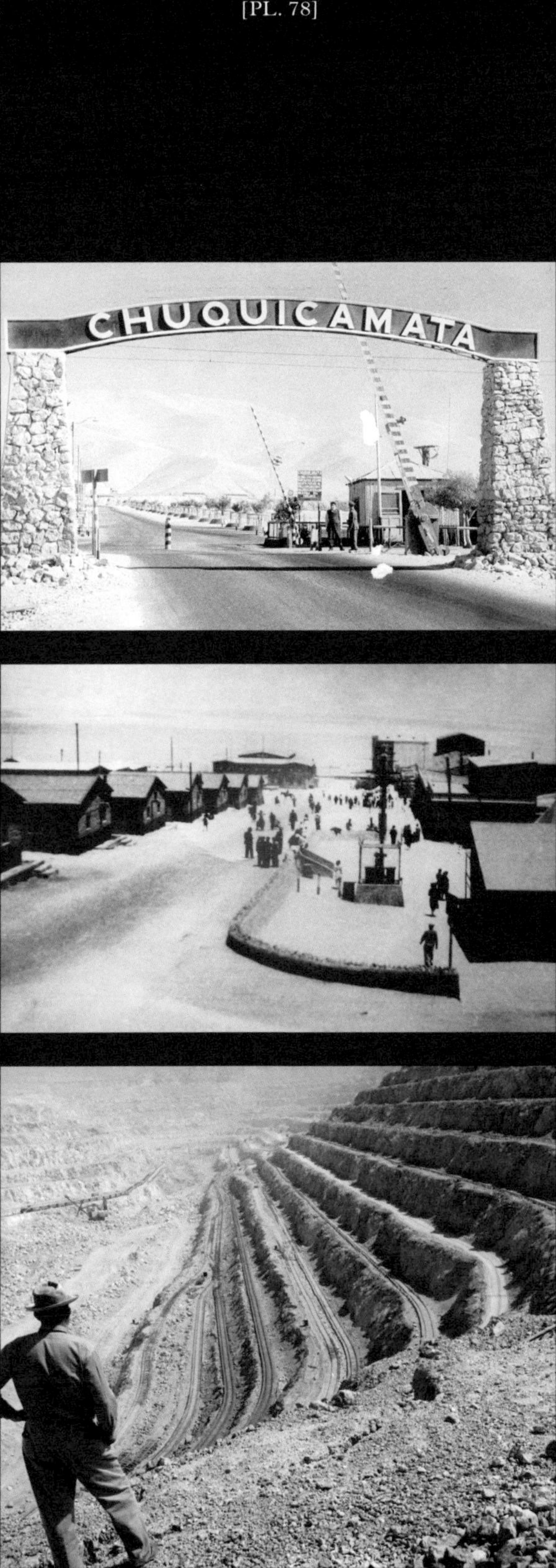
CHUQUICAMATA

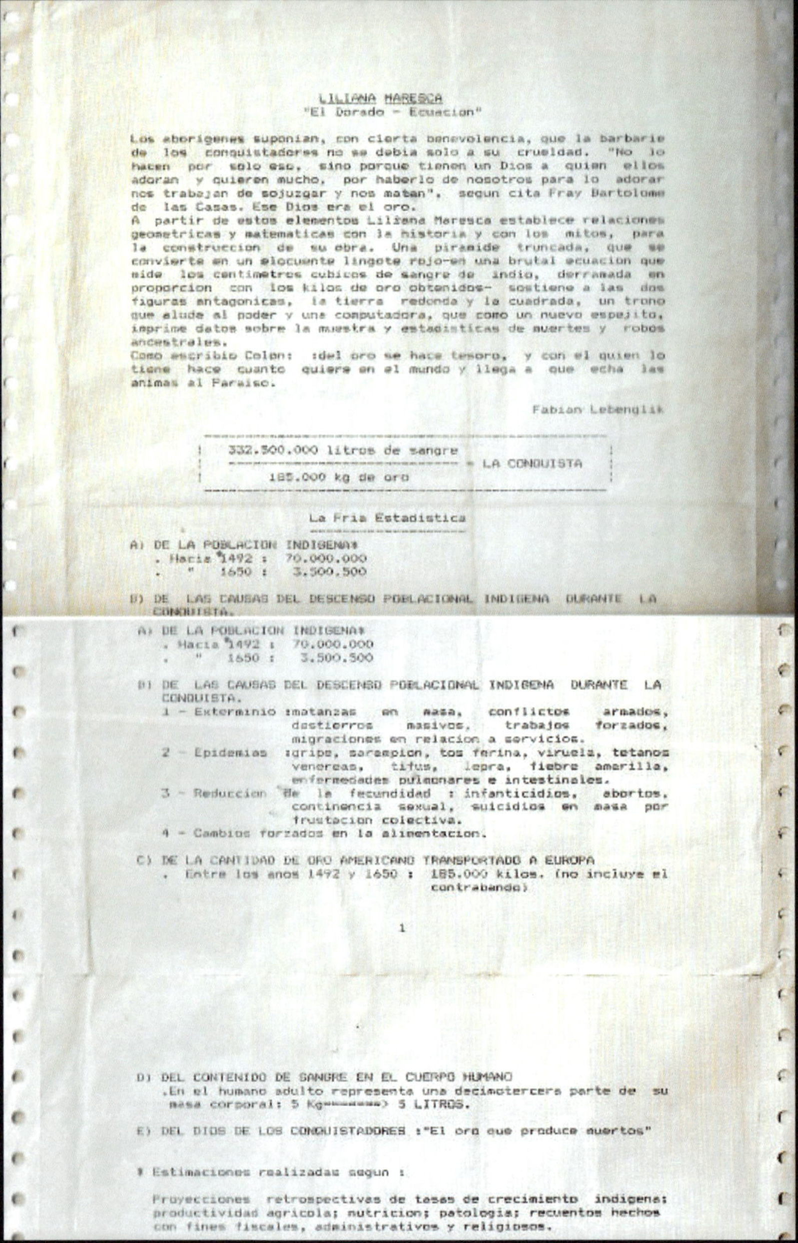

LILIANA MARESCA
"El Dorado - Ecuacion"

Los aborigenes suponian, con cierta benevolencia, que la barbarie de los conquistadores no se debia solo a su crueldad. "No lo hacen por solo eso, sino porque tienen un Dios a quien ellos adoran y quieren mucho, por haberlo de nosotros para lo adorar nos trabajan de sojuzgar y nos matan", segun cita Fray Bartolome de las Casas. Ese Dios era el oro.
A partir de estos elementos Liliana Maresca establece relaciones geometricas y matematicas con la historia y con los mitos, para la construccion de su obra. Una piramide truncada, que se convierte en un elocuente lingote rojo-en una brutal ecuacion que mide los centimetros cubicos de sangre de indio, derramada en proporcion con los kilos de oro obtenidos- sostiene a las dos figuras antagonicas, la tierra redonda y la cuadrada, un trono que alude al poder y una computadora, que como un nuevo espejito, imprime datos sobre la muestra y estadisticas de muertes y robos ancestrales.
Como escribio Colon: :del oro se hace tesoro, y con el quien lo tiene hace cuanto quiere en el mundo y llega a que echa las animas al Paraiso.

Fabian Lebenglik

$$\frac{\text{332.500.000 litros de sangre}}{\text{185.000 kg de oro}} = \text{LA CONQUISTA}$$

La Fria Estadistica

A) DE LA POBLACION INDIGENA*
. Hacia 1492 : 70.000.000
. " 1650 : 3.500.500

B) DE LAS CAUSAS DEL DESCENSO POBLACIONAL INDIGENA DURANTE LA CONQUISTA.

A) DE LA POBLACION INDIGENA*
. Hacia 1492 : 70.000.000
. " 1650 : 3.500.500

B) DE LAS CAUSAS DEL DESCENSO POBLACIONAL INDIGENA DURANTE LA CONQUISTA.
1 - Exterminio :matanzas en masa, conflictos armados, destierros masivos, trabajos forzados, migraciones en relacion a servicios.
2 - Epidemias :gripe, sarampion, tos ferina, viruela, tetanos venereas, tifus, lepra, fiebre amarilla, enfermedades pulmonares e intestinales.
3 - Reduccion de la fecundidad : infanticidios, abortos, continencia sexual, suicidios en masa por frustacion colectiva.
4 - Cambios forzados en la alimentacion.

C) DE LA CANTIDAD DE ORO AMERICANO TRANSPORTADO A EUROPA
. Entre los anos 1492 y 1650 : 185.000 kilos. (no incluye el contrabando)

1

D) DEL CONTENIDO DE SANGRE EN EL CUERPO HUMANO
.En el humano adulto representa una decimotercera parte de su masa corporal: 5 Kg======> 5 LITROS.

E) DEL DIOS DE LOS CONQUISTADORES :"El oro que produce muertos"

* Estimaciones realizadas segun :

Proyecciones retrospectivas de tasas de crecimiento indigena; productividad agricola; nutricion; patologia; recuentos hechos con fines fiscales, administrativos y religiosos.

Liliana Maresca, *Original printed document from the computer of El Dorado – Ecuación* (Equation), 1991–2

[PL. 80] Theodor de Bry, *In*

ARGVMENTVM.

Deß Ferdinandi vnd Petri de Contreras gefangene Kriegßknecht werden zu Ranama durch den Statt Schultheissen/mit einem Dolchen durchstochen.

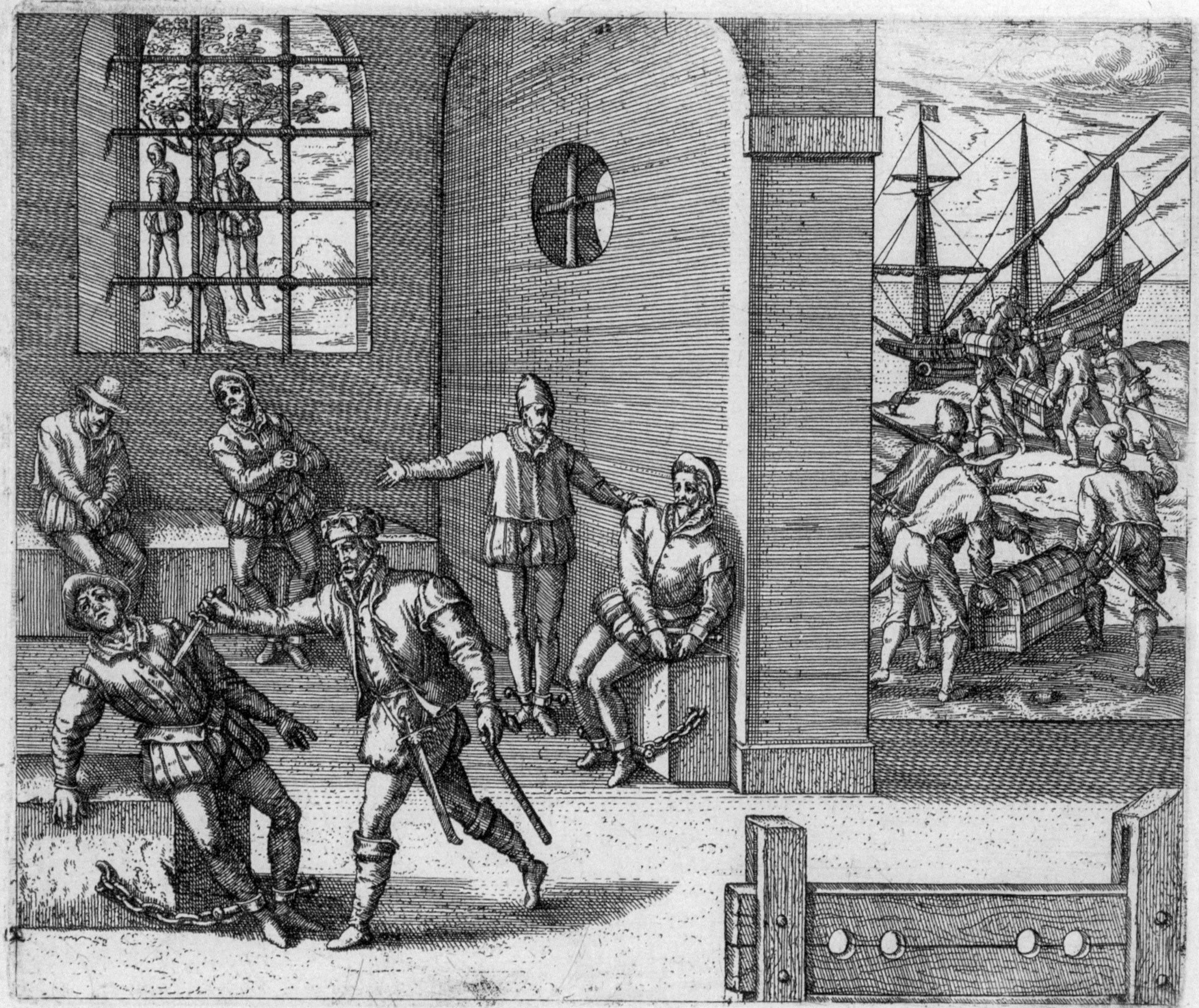

DEmnach in Peru frieden gemacht/rüstet sich der Præsident Gasca widerumb nach Spanien zu fahren/Zeucht derhalben gen Ranama, so bald er ankommen/schickt er deß Keysers gelt vorhin/zu der Stadt Nomen-Dei, vber den fluß Chagre, er selbst folgt so bald hernach/ließ hinder jhm zu Panama an Silber/auff die sechsmal hundert tausent Kronen werth/die er in mangel der fuhr nicht mit nehmen kundt Mitler weil rotten sich der meinste theil der Kriegßknecht zusammen/welche der Præsident in der außbeut vbergangen hatt/vnnd begaben sich zu dem Ferdinando vnnd Petro de Cantreras beyden leiblichen gebrüdern / vnnd deß Roderii de Contras Söhnen/welche ohn das vbel content waren/von wegen daß jhr Vatter seines Ampts entsetzt worden/kommen also auff die drey hundert Kriegßknecht zusammen / lassen sich mit Schiffen an den Pfort zu Panama führen/weil sie kundtschafft eingenommen / daß der Præsident mit deß Keysers gelt allda ankommen were. Da sie nahe herzu kamen/hielten sie still biß auff die Nacht/Wie es nun finster worden/fielen sie stillschweigens in den hauffen / in hoffnung den Præsidenten mit dem Gelt allda zu erdappen/Wie sie aber vernahmen/daß er nach der Stadt Nomen-Dei verruckt/fielen sie mit Gewalt in die Behausung deß Königlichen Schultheissen Martin Ruiz, bekommen das hinderlegte Gelt / führen dasselbige zugleich mit allem dem Goldt/vnd anderm gut/so sie in der Stadt geraubt/in jhr Schiff/beschlossen demnach bey sich/sich notwendig nach der Stadt Nomen-Dei zubegeben/vnnd den Presidenten zu vberfallen/ehe dann er erführe/wie sie zu Panama gehaust hetten. So bald sie die Statt hinauß kamen/liessen sie den Ioannem de Bermeio mit hundert Fußknechten sich auff einem hügel/nicht weit von der Statt lägern. Ferdinandus aber zog selbst in Person mit dem vbrigen volck nach dem Presidenten, jedoch ohn die jenigen / welche er seinem Bruder Petro zugeben / die Schiff mit dem geraubten gut zu bewahren. Wie der Königliche Statt Schultheiß vnd Ioannes de Larez sahen / daß sie sich zertrennet hatten / gedachten sie/sie wolten sie nun wol bestehen oder verjagen. Derwegen beruffen sie die Burgerschafft/machtn sie wehrhafftig/ziehen mit denselbigen dem Ioanni de Bermeio entgegen. Auch hatten sie zuvor zwo Landtkündige person/ auff zween vnderschiedliche weg abgefertiget / dem Præsidenten vnnd der Burgerschafft zu Nomen-Dei allen zustand zu Panama anzumelden/ vnnd sie für dem Ferdinando zu warnen. Sie fielen den Bermeium mit einem Sturm an/schlugen jn in die flucht/fiengen viel seines Volcks/Darauff der Schultheiß so bald dem Ferdinando auff dem Fuß nach der Stadt Nomen Dei zu eylet/in meinung jhn zu erlangen/Aber derselbige war schon zuuor von den entrunnen Knechten vnder wegen verstendiget worden/wie der Schultheiß die vberhand gehabt/vnd jhm auff dem Fuß nacheylete. Derhalben läst er so bald sein volck von sich / ermahnet sie/daß sie eylends sich/vnd durch was wege sie jmmer kündten/zum Meer verfügen/da sein Bruder die Schiff mit dem Gelt verwahret. Aber sie wurden meinstentheils gefangen. Vnnd wie Petrus seines Bruders vnd deß Bermei zustand vernahm/satzte er sich in einen Nachen/verließ die Schiff mit dem Raub/vnd gab die Flucht/die gefangenen führet man in einen Thurn/ allda seind sie von dem Profosen mit einem Dolchen durchstochen worden.

Indi cuiusdam Gnomologia insignis de Christianorum auaritia. XXI.

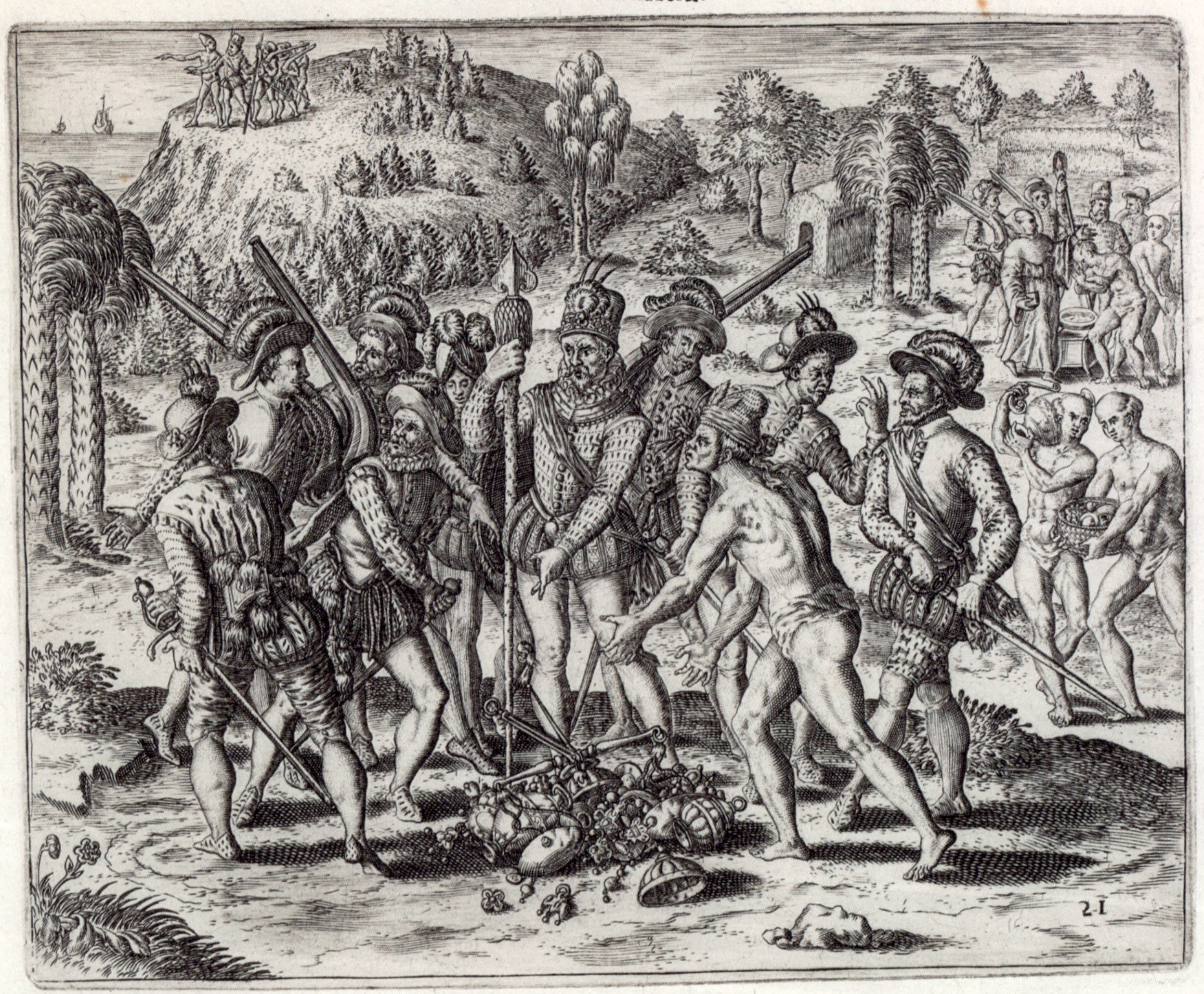

PANCHIACO Regulus amicitia cum Valboa contracta, illi grandem auri vim elaborati in vasa & monilia, dat. Verum conspicatus Hispanos, dum aurum hoc penditur, inter se rixari, & eductis gladijs sese mutuo ferire velle, aurum cum trutina euertit, illorum auaritiam acerbe carpens. Atq; si tanta auri cupiditate arderent, regiones demonstraturum in quibus abundantissime id inuenirent. Valboam deinde per difficilia itinera ad summa montium iuga deducit è quibus mare Australe ipsi demonstrat. Reuersus Panchiacum baptisandum curat & Carolum nuncupat.

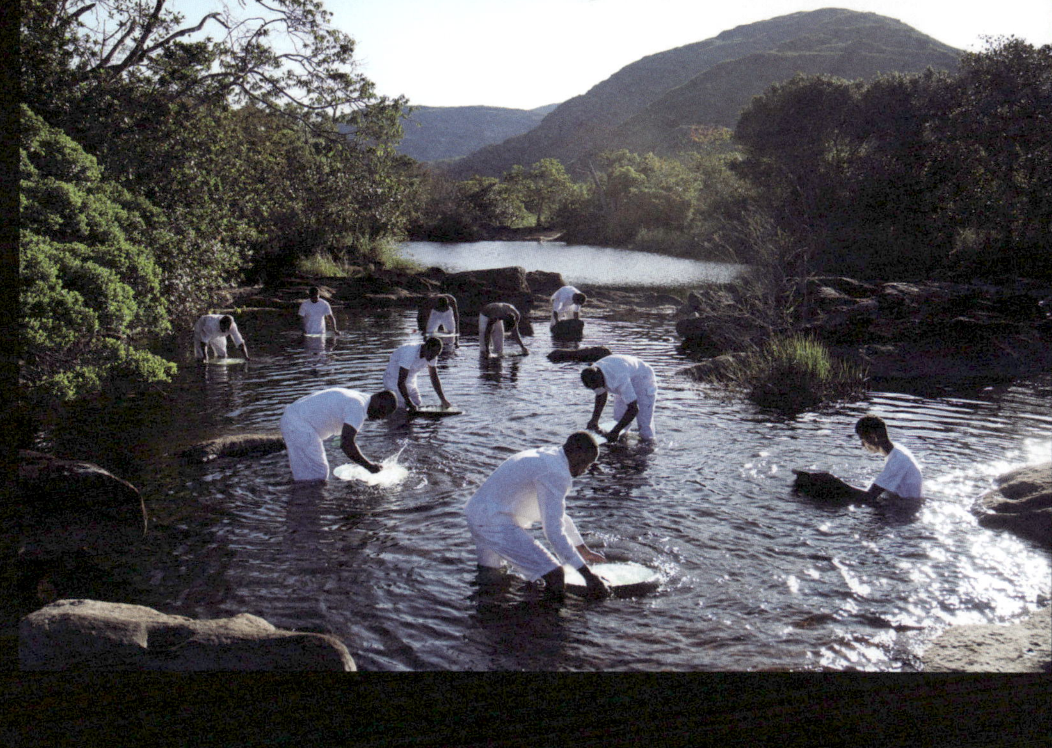

Tiago Sant'Ana, *Chão de estrelas* (Ground of stars), 2022

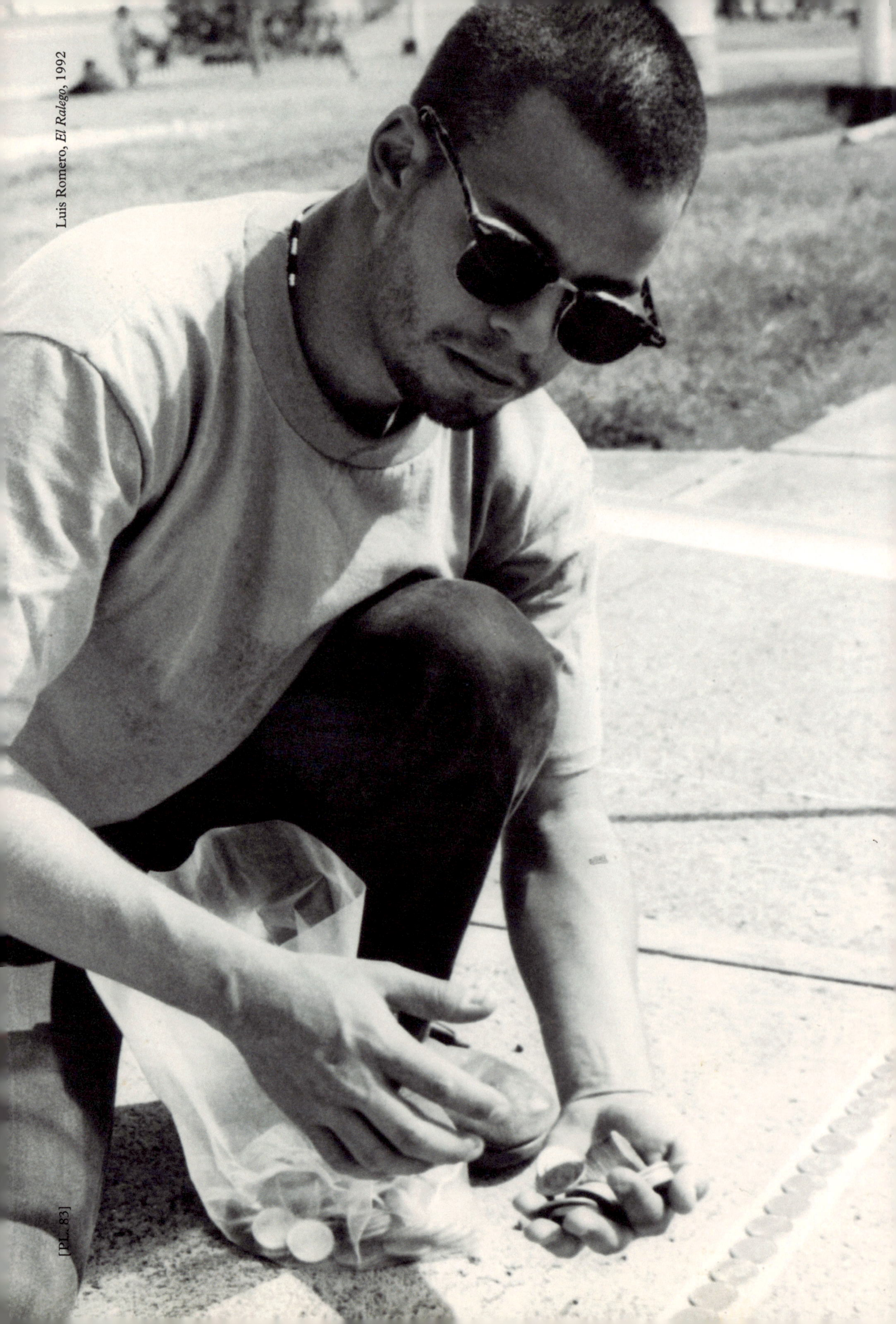

Luis Romero, *El Ralego*, 1992

[PL. 83]

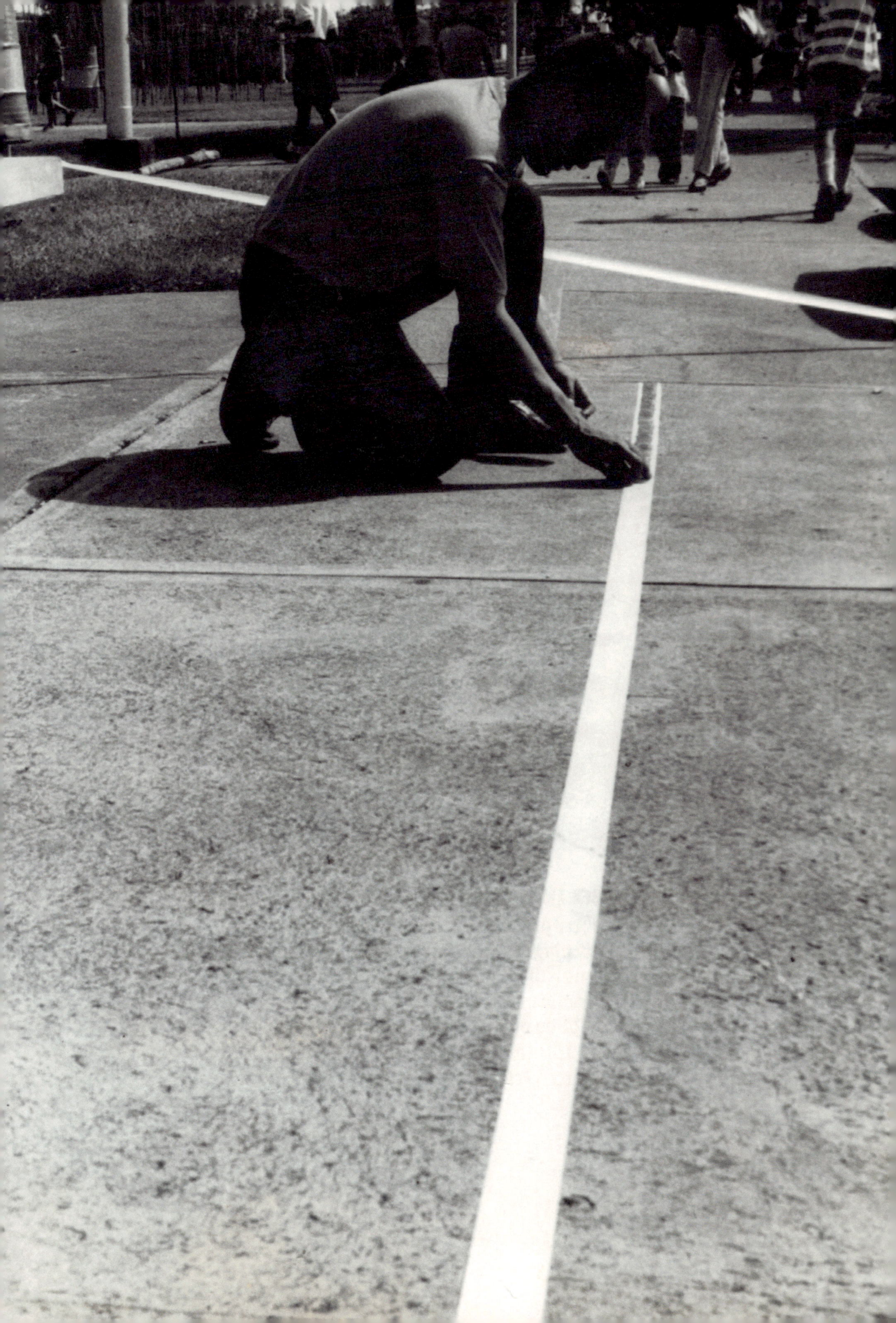

Die Indianer giessen den Spaniern zuersättigung jhres Geitzes geschmeltzt Goldt in den Mund. XX.

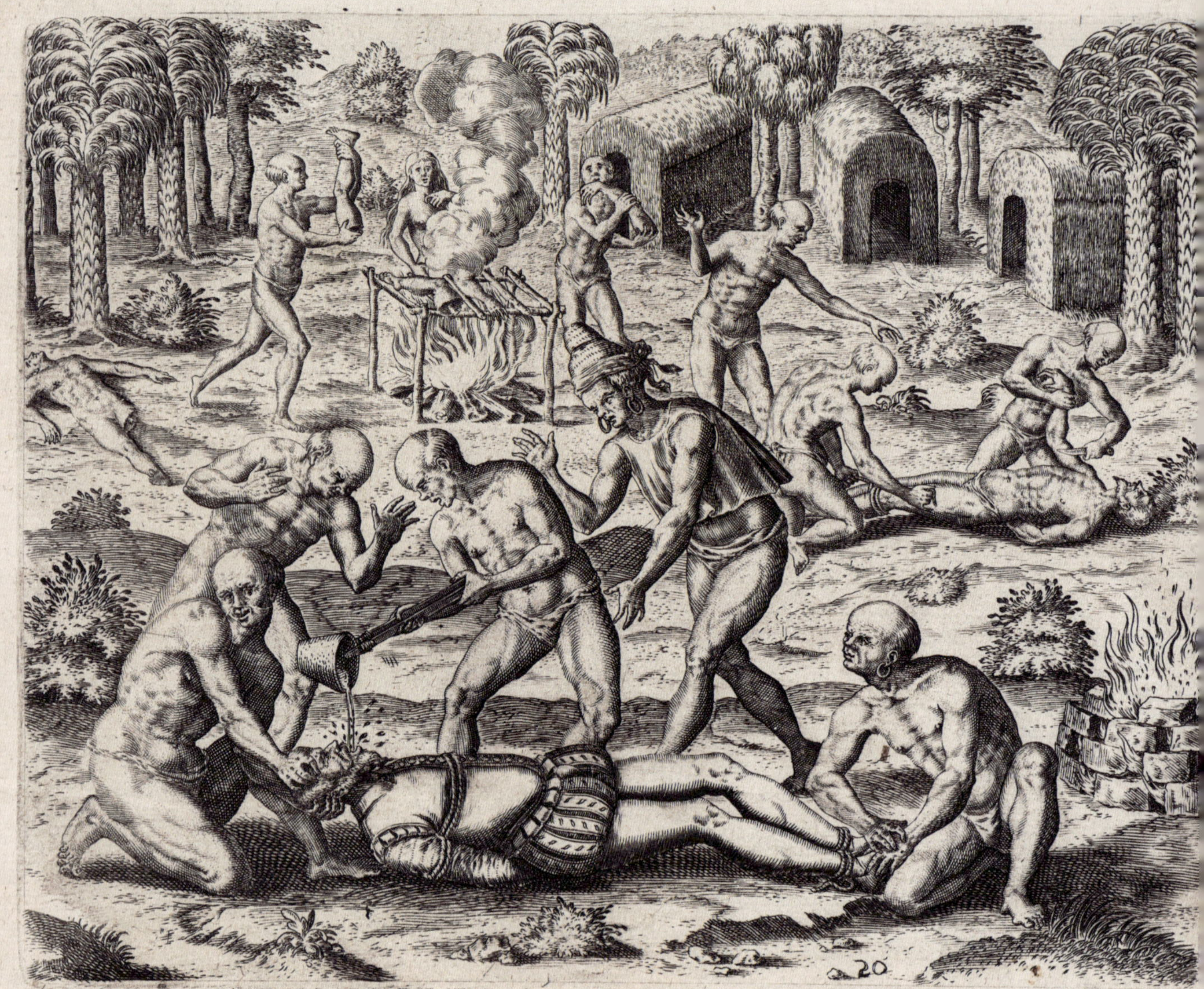

DJe Indianer zu Neidt vnd Zorn gegen die Spanier bewegt/von wegen jhrer zuviel grossen Tyranney vnd Grausamkeit vnd Geitz/ so viel sie deren lebendig fiengen/ fürnemblich aber die Hauptleuth/ denen bunden sie Händ vnd Füß/ vnd warffen sie auff die Erden nider/ vnd gossen jhnen zerschmeltzt Goldt ins Maul/ vnd rupffeten jhn jhren Geitz mit solchen Worten auff: Jß Goldt/ jß Goldt du vnersättiger Christ. Ja zu grösserer Marter vnnd Schmach schnitten sie etlichen also lebendig mit scharpffen Instrumenten auß Steinen gemacht/ die Arm/ etlichen die Schultern/ etlichen die Bein ab/ vnd legten sie auff die Kolen/ brieten vnd assen sie. 23. Cap.

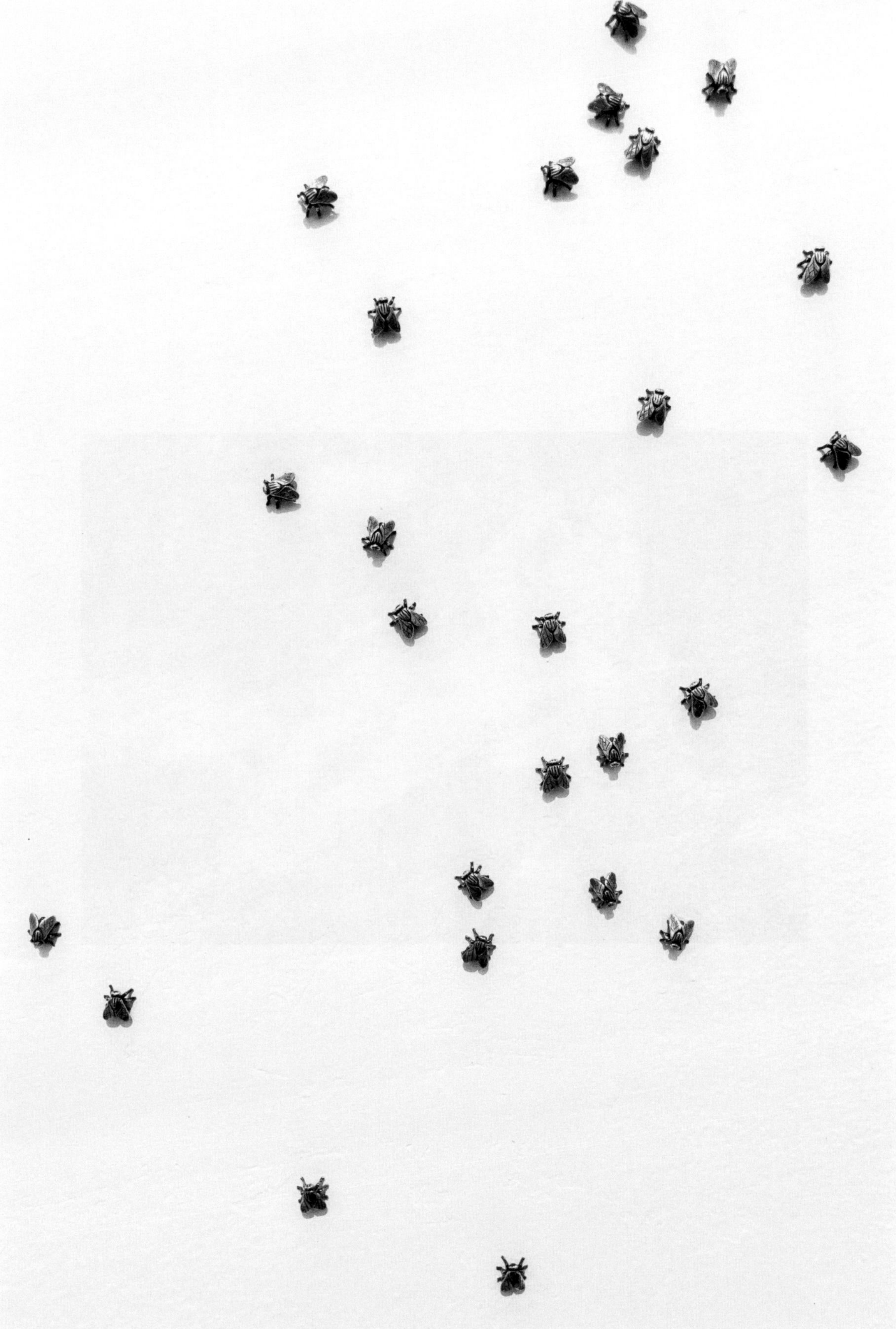

Andrés Bedoya, *Moscas* (Flies), 2022

↑ [PL. 84]

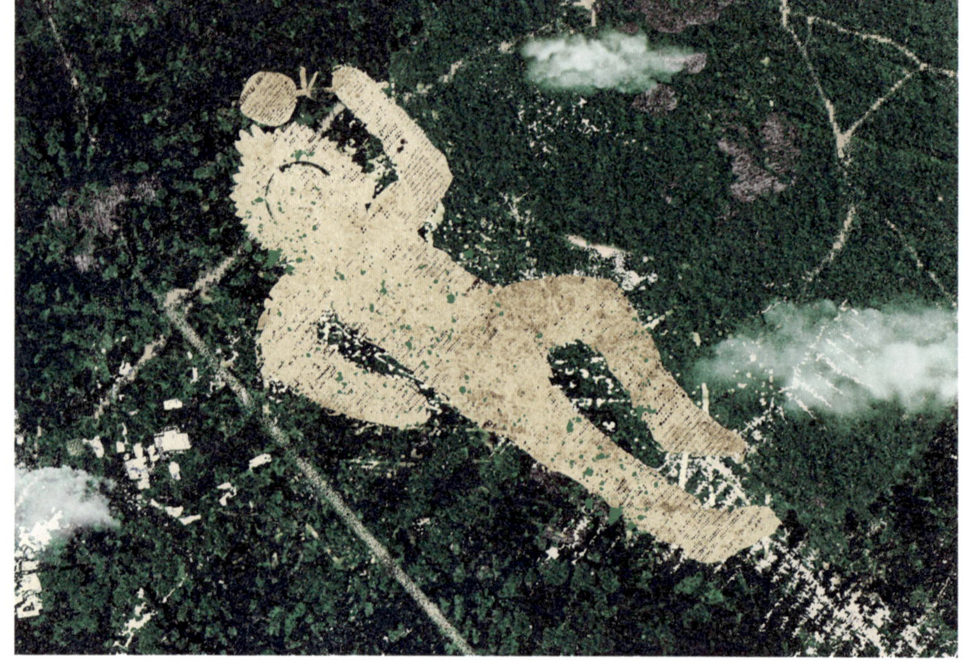

Denilson Baniwa, *Natureza morta 1* (Still life 1), 2016

↓ [PL. 87]

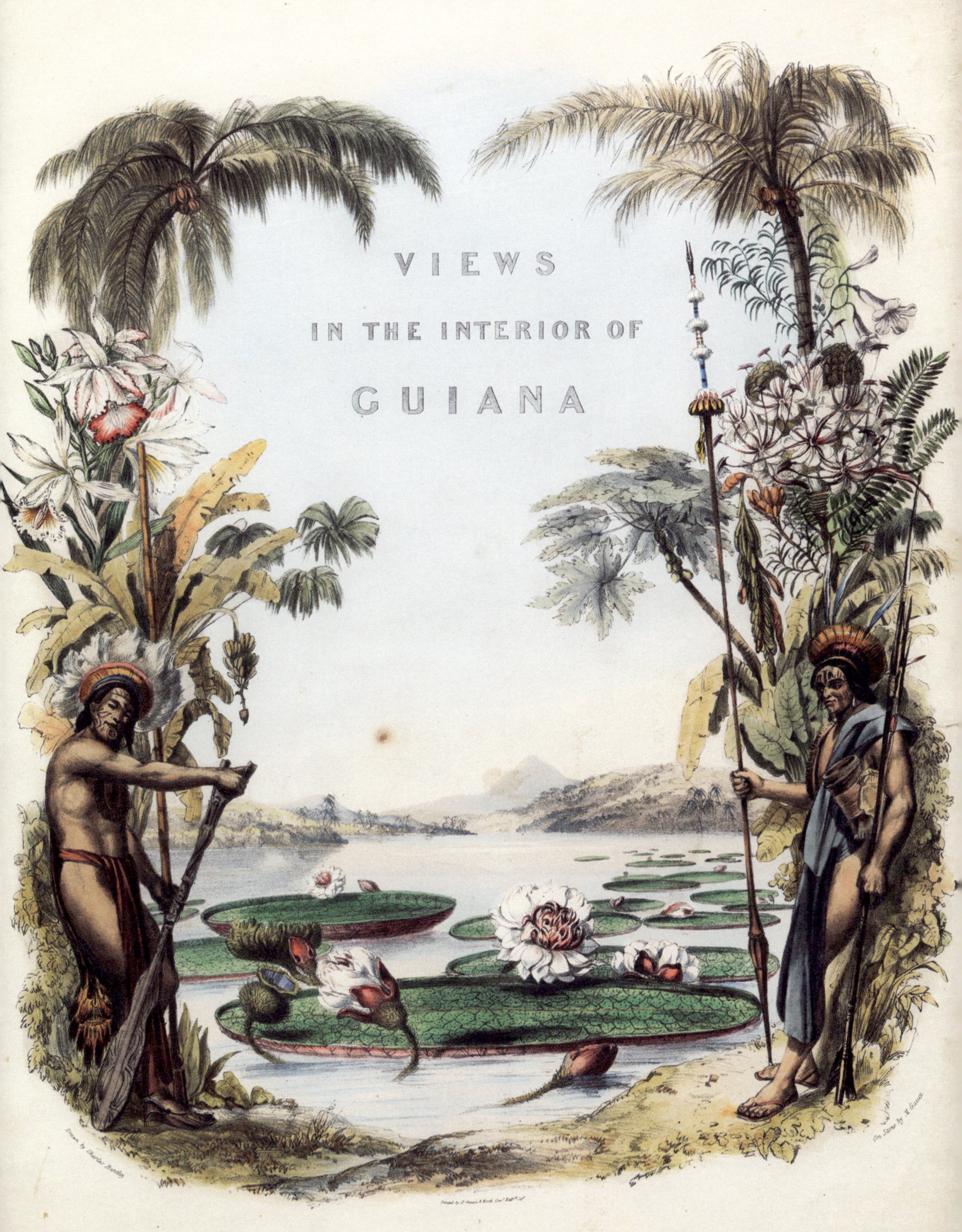

London, Published by Ackermann & Co. 96, Strand, 3rd Augt. 1840

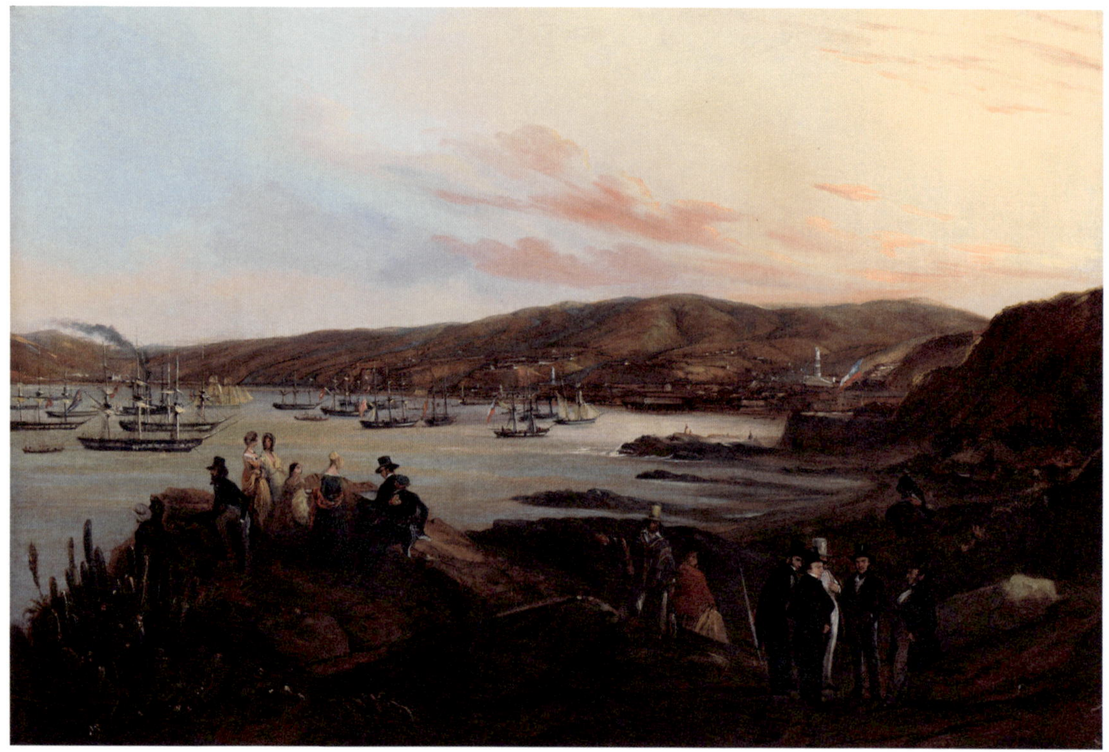

Johann Moritz Rugendas, *View of Valparaíso*, 1842

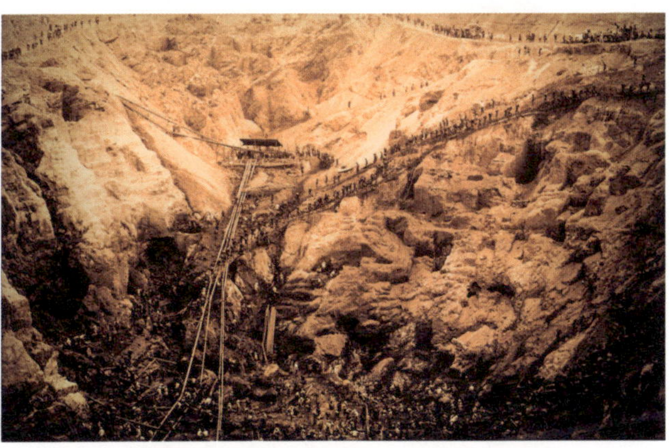

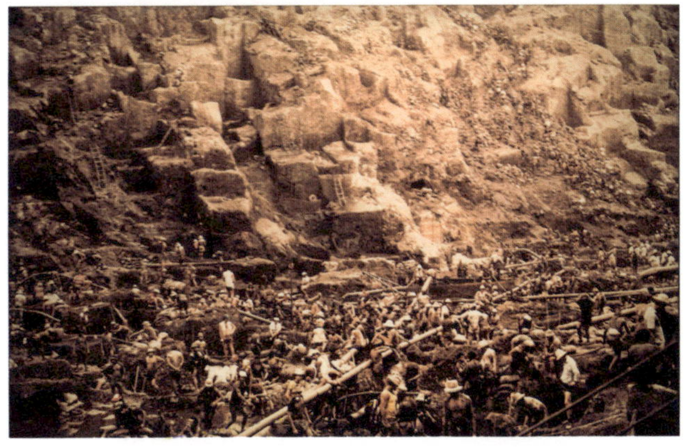

Alfredo Jaar, *Gold in the Morning*, 1985

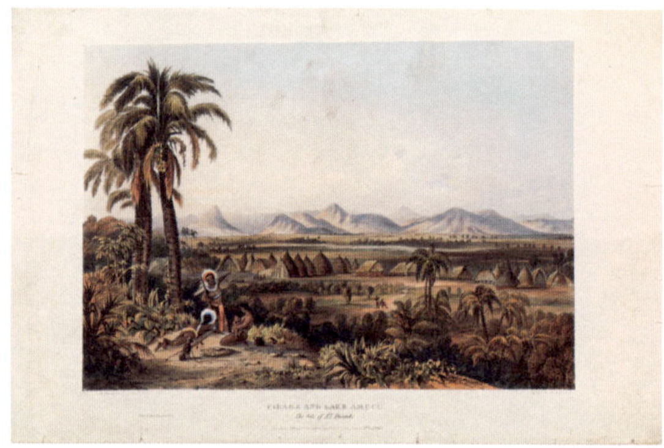

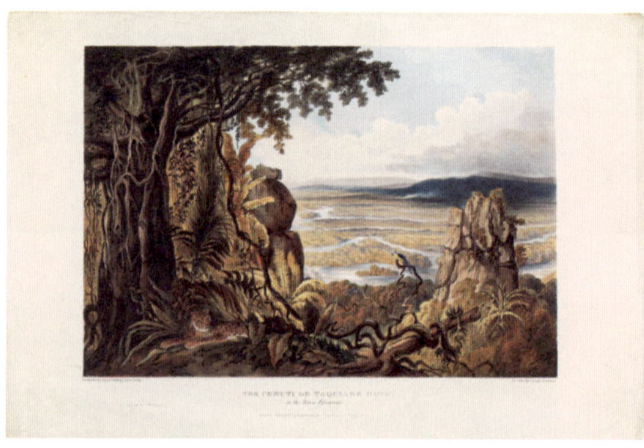

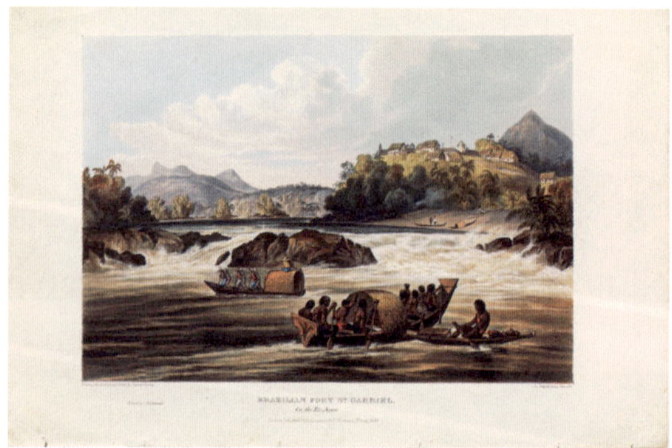

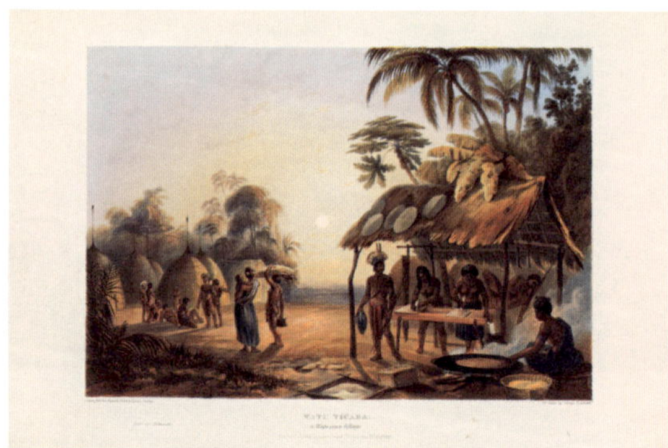

Charles Bentley and Robert H. Schomburgk, *Twelve Views in the Interior of the Guianas* (London: Ackermann & Co., 1840)

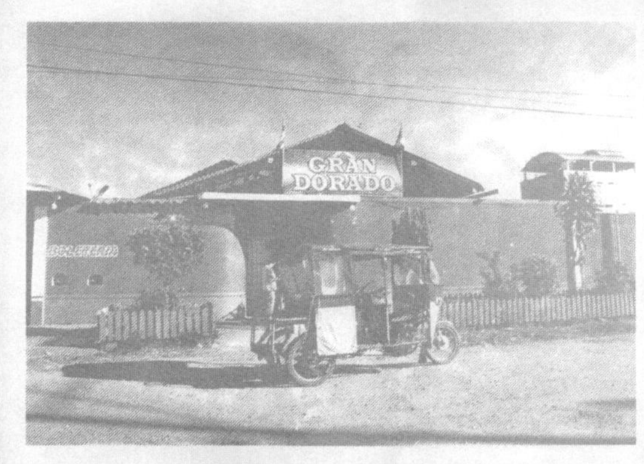

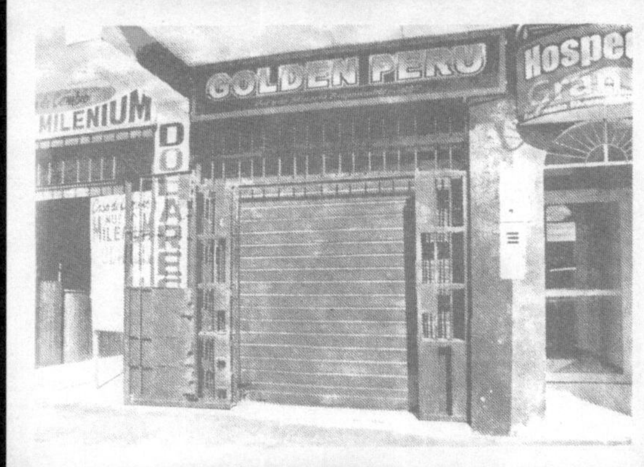

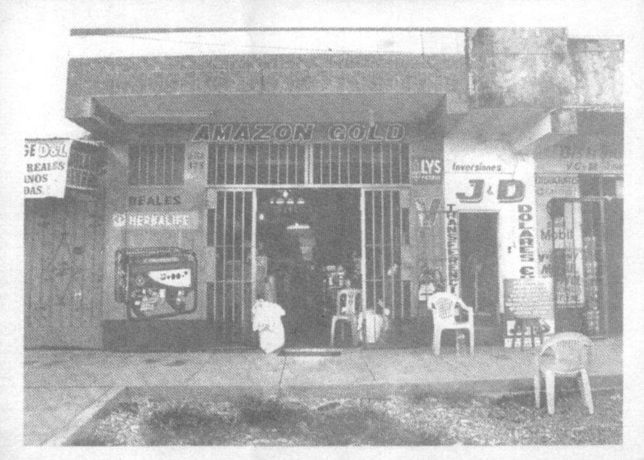

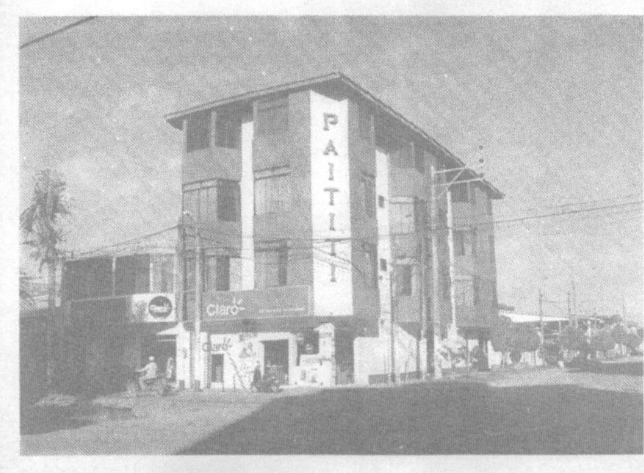

Nancy La Rosa and Juan Salas Carreño, *Mirages (Espejismos)* (Mirages), 2015

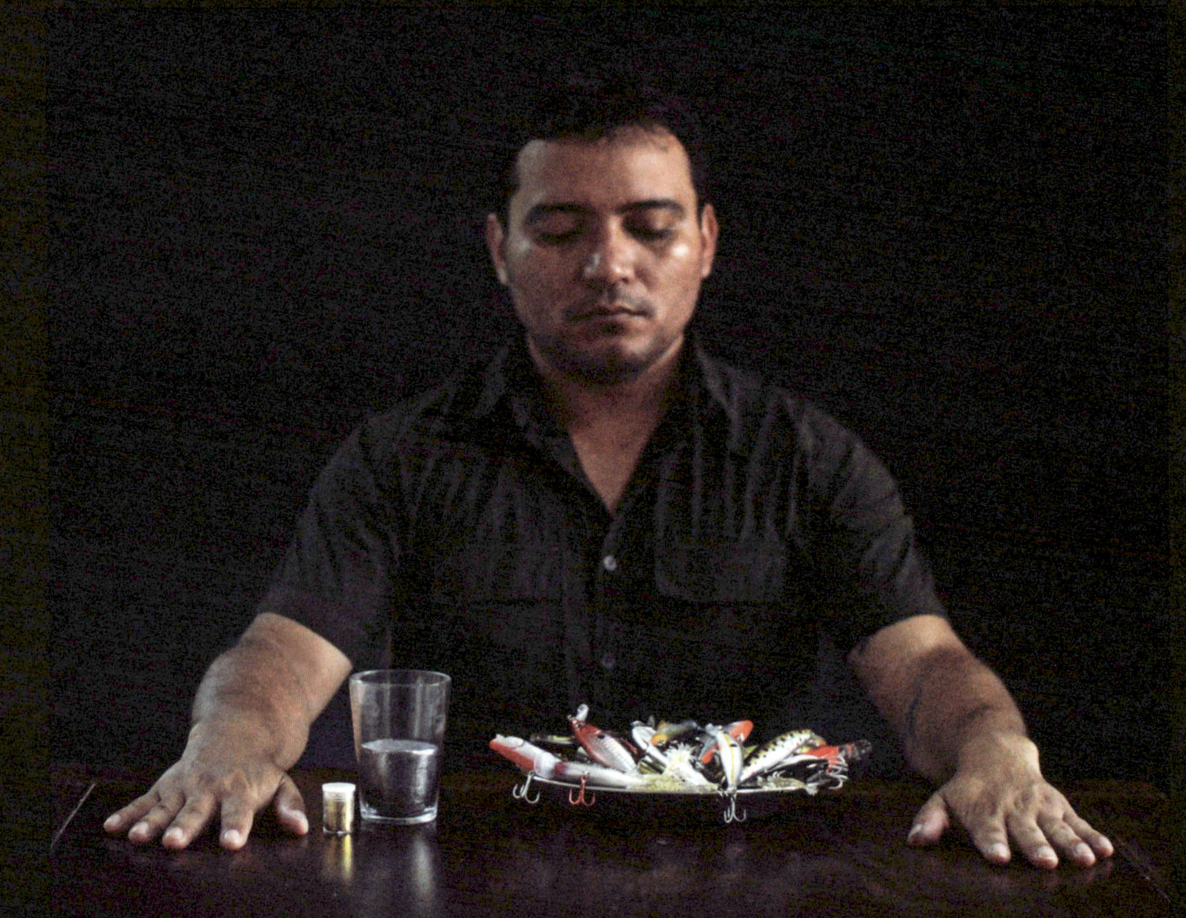

Denilson Baniwa, *Azougue 80*, 2019

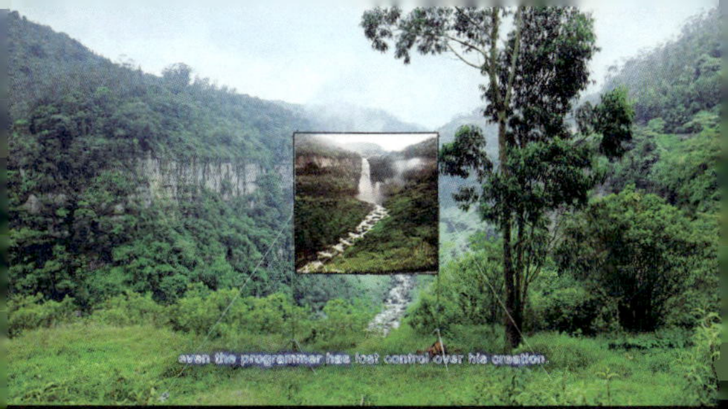

even the programmer has lost control over his creation.

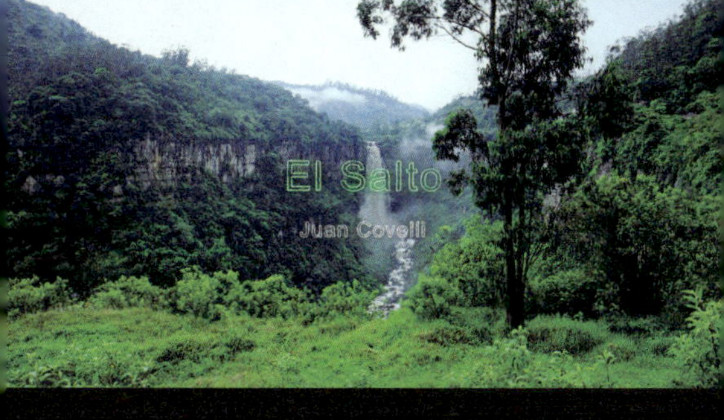

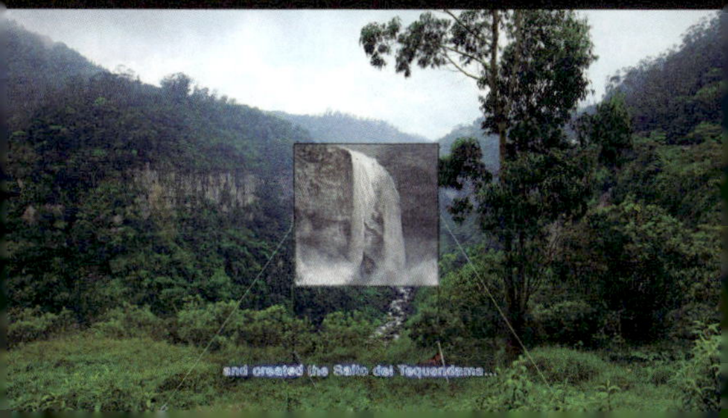

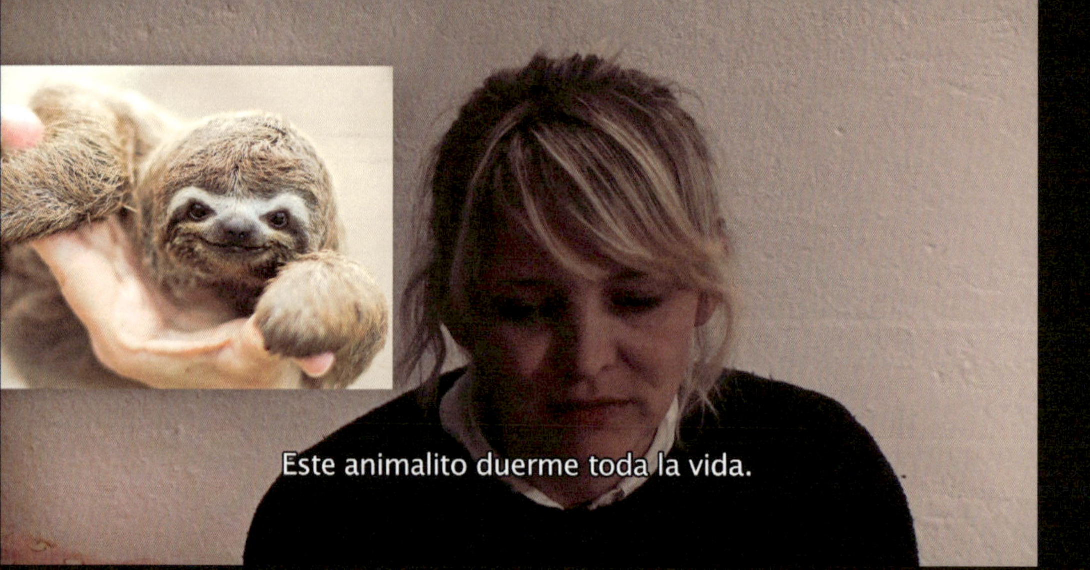
Este animalito duerme toda la vida.

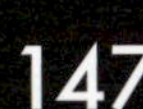

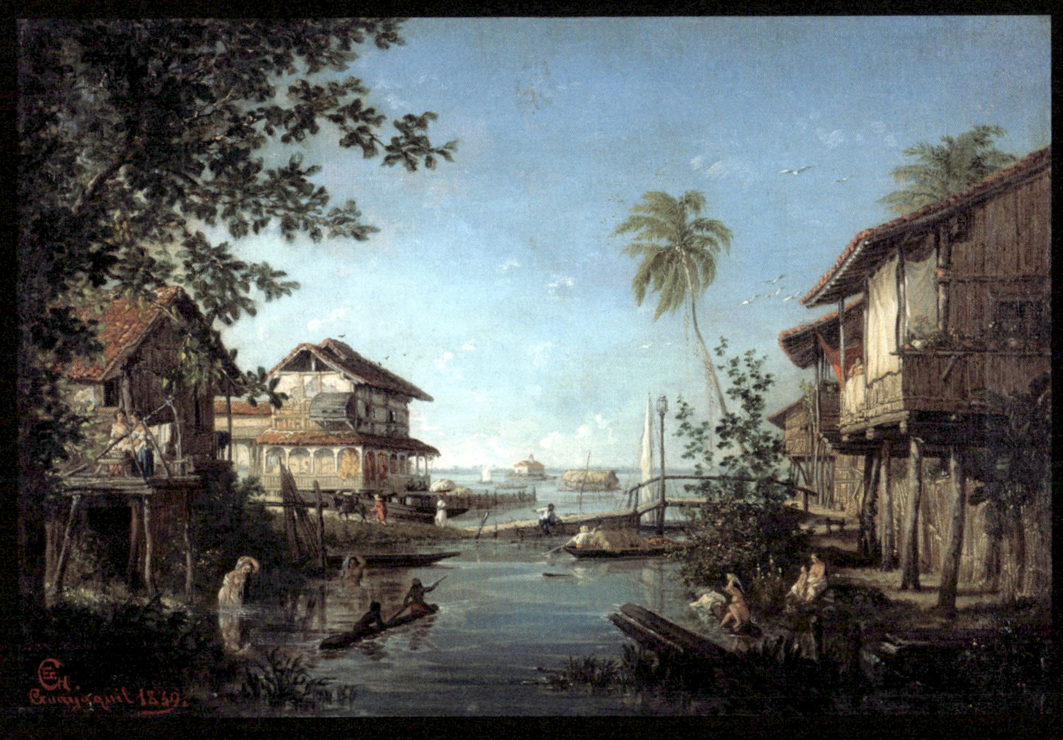

Ernest Charton de Treville, *Guayaquil*, 1849

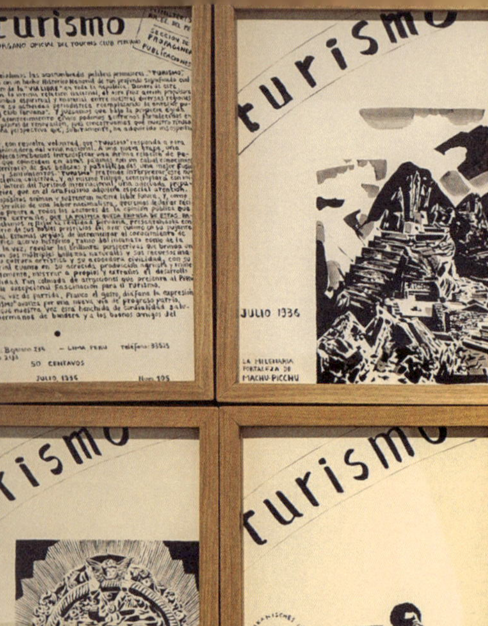
turismo
turismo
JULIO 1936
LA MILENARIA FORTALEZA DE MACHU-PICCHU

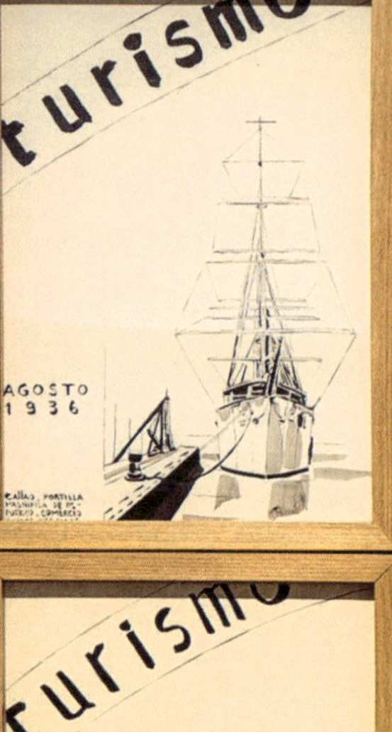
turismo
AGOSTO 1936

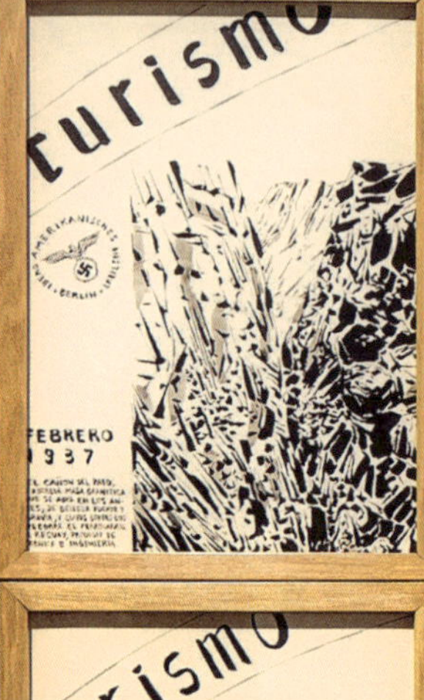
turismo
FEBRERO 1937

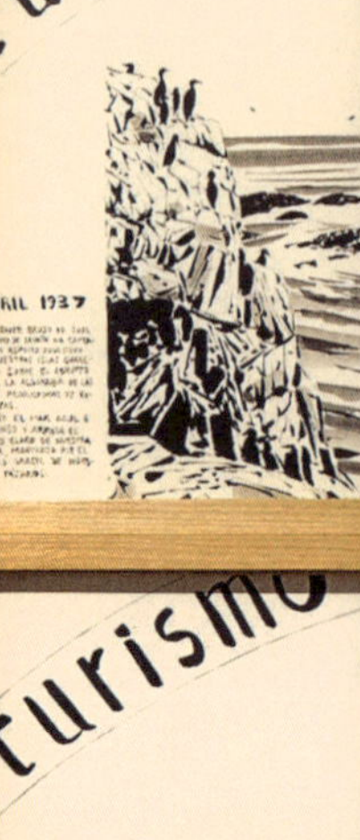
turismo
ABRIL 1937

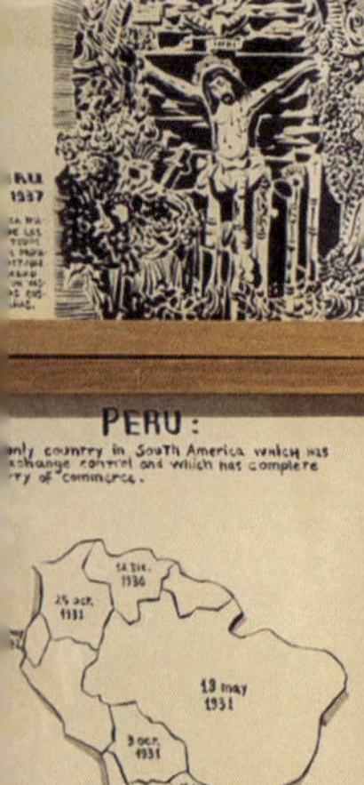
turismo

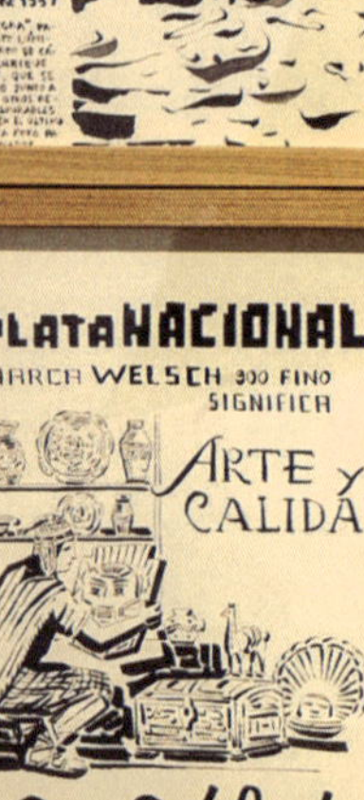
turismo
LIMA-PERU
NOVIEMBRE 1937

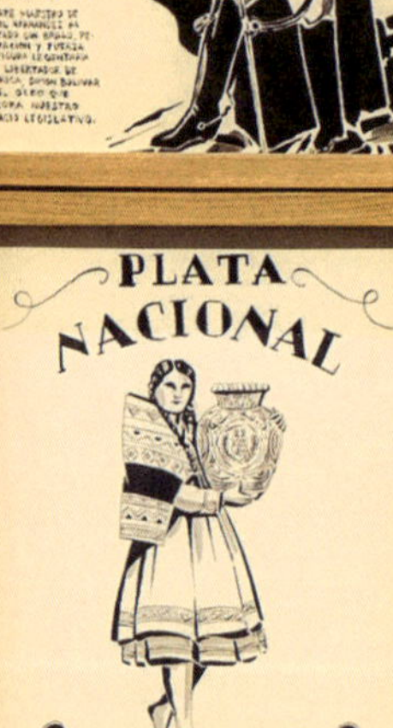
turismo
DICIEMBRE 1937
LIMA-PERU

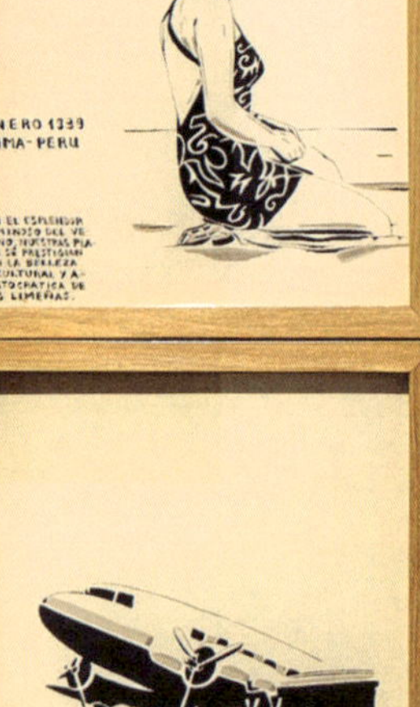
turismo
ENERO 1939
LIMA-PERU

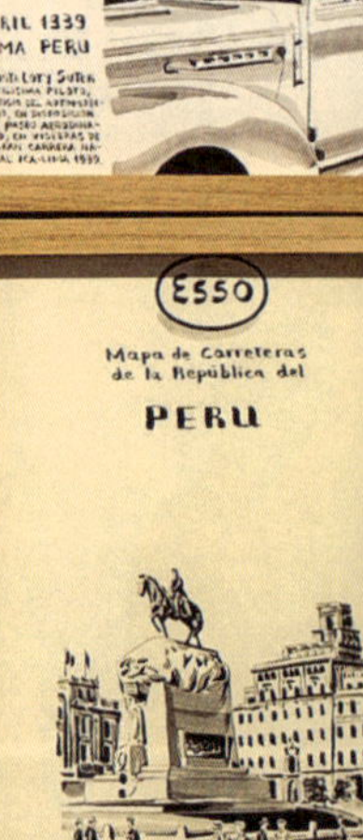
turismo
ABRIL 1939
LIMA PERU

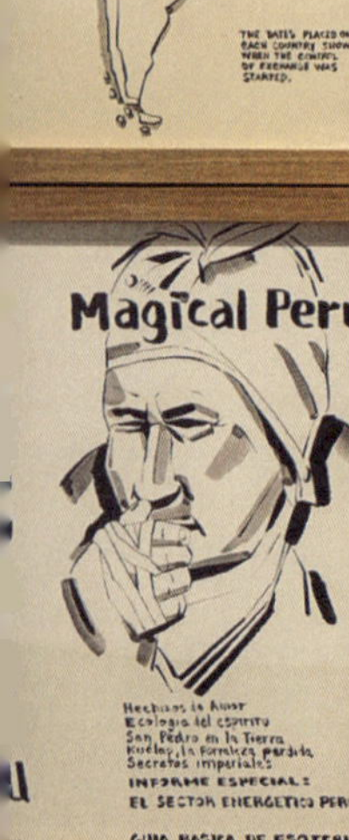
PERU:
PLATA NACIONAL
MARCA WELSCH 900 FINO SIGNIFICA
ARTE y CALIDAD
Casa Welsch
PLATA NACIONAL
CASA WELSCH
Pan American Grace Airways, Inc
ESSO
Mapa de Carreteras de la República del
PERU
INTERNATIONAL PETROLEUM COMPANY LTD.
Magical Peru
EL DORADO
PERU
A Dancing Nation
EL DORADO
PERU
Peruvian Creativity
A Lively Force
EL DORADO
PERU
LOS ANDES: UNA DIVERSIDAD INTEGRADORA
EL DORADO

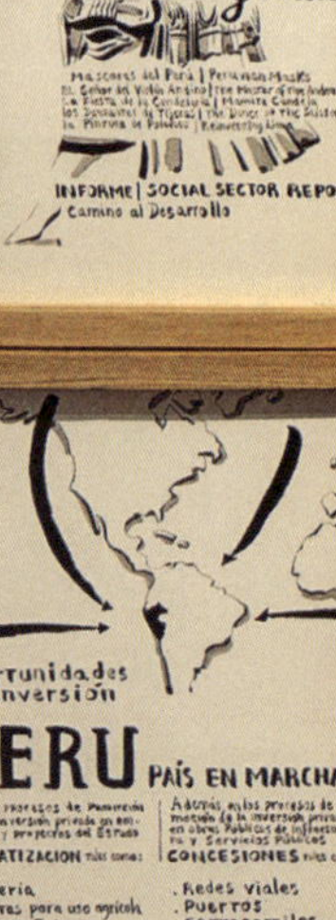
oportunidades de inversión
PERU PAÍS EN MARCHA
PRIVATIZACION
CONCESIONES

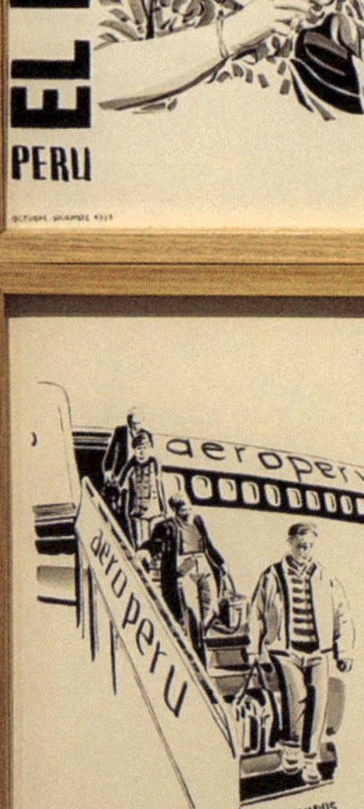
aeroperu
aeroperu
BIENVENIDOS

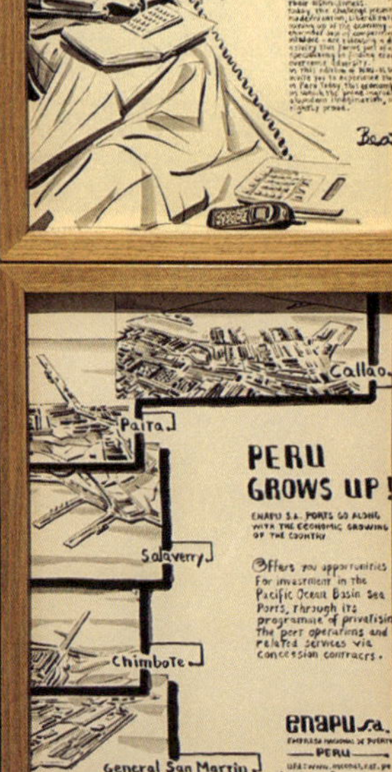
Callao
Paita
PERU GROWS UP!
Salaverry
Chimbote
General San Martin
enapu s.a.

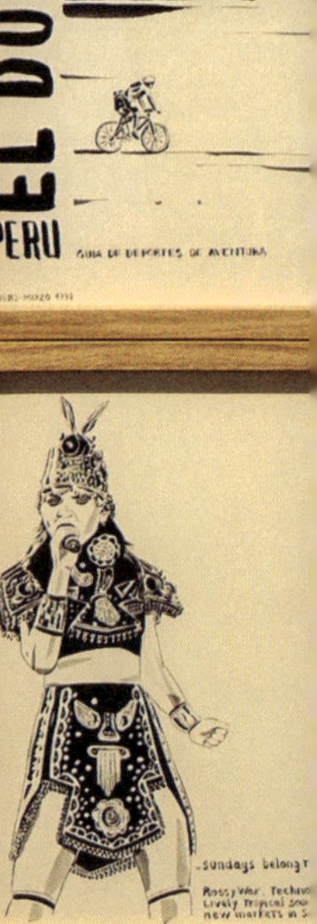

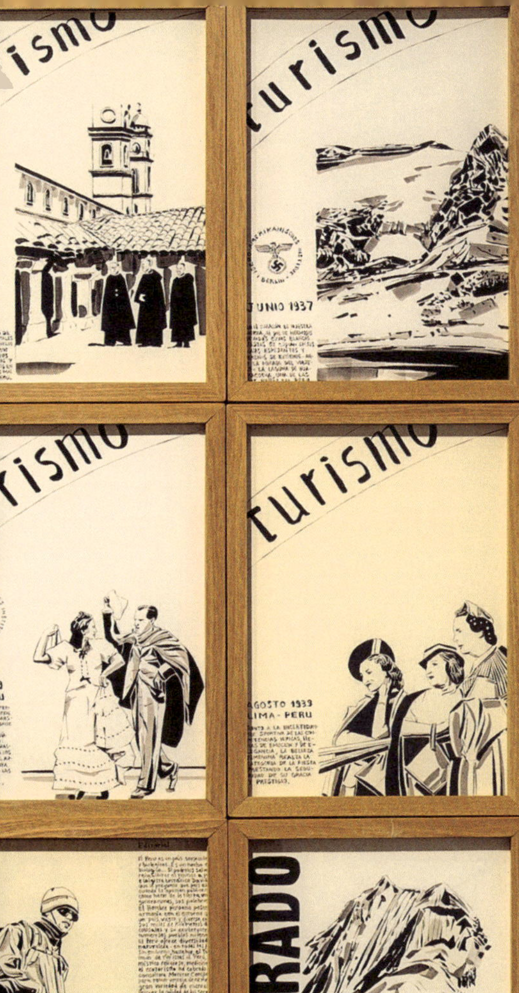
turismo
JUNIO 1937
turismo
AGOSTO 1938
LIMA-PERU

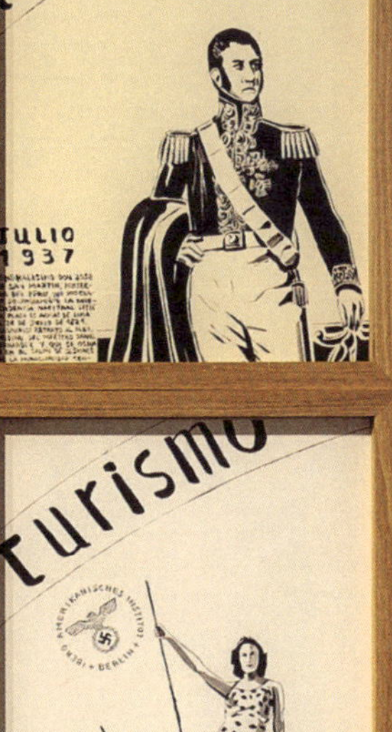
turismo
MARZO 1940
LIMA-PERU

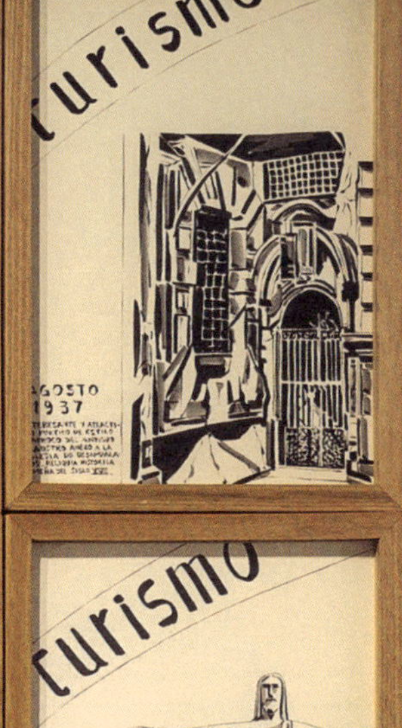
turismo
JULIO
1937

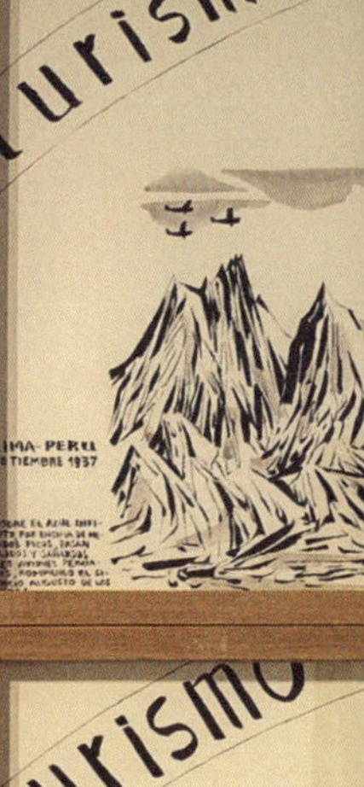
turismo
LIMA-PERU

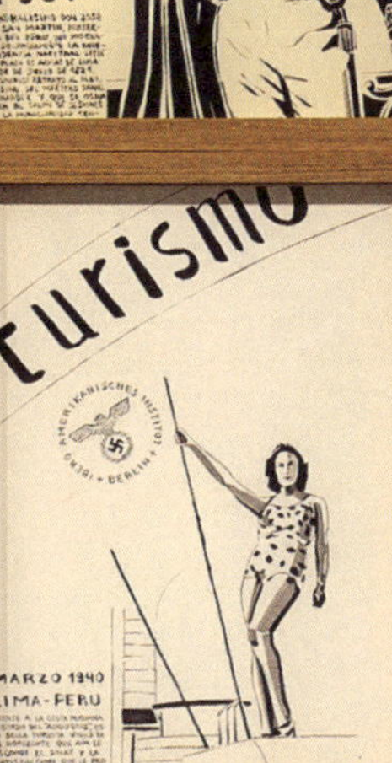

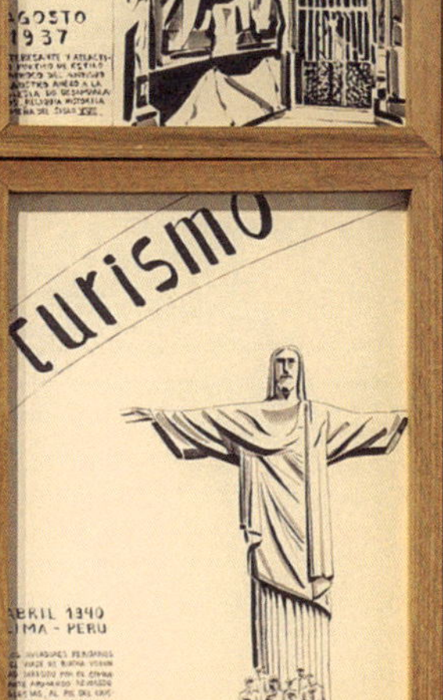
turismo
AGOSTO
1937

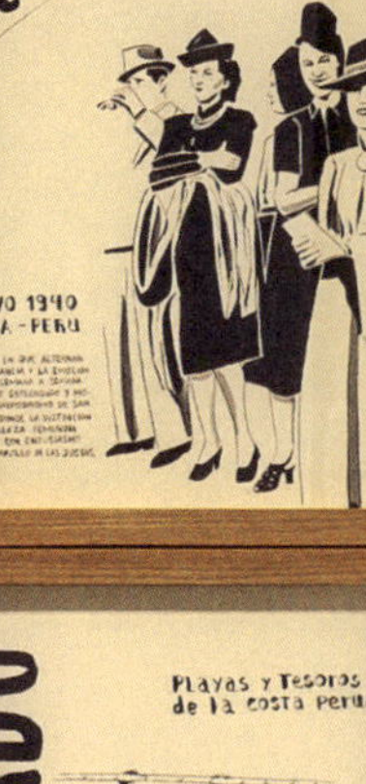
turismo
MAYO 1940
LIMA-PERU

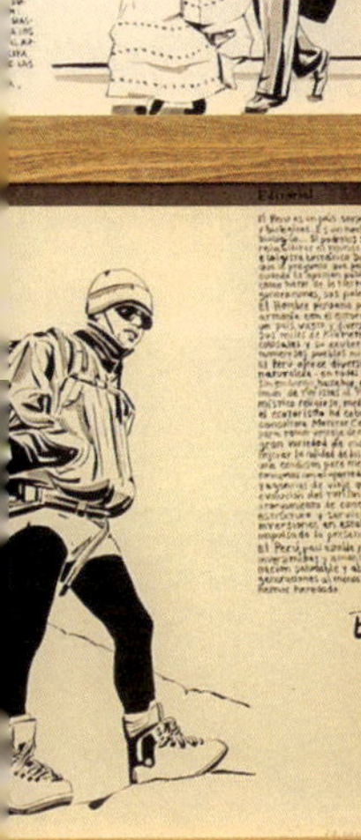

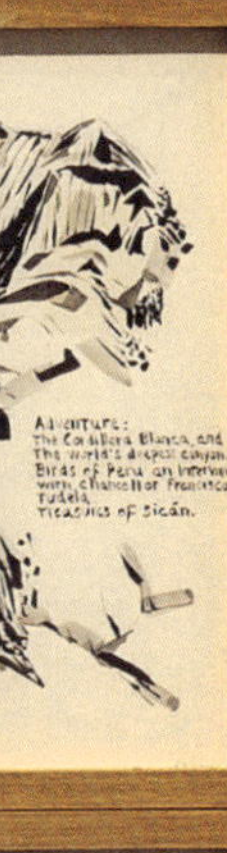
EL DORADO
PERU

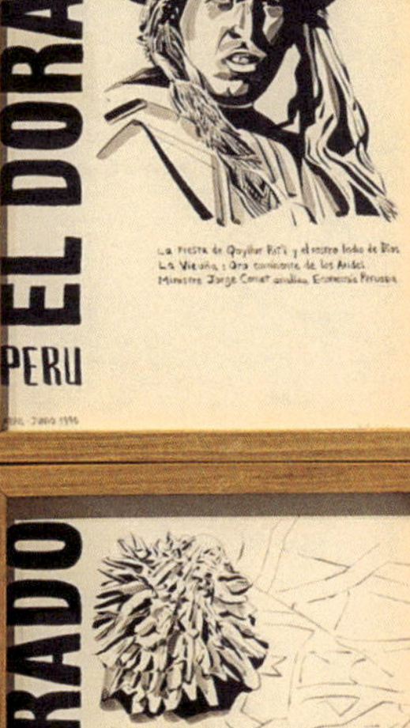
EL DORADO
PERU

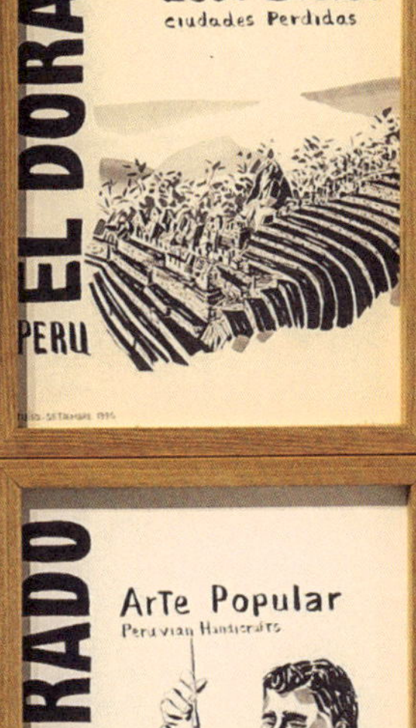
EL DORADO
PERU
Lost Cities
ciudades Perdidas

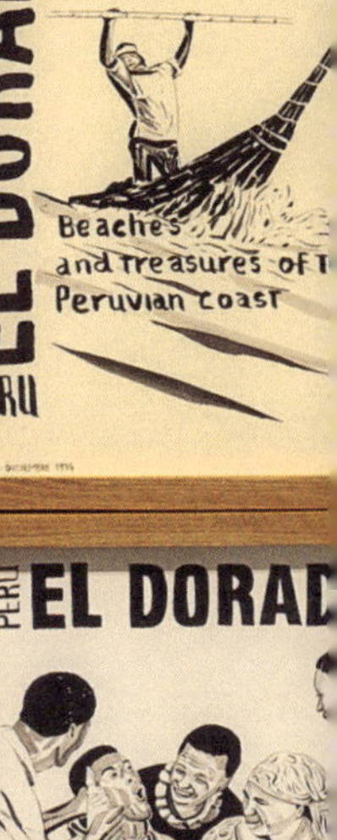
EL DORADO
PERU
Beaches and treasures of the Peruvian coast

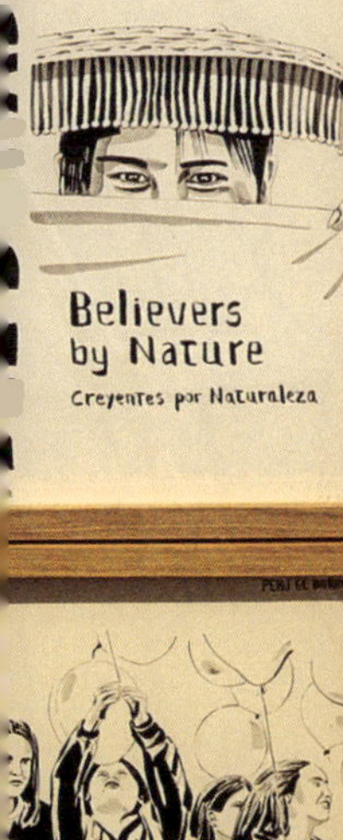
Believers by Nature
Creyentes por Naturaleza

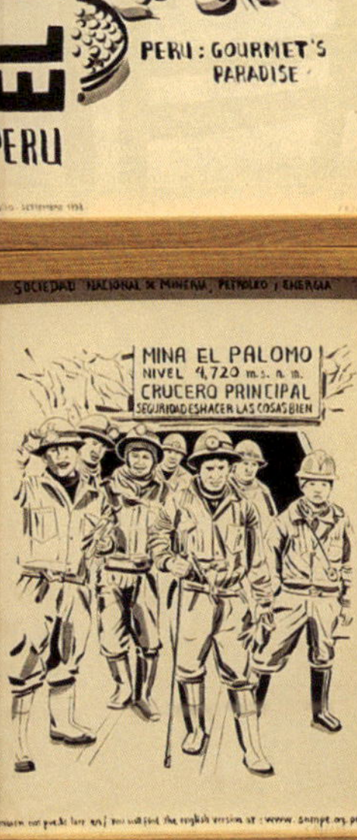
MINA EL PALOMO
CRUCERO PRINCIPAL

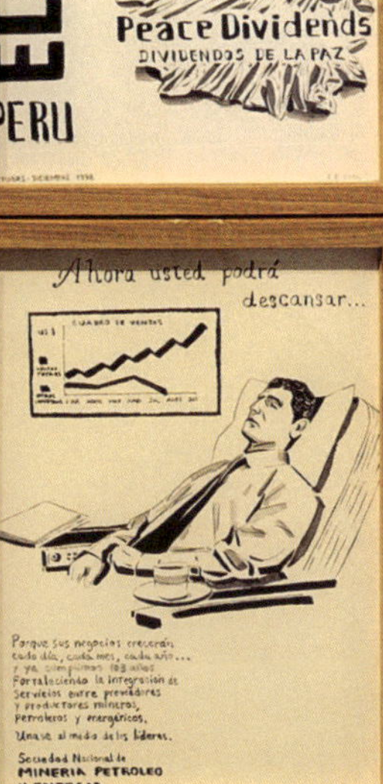
Ahora usted podrá descansar...

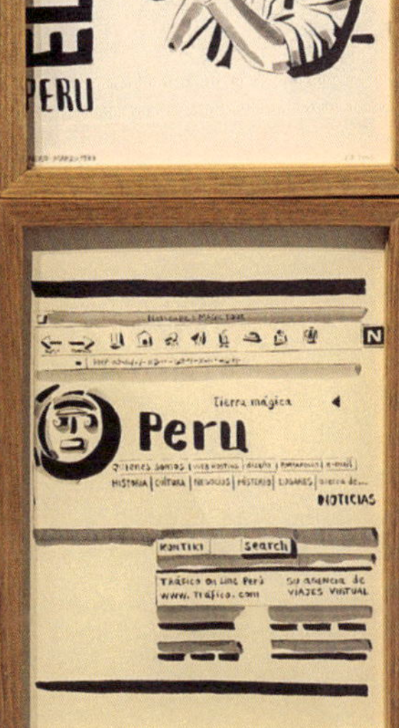
Peru

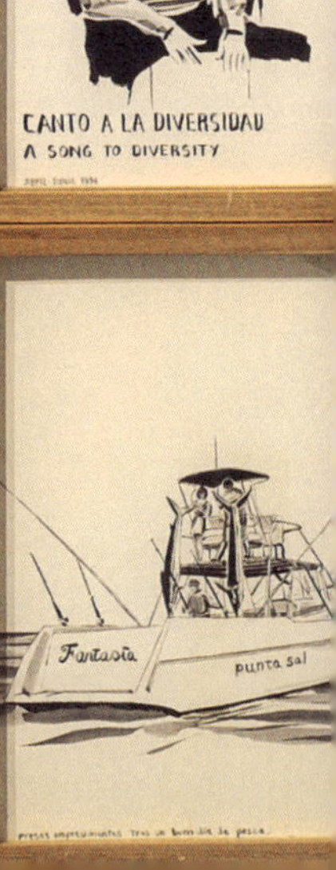
Fantasía

↑ [PL. 96] Fernando Bryce, *Turismo El Dorado* (El Dorado tourism), 2000
[PL. 97] Ronny Quevedo, *los desaparecidos (the arbiter of time)* (The disappeared [the arbiter of time]), 2018

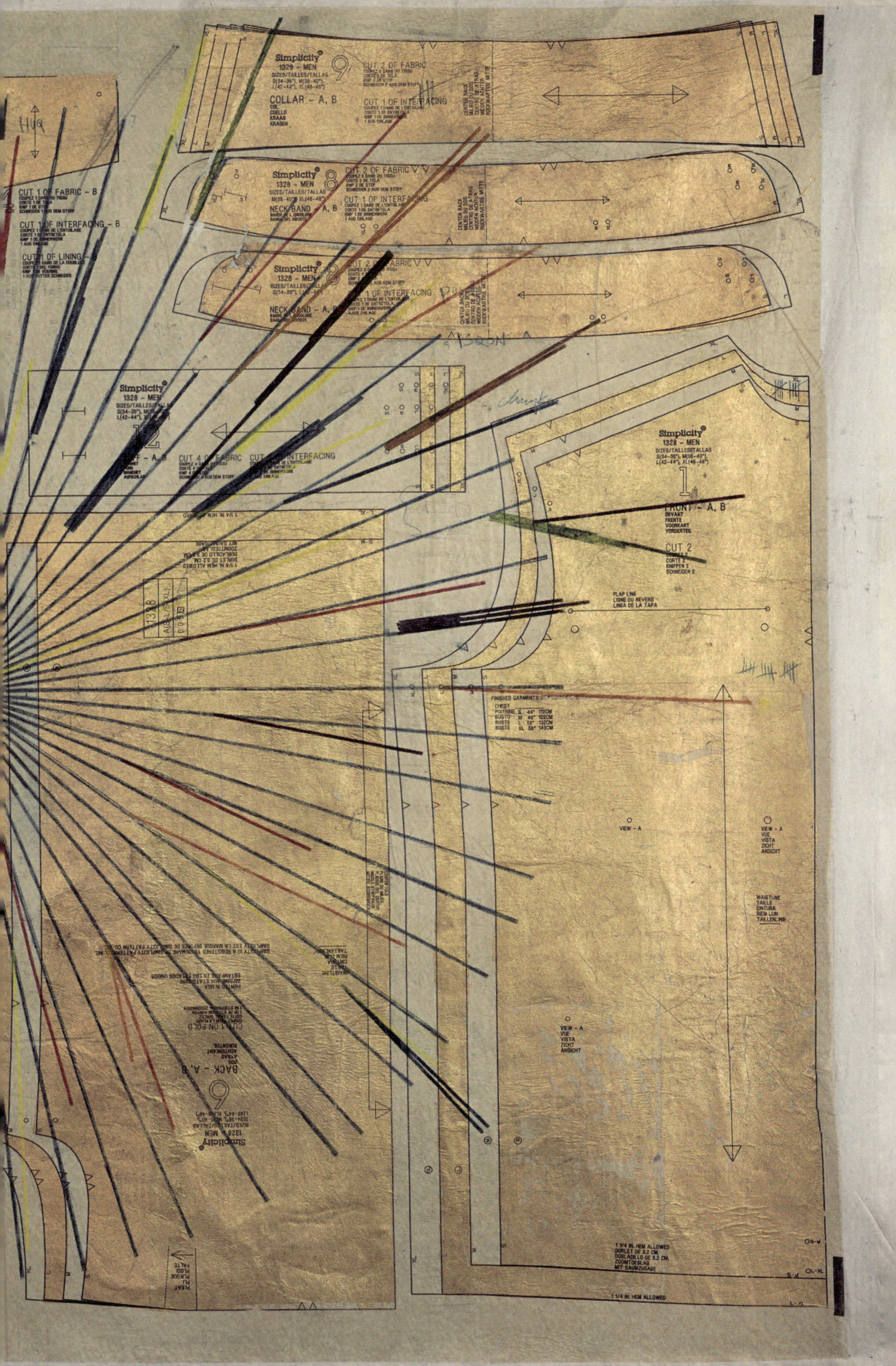

Simplicity
1328 - MEN
COLLAR - A, B
CUT 2 OF FABRIC
CUT 1 OF INTERFACING
NECK BAND - A, B
CUT 1 OF FABRIC - B
CUT 1 OF INTERFACING - B
CUT 1 OF LINING - B
CUFF - A, B
CUT 4 OF FABRIC
FRONT - A, B
CUT 2
FLAP LINE
FINISHED GARMENTS
VIEW - A
WAISTLINE
BACK - A, B
CUT 1 ON FOLD
1 1/4 IN. HEM ALLOWED
PLEAT

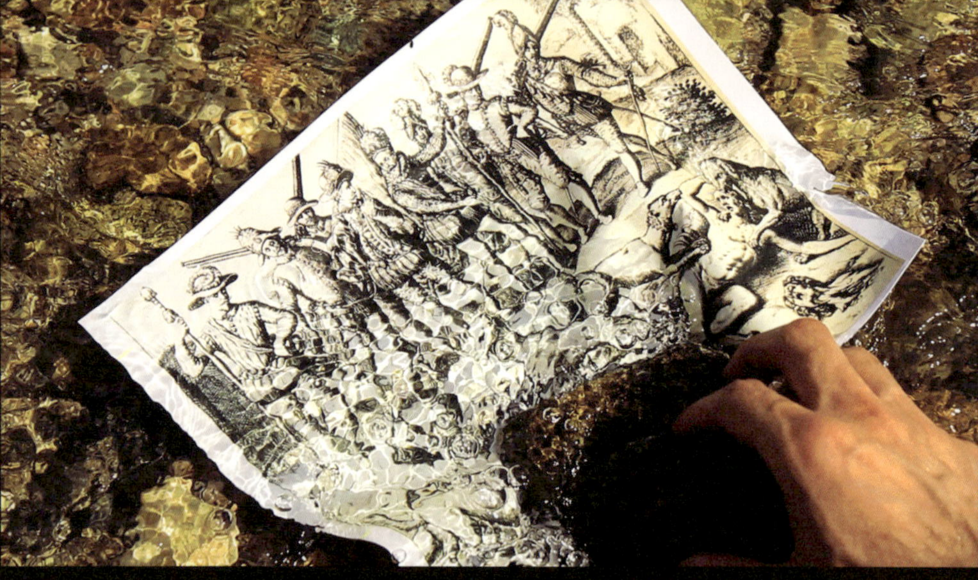

[PL. 99]

153

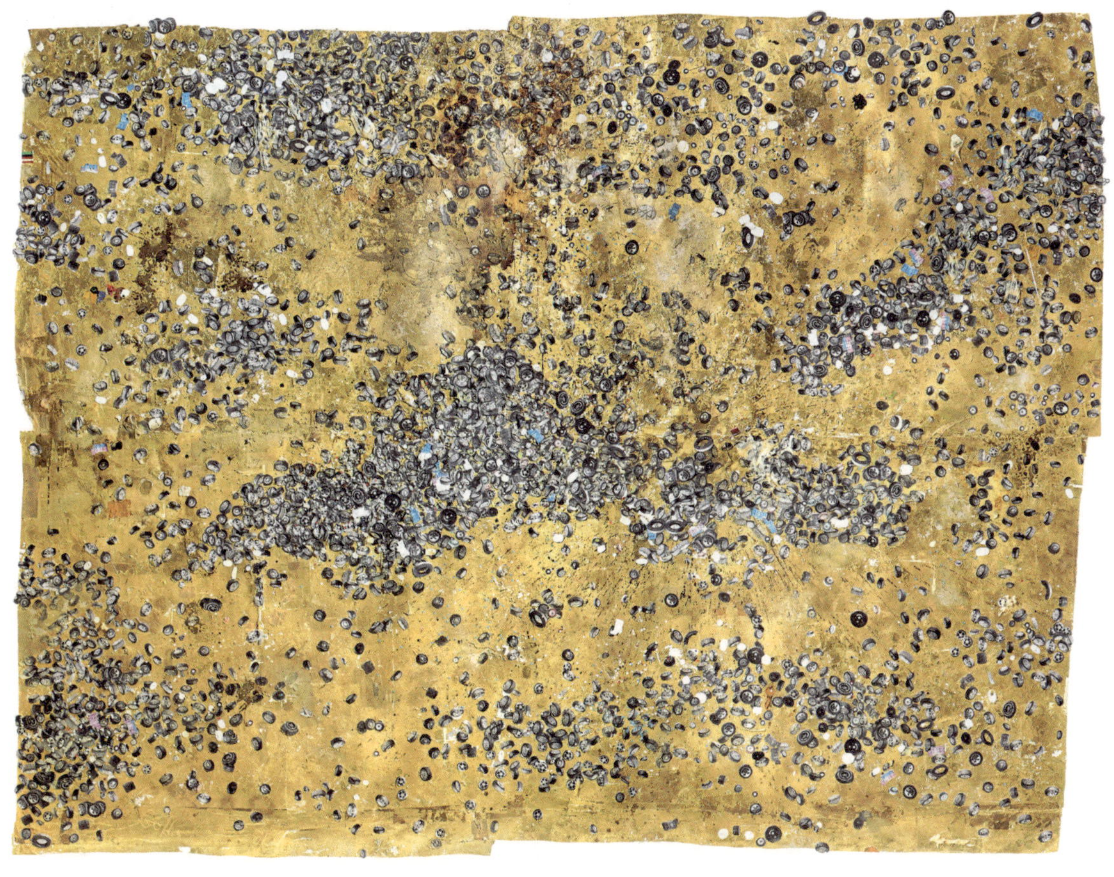

william cordova, *daniel boone, pat boone y mary boone (or firestone pero los olmecas venceran!)*, 2008

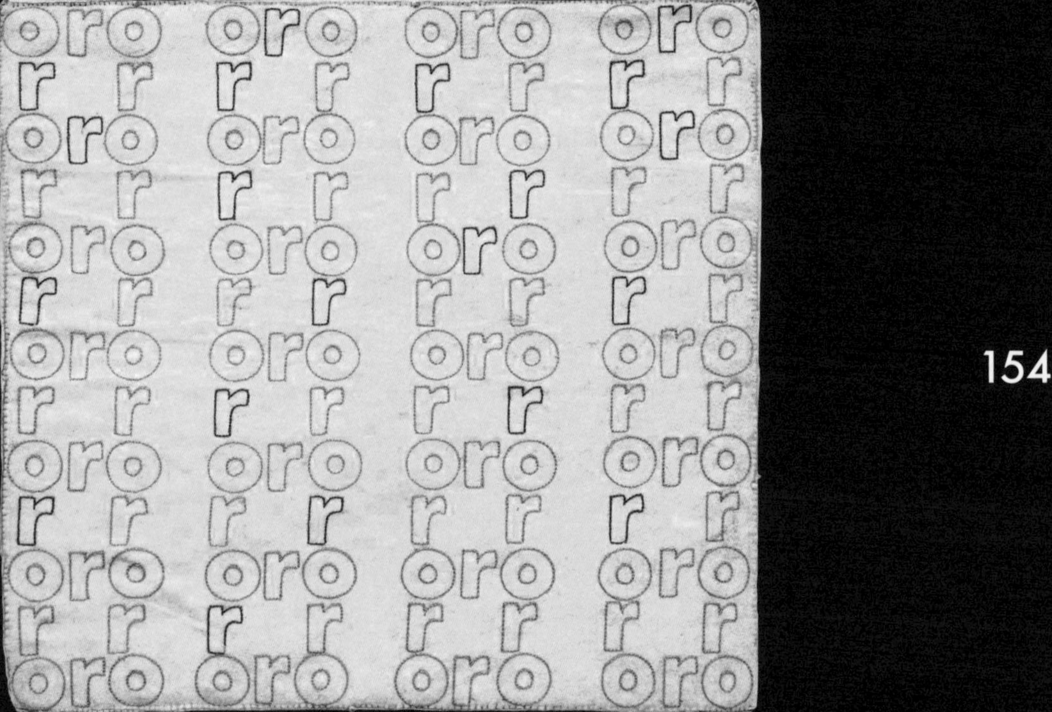
oro oro oro oro
r r r r r r r r
oro oro oro oro
r r r r r r r r
oro oro oro oro
r r r r r r r r
oro oro oro oro
r r r r r r r r
oro oro oro oro
r r r r r r r r
oro oro oro oro
r r r r r r r r
oro oro oro oro

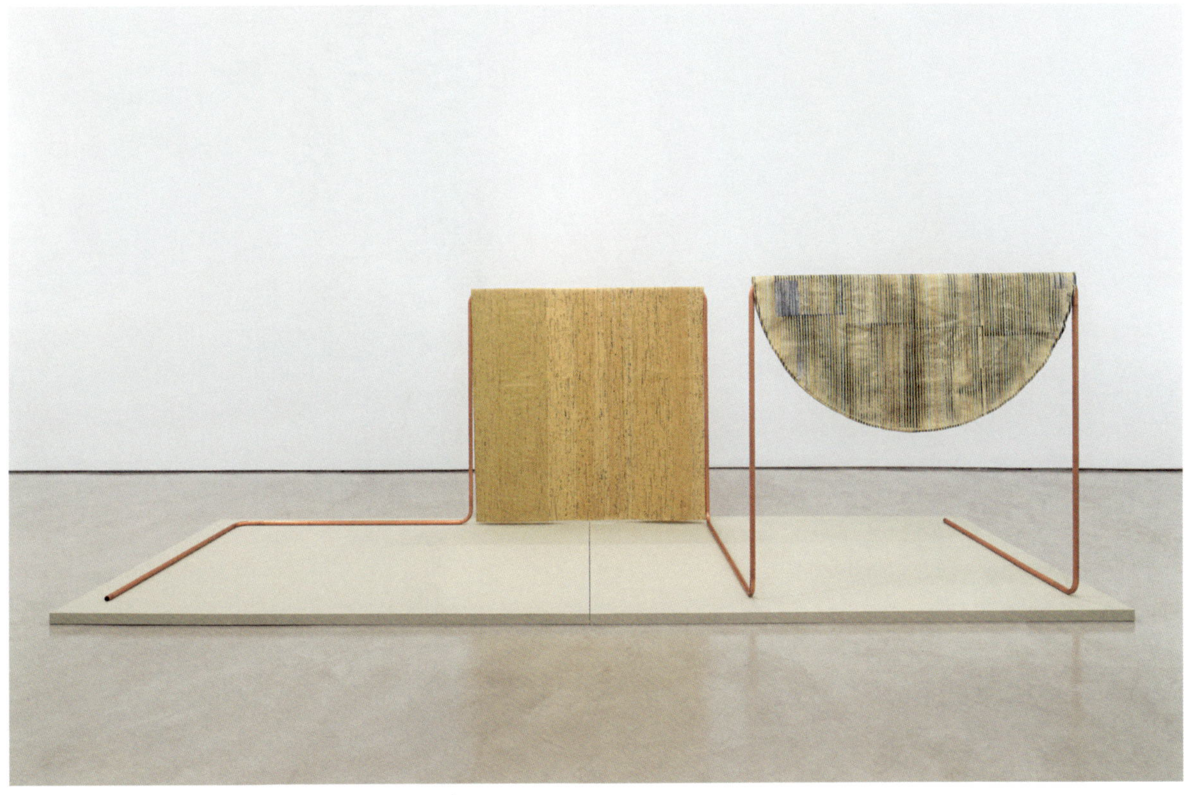

Ronny Quevedo, *el guarda meta de los cosmos (from the abyss)* (Meta guardian of the cosmos [from the abyss]), 2022

[PL. 102]

Olga de Amaral, *Estelas* (Stelae), 1996–2018

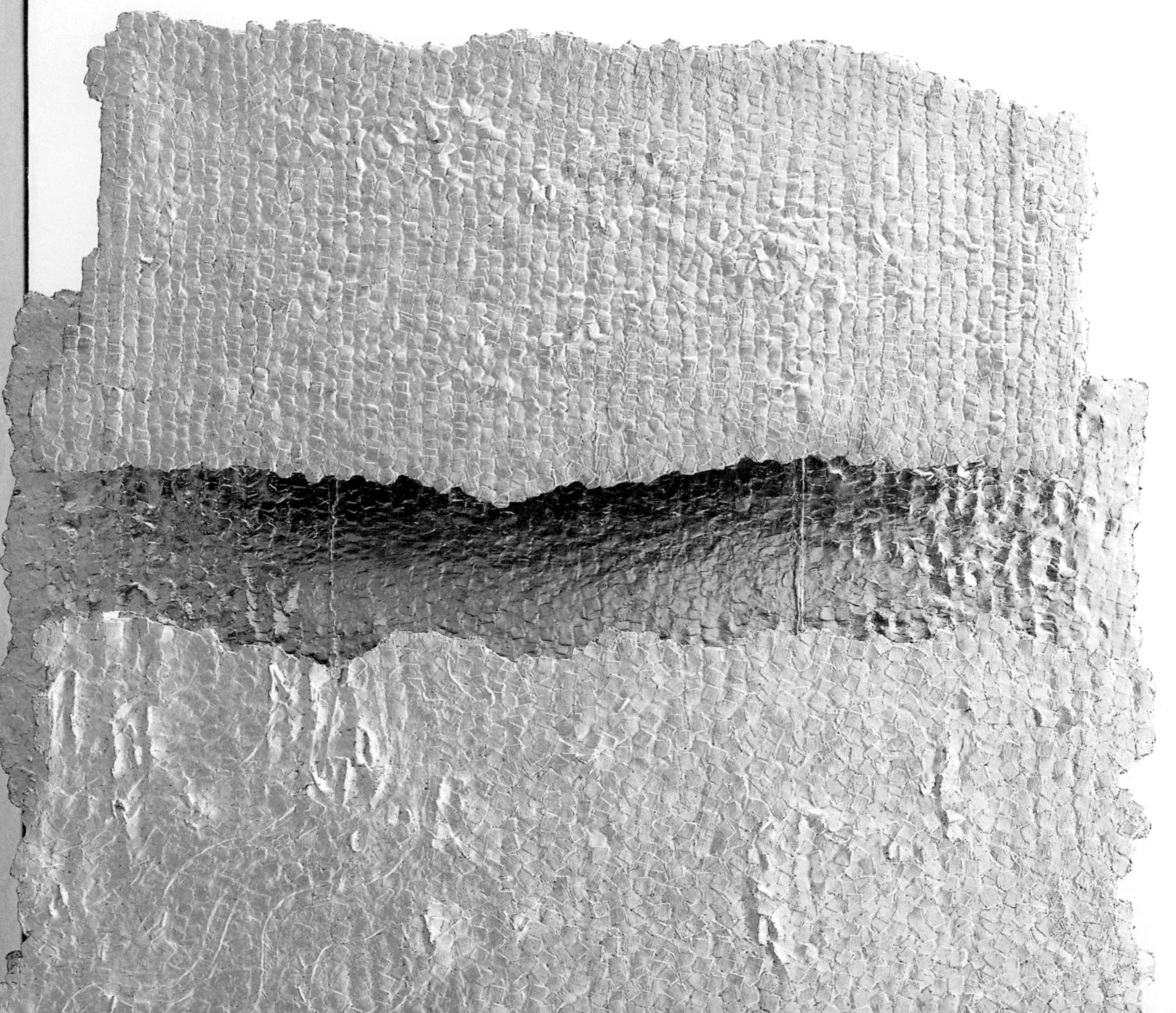

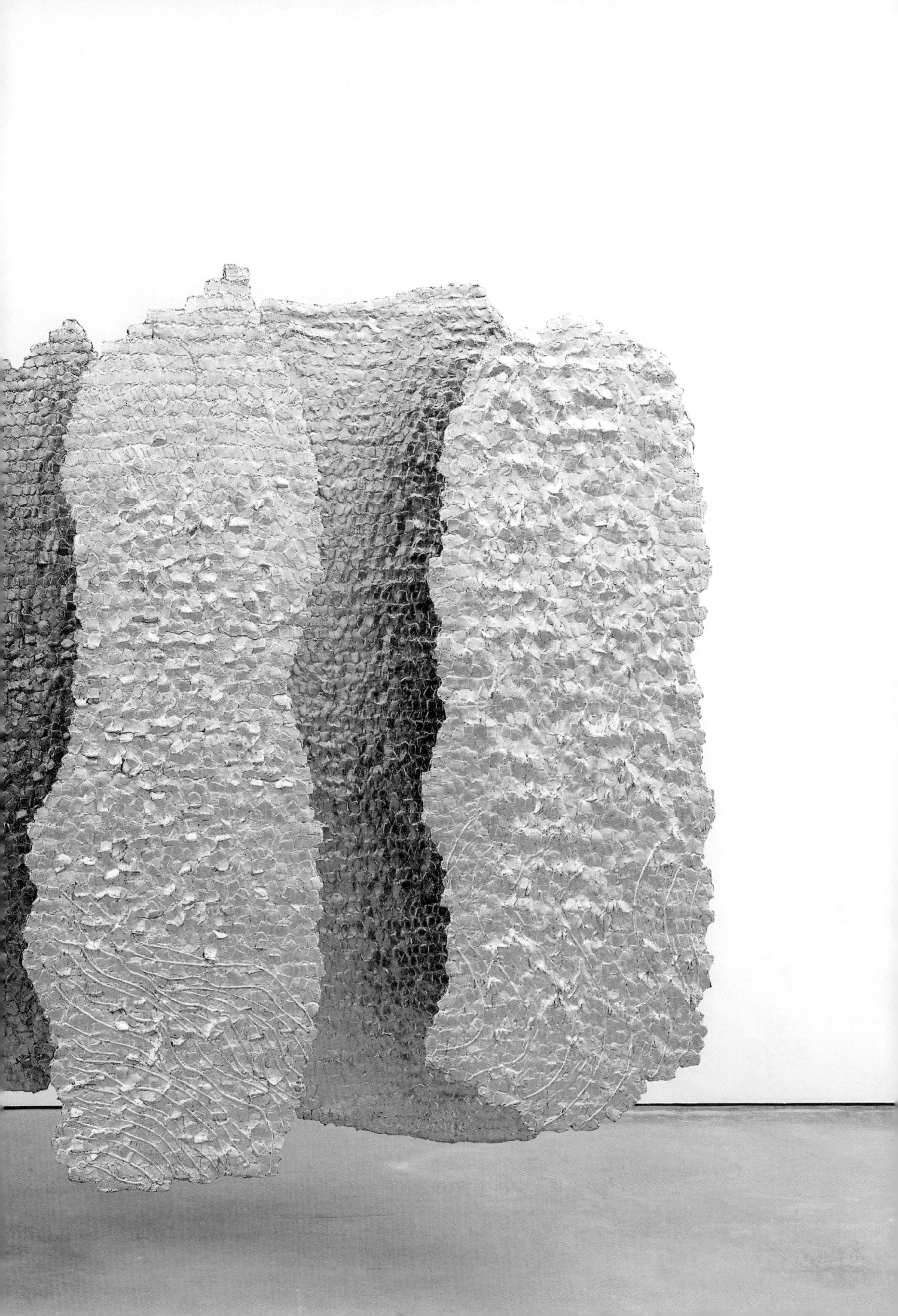

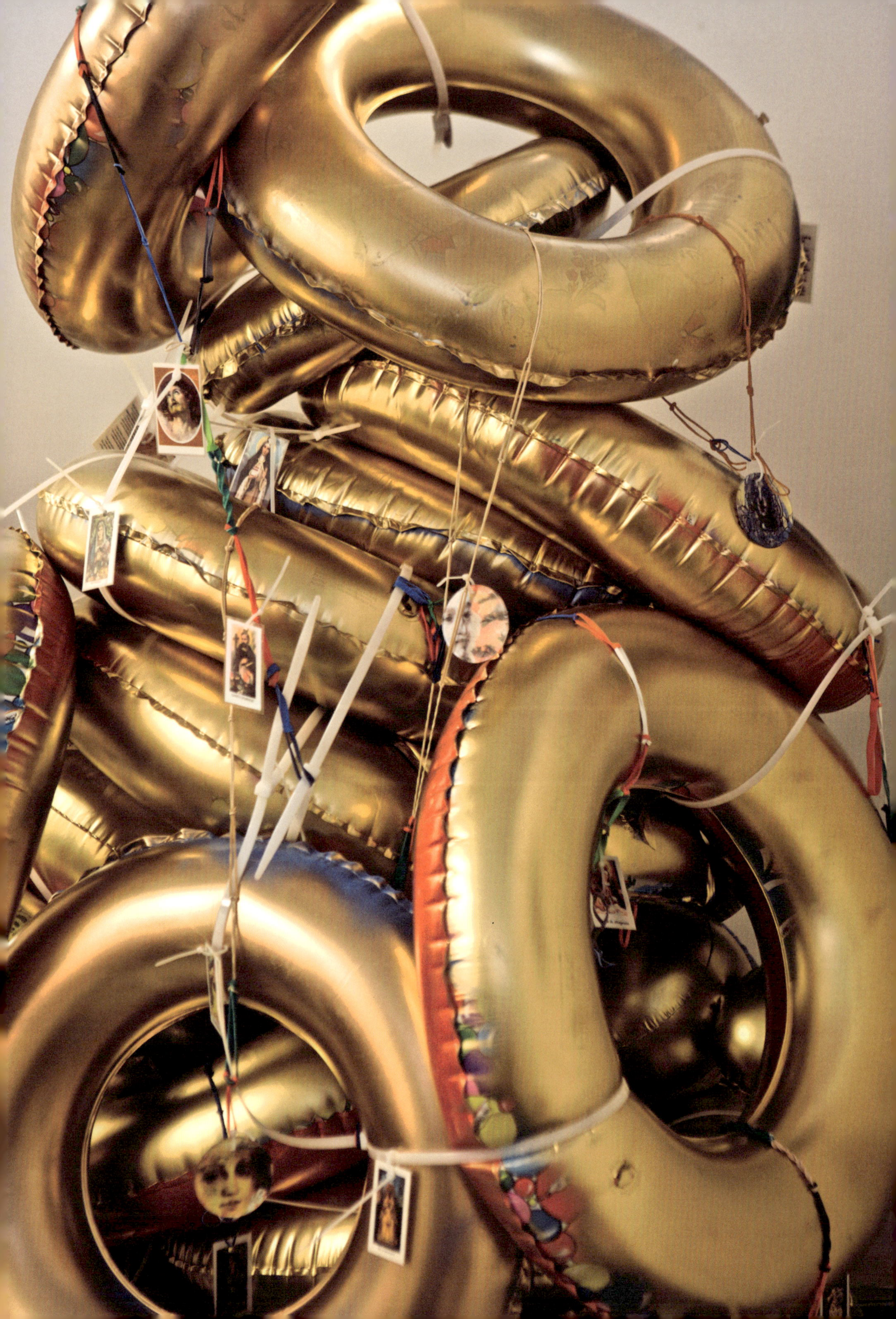

Scherezade Garcia, detail of *Cathedral* from the series *Theories of Freedom*, 2009–2014

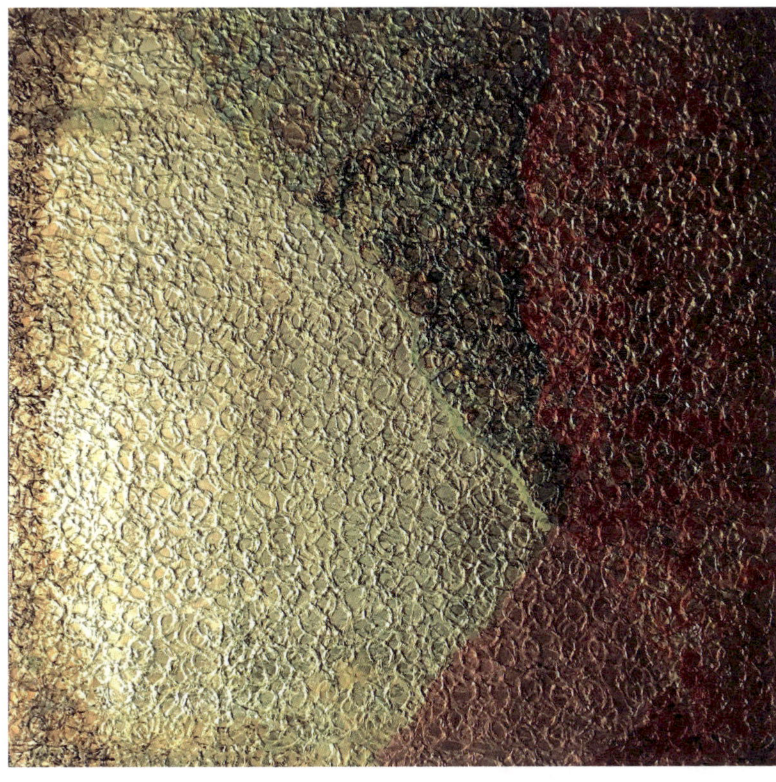

↑ [PL. 103]

Julia Santos Solomon, *Cresta*, 2016

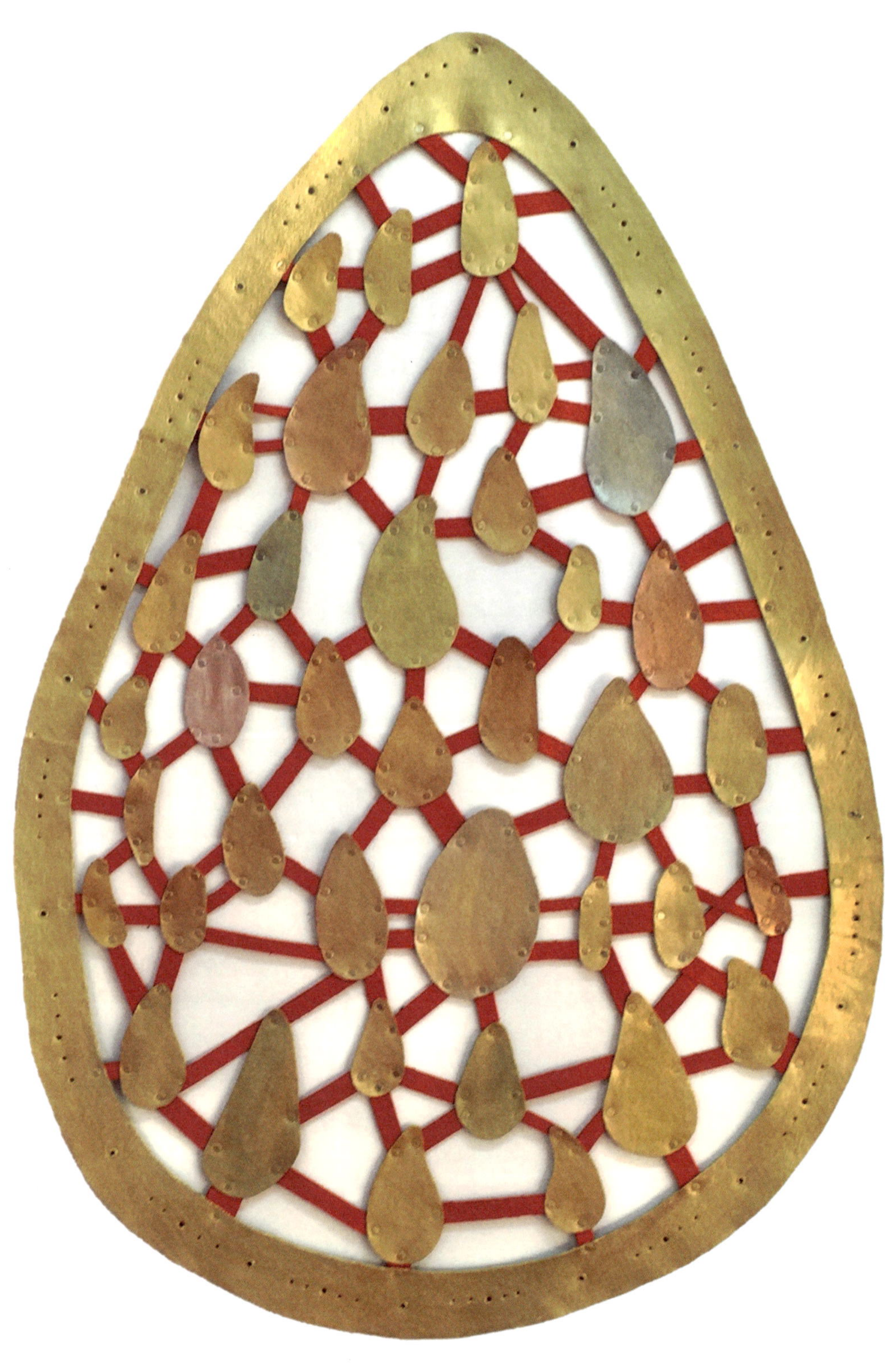

Leda Catunda, *Ovo Rei* (King egg), 2018

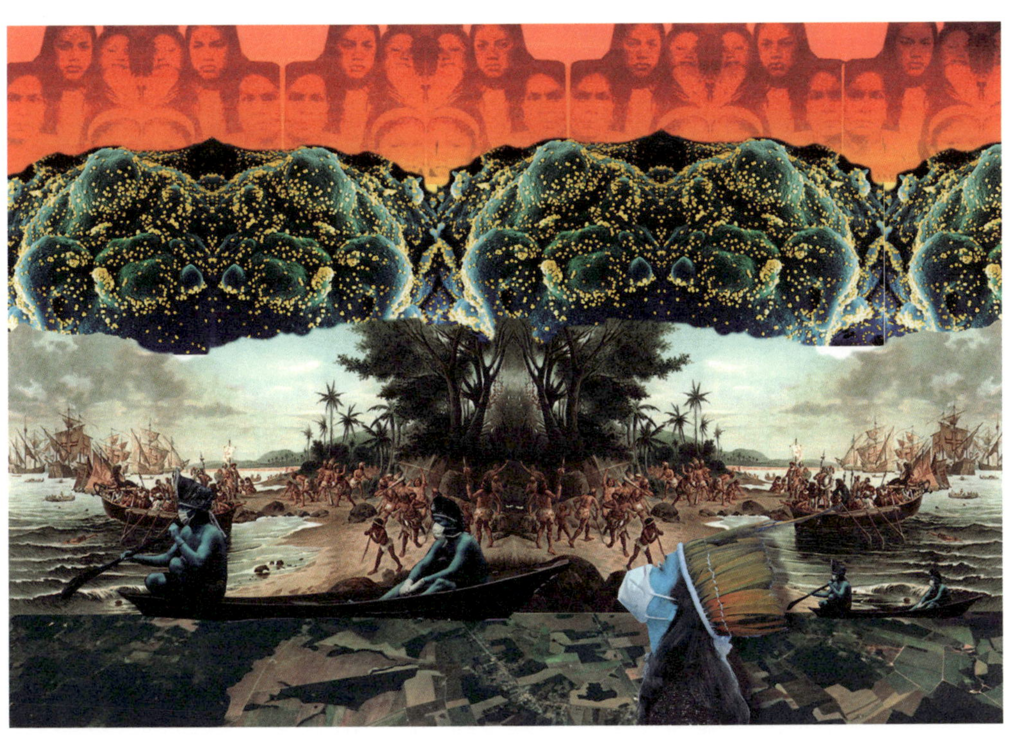

Moara Tupinambá, *Kuêra*, 2021

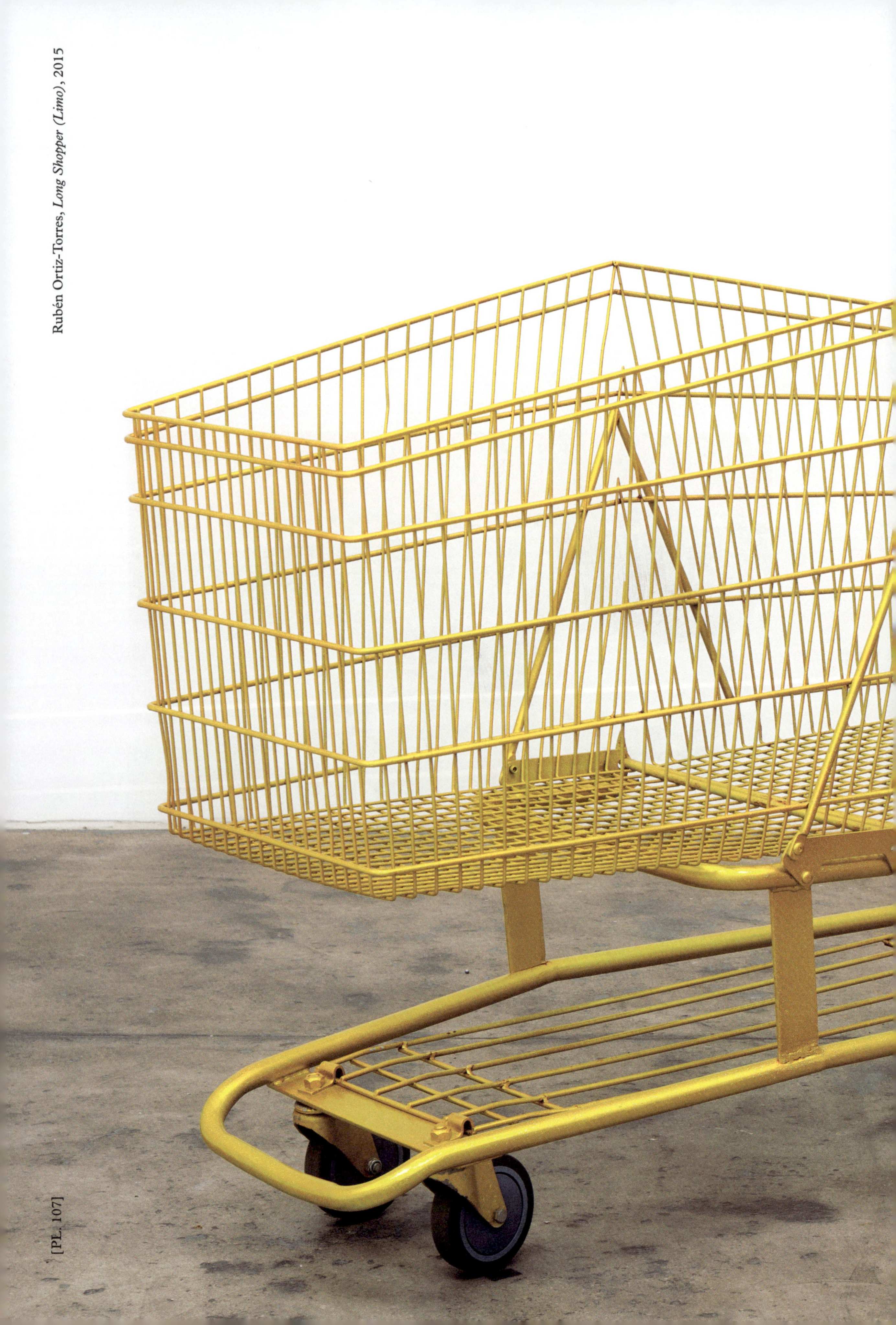

Rubén Ortiz-Torres, *Long Shopper (Limo)*, 2015

[PL. 107]

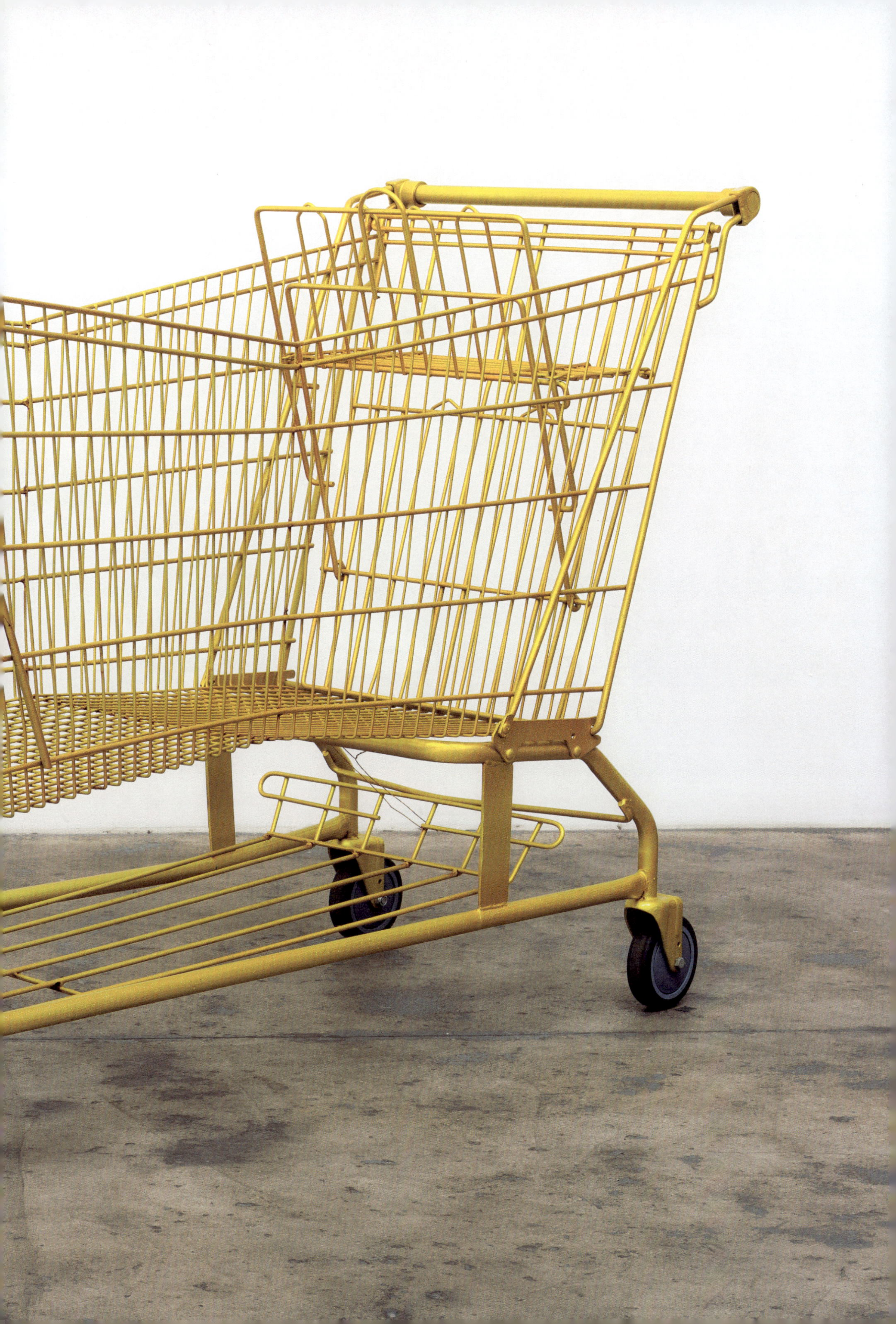

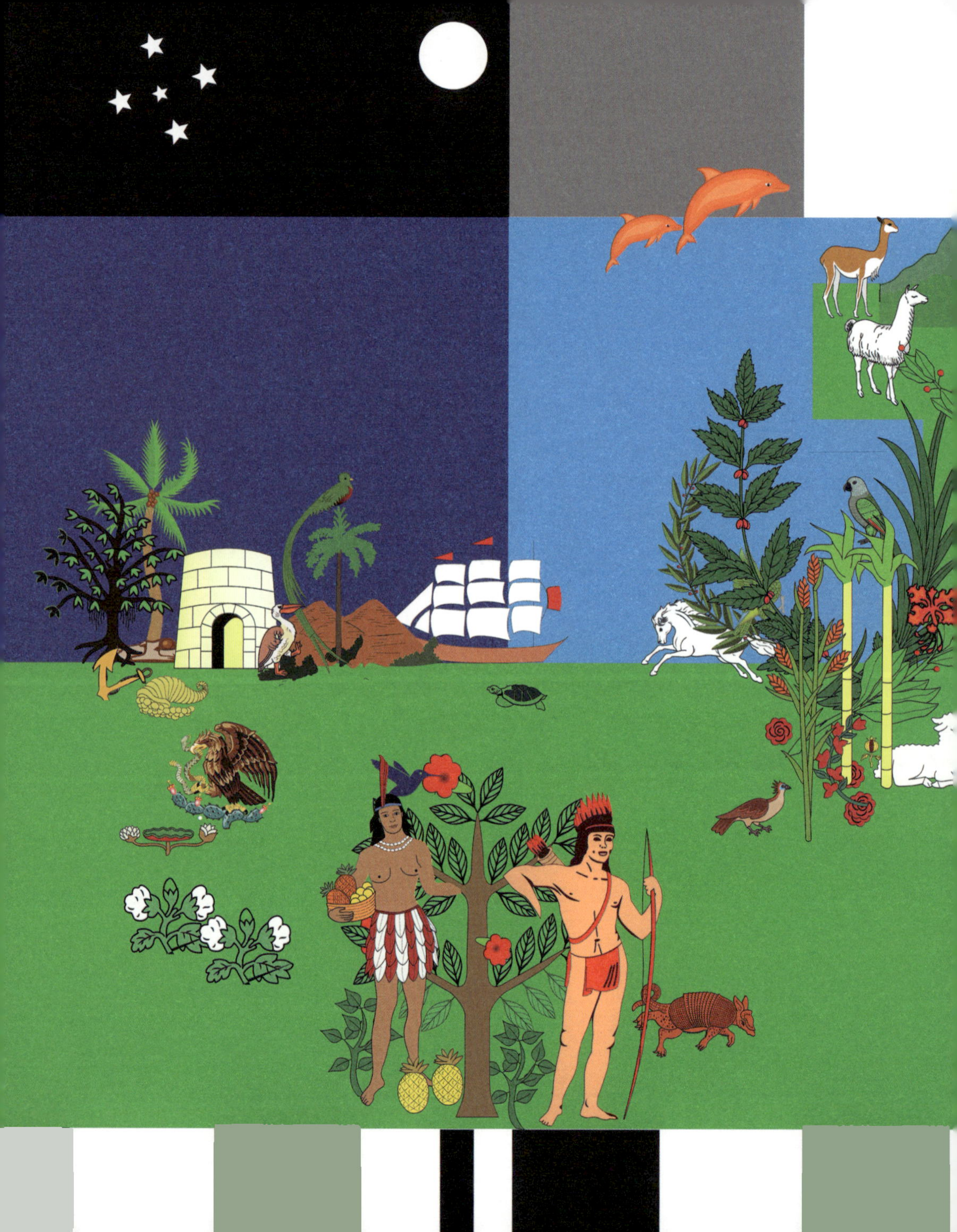

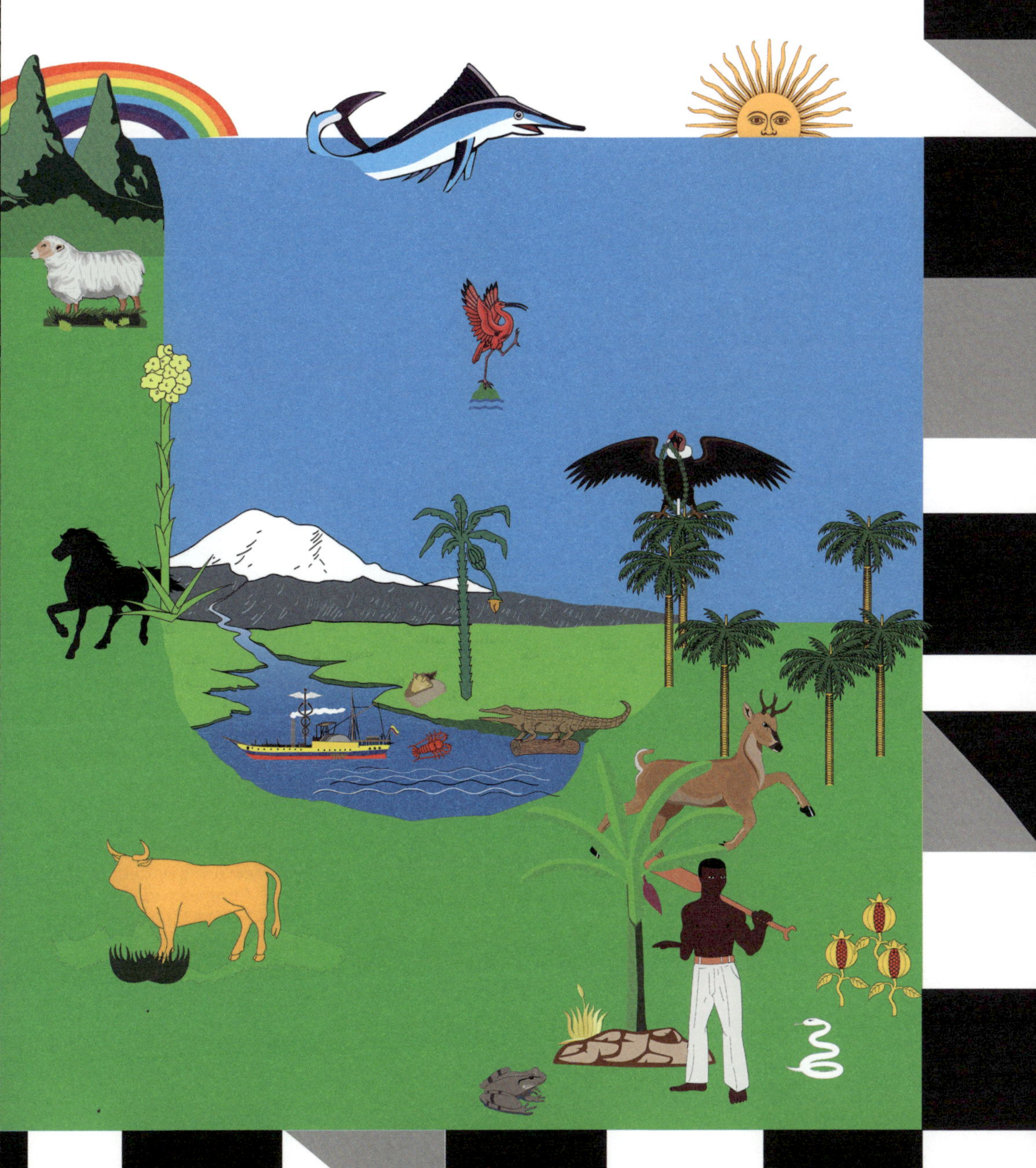

El Dorado: The Myth of Gold was organized in two parts. The first part was on view from September 6 to December 16, 2023 and the second part from January 24 to May 18, 2024. See indications in parentheses at the beginning of each caption.

PL. 75 P. 126
Alberta Whittle

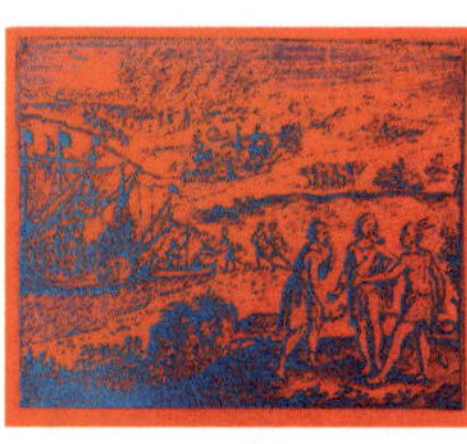

PL. 77 P. 127

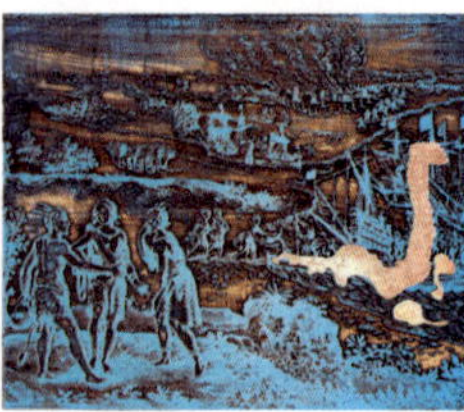

(I)
Jamestown Mythology: Amonute, 2023.
Laser-engraved woodblock print on Somerset Satin 300 gsm paper with saliva embossed in gold, 23 ⅝ × 26 ⅝ inches (60 × 67.5 cm).
Courtesy of the artist and The Modern Institute/Toby Webster Ltd., Glasgow

(I)
Jamestown Mythology: Amonute (turquoise), 2023.
Laser-engraved woodblock matrix with photo etched copper additions, 17 ⅜ × 20 ¼ inches (44 × 51.5 cm).
Courtesy of the artist and The Modern Institute/Toby Webster Ltd., Glasgow

← Alberta Whittle (b. 1980, Bridgetown) is an artist, researcher, and curator. Her work engages with the history of race and colonialism, often utilizing historical imagery. Whittle's *Jamestown Mythology: Amonute* reimagines Georg Keller's seventeenth-century engraving *The Abduction of Pocahontas*, rendering the previously monochromatic work in bright reds and blues. The seventeenth-century print was made to accompany a German translation of *True Discourse of the Present State of Virginia* by Ralph Hamor and was reprinted by Theodor de Bry in his 1624 publication *Novi Orbis Pars Dvodecima sive Descriptio Indiae Occidentalis.* In all three engravings, multiple events are compressed into the singular print, illustrating multiple episodes that led up to the abduction of Pocahontas and the English burning of the Powhatan village. In Whittle's reinterpretation of this work, she utilizes a bright red backdrop and blue ink, effectively flattening the sense of depth within the image. This effect suggests the historic flattening of historical narratives through the lens of Western historiography.

–Esther Levy

PL. 76 P. 128
Theodor de Bry

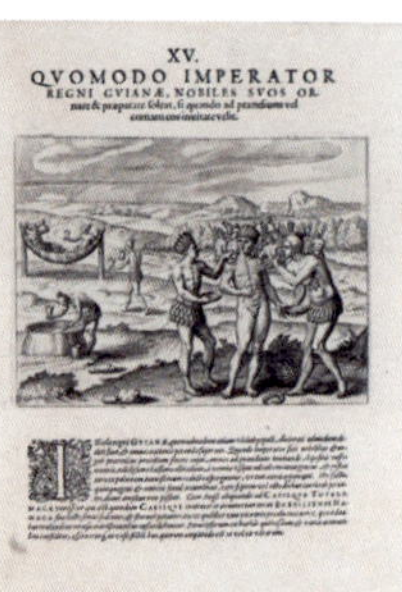

(I)
The Origin of the El Dorado Legend, 1599. Engraving, 12 ⅜ × 9 ⅛ inches (31.5 × 23.3 cm).
Courtesy of Proyecto Bachué Collection, Bogotá

← Although this printed image is rendered in black ink on white paper, we are meant to imagine the nude man in center foreground is covered with gold powder. The small black dots on his shoulders and torso represent shimmering gilt dust blown onto him by the man on the right. This scene, set in the landscape of "Guiana" (modern-day eastern Venezuela), reflects not an actual event but rather the imaginings of Englishman Sir Walter Raleigh. In 1595, Raleigh traveled to this territory, which he fervently believed was El Dorado. He found no gold but upon returning to England published a popular and apocryphal travel account largely accepted as fact. The de Bry family published a portion of Raleigh's text alongside this print in 1599.

Here Raleigh describes feasting and adornment rituals among "Guiana's" Indigenous elites. He never actually saw a gilded man, nor did the print's artist. Thus, the Indigenous peoples are fashioned as Tupinambá, who lived hundreds of miles to the south but for many European artists were the representational model for all Indigenous Americans. Raleigh's text borrowed from other colonizers' writings, which claimed that El Dorado was the realm of a powerful Indigenous ruler covered in gold. In (ostensibly) seeing such a person, the location and existence of the golden city could thus be confirmed. Raleigh's report, as fictional as the imagined gold in this print, was meant to encourage the painfully exploitative European search for El Dorado, which for many Indigenous groups was all too real.

–Sarah Mallory

PL. 84 P. 136
Theodor de Bry

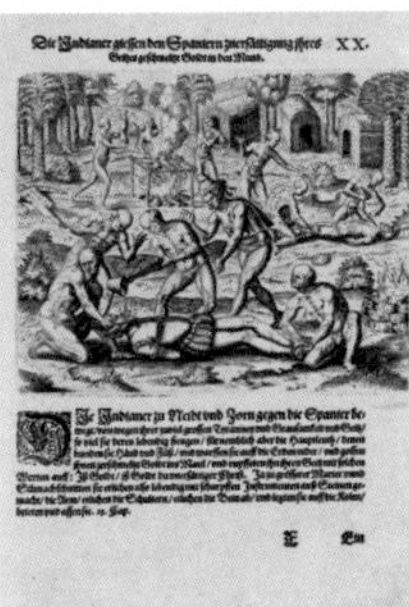

(I)
The Spanish Are Fed Liquid Gold, 1599.
Engraving, 13 ⅜ × 9 ½ inches (34 × 24 cm).
Courtesy of Proyecto Bachué Collection, Bogotá

← In the center foreground of this print, a man is forcefully restrained while liquid is poured into his mouth. The liquid is molten gold, and the man is a conquistador—a Spanish colonizer who, often through violent acts under the auspices of the Catholic Church, extracted wealth and labor from Indigenous Americans. In this print, however, we see what are meant to be Indigenous Americans attacking a Spanish man. The artist had limited knowledge of the Americas and thus imagined Indigenous peoples in the form of classical Roman statuary.

For some Europeans, this image would have equally villainized Indigenous Americans and the Spanish. The accompanying text claims that so offensive was the Spanish quest for gold, Indigenous men poured the molten metal down conquistadores' throats while telling them to "eat." Little evidence supports that the author of the book in which the print was published, Italian Girolamo Benzoni, or anyone else witnessed this event. However, Benzoni's story supported a common trope: chroniclers of the period described the notorious Spanish search for gold as an unquenchable thirst. This print scorns that thirst and falsely depicts Indigenous peoples as violently punishing such yens.

Myriad books and pamphlets recounted, and sometimes exaggerated, Spanish cruelties throughout the Americas. These publications, frequently authored or published by Protestants, question the morals of the Spanish Catholic regime, which was also waging war against Protestants throughout Europe. Such critiques often ignored mistreatment of Indigenous groups by Protestants. The de Bry family, supporters of Protestantism, published this image and Benzoni's text in 1594 as part of *Collectiones peregrinationum in Indiam Occidentalem et Indiam Orientalem* (Collected travels in the East Indies and West Indies), a book series about the Americas.

–Sarah Mallory

PL. 81 P. 132
Theodor de Bry

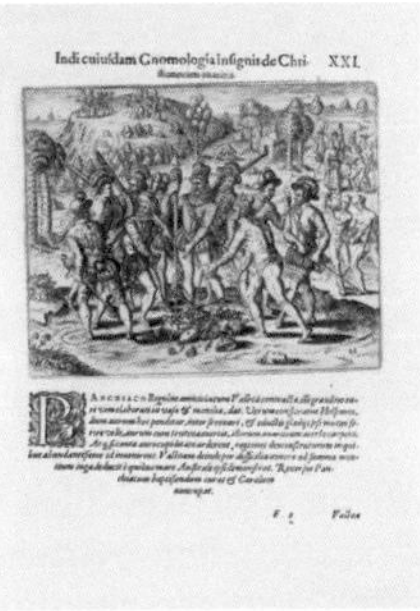

PL. 80 P. 131

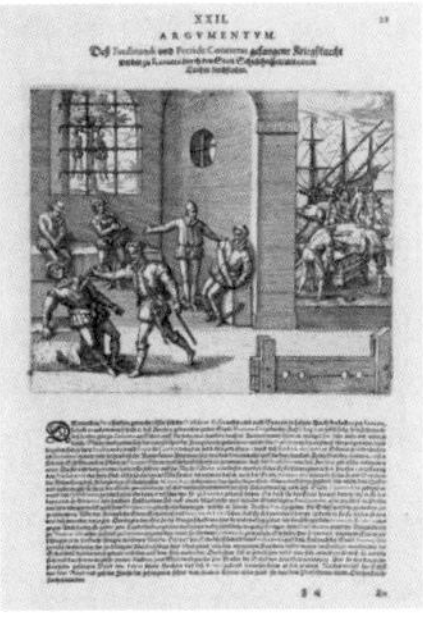

(I)
Balboa and His Men Quarrel Over Gold, 1594.
Engraving, 13 ⅜ × 9 ⅜ inches (34.1 × 23.7 cm).
Courtesy of Proyecto Bachué Collection, Bogotá

(I)
Inca Gold is Brought to Panama, 1596.
Engraving, 12 ⅝ × 8 ¾ inches (32 × 22.2 cm).
Courtesy of Proyecto Bachué Collection, Bogotá

PL. 78 P. 129
Pablo Helguera

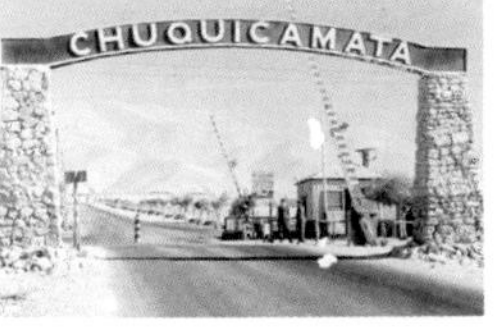

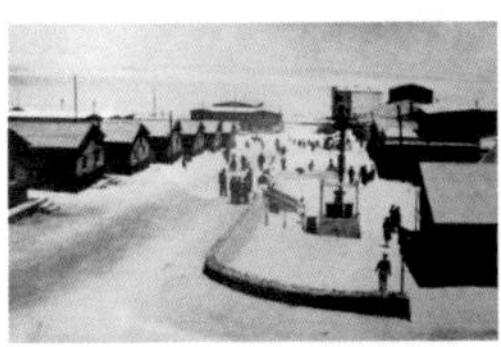

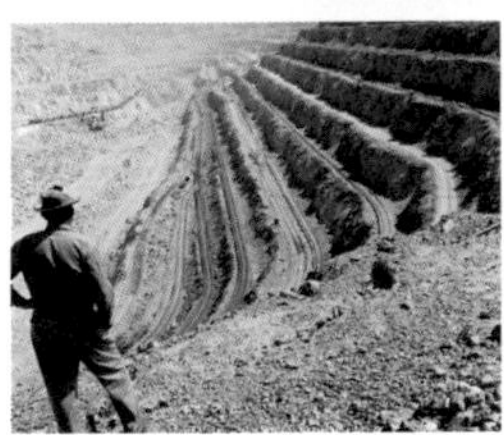

Pablo Helguera (b. 1971, Mexico City) is an artist, author, and educator who focuses on a wide range of topics including history, pedagogy, sociolinguistics, ethnography, memory, and the absurd. Helguera's artistic practice follows a pedagogic methodology by studying the relationship between language and art, as well as the social dynamics of contemporary art in our daily lives. Helguera's *Chuquicamata* (2023) focuses on the Chilean mine of the same name, which is the largest open-pit copper mine in the world. During the early twentieth century, the mine was owned and operated by the Guggenheim family, perhaps the most prominent family connected to cultural institutions around the world. The work links metal extraction to the wealth of art institutions with the power of creating cultural narratives for the Global South. The video consists of a slide show of archival photographs and images of the mine, surrounding desert landscape, and nearby infrastructure, and it includes a voice-over narration of a detailed socioeconomic account of the region in 1915.

–Sarah Lopez

(I)
Chuquicamata, 2023.
Video, 7 minutes, 48 seconds.
Courtesy of the artist

PL. 106 P. 161
Moara Tupinambá

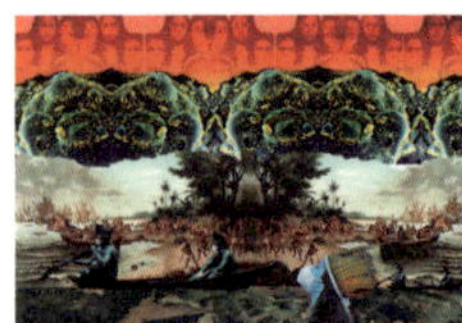

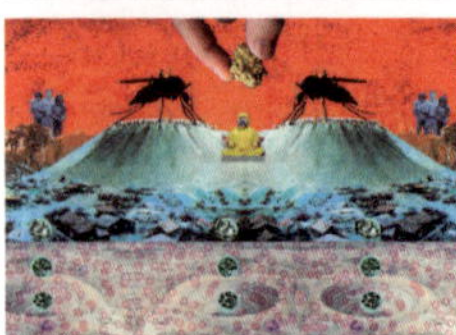

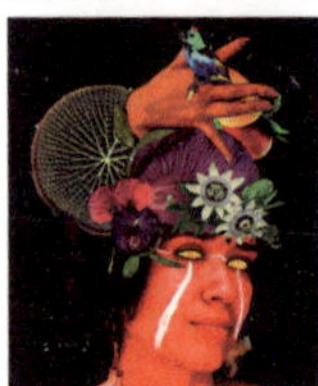

Moara Tupinambá (b. 1983, Belém) is an Indigenous artist from the Tupinambá people in Brazil interested in Indigenous Amazonian culture and activism. The artist creates landscapes by juxtaposing contemporary and historical images, such as exotifying photographs of unnamed Indigenous subjects. By so doing, she questions the continuity of colonialism into the present while engaging with a canonical art historical genre that often reproduced the white European projections onto a space. In her landscapes the artist depicts apocalyptic situations including mining pits, environmental and social degradation, symbols of disease such as mosquitoes and viruses, and industrial buildings. In her self-portrait, *Moara de Maery*, she portrays herself with a crown of flowers and a delicate hand holding a bird, and with golden eyes which, to the artist, symbolize transcendence.

–Tie Jojima

(I)
Kuêra, 2021.
Photographic print,
dimensions variable.
Courtesy of the artist

(I)
Takuá, 2021.
Photographic print,
dimensions variable.
Courtesy of the artist

(II)
Moara de Maery (Autoretrato),
2020. Photographic print,
dimensions variable.
Courtesy of the artist

PL. 82 P. 133
Tiago Sant'Ana

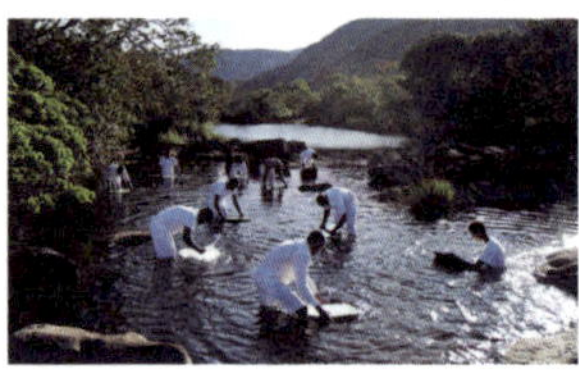

In his artistic practice, Tiago Sant'Ana (b. 1990, Santo Antônio de Jesusin) explores memory and history, especially those relating to the experiences of Afro-Brazilian populations and the legacy of colonialism in the country. In his video *Chão de estrelas*, shot at Chapada Diamantina in the state of Bahia, a historical site of gold and precious metal extraction, the artist references the history of mining in colonial Brazil. The video depicts Black men in the action of panning for gold in a river, but instead of holding pans or sieves, each of them holds a mirror. Addressing how the history of enslavement constructed the subjectivity of Black people in Brazil, the video also tells of strategies of survival, suggesting other possible narrative paths for Blacks in the country.

–Tie Jojima

(II)
Chão de estrelas (Ground
of stars), 2022.
Video, 8 minutes, 51 seconds.
Courtesy of the artist
and Leme Gallery

PL. 83 PP. 134–135
Luis Romero

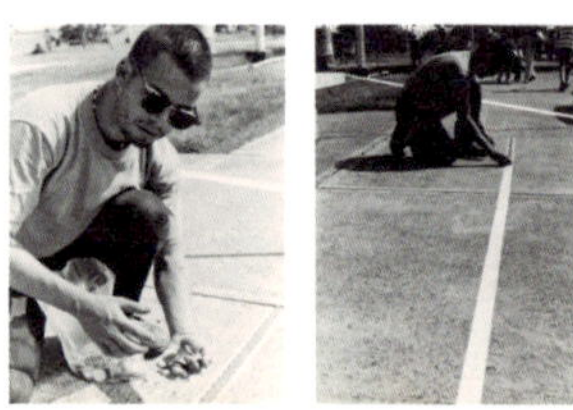

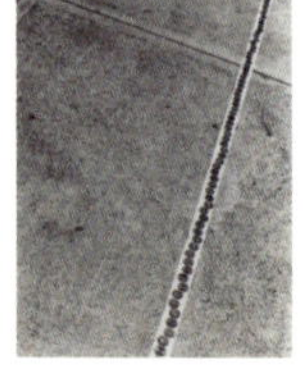

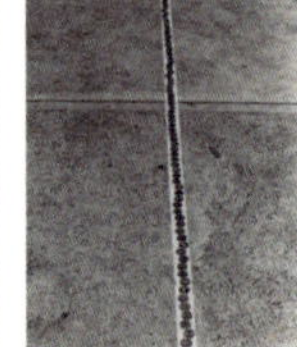

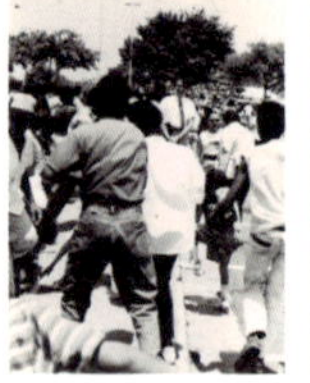

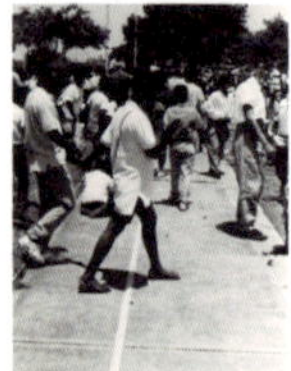

PL. 108 PP. 164–165

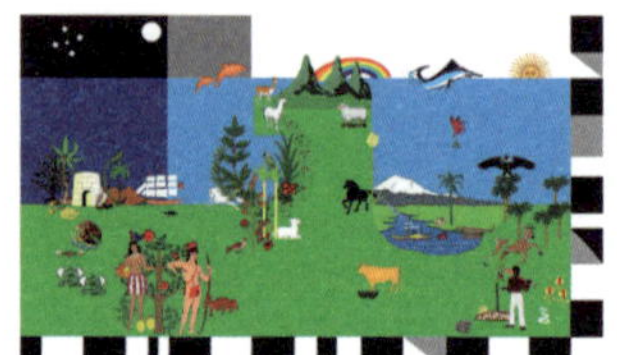

(II)
El Ralego, 1992.
Six black-and-white
photographs, 4 ⅝ × 3 ½
inches each (12.4 × 8.9 cm).
Courtesy of the artist

(I and II)
El Dorado, 2012–23.
Digital print on fabric,
60 ⅛ × 98 ⅛ inches,
(152.78 × 249.24 cm).
Courtesy of the artist

← Luis Romero's (b. 1967, Caracas) project *El Ralego* was created for the 1992 III Bienal Nacional de Arte de Guayana, and it is titled after the name the Spaniards gave to the English pirate and explorer Walter Raleigh (1552–1618), who explored the area in search of El Dorado. For his ephemeral intervention, Romero requested the 10,000 bolivars given to selected projects in the smallest denomination and placed the 2,000 coins in a line parallel to the Orinoco River, in the same direction that Raleigh navigated in 1594. Once all the coins were installed, the area was opened to the public, which chaotically ran to grab the coins, creating a parallel to the desperation for gold of the sixteenth-century explorers.

The flag *El Dorado*, whose first version was created in 2012, was conceived when the artist realized that most flags and emblems in the Americas used images that referred to idyllic representations of territory. Combining them into a Garden of Eden–like composition, Romero highlights the absurdity of this conception of the Americas as paradise and imagines an ironic flag for the Panamerican dream. The black-and-white guard follows the style of African flags and refers to the successes and losses of the continent's national histories at the same time as it evokes the abstract constructivist and geometric spirit that defined so much of modern Latin American art history.

–Aimé Iglesias Lukin

PL. 84 P. 137
Andrés Bedoya

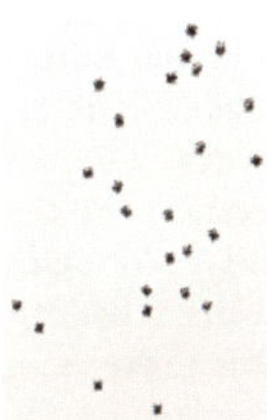

Andrés Bedoya's (b. 1978, La Paz) silver works address the importance of the metal for Bolivian history and the Alto Perú, where the Potosí mine defined the commerce and political history of the region for centuries and continues to do so, through the extraction of lithium and other soil materials. Using traditional jewelry techniques, Bedoya created small flies that inundate the gallery space like an undesirable plague or memento mori reminding us of the natural circles of life and death while also evoking the thousands of lives affected by mining and the consequences of greed.

–Aimé Iglesias Lukin

(II)
Moscas (Flies), 2022.
Silver, 9 ⅞ × 9 ⅞ inches
(25 × 25.5 cm).
Courtesy of the artist

PL. 87 P. 139
Charles Bentley and Robert H. Schomburgk

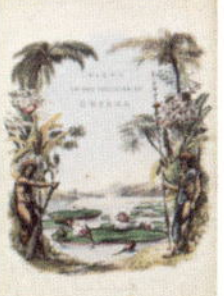

PL. 90 P. 142

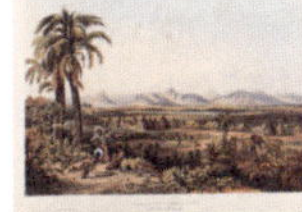

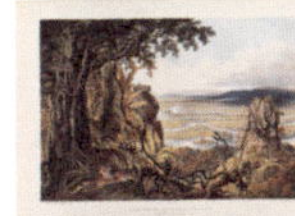

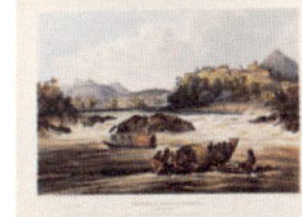

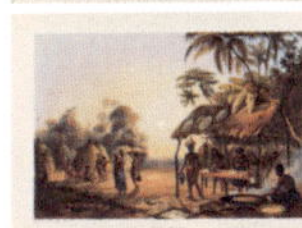

PL. 87 P. 140
Johann Moritz Rugendas

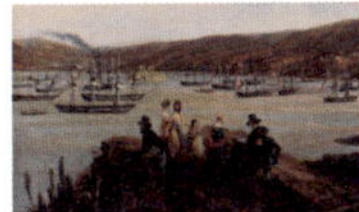

PL. 94 P. 147
Ernest Charton de Treville

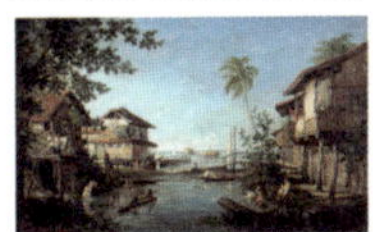

(I)
Charles Bentley and Robert H. Schomburgk, *Twelve Views in the Interior of the Guianas* (London: Ackermann & Co., 1840).
Lithograph (decorated title),
14 ¾ × 21 ½ inches
(37.5 × 54.6 cm).
Colección Patricia Phelps de Cisneros

(I)
Johann Moritz Rugendas, *View of Valparaíso*, 1842.
Oil on canvas, 25 × 36 ¼ × 1 inches (63.5 × 92 × 2.5 cm).
Colección Patricia Phelps de Cisneros.
Photo: Carlos Germán Rojas

(I)
Ernest Charton de Treville, *Guayaquil*, 1849.
Oil on canvas, 15 ¾ × 23 ¼ inches (40 × 59.1 cm).
Colección Patricia Phelps de Cisneros.
Photo: Gregg Stanger

PL. 89 P. 141
Alfredo Jaar

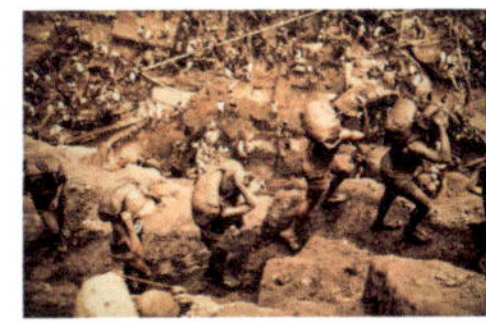

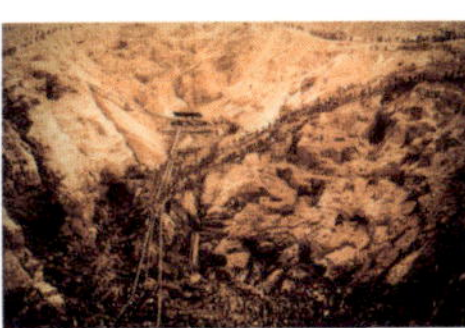

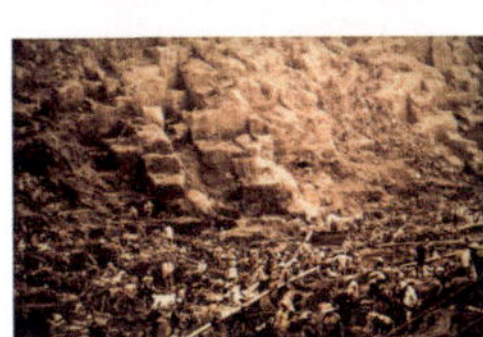

Alfredo Jaar (b. 1956, Santiago de Chile) is a multidisciplinary artist who engages with themes of inequity, discrimination, and migration in the Americas and beyond. Jaar utilizes often frank depictions of his subjects as a means by which to unearth the realities of those who are often overlooked or underrepresented in mainstream American media. For the series *Gold in the Morning*, Jaar traveled to the Serra Pelada gold mine in Brazil to photograph the conditions of the independent miners, or *garimpeiros*, that labored there. The Serra Pelada was an open pit, hand dug by the thousands of *garimpeiros* who sought to profit from its resources. Jaar's series sheds light on the extraction not only of Latin America's natural resources but also of the individual risk taken for the sake of profit. By mounting the photographs on lightboxes typically used for advertisements, Jaar adds an ironic twist to the display of dozens of mud-covered laborers and the lure of potentially finding riches from their toil.

–Esther Levy

(I)
Gold in the Morning, 1985.
Lightbox with color transparency, 12 ⅝ × 18 ½ × 5 ⅛ inches
(32 × 47 × 13 cm) each.
Proyecto Bachué Collection, Bogotá

PL. 91 P. 143
Nancy La Rosa and Juan Salas Carreño

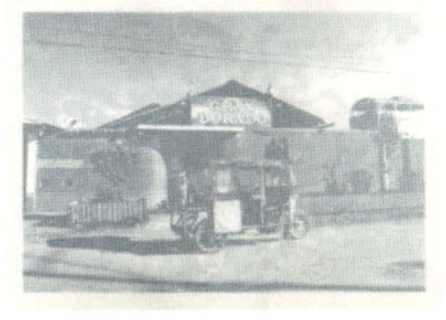

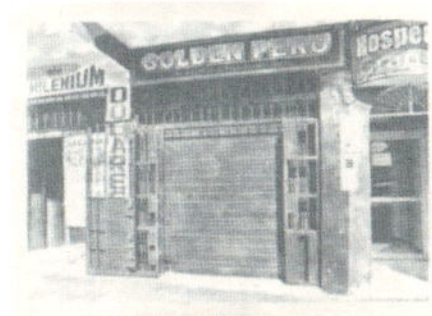

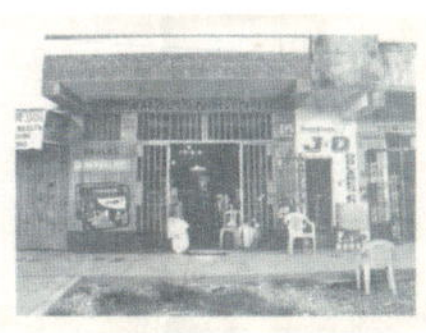

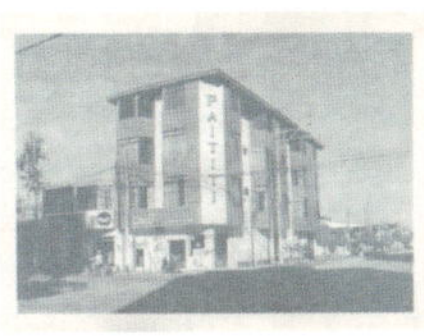

Peruvian artists Nancy La Rosa (b. 1980, Lima) and Juan Salas Carreño (b. 1982, Cusco) are interested in researching and exploring social, economic, and environmental issues resulting from metal extraction in the Amazon. During the Hawapi arts residency in the mining town of Madre de Dios in the Peruvian Amazon, the artists photographed storefronts, hotels, bars, and other commercial spaces, all of which were given names referring to gold extraction or to the myth of El Dorado, including the Quechua word for "El Dorado," *Paititi*.

–Tie Jojima

(I)
Mirages (Espejismos), 2015.
Silk screen prints on paper, 9 ¼ × 12 ⅝ inches
(23.5 × 32 cm) each.
Courtesy of the artists

PL. 94 P. 146

Ana María Millán

Ana María Millán (b. 1975, Cali) lives in Berlin and works with animation and video, often resulting in funny and ironic narratives that question the power behind established narratives. For *Dinastía*, she invited non-actors to read aloud selected lines from Werner Herzog's iconic 1972 film *Aguirre, the Wrath of God*, a film based on the deranged actions of Pedro de Aguirre in an expedition started in 1560 in search of El Dorado. The lines, decontextualized from the dramatic and tragic film from which they are extracted, are comically read by her friends to a pillow, while holding a dog, and in other disconcerting situations. The video thus invokes the madness of the historical character as portrayed by Herzog, at the same time that it puts into evidence how the film reiterates the European point of view of America as a land up for grabs by giving voice and protagonism to the conquistadores over the Indigenous people they encountered. The selection of speakers, some Colombian and others German, connects with the artists' original and chosen homes and at the same time refers to Herzog's point of view as a European himself.

–Aimé Iglesias Lukin

(I)
Dinastía (Dynasty), 2014.
HD video, 3 minutes,
55 seconds.
Courtesy of the artist and
Instituto de Visión

PL. 96 PP. 148–149

Fernando Bryce

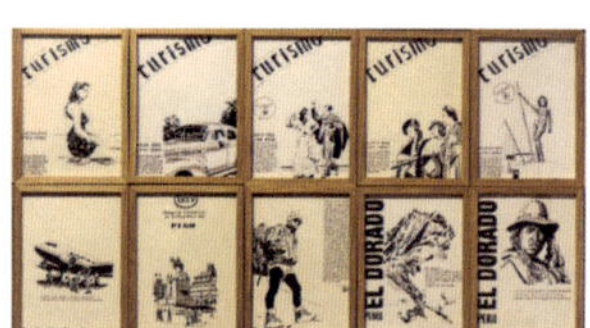

Fernando Bryce (b. 1965, Lima) has created a body of work in which he copies magazines and printed materials on Latin American and Western politics of the postwar period in ink drawings. In *Turismo El Dorado* he addresses the picturesque representations of Peru between 1932 and 2001 in advertisements and brochures promoting tourism in the country. The neutralized and controllable image of Peru promoted by these ads is emphasized by Bryce to demonstrate the double sword of tourism, an industry many populations rely upon but that is usually based on a view of the local population that is created for export and nonpoliticized. Continuing the stereotypes of travelers' books during the eighteenth and nineteenth centuries, touristic visual cultures neutralize the agency of the Indigenous populations to imagine the land as a peaceful, idyllic oasis to visit.

–Aimé Iglesias Lukin

(II)
Turismo El Dorado (El Dorado tourism), 2000.
Fifty ink on paper drawings,
11 ¾ × 8 ¼ inches
(29.8 × 21 cm) each.
Courtesy of Track 16
and the artist

PL. 97 PP. 150–151

Ronny Quevedo

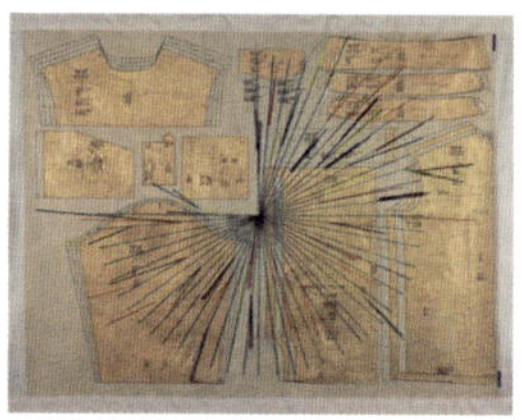

PL. 101 P. 155

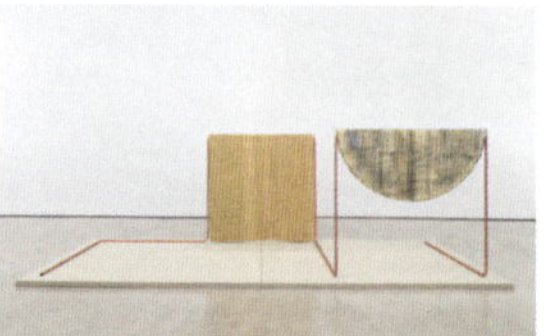

(II)
los desaparecidos (the arbiter of time) (The disappeared [the arbiter of time]), 2018.
Wax, pattern paper, and gold leaf on muslin, 48 × 60 inches
(121.92 × 152.4 cm).
Denver Art Museum:
Purchased with generous funds from the Marion G. Hendrie Fund, Ralph L. & Florence R. Burgess Trust, and Alianza de las Artes Americanas in honor of Ruth Tomlingson, 2019.85.
© Ronny Quevedo.
Photography courtesy
of Denver Art Museum

(I)
el guarda meta de los cosmos (from the abyss) (Meta guardian of the cosmos [from the abyss]), 2022.
Mixed media in three parts,
60 × 179 ¾ × 60 inches
(152.4 × 456.6 × 152.4 cm).
Courtesy of the artist and
Alexander Gray Associates,
New York

← Ronny Quevedo (b. 1981, Guayaquil) includes aspects of abstraction, sports imagery, and cartography in his painting, drawing, collage, installation, and print work. One of his primary interests is in the topographies and strategies of pathfinding utilized by migrants and how this movement creates a liminal geography and space. Through his work, Quevedo engages with ideas of identity and reframes pre- and postcolonial iconographies to create a unique exploration of personal and social histories. *El guarda meta de los cosmos (from the abyss)* (2022) further speaks to Quevedo's interest in cartography and migration. In this work, Quevedo deconstructs a grid to create a series of portal-like passageways, some of which are obscured by abstracted shapes. Encouraging circumnavigation, the sculpture repositions viewers in relation to its structure, allowing the piece to inhabit multiple perspectives. In *los desaparecidos (the arbiter of time)* (2018) Quevedo reflects on his family's story of migration, displacement, and adaptation within the greater history of conquest and colonization. The shirt pattern applied in gold leaf refers to his mother's career as a seamstress. The lines radiating from the center resemble the face of a clock that has stopped at the forty-five-minute mark, the minutes that make up a period in soccer, a reference to his father's career as a professional soccer player.

–Sarah Lopez

PL. 99 P. 153
william cordova

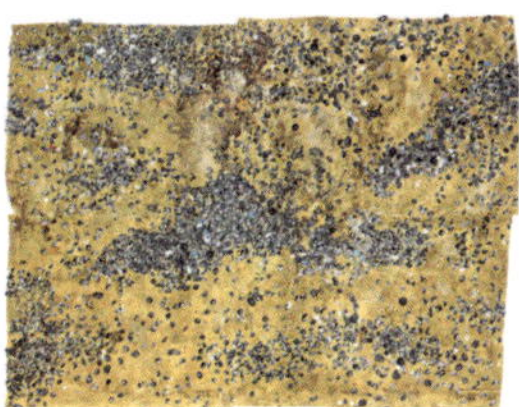

The oeuvre of william cordova (b. 1969, Lima) engages with the fluidity of cultural production based on time and place. His works utilize sound, sculpture, painting, and drawing to disentangle the complexities of multiculturalism, contemporary politics, and history. In works such as *daniel boone, pat boone y mary boone (or firestone pero los olmecas venceran!)* the artist uses two juxtaposing natural resources that have historically been used to colonize Latin America: gold and gasoline. The highly textured gold leaf background of the work suggests the complexity of the historic precedent of Latin American extractivism. The artist then forms undulating waves of tires, standing as a signifier for gasoline. This connection to gasoline is further compounded by the fluid forms these tires create as they pool, ripple, and splash across the golden backdrop. In this work, gold and gasoline are used as two historically separate yet symbolically similar natural resources that have been plundered from countries across the Americas. In doing so, cordova forms a historical parallel that interrogates concepts of neocolonialism and the history of extractivism in Latin America.

–Esther Levy

(II)
daniel boone, pat boone y mary boone (or firestone pero los olmecas venceran!), 2008.
Gold leaf on paper, mixed media on paper, 96 × 120 inches (243.84 × 304.8 cm).
Estrellita B. Brodsky Collection.
Photo: Arturo Sánchez

PL. 100 P. 154
Wendy Cabrera Rubio

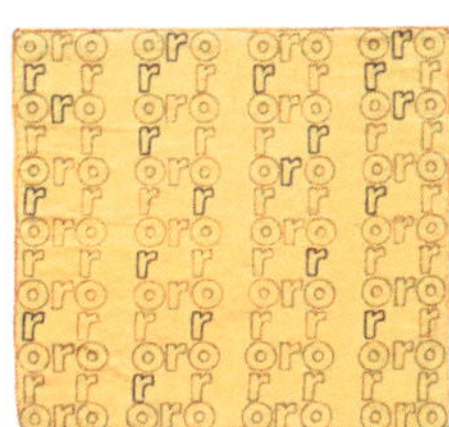

Wendy Cabrera Rubio (b. 1993, Mexico City) interrogates in her work the legacy of Mexican Modernism and of the ideological program behind the architectural and art projects developed for the 1968 Olympics in the city. Specifically, she questions Mathias Goeritz's political positioning and his lack of criticism of the Tlatelolco massacre. Goeritz used gold in his 1950s paintings to integrate spirituality and the power of religious icons into modern art. He extended the research on gold into concrete poetry, where he repeated the word *oro* (gold) as a prayer, using the font Helvetica, a staple of modern design. In Cabrera Rubio's interpretation, the word is reproduced and decomposed repeatedly in felt, an unluxurious element that grounds her work in everyday, ordinary life.

–Aimé Iglesias Lukin

(I)
Modern Art and Architecture in Cold War Mexico (series), 2022.
Felt, synthetic filling, 35 ½ × 35 ½ × 2 inches (90 × 90 × 5 cm).
Courtesy of the artist and Anonymous Gallery

PL. 103 P. 158
Scherezade Garcia

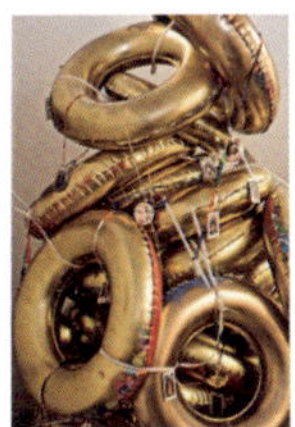

Scherezade Garcia (b. 1966, Santo Domingo) utilizes a multitude of different media to create diverse artworks that tackle themes of colonialism, migration, and history. She is also one of the co-founders of the Dominican York Proyecto GRÁFICA: a printmaking collective of artists of Dominican descent based in New York City. In works such as *Theories of Freedom,* Garcia spray-paints inflatable plastic inner tubes gold, fastening them together to create larger sculptural forms. Garcia's use of inner tubes recalls oceanic passageways traversed by refugees, slaves, immigrants, and colonizers alike and the ocean as a site that shapes and separates geographic territories. The inner tubes suggest the promise of future safety yet still denote the precariousness of their present circumstance as a passenger voyaging into the unfamiliar. The use of metallic gold paint further draws a connection between the idea of a promised land in the Americas and the image of the Americas as a continent in which gold and other valuable natural resources are to be found in abundance.

–Esther Levy

(I)
Detail of *Cathedral* from the series *Theories of Freedom*, 2009–11.
Golden inner tubes attached with safety ties, dimensions variable.
Courtesy of the artist.
Photo: William Vazquez Photography NYC

PL. 104 P. 159
Julia Santos Solomon

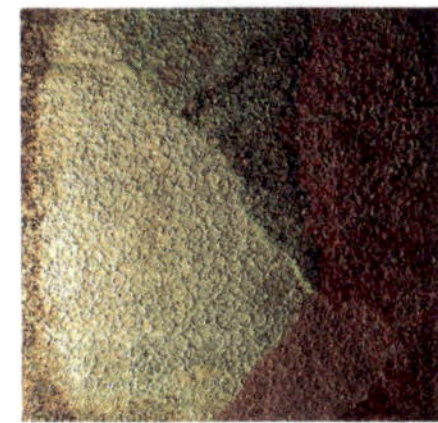

Julia Santos Solomon (b. 1956, Dominican Republic) uses gold leaf as a tool with which to explore European colonization in her home country of the Dominican Republic. Santos Solomon states that she aims to "re-appropriate" the gold that was historically stripped by the Spanish from the Caribbean. The artist's application of the leaf creates textures that resemble topographical forms, suggesting the shapes of islands interspersed with mountains and valleys. The illuminated, overhead view of these island forms suggests the reverence and divinity of the use of gold in traditional Catholic paintings. *Cresta* features an array of metallic tones with repetitive circular textures that recall the rippling of ocean waves, further compounded by the variety of shades cast by the highly textured surface. A chartreuse, serpentine line of paint meanders between gold and green portions of the canvas, suggesting a river running through the mountainous landscape Santos Solomon has created. Through works like *Cresta*, she repatriates the resources stripped from the Dominican Republic while utilizing the visual language of topography and cartography, suggesting a recontextualization of the tools that have historically been used to colonize.

–Esther Levy

(I)
Cresta, 2016.
Gold leaf, paper, paint on panel, 40 × 40 inches (101.6 × 101.6 cm).
Courtesy of the artist

AIMÉ IGLESIAS LUKIN is Director and Chief Curator of Art at Americas Society. Born in Buenos Aires, she received her PhD in art history from Rutgers University with a dissertation titled "This Must Be the Place: Latin American Artists in New York 1965–1975." Her research received grants from the Metropolitan Museum of Art, the Terra and Andrew W. Mellon Foundations, and the ICAA Peter C. Marzio Award from the Museum of Fine Arts, Houston. She completed her MA at The Institute of Fine Arts, New York University, and her undergraduate studies in art history at the Universidad de Buenos Aires. She has curated exhibitions independently in museums and cultural centers and previously worked for the Modern and Contemporary Art Department of the Metropolitan Museum of Art, the Institute for Studies on Latin American Art, and Fundación PROA in Buenos Aires.

TIE JOJIMA is Associate Curator and Manager of Exhibitions of Art at Americas Society and a PhD candidate in art history at the Graduate Center, CUNY, specializing in modern and contemporary Latin American art. At Americas Society she has cocurated the exhibition *Geles Cabrera: Museo Escultórico* (2022) and worked as associate curator for *Bispo do Rosario: All Existing Materials on Earth* (2023). Jojima has worked on the organization of several exhibitions and their corresponding publications and public events, including *Tropical is Political: Caribbean Art under the Visitor Economy Regime* and *This Must Be the Place: Latin American Artists in New York, 1965–75*. She has received fellowships and awards from the School of the Art Institute of Chicago, the Patricia Phelps de Cisneros travel grant, and the Graduate Center, CUNY. She has published academic and curatorial writings in journals including *Vistas: Critical Approaches to Latin American Art* (ISLAA) and *Arte & Ensaios*, as well as at Americas Society and El Museo del Barrio.

EDWARD J. SULLIVAN is the Helen Gould Shepard Professor in the History of Art at the Institute of Fine Arts and College of Arts and Sciences, New York University. A prominent scholar and curator in the field of modern and contemporary Latin American and Caribbean art, Sullivan is the author of numerous books and exhibition catalogues in this area. Among his publications are the books *Making the Americas Modern: Hemispheric Art 1910–1960*, *From San Juan to Paris and Back: Francisco Oller and Caribbean Art in the Era of Impressionism*, and *The Language of Objects in the Art of the Americas*. He recently curated the 2019 exhibition *Brazilian Modern: The Living Art of Roberto Burle Marx* at the New York Botanical Garden and the 2018 exhibition *Processing: Paintings and Prints by Roberto Juarez* at the Museum of Contemporary Art in Boulder, Colorado.

ESTHER LEVY, Research Assistant, Art at Americas Society

SARAH LOPEZ, Curatorial Assistant, Art at Americas Society

SARAH W. MALLORY, Predoctoral Fellow, Drawing Institute, The Morgan Library & Museum and PhD candidate, Harvard University

ERIC MAZARIEGOS, PhD candidate, Department of Art History and Archaeology, Columbia University

LOUISA M. RAITT, PhD candidate, The Institute of Fine Arts, New York University

RACHEL REMICK, Former Assistant Curator, Art at Americas Society

JI MARY SEO, PhD candidate, Department of History of Art and Architecture, Harvard University

We thank all the lenders and artists in the exhibition. Special thanks to Adriana Rosenberg from Fundación PROA in Buenos Aires and Ramiro Martínez from Museo Amparo in Puebla for their collaboration. We also thank Siobhan Angus, Pedro Barbosa, Clara Bargellini, Juan Gabriel Ramírez Bolivar, Julia Bozer, H.W. Brands, Monica Bravo, Estrellita B. Brodsky, Sherwin K. Bryant, Marcela Caruso, Jacopo Crivelli Visconti, James Doyle, Emily A. Engel, Álvaro Enrigue, Elizabeth Ferry, Andrew Finegold, Diana Flatto, Veronica Flom, Tatiana Flores, Ana Franco, Sonja Gandert, Florencia Giordano Braun, Laura Hakel, Alexa Halaby, Manuela Hansen, Israel Hernandez, Isabella Hutchinson, Cristóbal Jácome-Moreno, Cecilia Jaime, Jennifer Josten, Ronda Kasl, Ilona Katzew, Ileen Kohn, Abigail Lapin Dardashti, Pablo León de la Barra, Victoria Lyall, Lina Méndez, Walter Mignolo, Bernardo Mosqueira, Verónica Muñoz-Nájar Luque, Sean Nesselrode-Moncada, Maite Paramio, Valéria Piccoli, Joanne Pillsbury, Jennifer Raab, Horacio Ramos, Jorge Rivas Pérez, Nancy Rosoff, Sandra Rozental, Sharon Schultz, Gabriela Siracusano, Ana Sokoloff, Eugenia Sucre, Leon Tovar, Maria Wills Londoño, and Mayra Zolezzi.

The presentation of *El Dorado* and related programming has been made possible by generous support from the National Endowment for the Arts and by public funds from the New York City Department of Cultural Affairs and New York State Council on the Arts with the support of the Office of the Governor and the New York State Legislature. Additional support was provided by Furthermore: a program of the J. M. Kaplan Fund.

Americas Society acknowledges the generous support of the Arts of the Americas Circle contributors: Amalia Amoedo, Almeida & Dale Galeria de Arte, Estrellita B. Brodsky, Virginia Cowles Schroth, Emily A. Engel, Diana Fane, Isabella Hutchinson, Carolina Jannicelli, Diana López and Herman Sifontes, Antonio Murzi, Gabriela Pérez Rocchietti, Vivian Pfeiffer, Phillips, Erica Roberts, Sharon Schultz, and Edward J. Sullivan.

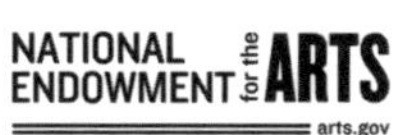

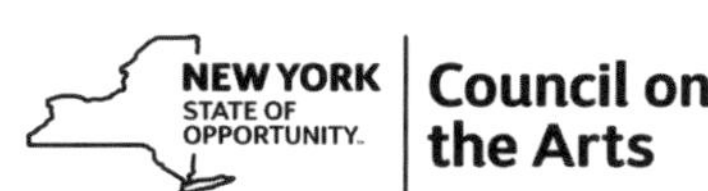

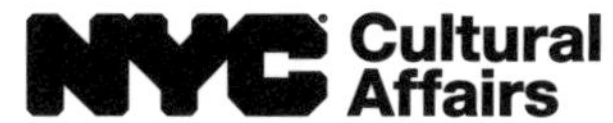

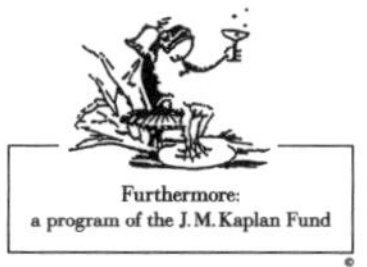

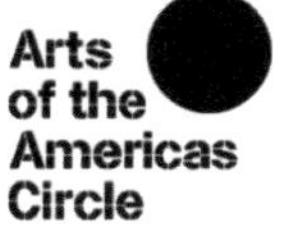

EL **DORADO:** MYTHS OF GOLD
Aimé Iglesias Lukin, Tie Jojima,
and Edward J. Sullivan

Sept 6, 2023 – May 18, 2024

Organized by Americas Society, in collaboration with Fundación PROA, Buenos Aires, Argentina, and Museo Amparo, Puebla, Mexico.

AMERICAS SOCIETY
680 Park Avenue, New York, NY 10065
www.as-coa.org

EXHIBITION

Curatorial Assistants
Esther Levy and Sarah Lopez

Research Assistant
Manuela Hansen

Exhibition Design
SAS/Solomonoff Architecture Studio

PUBLICATION

Editors
Aimé Iglesias Lukin, Edward J. Sullivan, and Tie Jojima

Consulting editor
Karen Marta

Research assistant
Esther Levy

Project manager and production
Todd Bradway

Design
Estudio Herrera, Mexico
Maricris Herrera, Israel Hernández

Copy editor
Flatpage

Printed and bound by
Faenza Printing Spa, Italy

Printed on Arena 120 g/m²
Typeset in Plantin STD, Futura PT, Millionaire and Roboto Mono

ISBN 978-1-879128-56-9
Library of Congress Control Number: 2023914614

Printed in Italy

ART/AMERICAS SOCIETY

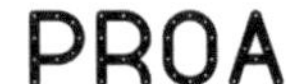

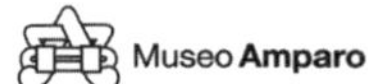